Scholarship in the Sandbox:

Academic Libraries as Laboratories, Forums, and Archives for Student Work

Amy S. Jackson, Cindy Pierard, and Suzanne M. Schadl, editors

Association of College and Research Libraries
A division of the American Library Association
Chicago, Illinois 2019

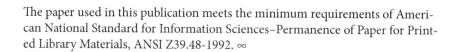

The paper used in this publication meets the minimum requirements of American National Standard for Information Sciences–Permanence of Paper for Printed Library Materials, ANSI Z39.48-1992. ∞

Cataloging-in-Publication data is on file with the Library of Congress.

Table of Contents

SECTION II. LIBRARY AS FORUM

SECTION IV. ARTICULATING THE VALUE OF STUDENT WORK

CONCLUSION

Introduction

CHAPTER 1

Students as Producers

Collaborating toward Deeper Learning

Derek Bruff

My Story

In the fall of 2010, I taught a first-year writing seminar for the first time. It is a little unusual for a mathematician to teach a writing seminar, but in the College of Arts and Science at Vanderbilt University, each undergraduate is required to take a first-year writing seminar, and each department is required to offer one. That means that departments not traditionally known for their writing instruction, like mathematics, have to figure out what it means to teach writing to non-majors. I volunteered to teach a seminar in part because I wanted a break from the statistics courses I usually taught, and in part because I wanted to put into practice a variety of teaching approaches I had learned about while working at the Vanderbilt University Center for Teaching.

The course I put together was called "Cryptography: The History and Mathematics of Codes and Codebreaking." I continue to teach it today, every other fall. It's a fun course, with an unusual blend of mathematics, puzzle solving, history, current events, and, of course, writing. I didn't have any experience teaching writing, but I was well read, thanks to my work at the Center for Teaching. I had learned that students often write better when they write for each other.[1] The theory is that when students write for their instructors, when they run into something they can't quite explain, they leave things a little vague, knowing their instructor, an expert in the field, can fill in the details. But when students write for other students, who don't know anything more than they do, they go the extra mile to explain their thoughts and perspectives more clearly.

That made sense to me, so I built some peer review into my new writing seminar. For one of the course assignments, students had to select a code or cipher from history, one that we hadn't covered much in the course, and write about it—its origin, use, mechanics, and influence. I took the students' papers and posted them on my course blog. The blog at the time wasn't much, just a place for me to share course resources without having to suffer through our course management system. I asked my students to read and comment on a couple of their peers' papers, using a few prompts I provided for this purpose. My students dutifully did so, offering surprisingly thoughtful responses to the prompts I had given them. Knowing their peers would read their essays seemed to motivate my students to write well. Mission accomplished.

It wasn't until after the assignment was over that the fun began. The next week, one of my students walked into class and told me he had been Googling his paper topic. He asked me to do so on the classroom projector. I did, and I was surprised to see that his paper on the Great Paris Cipher was now the number-three result on Google! And this was back in the day of universal Google results, before it personalized one's searches. My student said, "Dr. Bruff, some high school student is going to cite my paper!" He seemed a little worried, but I was excited. To be fair, the Great Paris Cipher is pretty obscure; my student didn't have a lot of competition. But knowing that his work turned up that highly in Google results made him reconsider the quality of his essay.

But the fun wasn't over yet. The next day, another student walked into class and shared with the class, "The dude from my footnotes read my paper!" He had written a paper on something called the Chaocipher, which is perhaps the cheesiest name for a cipher I can imagine. He had cited a particular cryptography researcher who had studied the Chaocipher, and that same researcher had somehow (likely a Google alert on the name of the cipher) found the blog post with the student's paper. He had read the paper and left a very helpful comment on the blog, responding to a few questions the peer reviewers had raised about the paper. I was blown away, and so was my student.

These two experiences in the fall of 2010 convinced me of the power of an idea that I've since come to call "Students as Producers." When we bring this approach to our teaching, we engage students not only as consumers of information, but also as producers of knowledge. Thanks to my course blog, I inadvertently connected my students to audiences beyond the course, including "the dude from my footnotes." This transformed what could have been a busywork assignment into authentic, meaningful work. And that transformation had an effect on my students, causing them to take the work more seriously and to own it in a way they didn't own other assignments.

The next time I taught the course, I planned ahead to leverage this audience effect. I partnered with Vanderbilt French professor Holly Tucker, who, at the time, edited a group blog called *Wonders and Marvels*.[2] She had a team of about a dozen scholars and journalists who blogged for the site, writing about curiosities from the history of medicine and science. Student essays exploring the history of cryptography were on-topic for the site, so she invited my students to pitch their essays to her for publication on *Wonders and Marvels*.

Holly spent an hour with my students talking about her site and its readers, giving my students a sense of their audience and what might engage them. My students submitted their first drafts to me for grading and feedback, then revised their essays and resubmitted them for a final grade from me. Then I passed the revised papers over to Holly, who provided another round of feedback. Students weren't required to revise and resubmit a second time, but most did, and Holly published the essays that made the cut. A total of seventeen student essays were published on *Wonders and Marvels* between the 2012 and 2014 offerings of my cryptography seminar,[3] and they were seen by hundreds of Holly's readers.

But wait, there's more! Holly was contacted by an editor from io9,[4] a website that covers science, fiction, and science fiction. io9 wanted to republish one of my student's essays, a piece about the Purple encryption machine used by the Japanese during World War II. Holly contacted me, and I contacted the student, and we all agreed we were comfortable with io9's request. So my student's work went up on the site and has been seen by more than 87,000 readers, as of the time of this writing.[5] That's quite an audience!

Students as Producers

As an instructor, one can't plan on student work being picked up by an outlet with tens of thousands of readers.[6] However, there are a variety of choices an instructor can make when designing assignments that tap into this "Students as Producers" idea. My colleagues at the Vanderbilt Center for Teaching and I wanted to understand these choices, so we designated "Students as Producers" as the theme for the 2013–14 academic year. Through a series of workshops, panels, teaching visits, teaching guides, and blog posts, we explored with our faculty and staff ways to help students engage in meaningful, generative work in the courses they take.

For our end-of-year event, we wanted to show our campus what "Students as Producers" could look like, so we held an event we called the Celebration of Learning, an exhibition of twenty-five student projects from across the university: Research by first- and second-year undergraduates conducted within a biology lab course. Original short stories written for a Spanish course. Video documentaries created by future teachers to explore social and philosophical aspects of education. A water conservation education program aimed at children, developed by students in a service-learning course. These were just some of the products of student learning on display at the Celebration of Learning. The projects, posters, presentations, and performances shared at the event represented significant learning experiences for students. They also represented courses that were thoughtfully and intentionally designed by faculty to foster deep learning, and that often involved collaborative work with librarians, technologists, community partners, and others outside the traditional classroom.

Our mission at the Vanderbilt Center for Teaching is to promote university teaching that leads to meaningful student learning. Our work focuses on helping members of the Vanderbilt community become more effective teachers. We go about that work in a variety of ways, including individual consultations, workshops, orientations, panel discussions, learning communities, and partnerships with departments and programs. We weave the "Students as Producers" approach throughout much of that work, but it is perhaps most explicit in the Course Design Institute we hold each May. During the three-day institute, participants design (or redesign) courses that engage students not only as consumers of information, but also as producers of knowledge. We draw on what we've learned about the "Students as Producers" approach as we support the institute participants, and, in turn, we learn more about engaging students in this kind of work as we follow up with participants when they implement and assess their new courses.

I first heard the term "student as producer" in a keynote by Mike Neary of the University of Lincoln at a 2011 conference in Ireland. Mike Neary was Dean of Teaching and Learning at Lincoln and directed Lincoln's Student as Producer initiative.[7] He argued that students should move from being the object of the educational process to its subject. That is, students should have an active role in shaping their own educational experience and should be engaged in knowledge production alongside university faculty and staff. The work at Lincoln was a campus-wide effort to build research and research-like activities into the undergraduate curriculum. It was initially funded by an external grant, but it took on a life of its own as the "student as producer" idea resonated with faculty there.

Listening to Mike Neary describe the work at Lincoln, it occurred to me that students on my campus were frequently involved in knowledge production in various cocurricular settings, such as undergraduate research, internships, entrepreneurial activities, and student organizations. What appealed to me about the University of Lincoln's initiative, and what we tried to explore through our "Students as Producers" work at Vanderbilt, is the involvement of students as producers in more traditional academic settings, such as semester-long courses and library-based research. That seemed like more of a challenge, but also an opportunity to transform learning experiences that traditionally involved connecting students to existing information into ones that engaged students in knowledge production and, thus, deeper learning.

The University of Lincoln and Vanderbilt University were not the only higher education institutions to hit upon this idea. As part of its 2013 Flexible Learning Initiative, the University of British Columbia provided resources for undergraduate course transformation. Among the themes that emerged from the proposals was the idea of students as producers of content.[8] In fact, my colleagues at the UBC Centre for Teaching, Learning, and Technology asked me to speak on their campus in the summer of 2014 about the Vanderbilt "Students as Producers" initiative. Back in the States, Georgetown University's Students as Scholars initiative tapped into the same idea.[9] Many of the Students as Scholars activities focused on undergraduate research and creative projects outside of the classroom, but the initiative also featured an internal grant program aimed at building this kind of work into regular courses. And faculty at a number of institutions are involved in developing what are known as course-based undergraduate research experiences (CUREs) in biology, thanks in part to organizations like CUREnet.[10] Thanks to these efforts and others, the 2014 *Horizon Report*, an annual report from the New Media Consortium and Educause, identified the shift from students as consumers to students as creators as one of six key trends in technology in higher education.[11]

Essential Elements

The notion of engaging students as producers may not be new, but I have found the "Students as Producers" framing to be particularly useful in talking with faculty and staff about the design of learning experiences that move students from the object of education to its subject. And our ongoing work in this area at the Vanderbilt Center for Teaching has revealed a few dynamics typically at play in courses and projects that adopt the "Students as Producers" approach. The idea of students as producers plays out differently in different teaching and disciplinary contexts—sometimes students are producers, sometimes scholars, creators, researchers, performers, designers, or problem solvers—but there are a few elements that seem to define a "Students as Producers" assignment.

Open-Ended Problems

If we give our students a problem for which the correct answer is known and the path to reaching that answer is well laid out, having students solve that problem might be useful in some situations, but it won't prepare them for the kind of hard problems they will encounter when they leave us. If we want to prepare our students to take what they've learned in our courses and apply it to new context and new problems (a process called *transfer* in the literature on teaching and learning),[12] we have to give them the chance to practice solving hard problems now. Engaging students as producers typically involves having them tackle *open-ended problems* of some kind, problems where the answer isn't fully known, problems that permit multiple possible solution approaches, problems where failure is quite possible.

Holly Tucker, professor of French at Vanderbilt and my collaborator on the cryptography writing project, started her honors seminar, "Leeches and Lancets: Early Medicine in Cultural Contexts," in a fairly traditional way, with readings and discussions each week. However, the second half of the course was what Tucker called a "collaborative lab," in which students worked in groups to create public-facing websites exploring fertility and birth control, witchcraft and medicine, and poison. The students selected topics, identified relevant resources, constructed arguments, and determined how to present their work through various digital tools. Tucker hosted the students' work on a website called Imagining the Past, a site that she built with fellow French professor Lynn Ramey to provide a platform for public-facing student projects.

Helping students engage in this kind of open-ended work required a different instructional approach for Tucker. "I was there—not as an intractable 'expert' but instead as a guide," she wrote.[13] "My job was to guide them toward appropriate resources and to ask the right questions at the right time—as well as help shape tasks and assignments to help them move their projects forward." Class time changed, too, as students worked in groups during class to research their projects and build out their websites. Since that work was central to the students' learning in the course (and preparing them for future transfer to other projects), Holly moved that work into the shared, collaborative space of the classroom. This gave students the chance to practice tackling problems and questions where the way forward wasn't always clear.

The second half of Tucker's course felt to the students more like a lab course. Over in the biology department, where students traditionally take lab courses, lab coordinator Steve Baskauf spent several years overhauling the "cookbook" style labs he was using into inquiry-based labs in which students did original biology research. This wasn't a special course; it was the second-semester intro biology lab. Providing early-career students the chance to tackle open research questions within a single semester meant selecting those questions for students with care and providing students a lot of support, largely in the form of well-trained teaching assistants. But more often than not, students in Steve's labs are able to conduct original research and get at least provisional results.

Baskauf has his students present their work at the end of the course in a poster session open to the campus. I've been a few times, and I've enjoyed hearing about the students' work. The first time I attended, I noticed a pattern in the students' presentations. They were all working with simple organisms—algae, bacteria, plants, insects, and so on. They had all designed some kind of experiment to test some hypothesis using these organisms. Without exception, every student group I talked to said, at some point in their presentation, something very much like, "And then they all died." Baskauf summarized my experience with some understatement: "There are always a fair number of failures."[14] Every group had the experience of a failed experiment, and every group had the chance to go back to the drawing board and try something different. Those second attempts didn't all work, but the chance to try again, to learn from a mistake and engineer a solution, that was invaluable.

The chance to confront failure, to learn from it, to keep working a solution, that's what open-ended problems provide for students. It's hard work, for both students and instructors, but it's important to provide students these opportunities to prepare them for hard problems they will face in the future.

Authentic Audiences

Consider the traditional five-page research paper. A student spends a week or more working on a document that's read by just one person on the entire planet—the instructor. What's the point? Sure, practicing a particular set of skills in gathering, evaluating, and synthesizing information and receiving feedback on that practice is certainly useful. But if we are the only audience for our students' work, we have missed an opportunity to move beyond what they may see as "busywork" and to motivate them to create something of lasting value.

While teaching an introduction to Portuguese language course at Vanderbilt a couple of years ago, doctoral student Tim Foster decided to provide his students with an authentic language production task. He showed his students the Portuguese Wikipedia page for Nashville, the city in which Vanderbilt is located. There wasn't much to it at the time, much less than the English version of the page, which helped his students get past a misconception they had that language-specific versions of Wikipedia were just translations of English language Wikipedia pages. To drive home this point—and give his students some authentic language production practice—Foster had them write content for the Portuguese Wikipedia page for Nashville. Foster and his students spent a week brainstorming potential content for the page, then researching information about the city of Nashville, then summarizing that information in the target language in ways consistent with Wikipedia writing practice (neutral tone of voice and so on). The result was a much more robust representation of the city of Nashville on Portuguese Wikipedia.

If my cryptography student was excited when he saw his paper show up in Google search results, you can imagine how motivated Foster's students were to know that their work would appear on Wikipedia. They knew how often they consulted "the Free Encyclopedia." Portuguese speakers across the world interested in learning more about Nashville would read and hopefully benefit from their work. Some of his students were so excited by this prospect that they went above and beyond what was asked of them in the assignment, adding additional data to the Nashville page. "I don't think I would have seen that extra effort had this been something that just got turned in to me," Foster said.[15] "I think students want their work to be impactful."

Increased student motivation is one reason to have students produce work for authentic audiences. Another is that by asking students to represent what they are learning for an authentic audience, students get the opportunity to shape and refine their own understanding of what they are learning.[16] Consider a podcast assignment used by Vanderbilt health policy professor Gilbert Gonzales, a participant in one of our Course Design Institutes. Gonzales wanted his students to encounter recent health policy research articles, understand the research they conveyed, and make sense of its implications for policy and personal health-care decisions. He could have asked students to do so in a traditional five-page paper, but instead, he asked his students to create fifteen-to-twenty-minute podcast episodes in the style of National Public Radio stories. Each student selected an article from a list provided by Gonzales, then worked to produce creative audio stories summarizing the research and making clear its implications. Some interviewed local faculty with relevant expertise, others interviewed students ("man on the street" style) or health-care providers, and still others put together audio dramas that helped communicate their findings.

Gonzales shared the results on his SoundCloud page, Health Policy Radio with Gilbert Gonzales.[17] Not only were the student-produced podcast episodes available to anyone searching SoundCloud or iTunes for health policy content, Gonzales shared the episodes with his Twitter network and with the researchers the students cited, many of whom were quite excited to hear the students' summaries of their work. Just as Holly Tucker's *Wonders and Marvels* readers presented an authentic audience for my cryptography students that helped shape their writing, the Health Policy Radio podcast provided

Gonzales's students with a real audience outside the course. By representing their understanding of the health policy research they were studying through audio, they had to more deeply understand that research and its implications. And knowing their work would be public made a difference. "I think that really raised the stakes on the quality of the work," Gonzales said, "because they knew that whatever they submitted to me at the end would be available for the world to hear."[18]

Student Autonomy

Much of the "Students as Producers" approach to learning design involves finding ways to motivate students to engage in meaningful, generative work, the kind of work that leads to deeper learning. Open-ended problems can be motivating, as can authentic audiences. Also motivating, as we know from psychological science research: having a degree of autonomy in the work one does.[19] When we give students some choices in what work they do or in how they go about that work, we help them embrace the work as their own and engage more deeply in it.

Consider that other course I teach, the one that isn't quite as interesting as my cryptography course—my introduction to statistics. It usually enrolls about a hundred students, most of whom aren't particularly excited to be taking a statistics course. The course has always featured an application project of some kind, in which students find or generate some authentic data and then ask and answer questions of the data using the statistical techniques they have learned in the course. In years past, the deliverable for this project was a five-page paper. That was fine, but a few years ago, I realized the increasing importance of data visualization in a variety of professional contexts, and so I replaced that traditional assignment with an infographic project. Students still had to apply statistical techniques to real-world data, but now they also had to communicate their results in visually meaningful ways, paying careful attention to size, color, positioning, and more to share the stories their data analysis uncovered.

This is challenging work for students, mainly because most of them haven't thought too hard about visual communication strategies. To get them a little more excited to take on this project, I let them pick the topic, the questions, and the data. For what follows, it is important to know that I am not a sports guy. I will occasionally notice that Vanderbilt football has a game coming up, but if my children aren't on the field, it's a safe bet I'm not paying attention. That said, the last time I taught this statistics course, almost half of my students chose sports for their topics. Sports is a great topic for a project like this. There's a recent but strong tradition of statistics in baseball (sabermetrics, as it is known), and a wide variety of interesting sports-related questions can be addressed through basic statistical techniques—Is there such a thing as a home field advantage in baseball? Does offense or defense matter more in basketball?—and other sports questions.

I would never pick sports for a topic for myself, but many of my students did. And because they picked a topic that they found interesting, they brought more energy and enthusiasm for the work. And I believe that many of them produced stronger infographics—with more intentional visualizations—because they took their research questions so seriously.

Topic choice is one way to give students more autonomy in the work they do. Medium choice is another. Consider my Vanderbilt colleague Larisa DeSantis, who teaches in our earth and environmental science program. In most of her courses, she asks her students to produce some creative work communicating something they've learned in her course. She has had students make podcasts, children's books, lesson plans for middle school teachers, and more.[20] One of her students, a member of a campus a cappella singing group, created a YouTube video in which he explained the expansion of grasslands during the Miocene epoch through a song with six-part harmony.[21] He sang all six parts himself, and DeSantis tells me his science was 100 percent accurate.

Giving students the option to decide what they produce for an assignment or project can feel a little risky to an instructor, since it can be challenging to support a student working in an unfamiliar medium and it can be hard to grade a more open-ended assignment. But allowing students to leverage their existing knowledge and skills (in, say, lesson plan design by preservice teachers or six-part harmony by a music major) can lead them to create work that is interesting, compelling, and worth sharing. And by encouraging students to find personal or professional connections to the material in a course or other learning experience, we help students see the relevance of what they are learning beyond the immediate university context.

A Call to Action

Steve Baskauf's students leave their biology lab with a firsthand experience of the process of science and how important learning from failure is to that process. Tim Foster's students left his course with a deeper understanding of Wikipedia and how it functions as a crowdsourced encyclopedia. And my statistics students pay more attention to the ways spatial and color relationships can convey meaning in data visualizations they encounter. We often want our students to be more savvy consumers of information, whether they are reading a scientific research article or using Wikipedia to teach themselves something or trying to make sense of a chart in an annual report. Engaging students as producers of knowledge helps to equip them to be better consumers of information. Whether or not Gilbert Gonzales's students go on to make more podcasts (and they might—it's a useful skill!), they will be more critical consumers of podcasts and other audio storytelling in the future.

Making something helps you understand that thing more deeply. This is one reason to ask students to take on these nontraditional projects. Another is that doing so prepares students to make a difference in their professional and personal lives when they leave us. We want our students to be problem solvers, to take what we have taught them and do useful things with it. That requires giving them the chance to practice doing so and opportunities to see themselves as researchers, designers, creators, performers, and innovators. And that means giving students open-ended problems, putting them in front of real audiences, and helping them find their own connections to what we are teaching them.

Designing such learning experiences and supporting students as they move through them is not easy. Doing so often requires what Bass calls a "team-based design," in which instructors, librarians, technologists, teaching center staff, and others collaborate in the design, implementation, and assessment of meaningful student learning experiences.[22] I can speak to the collaborative role of teaching center staff, but this volume attests to the growing importance of librarians and libraries in engaging students as producers of knowledge. Libraries can be laboratories, where students and faculty go to learn and practice the skills they need to take on open-ended problems. Libraries can be forums, where students and their projects are connected to authentic audiences on campus and beyond. Libraries can be archives, where the products of student work are made both public and persistent. And libraries, especially their special collections, can be sources of rich student projects.

I want to share one more story that features all of these collaborative roles. The Buchanan Library Fellows Program at Vanderbilt University provides support for undergraduates to take on immersive projects of strategic value to the library, mentored by both librarians and faculty members. Ellen Dement was a 2017 fellow who worked with Mary Anne Caton, library consultant for educational and interpretive programs, and Kevin Murphy, professor and chair of history of art. Murphy led an effort by the Vanderbilt Fine Arts Gallery to acquire a collection of almost 180 architectural drawings of the Woolworth Building in New York City by the office of its architect, Cass Gilbert. When it opened in 1913, the Woolworth Building was the height of innovation and the world's tallest building for almost two decades, and it fascinated architects, artists, and the general public alike. Although other collections of similar Woolworth documents exist, none are both well cataloged and available online. Dement's task as a library fellow was to create an online exhibit focused on the Vanderbilt document collection, one that would be useful to historians and students of architecture, including students in a course taught by Murphy called "The Skyscraper: Modern Urban Icon."[23]

Dement spent the semester learning and using Scalar, an open-source platform for creating online exhibits and stories, to build an exhibit around photographs and catalog information from the Vanderbilt collection. She had never used Scalar before, but she learned it well enough, with help and support from Caton as well as director and curator of visual resources Millicent Fulmer, to teach Murphy's students to use it the following semester. (Library as laboratory.) Caton had selected Scalar for the project, in part because it provided the nonlinear, multimedia exhibit space the project needed and in part because it played well with other online resources, allowing the creation of a public exhibit that drew on items in other digital library connections. (Library as forum.) Caton also helped design the data structure for the Scalar exhibit to conform to the right standards so that the project could live beyond the following semester, when Murphy's skyscraper students were to add to and enhance Dement's initial Woolworth exhibit, and even migrate from Scalar to other platforms, if the need was there over time. (Library as archive.) And while the Woolworth documents weren't actually part of the library's special collections (they live at the fine arts gallery), the individual student project and the collaborative class project came about because of a local campus collection. (Library as inspiration.)

The Woolworth Building project was possible because of the collaboration that launched it—faculty, librarians, students, and gallerists, not to mention all the technologists that helped to create Scalar. In our work exploring the "Students as Producers" idea, we have seen many creative student projects guided and supported by faculty members, but those instructors almost never acted alone. Holly Tucker worked with a faculty colleague, a graduate assistant, and a web hosting company to build out the Imagining the Past site. Gilbert Gonzales got the idea for his podcast assignment at our Course Design Institute, worked with a graduate assistant to learn the technology and teach it to his students, then shared the word about his students' work thought his extensive Twitter network. And to make his inquiry-based labs work, Steve Baskauf and his fellow lab staff members recruit, train, and mentor a team of talented graduate teaching assistants.

Collaboration plays a critical role in engaging students as producers of knowledge, and libraries are increasingly both collaborators and sites of collaboration. Faculty and students need new tools and new skills to create these nontraditional and often digital projects, and they need help finding, building, and sustaining platforms for sharing student work and connecting it with authentic audiences. Libraries and librarians are uniquely positioned to provide this kind of collaboration, support, and leadership. I am excited by the student scholarship represented by the contributions this volume, and by the future student work that will be guided and facilitated by faculty, staff, librarians, and others who are inspired by this volume.

Notes

1. Richard J. Light, *Making the Most of College* (Cambridge, MA: Harvard University Press, 2001).
2. Holly Tucker, *Wonders and Marvels* (blog), last modified June 23, 2017, http://www.wondersandmarvels.com.
3. Holly Tucker, post category: "Cryptography (Vanderbilt)," *Wonders and Marvels* (blog), accessed March 22, 2018, http://www.wondersandmarvels.com/category/cryptography-vanderbilt.
4. io9: We Come from the Future homepage, accessed March 22, 2017, https://io9.gizmodo.com/.
5. Alberto Perez, "How the U.S. Cracked Japan's 'Purple Encryption Machine' at the Dawn of World War II," io9: We Come from the Future, March 22, 2013, https://io9.gizmodo.com/how-the-u-s-cracked-japans-purple-encryption-machine-458385664.
6. Portions of this section were adapted from Derek Bruff, "Students as Producers: An Introduction," Vanderbilt University, Center for Teaching, September 3, 2013, https://cft.vanderbilt.edu/2013/09/students-as-producers-an-introduction/.
7. University of Lincoln, Student as Producer website, last modified 2014, http://studentasproducer.lincoln.ac.uk/.
8. Heather McCabe, "UBC Course Offerings Feature Students as Producers of Content," *Centre for Teaching, Learning and Technology* (blog), September 27, 2013, University of British Colombia, Vancouver Campus, https://ctlt.ubc.ca/2013/09/27/ubc-course-offerings-feature-students-as-producers-of-content/.
9. George Mason University, *Students as Scholars* (blog), accessed March 22, 2018. http://studentsasscholarsgmu.blogspot.com/.
10. University of Texas at Austin, College of Natural Sciences, CUREnet: Course-Based Undergraduate Research Experience website, accessed March 22, 2018. https://curenet.cns.utexas.edu/.
11. L. Johnson et al., *NMC Horizon Report: 2014 Higher Education Edition* (Austin, TX: New Media Consortium, 2014).
12. Susan A. Ambrose et al., *How Learning Works* (San Francisco: Jossey-Bass, 2010).
13. Holly Tucker, "Medicine and Magic—or, What I Did This Spring Semester," *Wonders and Marvels* (blog), April 2014, http://www.wondersandmarvels.com/2014/04/medicine-and-magic-or-what-i-did-this-spring-semester.html.
14. Steve Baskauf, quoted in David Salisbury, "Laboratory Throws Away Cookbooks in Pursuit of Discovery," Research News @ Vanderbilt, May 20, 2011, https://news.vanderbilt.edu/2011/05/20/laboratory-throws-away-cookbooks-in-pursuit-of-discovery/.
15. Derek Bruff (producer), "Episode 13: Tim Foster," February 20, 2017, in *Leading Lines* (podcast), 36:48, http://leadinglinespod.com/episodes/episode-013-tim-foster/.

16. Randy Bass and Heidi Elmendorf, *Designing for Difficulty: Social Pedagogies as a Framework for Course Design* (New York: Teagle Foundation, 2011).

17. Gilbert Gonzales, *Health Policy Radio with Gilbert Gonzales*, Soundcloud podcast, accessed March 22, 2018. https://soundcloud.com/user-175461561.

18. Derek Bruff (producer), "Episode 27: Gilbert Gonzales," October 16, 2017, in *Leading Lines* (podcast), 36:46 http://leadinglinespod.com/episodes/episode-027-gilbert-gonzales/.

19. Richard M. Ryan and Edward L. Deci, "Self-determination Theory and the Facilitation of Intrinsic Motivation, Social Development, and Well-being," *American Psychologist* 55, no. 1 (2000): 68–78.

20. "Podcasts, Music, Children's Books, and More," DeSantis DREAM Lab, accessed March 22, 2018. https://sites.google.com/site/larisadesantisdreamlab/Podcasts-Childrens-Books-and-More.

21. Augie Phillips, "Miocene: Augie Phillips," posted by Larisa DeSantis, April 21, 2015, YouTube video, 2:52, https://www.youtube.com/watch?v=WDaopt5dYBI.

22. Randy Bass, "Disrupting Ourselves: The Problem of Learning in Higher Education," *Educause Review* 47, no. 2 (2012): 23–33.

23. Ellen Dement, Cass Gilbert's Woolworth Building homepage, last modified January 28, 2018, http://scalar.usc.edu/works/cass-gilberts-woolworth-building/index.

Bibliography

Ambrose, Susan A., Michael W. Bridges, Michele DiPietro, Marsha C. Lovett, and Marie K. Norman. *How Learning Works: Seven Research-Based Principles for Smart Teaching.* San Francisco: Jossey-Bass, 2010.

Bass, Randy. "Disrupting Ourselves: The Problem of Learning in Higher Education." *Educause Review* 47, no. 2 (2012): 23–33.

Bass, Randy, and Heidi Elmendorf. *Designing for Difficulty: Social Pedagogies as a Framework for Course Design.* Teagle Foundation white paper. New York: Teagle Foundation, 2011.

Bruff, Derek, producer. "Episode 13: Tim Foster." February 20, 2017. In *Leading Lines,* podcast, 36:48. http://leadinglinespod.com/episodes/episode-013-tim-foster/.

———, producer. "Episode 27: Gilbert Gonzales." October 16, 2017. In *Leading Lines,* podcast, 36:46. http://leadinglinespod.com/episodes/episode-027-gilbert-gonzales/.

———. "Students as Producers: An Introduction." Vanderbilt University, Center for Teaching, September 3, 2013. https://cft.vanderbilt.edu/2013/09/students-as-producers-an-introduction/.

Dement, Ellen. Cass Gilbert's Woolworth Building homepage. Last modified January 28, 2018. http://scalar.usc.edu/works/cass-gilberts-woolworth-building/index.

DeSantis DREAM Lab. "Podcasts, Music, Children's Books, and More." DeSantis DREAM Lab. Accessed March 22, 2018. https://sites.google.com/site/larisadesantisdreamlab/Podcasts-Childrens-Books-and-More.

George Mason University. *Students as Scholars* (blog). Accessed March 22, 2018. http://studentsasscholarsgmu.blogspot.com/.

Gonzales, Gilbert. *Health Policy Radio with Gilbert Gonzales*. Soundcloud podcast. Accessed March 22, 2018. https://soundcloud.com/user-175461561.

io9: We Come from the Future homepage. Accessed March 22, 2017. https://io9.gizmodo.com/.

Johnson, L., S. Adams Becker, V. Estrada., and A. Freeman. *NMC Horizon Report: 2014 Higher Education Edition*. Austin, TX: New Media Consortium, 2014.

Light, Richard J. *Making the Most of College: Students Speak their Minds*. Cambridge, MA: Harvard University Press, 2001.

McCabe, Heather. "UBC Course Offerings Feature Students as Producers of Content." *Centre for Teaching, Learning and Technology* (blog), September 27, 2013. University of British Colombia, Vancouver Campus. https://ctlt.ubc.ca/2013/09/27/ubc-course-offerings-feature-students-as-producers-of-content/.

Perez, Alberto. "How the U.S. Cracked Japan's 'Purple Encryption Machine' at the Dawn of World War II." io9: We Come from the Future, March 22, 2013. https://io9.gizmodo.com/how-the-u-s-cracked-japans-purple-encryption-machine-458385664.

Phillips, Augie. "Miocene: Augie Phillips." Posted by Larisa DeSantis, April 21, 2015. YouTube video, 2:52. https://www.youtube.com/watch?v=WDaopt5dYBI.

Ryan, Richard M., and Edward L. Deci. "Self-determination Theory and the Facilitation of Intrinsic Motivation, Social Development, and Well-being." *American Psychologist* 55, no. 1 (2000): 68–78.

Salisbury, David. "Laboratory Throws Away Cookbooks in Pursuit of Discovery." Research News @Vanderbilt, May 20, 2011. https://news.vanderbilt.edu/2011/05/20/laboratory-throws-away-cookbooks-in-pursuit-of-discovery/.

Tucker, Holly. "Medicine and Magic—or, What I Did This Spring Semester." *Wonders and Marvels* (blog), April 2014. http://www.wondersandmarvels.com/2014/04/medicine-and-magic-or-what-i-did-this-spring-semester.html.

Tucker, Holly. Post Category: Cryptography (Vanderbilt). *Wonders and Marvels* (blog). Accessed March 22, 2018. http://www.wondersandmarvels.com/category/cryptography-vanderbilt.

Tucker, Holly. *Wonders and Marvels: A Community for Curious Minds Who Love History, Its Odd Stories, and Good Reads* (blog). Last modified June 23, 2017. http://www.wondersandmarvels.com.

University of Lincoln. Student as Producer website. Last modified 2014. http://studentasproducer.lincoln.ac.uk/.

University of Texas at Austin, College of Natural Sciences. CUREnet: Course-Based Undergraduate Research Experience website. Accessed March 22, 2018. https://curenet.cns.utexas.edu.

CHAPTER 2

Learning with Students in the Sandbox
Our Stories

Amy S. Jackson, Cindy Pierard, and Suzanne M. Schadl

Amy

My introduction to the library came as a music performance student. Although the library was the natural connection to the repertoire (scores) and interpretations of the repertoire (recordings), this connection ended with the circulation transaction. As I became more serious about performing a piece of music, it was expected that I would purchase the score and recordings as an investment in my art. At this point, I would return the music to the library, and the library was no longer my connection to the music. However, in my role as Performing Arts Librarian, I questioned why it needed to end at this point. Was a student interpretation of a piece of the repertoire any less of an interpretation than the recordings in the library? Professional recordings may be held in higher regard by other musicians, but how can students advance without the opportunity to practice their art? How can the library be more supportive of the initial match between performer and composer when the student checks out a score? The natural extension of the circulation transaction should be a performance in the library demonstrating how the student engaged with the music we made available to them. Expanding from my role as the Performing Arts Librarian to the Director of Instruction and Outreach, this support of student performances extends to student lectures in the library, and finally to archiving student work in the archive or repository. By making capstone projects, dissertations and theses, artwork, music performances, and other student works available in the library, we demonstrate our continued support and interest in how students are engaging with our resources. By engaging with these students, we show interest in the entire cycle of their research and learning, becoming a place to create and preserve their work, and more than gatekeepers of the "great works."

Cindy

I'm the daughter of a librarian and a historian. I grew up in libraries and archives, and I've always been drawn to the stories found in these spaces. As a librarian myself, I've become interested in how libraries can provide students with venues for practicing and sharing their work, whether that work is an experimental art project or a scientific poster. Many students have grown up with access to technology that encourages them to create and share—whether the subject is a remix of favorite samples or a Halloween costume hack. And yet we don't do much to foster a student-centered culture of creative and scholarly sharing within library spaces. This is a missed opportunity, especially when we consider how *publicly displaying competence* has been shown to reinforce learning.[1] The strategies that libraries can use to facilitate tinkering and sharing by students are many. Libraries with makerspaces can provide tools, materials, and problems that inspire students to produce and even teach solutions. Libraries with gallery space—or even a blank wall and some seating—can move beyond showing the products of a class project to inviting student artists to discuss the role of inspiration and frustration in the creative process. Capturing and supporting the process as well as the product, whether in a repository, in a zine, or as part of an affinity group, can provide a source of inspiration and a sense of community for students who are finding their voices and adding their stories to broader discourse.

Suzanne

I came to the library from the classroom where I taught history, literature, and Portuguese. Training in Latin American studies introduced me to Brazilian playwright Augusto Boal, who applied critical pedagogy to group theatre.[2] He transformed individuals in audiences into "spect-actors" who intervened with and changed the action on stage. Transferring this concept to library instruction requires me to reject the typical request from classroom instructors to "show" library databases. Instead I invite them and their students to join me on the library platform. Rather than showing them databases, we collectively examine the metadata in their syllabi and link that information with students' inquiries in the moment. This method turns instructors' syllabi into scripts, students' research questions into stage directions, and facilitated library linking into action. Databases barely announce their presence, serving only as backdrops for the content linking students' keywords with the authors, journals, presses, call numbers, and collections identified on professors' syllabi. Adapting this Boalean role (as in Boal and boolean) within a library learning setting enables me to work with students and teaching faculty in the disjunctures between traditional and emerging practice.[3] In this middle—or third space—I learn with others through processes of communal exploration and consciousness raising, or critical pedagogy—where students and instructors are necessarily and simultaneously producers and consumers of information and learning. Together with students, I have argued elsewhere for the option of using library space to practice, rather than just study, disciplines.[4] These opportunities enable students to learn as they contribute further to academic discourse.

A Response: For Action

The title of this book, *Scholarship in the Sandbox*, was inspired by our mutual desire to create a welcoming environment for students practicing the art of scholarly discourse surrounded and inspired by works of others. Although we use the term *scholarship*, we do not limit our definition of scholarship to text-based resources. We embrace all types of scholarly and creative works, including, but not limited to, written works, performed works, spoken works, and created objects. Information professionals use the term *sandbox* to identify restricted physical and virtual spaces for experimenting with new services, workflows, or products. While some situate this enclosure in library learning commons, others use the term to denote private electronic spaces that enable programmers to experiment, testing code and developing software without impacting publicly accessible systems.[5] In this book, the sand is emerging scholarship, which ultimately finds its way out of the box—perhaps best described here as university learning spaces. The collection of stories accumulated in this book demonstrate that the sand and the box intersect with one another in varied spaces that link classroom learning with physical and virtual locations as well as with information systems and communities that extend far beyond our campuses.

The linking mechanisms that Derek Bruff identifies as inadvertent connections between students, their course work, and audiences beyond their reach—"the dude" from his student's footnotes—underscore important connections between people and their scholarship or creativity. Whether students share this production in blogs, performances, repositories, zines, makerspaces, galleries, or "spect-acting" with their professors on library platforms, the experience—as Bruff illustrates—is transformative because production ties classroom learning into a meaningful knot with research or practice done outside of the classroom. This anchor enables students to employ their own academic or creative practices, establish stronger footholds in their disciplines, and publicly display competence. Engaging library spaces and services in creating, preserving, and sharing these kinds of experiences expands the confines of the sandbox to create more diverse, inclusive, and impactful innovations.

This book is divided into four sections: library as laboratory, library as forum, library as archive, and a final section about articulating the value of these roles. Each section includes diverse perspectives, including those of students, classroom professors, academic staff, and librarians, on its topic. Institutions represented include research universities and undergraduate colleges from the United States and Canada. Contributors from the North Carolina State University Libraries are included in each section as "spotlights" because of their long-term commitment to student success in learning spaces that inspire innovation. Part 4 of these spotlights describes the values and principles that unify these contributions. Collectively, all chapters in this book address how libraries are currently expanding their engagement and occupying more central spaces as practical laboratories outside of the classroom. They reveal efforts to curate student work and tips for promoting and preserving access to this production through programming and services that affirm libraries' roles in intellectual processes. Following Bruff's focus on collaborative open-ended problem solving as essential for engaging students as producers of knowledge, these chapters reflect on collective learning in a sandbox where the answers are far less important than the multiplicity of prospective solutions.

On Essential Elements: Open Ends, Audiences, and Student Autonomy

As Bruff notes, preparing students to take what they learn and apply it in differing contexts requires opportunities to practice, fail, troubleshoot, and try again. The student voices in this book confirm the value in this approach. Temnyalova, for instance (chapter 4), concludes that pathways leading to failure underscore the importance of the journey and the map. Morse and

Gordon (chapter 4) value the experimentation required for a final product over the end results, shifting the focus of learning from the final product to the process. Hackenberger (chapter 21) illustrates how tackling problems and questions without a clear way forward illuminates the pitfalls of theoretical understanding without praxis.

Bruff also makes a case for students having an audience outside of class. Students' writing in this book confirms his claim that sharing academic production publicly raises the stakes. Beyond the connections Bruff highlights between student projects, media systems, and potential outside interests, students speaking throughout this book address the ethics of information sharing and the broad impact of making their work available in open-access environments. Kramer (chapter 21), for example, reflects on accountability, acknowledging that making academic work accessible online ties students' conclusions directly to their subjects, ultimately exposing both. Separately, Cain (chapter 10) acknowledges that student research influences the way people frame, understand, contribute to, and challenge norms, also addressing accountability.

On autonomy, Bruff argues that giving students choices in their approaches and methods helps them own the final result and engage more deeply in its effects. One student featured in this book adds an important twist to this equation: Apata (chapter 11) demonstrates the application of classroom theory in library programming, blending her understanding of a disciplinary text addressing doing good as opposed to sounding good with important questions about silence and advocacy among librarians. In her case, and in many others addressed throughout this book, opportunities are taken by students rather than given—underscoring the importance of opening doors for collaboration and opening minds to help identify prospective collaborators on campus and off. Acknowledging the power of these connections enables students, faculty, and librarians to work and learn together in community, ultimately reaching beyond the sandbox to pave a way toward greater diversity and equity in higher education.

Each section of this book brings together varied perspectives on the importance of sharing student scholarship and creative work, as well as case studies illustrating how it can be done. Rather than focusing exclusively on any single part of the community, the book incorporates the viewpoints of teaching faculty, academic staff, community members, and students themselves. The idea is to illustrate the benefits of extending teaching and learning beyond instructor/student or library/student binaries to a multidirectional map. The goal is to create a dialogue around the idea of the academic library as a laboratory for emerging scholars and creatives to practice and test their disciplinary work, as a forum for sharing that work, and as an archive where work can be sustained and curated to continually inspire new audiences.

On Libraries as Labs, Forums, and Archives

In our model we propose new roles for libraries based on current practices, expanding our scope to embrace student-produced content as a significant addition to the existing library. We examine our current roles as laboratories, forums, and archives, documenting ways in which participating in these spaces benefits student learning and engagement. And we consider gaps in learning practices that the library is well positioned to fill.

If we start with the idea of the laboratory, we immediately have a concept that looms large in popular imagination, whether one's individual picture is that within Dr. Frankenstein's gothic castle, Batman's Cave, or the *USS Enterprise*'s Holodeck.[6] Interestingly, and despite laboratories' central role in science education, few scholars defined student learning objectives for the laboratory before the early 1980s. Many schools and colleges had labs in which students practiced specific methods or techniques, but little was known about how or why such practices supported broader goals of scientific learning.[7] And yet labs certainly have capacity to support learning. The scientific method involves observing something that inspires questions, doing background research, developing a hypothesis about possible answers, testing the hypothesis through experiments, and analyzing the data to draw conclusions or pose more questions. Library-based labs recognize the value of process by offering spaces that encourage testing ideas and analyzing data as a pathway to connecting to broader ideas. Indeed, many libraries provide labs to support specific areas of digital scholarship, with the digital humanities standing out as the primary focus of this literature.[8]

Seymour Papert has argued that the process of knowledge creation works particularly well when learners have the opportunity to design, create, and construct (constructionism), especially when the process of creation holds personal meaning for them.[9] Papert's ideas are championed through the emergence of makerspaces, community work spaces outfitted with tools and materials that share a goal of encouraging participants to learn through making. Makerspaces have spread rapidly since the concept emerged in the mid-2000s, and they are now found in a variety of settings, including schools, museums, and libraries.[10] For student makers or producers, this type of library lab offers a chance to experiment, to learn or teach a new skill, to test a process or build a prototype, and to come together with others to share ideas, problems, and solutions.

Knowledge is also developed and refined socially, as Vygotsky notes, through social contexts that involve student-student and expert-student interactions in real-world situations that build on diverse languages, skills, and experiences.[11] Thus, while laboratories can support the development of understanding through the acts of observing, designing, and creating (and failing), forums facilitate interactions that lead to knowledge creation as a result of community. Libraries are recognized as hearts and brains, bringing learning in and pushing it back out into the community, but the phrase "library as forum" is recent and limited to literature on public libraries, particularly those engaged with K–12 students in science, technology, engineering and math (STEM) learning.[12]

In the language arts, also in reference to K–12 teaching, Lewison, Flint, and Van Sluys illustrate four dimensions for engaging critical literacy. Each of these finds its way into critical librarianship. They are (1) disrupting the commonplace, (2) interrogating multiple viewpoints, (3) focusing on sociopolitical issues, and (4) taking action and promoting social justice.[13] Without naming it, librarians engage the concept of forum in the *Framework for Information Literacy*, noting that scholarship is conversation.[14] Even so, many framework studies fall short of critically assessing who these conversations include and exclude. Critical literacy and pedagogical theory, which surfaced in librarianship in the aughts, has enabled more discussion of inequitable access to information and its modes of production and dissemination.[15] In addition to underscoring the uneven nature of constructed and contextual authorities and the legitimacy of information, critical librarianship advocates for practicing socially just librarianship through more inclusive practices like those Boal embraced in group theatre.[16]

Laboratories and forums support experiential learning and conversation in the present. However, libraries also provide access to learning and conversations from the past, archived for present and future learners. "Throughout recorded history archives, libraries, and other repositories have evolved to provide access to and preserve traces of the past for the future."[17] Although most librarians and archivists understand the subtle distinctions between libraries and archives, recent conversations in the literature provide a deep discussion regarding the role of the archive versus the role of the library, and the place and value of the archive. Traditionally, the role of archives has been the preservation of unique items, while libraries emphasize dissemination of widely published materials. However, according to Manoff, the impact of digitally reproducing historical artifacts, recontextualizing them, and making them widely available disrupts this traditional divide between the library and the archive.[18] Paulus believes that "academic librarians and archivists have the opportunity to build on the recognized value of the library as an archive, to position the library as a site of creation, to confront the reality of digital 'archives in the wild,' and to reconceptualize their roles within the archival life cycle."[19] Grafton's 2007 essay in the *New Yorker* brings this full circle by pointing out that medieval libraries were sites of both creation and preservation.[20] As new platforms and technologies evolve, lessening demands on physical space, libraries have the ability to participate in the cycle of information production, creating a natural flow in conversation with students from the creation to the preservation of their work. This book uses the term *archive* in a metaphorical sense, meaning a repository of works and artifacts, digital or physical. The Library as Archives section of this book focuses on collecting intellectual property and the rights associated with this intellectual property. Most case studies involve use of an online institutional repository managed by librarians. However, we do not limit our discussion to institutional repositories specifically and also consider the collection of physical objects created by students. By situating student work within the sphere of work from other scholars, we can provide an authentic audience and expand the reach of this research.

Answering the Call

Derek Bruff calls for the library to be an inspiration for emerging scholars. He describes libraries as both places of collaboration and collaborators on campus. As Inayatullah notes, our current historical moment "of edutainment and peer-to-peer information sharing" presents libraries with a challenge to expand on their roles as warehouses of knowledge and to embrace the additional roles of being laboratories for creating knowledge.[21] Following that idea, this book presents several models for providing a supportive sandbox environment in which students, teaching faculty, and librarians can practice their academic work through collaboration. If libraries do this successfully, we will enhance our value to our students, our collaborators, and our institutions.

Notes

1. George D. Kuh, and Ken O'Donnell, *Ensuring Quality and Taking High-Impact Practices to Scale* (Washington, DC: Association of American Colleges and Universities, 2013).
2. Paulo Freire, *Conscientização* (São Paulo, Brazil: Cortez & Morales, 1979); Augusto Boal, *Theater of the Oppressed* (London: Pluto Press, 2000).
3. Sohail Inayatullah, "Library Futures: From Knowledge Keepers to Creators," *Futurist* 48, no. 6 (2014): 24.
4. Suzanne Michele Schadl, Molly Nelson, and Kristen S. Valencia, "Uncommons: Transforming Dusty Reading Rooms into Artefactual, 'Third Space,' Library Learning Labs," *Journal of Learning Spaces* 4, no. 1 (2015): 41–52.
5. D. Russell Bailey and Barbara Gunter Tierney, *Transforming Library Service through Information Commons* (Chicago: ALA Editions of the American Library

Association, 2008); Margaret Brown-Sica, Karen Sobel, and Erika Rogers, "Participatory Action Research in Learning Commons Design Planning," *New Library World* 111, no. 7/8 (2010): 302–19.

6. Colin Lecher, "The 10 Best Fictional Laboratories, Ranked," *Popular Science*, August 29, 2013, https://www.popsci.com/science/gallery/2013-08/10-greatest-fictional-laboratories.

7. Avi Hofstein and Vincent N. Lunetta, "The Role of the Laboratory in Science Teaching: Neglected Aspects of Research," *Review of Educational Research* 52, no. 2 (1982): 201–17.

8. Tim Bryson et al., *Digital Humanities: SPEC Kit 326* (Washington, DC: Association of Research Libraries, 2011).

9. Seymour Papert, "A Word for Learning," in *Constructionism in Practice: Designing, Thinking, and Learning in a Digital World*, ed. Yasmin B. Kafai and Mitchel Resnick (Mahwah, NJ: Lawrence Erlbaum, 1996), 1–24.

10. Micah Altman et al., *Rapid Fabrication/Makerspace Services: SPEC Kit 348* (Washington, DC: Association of Research Libraries, 2015).

11. Lev Vygotsky, *Mind in Society* (Cambridge, MA: Harvard University Press, 1978).

12. Marlete Kliman, Nuria Jaumot-Pascual, and Valerie Martin, "How Wide Is a Squid Eye? Integrating Mathematics into Public Library Programs for the Elementary Grades," *Afterschool Matters*, no. 17 (Spring 2013): 9–15.

13. Mitzi Lewison, Amy Seely Flint, and Katie Van Sluys, "Taking on Critical Literacy: The Journey of Newcomers and Novices," *Language Arts* 79, no. 5 (2002): 382–92.

14. Association of College and Research Libraries, *Framework for Information Literacy for Higher Education* (Chicago: Association of College and Research Libraries, 2016), http://www.ala.org/acrl/standards/ilframework.

15. Shana Higgins and Lua Gregory, *Information Literacy and Social Justice* (Sacramento, CA: Library Juice Press, 2013).

16. Boal, *Theater of the Oppressed*.

17. Michael. J. Paulus, Jr., "Reconceptualizing Academic Libraries and Archives in the Digital Age," *portal: Libraries and the Academy* 11, no. 4 (2011): 944.

18. Marlene Manoff, "Archive and Database as Metaphor: Theorizing the Historical Record," *portal: Libraries and the Academy* 10, no. 4 (2010): 385–98.

19. Paulus, "Reconceptualizing Academic Libraries," 940.

20. Anthony Grafton, "Future Reading: Digitization and Its Discontents," *New Yorker*, November 5, 2007, https://www.newyorker.com/magazine/2007/11/05/future-reading.

21. Inayatullah, "Library Futures," 24.

Bibliography

Altman, Micah, Matthew Bernhardt, Lisa R. Horowitz, Wenqing Lu, and Randi Shapiro. *Rapid Fabrication/Makerspace Services: SPEC Kit 348*. Washington, DC: Association of Research Libraries, 2015.

Association of College and Research Libraries. *Framework for Information Literacy for Higher Education*. Chicago: Association of College and Research Libraries, 2016. http://www.ala.org/acrl/standards/ilframework.

Bailey, D. Russell, and Barbara Gunter Tierney. *Transforming Library Service through Information Commons.* Chicago (ALA Editions of the American Library Association, 2008).

Boal, Augusto. *Theater of the Oppressed.* London: Pluto Press, 2000.

Brown-Sica, Margaret, Karen Sobel, and Erika Rogers. "Participatory Action Research in Learning Commons Design Planning." *New Library World* 111, no. 7/8 (2010): 302–19.

Bryson, Tim, Miriam Posner, Alain St Pierre, and Stewart Varner. *Digital Humanities: SPEC Kit 326.* Washington, DC: Association of Research Libraries, 2011.

Freire, Paulo. Conscientização: Teoria e Prática da Libertação: uma Introdução ao Pensamento de Paulo Freire. São Paulo, Brazil: Cortez & Morales, 1979.

Grafton, Anthony. "Future Reading: Digitization and Its Discontents." *New Yorker*, November 5, 2007, https://www.newyorker.com/magazine/2007/11/05/future-reading.

Higgins, Shana, and Lua Gregory. *Information Literacy and Social Justice: Radical Professional Praxis.* Sacramento, CA: Library Juice Press, 2013.

Hofstein, Avi, and Vincent N. Lunetta. "The Laboratory in Science Education: Foundations for the Twenty-First Century." *Science Education* 88, no. 1 (2004): 28–54.

———. "The Role of the Laboratory in Science Teaching: Neglected Aspects of Research." *Review of Educational Research* 52, no. 2 (1982): 201–17.

Inayatullah, Sohail. "Library Futures: From Knowledge Keepers to Creators." *Futurist* 48, no. 6 (2014): 24–28.

Kliman, Marlene, Nuria Jaumot-Pascual, and Valerie Martin. "How Wide Is a Squid Eye? Integrating Mathematics into Public Library Programs for the Elementary Grades." *Afterschool Matters,* no. 17 (Spring 2013): 9–15.

Kuh, George D., and Ken O'Donnell. *Ensuring Quality and Taking High-Impact Practices to Scale.* Washington, DC: Association of American Colleges and Universities, 2013.

Lecher, Colin. "The 10 Best Fictional Laboratories, Ranked." *Popular Science*, August 29, 2013, https://www.popsci.com/science/gallery/2013-08/10-greatest-fictional-laboratories.

Lewison, Mitzi, Amy Seely Flint, and Katie Van Sluys. "Taking On Critical Literacy: The Journey of Newcomers and Novices." *Language Arts* 79, no. 5 (2002): 382–92.

Manoff, Marlene. "Archive and Database as Metaphor: Theorizing the Historical Record." *portal: Libraries and the Academy* 10, no. 4 (2010): 385–98.

Papert, Seymour. "A Word for Learning." In *Constructionism in Practice: Designing, Thinking, and Learning in a Digital World.* Edited by Yasmin B. Kafai and Mitchel Resnick, 1–24. Mahwah, NJ: Lawrence Erlbaum, 1996.

Paulus, Michael J., Jr. "Reconceptualizing Academic Libraries and Archives in the Digital Age." *portal: Libraries and the Academy* 11, no. 4 (2011): 939–53.

Schadl, Suzanne Michele, Molly Nelson, and Kristen S. Valencia. "Uncommons: Transforming Dusty Reading Rooms into Artefactual, 'Third Space,' Library Learning Labs." *Journal of Learning Spaces* 4, no. 1 (2015): 41–52.

Vygotsky, Lev. *Mind in Society: The Development of Higher Psychological Processes.* Cambridge, MA: Harvard University Press, 1978.

Section I
Library as Laboratory

CHAPTER 3

The Library as a Lab for Student Work

Amy S. Jackson, Cindy Pierard, and Suzanne M. Schadl

This section recognizes the practice of research as a social and experiential craft. The library as laboratory supports this practice through makerspaces, exhibition areas, lecture spaces, digital design studios, large-scale visualizations, and collaborative learning spaces. The idea of a lab also transcends the characteristics of a particular physical space or a set of tools to encourage an ethos of exploration and experimentation.

Neither labs nor libraries have always welcomed students as participants in their spaces. It was not until the late nineteenth century that student labs were constructed in high school and college settings. Even then, the aim was primarily focused on training students to follow specific protocols and carry out highly prescribed experiments with the idea that learning the process of scientific reasoning and discovery would naturally follow.[1] Similarly, academic libraries did not begin programs of bibliographic instruction until the early part of the twentieth century, with the focus of teaching students how to navigate large print-based collections as a means of uncovering knowledge.[2] In both settings, it was not until the late twentieth century that the idea of using these settings as spaces to teach research as an intellectual process—and not just a set of tools and techniques—began to take hold.

Library labs serve a vital role for Derek Bruff's "students as producers" frame. They are settings where students can engage with open-ended problems, make choices about how they might try to address those problems, and experience successes (along with failures) as essential components of learning and discovery. Accordingly, chapters in this section respond to Bruff's call to action in a number of ways: by addressing the value of productive failure as an element of scholarship (Morse, Temnyalova, and Gordon, chapter 2), by exploring the power of high-visibility and high-tech spaces as a canvas for student work (Evans Groth, chapter 7), by extolling the transformative role of students as lab leaders within a makerspace setting (Wong-Welch, Casabar, Ghazala, and White, chapter 5), and by encouraging library space planners and service providers to embrace ongoing risk taking and assessment as the working ingredients of a successful lab space (Wofford and Milewicz, chapter 6).

Experimentation is core to the laboratory process with recognition that not all testing will result in success. Digital humanities, which—at a basic level—uses digital technology to advance knowledge across the humanities disciplines, encourage serendipitous discovery and the testing and retesting of approaches to a particular research question. Ian Morse, Will Gordon, and Mila Temnyalova, all alumni of Lafayette College's Digital Humanities Summer Scholars program, discuss their experiences as emerging digital humanities scholars and how their encounters with productive failure shaped their individual processes and projects, as well as their overall appreciation for the role of difficult learning and setbacks in scholarly work. The power of this experience, as the students describe, was that their program was one of the few places where they had the chance to develop and work out questions of their own design. Also striking in this case is how the student scholars describe the library as "a natural home for the program" and a place where they were supported in developing and refining their research questions, exploring tools to help them investigate those questions, and sharing their successes and failures with both student peers and faculty and library mentors.

Evans Groth shifts the lab focus back to the physical space in the NCSU Spotlight chapter, sharing examples of how he and his colleagues at the Hunt Library have leveraged the characteristics of the library's physical design to offer students working production spaces as well as highly visible stages for sharing those products. Of particular interest is the inclusive approach to the library's audio studios, one that encourages participation, whether users are novices or possess extensive experience. The lab setup includes a robust suite of hardware and software, but it is also coupled with support from library staff and student employees and has developed a community of peer creators who come together for regular Music Meetups. Projects inspired by classroom assignments—designed collaboratively by classroom faculty and library staff—have now been converted into public workshops, expanding the opportunities for students to experience the power of creating and sharing original music. The public nature of the studio spaces, which make extensive use of glass, exposes the often-private process of music creation and welcomes new students to participate in that process of creation.

Though seemingly ubiquitous in 2018, the phenomenon of makerspaces is relatively recent. Both the term *makerspace*, defined as "[a] publicly-accessible space ...to design and create," as well as a publication devoted to the movement, *Make:* magazine, debuted around 2005.[3] While makerspaces exist in a variety of settings, libraries have become particularly engaged with the makerspace movement, perhaps drawn by a similarity of mission: to provide resources and technologies otherwise unavailable to a community.[4] Within academic settings, the library is charged with supporting all disciplines and can act as neutral ground in providing access to resources that might otherwise be available to only specific segments of the campus population. For student producers, this type of neutral space offers a powerful opportunity to engage with open-ended problems and to design strategies and solutions. Jenny Wong-Welch, Charles Joseph Casabar, Rita Ghazala, and Lindsay White of the buildIT Makerspace @ San Diego State University Library share their experience co-creating a library makerspace in which student master builders from multiple disciplines lead efforts to support learning, making, and sharing approaches to design and fabrication. This case study exemplifies how a library makerspace has forged and sustained a community of practice, wherein participants exchange information and develop knowledge based on common practices. Master Builders share how they have found authentic audiences for their work through the experience of teaching peers and creating products to address defined needs.

Designing a lab space is an exciting and challenging proposition. How can a space help to drive social interaction, offer flexible configurations, support diverse projects, and serve as a showcase for products as well as processes? Brittany Wofford and Liz Milewicz discuss the multiyear process of envisioning, planning, implementing, and editing the Ruppert Commons for Research, Technology, and Collaboration at Duke University. They share how the experience of building a library lab has led them to embrace a spirit of experimentation with a constant need to tinker and adjust spaces, staffing, services, and programs to respond to failures and to better support student researchers and research teams. This spirit has been infused into all aspects of offering this space as service. New service models prompted by the creation of the lab led to the retooling of a student intern position that now involves developing proficiency with digital technology as well as its application to different disciplinary questions. Requests to use the lab have helped to drive changes to policies and procedures, as well as encourage networking and cross-referrals with other campus lab spaces. Lab programming is designed to foster curiosity (DataFest) and to encourage open discussion of research realities, such as how students have overcome setbacks and obstacles in the research process (Edge Research Talks).

These library labs support student researchers by providing a space where theory and practice coalesce, where students can pose open-ended questions, learn about the application of research tools and methods, and find their own pathways to discovery. Labs described here are inclusive and welcoming to novice and expert researchers and creators, offering opportunities for interaction and informal learning from disciplinary experts, librarians, or fellow students. Programs or exhibits held within lab spaces make public the work of scholarship, serving to spark curiosity and inspire.[5] In addition to the end product, sharing the process of the work's creation—a discussion of a computer science student's process for developing a tool to analyze the text of Supreme Court opinions, or the steps undertaken by an art student to design digital maps of her university library—provide the opportunity for others to take in that information and consider it within the framework of their own experience and ideas. In addition to sharing successes, library labs offer a safe space to share the types of failures and challenges that are frequently core to research and creation. These labs also call us to embrace a reflective practice, considering how libraries might continually reinvent our services and spaces in support of authentic learning.

Notes

1. National Research Council, *America's Lab Report* (Washington, DC: National Academies Press, 2006), 13, https://doi.org/10.17226/11311.
2. Susan Ariew, "How We Got Here: A Historical Look at the Academic Teaching Library and the Role of the Teaching Librarian," *Communications in Information Literacy* 8, no. 2 (2014): 212–13.
3. Gui Cavalcanti, "Is It a Hackerspace, Makerspace, TechShop, or FabLab?" *Make: magazine*, May 22, 2013, https://makezine.com/2013/05/22/the-difference-between-hackerspaces-makerspaces-techshops-and-fablabs/.
4. John Burke, "Making Sense: Can Makerspaces Work in Academic Libraries?" (presentation, Association of College and Research Libraries Conference, Portland, OR, March 25–28, 2015), http://www.ala.org/acrl/sites/ala.org.acrl/files/content/conferences/confsandpreconfs/2015/Burke.pdf.
5. Siu Hong Yu, "Just Curious: How Can Academic Libraries Incite Curiosity to Promote Science Literacy?" *Partnership: The Canadian Journal of Library and Information Practice and Research* 12, no. 1 (2017): 4–5.

Bibliography

Ariew, Susan. "How We Got Here: A Historical Look at the Academic Teaching Library and the Role of the Teaching Librarian." *Communications in Information Literacy* 8, no. 2 (2014): 208–24.

Burke, John. "Making Sense: Can Makerspaces Work in Academic Libraries?" Paper presented at the Association of College and Research Libraries Conference, Portland, OR, March 25–28, 2015. http://www.ala.org/acrl/sites/ala.org.acrl/files/content/conferences/confsandpreconfs/2015/Burke.pdf.

Cavalcanti, Gui. "Is It a Hackerspace, Makerspace, TechShop, or FabLab?" *Make: magazine*, May 22, 2013. https://makezine.com/2013/05/22/the-difference-between-hackerspaces-makerspaces-techshops-and-fablabs/.

National Research Council. *America's Lab Report: Investigations in High School Science*. Washington, DC: National Academies Press, 2006. https://doi.org/10.17226/11311.

Yu, Siu Hong. "Just Curious: How Can Academic Libraries Incite Curiosity to Promote Science Literacy?" *Partnership: The Canadian Journal of Library and Information Practice and Research* 12, no. 1 (2017): 1–8.

CHAPTER 4

The Good Side of Failure

Explorative Yet Productive Failure in Digital Humanities Projects

Ian Morse, Mila Temnyalova, and William Gordon

Introduction

A project is oftentimes not about the final result. The majority of research rarely makes it into publication or wider distribution. This learning—about the process, the tools, the limitations, and the impossibilities—can be more valuable than an end product. Such was the case with our research as members of the Digital Humanities Summer Scholars (DHSS) program, an intensive six-week Mellon-funded research program run by Lafayette College's Skillman Library. The digital humanities (DH) is a relatively new field with a diverse community of scholars and practitioners. While there is not one single definition that encapsulates it, its spirit is best described with continual rethinking, questioning, and demonstrating through a plethora of projects and collaborations. If our own DHSS projects were judged only by our initial aims, they would be failures. Yet it was in that failure that we learned the most.

Through discussions with students in our cohort, experimenting with college and library resources, and critical feedback from librarians and professors, we learned how to conduct research and clearly communicate our ideas. Equally critical to this process was experimentation—the ability to explore across disciplines, different methodologies, and tools. Here, we can see productive failure as Manu Kapur articulated it, as the value that can be realized by allowing struggle and even failure as pieces of the problem-solving and learning process.[1]

Many scholars writing about digital humanities pedagogy emphasize the benefits of experimentation, or what Stephen Ramsay calls "screwing around," as a means of learning serendipitously rather than only through specific and purposeful acts.[2] It is through acts of unplanned screwing around that some of the greatest discoveries are made and some of the greatest questions posed. Cathy Davidson provides one example of this, referencing a class she taught at Duke University where students were given the freedom to create their own ways to learn the material. When students were able to design the ways they learned, Davidson found they were also better at *unlearning* or connecting information and knowledge in new and different ways. She also discusses the importance of being free to court failure: "We spent a good deal of time thinking about how accident, disruption, distraction, and difference increase the motivation to learn and to solve problems, both individually and collectively."[3] Importantly, this approach enhanced rather than diminished the class. Students were more motivated to participate—at one point they took initiative to invite a guest lecturer to a class session that they hosted themselves as Davidson was out of town—they engaged in the readings, and even their writing was better. This environment that *allowed* for failure expanded the students' minds.

Davidson's students, in essence, experimented with different ideas as a means of learning. Jentery Sayers has referred to this approach as "tinker-centric pedagogy,"[4] which he has described as introducing unfamiliar modes of learning through testing and tinkering. This kind of learning through experimentation inevitably results in some degree of failure; however, failure is not necessarily seen as a problem since tinkering is not a process intended to reach a certain goal after constantly building on an idea. Instead, tinkering can offer insight even during failure. The process of tinkering is also not necessarily linear, as Sayers shows in his discussion of "change-logs,"—the idea of saving different versions of a project or an assignment and making note of what one changes as well as how one's ideas change over time. For Sayers, the idea that the first version of the assignment or project could be better than the later versions is important and learners should become comfortable with moving forward or backward across the versions they have created in an effort to determine what ultimately seems to work best.[5]

Lindsay Thomas and Dana Solomon describe a similar approach taken as they sought the help of undergraduate students in developing RoSE (research-oriented social environment), a web-based project designed to present humanities research organized as a social network of knowledge. By allowing students to give feedback on design and goals of the RoSE project, they found that RoSE became a kind of pedagogical tool and created "a stage or vehicle for the exploration and discovery of knowledge."[6] Discovery and exploration involves tinkering, and that's exactly what undergraduate students working on the RoSE project were doing. Like Davidson, Thomas and Solomon illustrate an example of tinkering or screwing around in practice.

In the remainder of this chapter, we will illustrate how each of our projects as DHSS relates to these ideas about the power and value of productive failure, experimentation, tinkering, and screwing around. Ian found he had to push the limits of digital humanities to find questions answerable with a sound methodology. Mila could not find a data set and had to create her own, tinkering with how to present it. Will had to grapple with results that either didn't make sense or were inconclusive. A lot of trial and error took place to create his project and figure out how to present his results.

Digital Humanities Summer Scholars (DHSS) Program

The DHSS program was, more than anything, a learning process. We were a cohort, the first of its kind on Lafayette's campus. As students, we learned about digital humanities. As DH advocates, we learned how to construct such a program. On a campus where student researchers usually work on a professor's project, the DHSS is one of the only opportunities for students to develop and work on research questions of their own. The student group—consisting of seven students the first year, eight the second—gathered three times a week in a collaborative environment. Each student pursued his or her own project in the span of six weeks, but peer review and constant critical feedback were a significant part of the program from the very beginning.

Each year, students were chosen to be a part of the cohort after a rigorous selection process. There were no prerequisites regarding experience in digital humanities. Nor were there requirements that related to computing skills, field of study, or prior experience in academic research. All students had the opportunity to apply, but selection to the program largely depended on the strength of the initial research question itself. Because of this, the selected group of students came from various backgrounds with a plethora of different skill sets and were put in an environment that encouraged exchange of information and knowledge.

In 2012, Skillman Library staff were awarded a Mellon Foundation grant for its proposal to create a program that would support student engagement with digital scholarship.[7] The resulting DHSS program was run by members of the library's Research and Instruction Department, with full support from the library's Department of Digital Scholarship Services, whose staff played a key role in introducing student scholars to specific tools and their potential applications. Student scholars were also encouraged to engage faculty members from across Lafayette College, drawing on their expertise in various disciplines including the humanities and social sciences, as well as science, technology, engineering and math (STEM) fields. While these faculty members were not all officially affiliated with the DH program, they opened their offices to the DHSS participants whenever they needed help finding relevant information or checking the validity of their theories.

The DHSS program was a place where different disciplines met head-on, a variety of methodologies were put to the test, and research questions of different fields found points of intersection. More than anything, DHSS was a place to break down walls and bring scholars together. The library, as a place that brings scholars from different fields under the same umbrella, was the perfect platform to launch such a project and further nurture its growth. According to Sarah Morris, the mentor for the 2016 and 2017 cohorts, "As the place where disciplines, methodologies, and research expertise intersect, the library is the natural home for the program." This statement could not ring more true.

The discursive process was supplemented by the resources the library provided. For instance, research librarians played key roles as mentors in the learning process, providing the students with critical feedback on all stages of their research projects. The librarians were the people on campus who had been exposed to the widest variety of research ideas—the people who had seen success and failure alike and could recognize a strong idea when they saw one. They made themselves available to the students with utmost enthusiasm, joining the open laboratory hours to offer feedback on how students might refine their research ideas and to assist in finding and evaluating resources. The librarians' ability to grapple with different digital tools, their knowledge of databases, and their connections to faculty and research projects granted scholars the freedom to experiment with their ideas, understand possibilities, and confidently interpret results.

At the beginning of each program term, the cohort had the opportunity to set its goals and values. The second cohort, for instance, drew on arguments put forth in the University of Minnesota's *Debates in the Digital Humanities* series, particularly Lisa Spiro's article on the shared values of digital humanities, and proposed the following elements as guiding values for community interactions and project constructions: constructive critique, access, experimentation, and rigor.[8] Afterwards, the DHSS group met, led by a research and instruction librarian, three times a week—twice as a small class and once in a laboratory setting, which was open to the public. There were three different types of assignments: research elements, project elements, and reflection elements. These were all heavily emphasized, especially at the beginning of the program when students had little idea of what DH was or how to go about navigating the world of academia and developing their self-guided research projects. Ultimately, that is where the assignments truly helped, giving them ideas as to where they should start.

The research elements were meant to help the students lay the building blocks of a solid research paper. Everything was done gradually and step by step, starting with the literature review, going through the methodology, and ending with the design. This allowed the students to write strong research papers grounded in many weeks' worth of reading and analysis. However, the process of writing the papers came hand-in-hand with the process of building the projects themselves. That is where the assignments centering on project elements came in. They were incorporated into the program in order to scaffold toward the final project. They started off with students reviewing other DH projects found through open databases and ended with student peer review of each other's final work.

Finally, the reflection elements were carried out through the maintenance of weekly blogs. At the end of each week, each student had the opportunity to review and assess his or her experiences. This was a completely unstructured activity, one that gave students the freedom to express themselves as they desired. This part of the program best exemplifies the personal and academic journey each student went through. It not only allowed the students to share their experiences, but also gave them the opportunity to revisit moments in time and gain awareness of how much they had grown, as scholars and as people, in these six weeks. One excerpt illustrating this awareness came from a member of the summer 2017 cohort, who wrote the following in his first entry: "My peers will definitely be an important part of this experience as we will struggle, learn, lead, and succeed together, or not at all. These six weeks are also weeks of self-discovery as undergraduates, researchers, and human beings capable of independent thought." Similar sentiments can be found across multiple cohorts of scholars, whose reflections are captured on Lafayette College's DHSS website.[9]

From the beginning, students have the mind-set that they may or may not reach their end goal, and that that is perfectly fine. While having a tangible project to show their work at the end of the six weeks is important, what's more important is showing what they learned in the whole process. It is a program not just about finding conclusive results, but about nurturing young, inexperienced students into scholars who are capable of tinkering with different designs and methodologies, creating databases, and building things from scratch time and time again. It is a program that encourages students to delve into their projects and experiment in finding the best ways to articulate themselves and present their projects. Consequently, productive failure was a vital part to this journey.

A similar train of thought followed scholars toward the end of their six-week experience, as told by a member of the summer 2016 program in his final blog entry: "A little deserves to be said about the collective analytical setting of our cohort. A striking lesson that I take away from this gem of an experience is the purely analytical and conceptual merging of our works for mutual critique. Not the act of critique itself, but the setting that fostered an intellectually inspiring atmosphere."

Reading the students' weekly reflections, one can truly feel the eagerness with which they started this endeavor and the sense of satisfaction that came toward the end of it, even if the students' original goals had not been met. This is because the process of the scholarship, rather than the actual results, was the main takeaway. Of course, all the skills and knowledge gained throughout the six weeks will remain with the students for a long time, but more important is the sense of purpose each budding academic found.

Ultimately, students had the freedom to explore new approaches and articulate them in otherwise unfamiliar areas precisely as a result of these three types of assignments, the diversity of the cohorts' scholarly interests, and the unconditional support of the research librarians and faculty mentors alike. But while this was a collaborative process conducted in a social and learning environment, it was also an individual growing and learning experience for each student. Because the research projects were largely self-guided, they were rooted in tinkering and experimentation and allowed for many discoveries. Failure was not frowned upon. If anything, students were encouraged to remember and built upon the takeaways of their failures, which ultimately made that failure productive.

Ian's Exploration Back to Basics

Project may be found at https://sites.lafayette.edu/dhss/ian-morse/.

I enrolled in the program's inaugural year in 2015 and began the six weeks as many other students did: with lots of interest in a large question and little experience with the tools to pursue it. Emily McGinn, the program convener and at that time a postdoctoral fellow at Lafayette College, had prepared a syllabus that guided us through our project in a short time frame. My interests were in the press and its freedom to publish. I believed a digital humanities project could add another, perhaps explanatory, dimension to the following question: Does press freedom deteriorate more strongly with economic, political, or legal change? Regardless of the specific question, I knew

I wanted to combine a few main interests—maps, statistics, and the press—and I knew these topics intersected perfectly in the DH. Of several online projects from which I drew inspiration, the closest to my vision was likely the Mapping Media Freedom Project.[10] Organized by Index on Censorship and funded by several organizations across Europe, the project logs verified violations of press freedom across the continent so the viewer is able to interpret press freedom over time, space, and category. Other projects, I saw, produced similar engaging and revealing interactive visuals that depicted the pieces of the world or a slice of time.[11] Confident in my library's ability to provide and teach skills, I thought I could find a way to combine big data and visuals. That was my project in its embryonic stages: explain press freedom through several indices and variables and translate it onto a map.

Yet there was a problem with my understanding of digital humanities. I had seen the products of projects, not the process and work. An analogy may be that one would rarely begin a research project, whether in the natural sciences or the humanities, knowing exactly what the result would be and striving to produce only that result. Such methods would taint the integrity of the answers or conclusions that would come from the final project. A research project without a question or hypothesis may be circular or even specious. My goal was not to create a product, but to answer a question. Yet, like the seven other undergraduates in the program, I approached the field with little understanding of what it was. We understood only the products and that it was supposed to be a field open to all disciplines and methods. We had reason to be enthusiastic because we thought our projects could have no limits. Because I was a student with little experience in the field, my biggest problem was not simply the integrity of the research methods used, but the ability to complete the project within the six weeks. I spent too much time figuring out what was possible in the field and what I wanted to do with my project.

The first two weeks of the program focused on readings in digital humanities as well as discussions of each member's project. We read John Unsworth's blog post "What's 'Digital Humanities' and How Did It Get Here?" and selections from Matt Gold and Lauren Klein's 2015 edition of *Debates in the Digital Humanities* published online.[12] We searched the web for other digital humanities projects and dissected their questions and methods. We also searched the web for tools to create projects, like the maps, time lines, and text analyses we found. The searching was neither superficial nor meaningless; we prepared presentations about the projects and tools for a discussion that dove into each. We were all getting a sense of the possibilities (which seemed immense) and a bit of what was required to produce each project. Some of us had little background in formatting spreadsheets or writing code to produce a visual, but that meant little because of the amount of help we could receive from both the library and online tools. Members of the research team occasionally held small meetings with us to explain their roles and the resources they had, but the whole library was available to us: we only had to ask. Later in my project, when I needed to pull content from a large spreadsheet into .txt files, I received crucial help from a digital production manager in the library.

However, by the end of the first two weeks, I still had not found a feasible question. While others in the DHSS program had begun to move on to methods and processes in the second week, my updates had remained largely static. I had learned from many of the projects presented within the group that large mapping projects often take years and several people to complete. I had also been torn between two interests: mapping and statistics. I latched onto political science papers that used publicly available data in large-N regressions to create interactive maps and find support for political theories. I found publicly available data sets and contacted others to find more, but some were not in an accessible format for the tools I knew. I became focused on learning secondhand, rather than producing or learning firsthand. Combining both my interests into one project would mean a several-layered world map, or a rigorous handling of dozens of indices and variables in explaining press freedom, or both. I had planned my project to be as engaging and cross-disciplinary a DH project as the dozens I saw online. Was I really trying to accomplish my own project and pursue my own questions? Emily, who had helped me explore dozens of tools that could be used for my interests, told me to take a big step back.

Emily provided a surprisingly helpful piece of guidance. She worked with me to go through the steps to a research question, a process I had done several times in academic positions I had held. Every thesis is composed of the claim and reason, she told me, and there were several different types of claims: a fact, definition, interpretation, value (whether something is good or bad), consequence, and policy. I really had to go back to basics. From this framework, I made my goal much more local and similar to the academic projects I had read about. I spent a day in a room with a large whiteboard, diagramming the connections across things I had read and across my interests. I had already read substantially. One country, Finland, consistently ranked high in press freedom indices, while a country I was familiar with, Turkey, was far lower in the ranking. What could explain that difference? Certainly, I could read of governmental or nongovernmental interference, but it is difficult for advocates to address such powerful forces. What if advocates looked more locally? What were the journalists experiencing, and how did that affect their journalism?

I found I had to really define the press freedom as well as its causes and effects. I found that there was a low possibility that amassing a lot of data would allow me to do what I really wanted to do. Press freedom violations were too individually determined and indices varied too greatly across organizations and time, making it unlikely that a global look could be meaningful. My interest was really in addressing press freedom and providing real insight. I found I had to continually narrow my focus to ensure I could complete it adequately. I could combine mapping, time lines, and text analysis, but each larger scale depended on precise information from its smaller counterpart. Most importantly, what I found was that the question was not inherently one of digital humanities. But it did use DH to address an old problem in a new way. Very few people seemed to have approached the problem of press freedom from a pretty crucial angle: from the perspective of those active in the press. The reason advocates care about freedom is because they are afraid it will alter or diminish information in an environment. How does press freedom affect the quality of journalism?

I now had a question from which I could form a hypothesis, and it was apparent how digital humanities could aid the answer. It was a project that required a bird's-eye view of journalistic texts. Through the several text analysis tools I had researched and explored, I could develop a methodology to discover how the press changed, or was affected by, press freedom violations. I would have to discover my own research process because other projects I had found typically viewed a corpus of text as a stationary unit, but I was interested in change within one. I settled on a newspaper with which I was familiar, *Today's Zaman* in Turkey, and I chose a turbulent period across which to measure its reporting, the Gezi Park Protests in 2013. The Lexis Nexis database did not cover that period for *Today's Zaman*, but after receiving help from the library, I created my own corpus and ran various analyses with Ant-Conc and some Voyant tools.[13] AntConc provides various text analysis tools based on frequency. For instance, one tool measures *keyness* or how unique a certain word is compared to another corpus (e.g., How unusual is the appearance of the word *media* after the protests, as opposed to before?). The online Voyant tools I used included RezoViz, which links words that appear together in a text (e.g., Do certain terms appear in an article together often?). My initial project was a failure. The final product looked nothing like what I had dreamed before the program started.

Yet even before I began using tools or collecting data, I tinkered. I worked off other projects, played with their interactivity, and experimented with the limits of tools in mapping, time lines, and text analysis. I found there wasn't a single tool that could accomplish exactly what I wanted, but that didn't mean that my project was unfeasible. Just as any traditional academic humanities project may find a dearth in evidence or a lack of ability to understand that evidence, you can work around it, acknowledging the shortcomings or nontraditional path. Having encountered the new digital humanities realm, screwing around allowed me to metaphorically echo-locate the walls that limited me. And each time I experimented, I would do so until I failed to do what I wanted. I found that tinkering can easily go on forever, so a helpful jolt back to basics let me find my feet again.

Mila's Mo(nu)ments of Productive Failure

Project may be found at https://ussrremnants.wordpress.com.

Going into the project, I was filled with determination and led by ambitious ideas. The original research proposal I wrote for my DHSS application revolved around communist-era monuments in Eastern Europe. Growing up in Bulgaria, I watched as a lot of monuments were abandoned, ridiculed, and destroyed by human aggression and passage of time. But I also saw how tourists stood in awe in front of bigger-than-life figures. I watched youth furiously scrub away the contempt painted upon men who, whether for good or bad, had made history. I witnessed how, piece by piece, meaning was brought back to monuments that had been left behind.

All of my adolescent years, I had been fascinated by how society's perception of ideological monuments was capable of changing from person to person and year to year. Yet no professor at Lafayette College was researching Eastern Europe's Soviet monuments, and so DHSS became the perfect opportunity for me to take matters into my own hands. Initially, I wanted to study why monuments were destroyed and what sparked the desire to bring life back to them. How did the treatment of monuments differ across borders, and why was this the case? Did the digital world—through its blog posts, videos, and viral images—play any role in the treatment of physical edifices in public spaces? By the second week of the summer program, I also became interested in tracking the establishment of communist-era monuments throughout the years.

Those were many questions to look into, and six weeks proved to be a highly insufficient time to work on an idea of this scale. As my mentors said—a project of this magnitude seemed better suited to a graduate school dissertation than a first-year student's summer fellowship. Day after day, I was encouraged to narrow the scope of my project, and each day, I claimed I was good enough to do it.

It was my first time conducting academic research. Since scope was but a foreign concept to me, the mentors' warnings fell on deaf ears for three weeks straight. By the third week, the pressure was on. I discarded the idea of Eastern Europe on the whole and chose to focus on Poland, Ukraine, East Germany, and Bulgaria instead. But by the start of the fourth week, when it became apparent there was no database of monuments for me to use and that I would have to build my own before beginning any analysis, I bit back the hurt and rather begrudgingly narrowed my area to Bulgaria. At that point, I felt a sense of disappointment. I had spent three weeks researching something that would be of very little use to me—a paragraph in the literature review, at most. To put this time span into perspective, three weeks was half of the entire length of the program. Needless to say, panic started creeping in. My reflection from the third week depicted my somber mood: "The past week has been rough. I had spent a lot of time researching monuments that I would not need and questions that were not essential."

However, after swallowing my hurt pride and severely narrowing my scope, my reflection of the fourth week ended with the following paragraph: "Overall, I have reached peace with the way this project is headed. A part of me fears potentially meeting with the History Department Head because he could discourage me from everything that I just rebuilt from scratch.... But another part of me knows that even if that happens, I have already learnt that rebuilding is not that bad, after all."

By then, I was not afraid of starting from scratch. Only scraps of my initial idea remained. If my project was to be judged by whether my final paper answered the initial research question that got me accepted into the program in the first place, my whole work would undeniably be deemed a failure. However, there is a sort of power in starting from scratch and building yourself up all over again. Yes, the first idea was a failure, and the second idea was still not doable. And I may have spent two solid weeks researching Tito's monuments in Yugoslavia (which had very little to do with Red Army monuments in Bulgaria), but I would in no way classify these two weeks as a waste. If anything, learning comes from trial and error. I had spent hours scrolling through blog posts and news accounts concerning erection, desecration, and destruction of monuments, and although I ultimately didn't use those exact monuments, I still learned through failure. Experimenting allowed me to explore different areas, try different methodologies, and incorporate different designs. None of them could be labeled as wrong. They were just not fit for the time frame of DHSS.

I tried and I erred, time and time again, but that motivated me to keep going until I found the right path. When I finally did find it—I started building a database of Bulgarian monuments using Google Maps and a time line of their desecration through Timeline JS (a tool I learned about from a fellow scholar in our cohort)—I also began to feel like I was back at square one. That feeling only intensified when I started analyzing the Soviet monuments I had compiled, only to find a link to another era's monuments in the inscriptions and realize that I would have to incorporate close to another 100 monuments in the database.

I spent many nights in front of the computer during that fourth week, just looking at monuments. At wrong pictures. Wrong locations. Wrong translations. My database had four monuments under the same name and in the same location, but photographs depicting radically different structures. Two monuments that looked completely identical in structure and shared the same name …in opposite sides of the country. The impossibilities were everywhere. To top that, I had added more than two dozen monuments for which I could not find a picture—or a correct location—at all. Of what use were they going to be if my new research question was rooted in the origin of Soviet monuments' sites and inscriptions? While Creative Commons photographs were many, I oftentimes resorted to asking bloggers' permission to use the photographs they themselves had taken. Not everyone, however, replied. Many monuments remain without an attached picture even to this day.

Building a database, I realized, is hard work. It is a road paved with mistakes and marred by failure, but it is still a road worth paving. One year after the official end date for DHSS, I have been contacted by two researchers who would like to use my database and a student who was looking for a similar database on Macedonian monuments. Coincidentally, the two weeks I had spent collecting Yugoslavian monuments had left me with more than twenty monuments in Macedonia—with locations, inscriptions, photographs, histories, and current state. And in the spirit of the digital humanities, I was more than willing to share. Even those two weeks, as it turns out, benefited somebody out there.

> Now I am grateful for the guiding hands on my shoulders, which steered me in the direction of the right path. I remember walking down the steps of Skillman Library and allowing myself but a few seconds to be disappointed: in my over-zealous ambition, in my jumping in head-first, in the fruitlessness of close to three weeks' worth of work. But I had seen others stumble and fall and get back on their feet right away—and that meant I was capable of that, too. So with a new-found strength in my steps, I made my way home.

That was part of my last reflection at the end of the six weeks, looking back at the obstacles we all had surmounted. I found motivation in seeing my cohort face failure and get back on their feet, and I was determined to not be left behind. That being said, I did not fear acknowledging the moments when I took a wrong turn or followed the shortcut instead of the main road. In retrospect, however, it is imperative to understand that while these were not a part of the road leading directly to the finish point, they were included in the broader map.

At the end, the takeaway of a journey is not the road we were supposed to follow, but the plethora of roads we took and the map we used itself. Experience lay in the journey—one filled with potholes and dirt roads and many wrong turns—and not merely in reaching the destination.

Will's Experiments with Code and Interpreting Results

Project may be found at https://sites.lafayette.edu/topic-modeling-scotus/.

Many of us thought that doing a digital humanities project in two weeks would be nearly impossible. Yet there was still enough time to build a small project—with room for some tinkering. For my project, I wanted to perform textual analysis on Supreme Court opinions to compare and contrast themes in liberal and conservative justices' opinions. In order to do this, I wanted to build a web-scraping tool to extract the text of Supreme Court opinions from the website FindLaw (https://caselaw.findlaw.com/) and put it into a text document. After that, I planned to run those documents through a program that performs textual analysis. How I would do this, though, and what I would use for my sample were two big questions to which I did not have ready answers.

Once I did some initial research for my project, I began to build the web scraper—a tool that allows me to pull text from a webpage and put it in a text file. After doing some research on the Internet, it occurred to me that this was the best way to go about pulling text without copying and pasting everything into a text file over and over again. This required a lot of experimentation. Because Python seemed to be the best language for the task, I chose it to begin programing. My previous experience coding was only in Java, so I first had to learn Python's syntax. That required a lot of experimentation. Programming pedagogy has a long history in tinkering, as Sayers notes, referencing the work of Annette Vee.[14] I tried out my own commands to see what I could get to work and used pedagogical tools such as Codeacademy and Learn Python the Hard Way, which are both online tutor programs for coding languages. These tools also gave room for error, especially Codeacademy. If I did not succeed in my first iteration of the code, the program would not punish me. Rather, it would give me another shot at performing the task. Shortly, I was proficient enough in Python to stumble through building a web scraper.

After looking at a couple of different libraries for web scraping with Python, I settled on Beautiful Soup. Essentially, this library expanded the toolbox of commands I could use in Python, giving me the ability to pull text from webpages. The documentation was fairly intuitive—perfect for messing around with to learn. It allowed me to pinpoint HTML tags in the webpage on FindLaw that indicated where the Supreme Court opinion began and ended. Figuring out how to code this part so the whole program worked effectively, however, required a bit more trial and error than just playing with Beautiful Soup. I also had to look for patterns in the HTML tags on FindLaw, which were inconsistent. At times, the opinion's start and end were marked with inconsistent tags. So I created a series of if-statements to catch these inconsistencies, which allowed me to find each part of the opinion. In the end, I developed a successful program that was able to pull Supreme Court opinions after 2009 from FindLaw. Playing with my code and constantly running and rerunning it was the only way to find all the inconsistencies in the program I was checking.

Finding a way to perform textual analysis of the documents I created was somewhat easier. Early in my research process I came across a tool called MALLET. The instructor of our program gave us a list of DH projects to look at during one of the first days of class. In one project, Topic Modeling Martha Ballard's Diary, digital humanities scholar Cameron Belvins used MALLET to find different topics Ballard discussed in her diary. I figured I could do something similar with the text of Supreme Court opinions. After going through a tutorial on The Programming Historian (https://programminghistorian.org/), I had a good handle on the program. Nevertheless, it still took a bit of experimentation to figure out exactly how it worked—to adjust the settings and properly read the table it printed out. Here, again, experimentation was valuable to the learning process.

In the end, my results proved inconclusive. There was too much legal and technical language in Supreme Court opinions to isolate language that may reveal the kind of topics a justice looks at when deciding constitutional cases or issues and that might reveal differences in the thinking of liberal or conservative justices. Judged on this standard, my digital humanities project would have been considered a failure. However, what I learned was found in experimenting with different tools in my project to achieve that result. My project resulted not only in me learning a new programming language, working with its libraries, and becoming better at reading HTML tags—I built a program to take texts of Supreme Court opinions off of a website. With some more tinkering, it could be applicable to more opinions on that website, since the basic structure of the code is already laid out. Failure, in this case, not only produced a useful tool, but also gave me a set of skills to apply to other projects. In other words, this kind of failure was productive.

Conclusion

At the start of the inaugural cohort, Ian's year, students were told they were guinea pigs for the program. The library had received approval to begin to stretch digital humanities funding into the undergraduate sphere, and after some applications, the group was set. At the end of the six weeks, few of the participants felt they had accomplished what they set out to do. In the final presentation to administrators and academics in the college, however, the group was told that they had been very successful. The program continues, at the time of writing, at least two more years.

A common thread lies in all our stories from working on digital humanities. Self-guided research projects can be challenging, especially to people who are new to the process. On the face of it, things usually seem simple enough, but in reality a lot of tinkering and experimentation are required in order to have a sound research question or project. Even then, the road to answering that question is hard and long. Failure is a natural part of it. Even if students do not reach their initial goals, what's important is they walk out of the DHSS program with new found skill sets and knowledge applicable elsewhere.

At Lafayette College, Skillman Library has encouraged the techniques of experimentation and productive failure by helping DHSS participants engage with digital scholarship on their own terms. DHSS proved to be the only opportunity for students to pursue independent research—not driven by faculty mentors, but by us, through our own interests and ideas. We don't have years of research experience and publications behind us—most of us were newcomers to the field who weren't aware of how intricate the process of building a project from scratch could actually be. Oftentimes, as research assistants to professors, students are not the ones directly experiencing setbacks and failures. They are merely witnessing it happen to the faculty member as the research goes on. The DHSS program led by Skillman librarians recognized the value in our scholarly ideas and in the occasional messiness of our scholarly processes. The program provided us with steady mentorship from the library's Research and Instruction Department, reliable peer review from within the student cohort, and shared experiences and support throughout the duration of the program, and even after its official end. That, ultimately, is where our success lies.

Acknowledgements

The authors wish to acknowledge Sarah Morris and Emily McGinn, whose support transformed our experience as digital humanities scholars and whose encouragement inspired this contribution.

Notes

1. Manu Kapur, "Productive Failure," *Cognition and Instruction* 26, no. 3 (2008): 380, https://doi.org/10.1080/07370000802212669.
2. Stephen Ramsay, "The Hermeneutics of Screwing Around; or What You Do with a Million Books," in *Pastplay: Teaching and Learning History with Technology*, ed. Kevin Key (Ann Arbor: University of Michigan Press, 2014), 115.
3. Cathy N. Davidson, "Collaborative Learning for the Digital Age," *Chronicle of Higher Education*, August 26, 2011, http://www.chronicle.com/article/Collaborative-Learning-for-the/128789.

4. Jentery Sayers, "Tinker-centric Pedagogy in Literature and Language Classrooms," in *Collaborative Approaches to the Digital in English Studies*, ed. Laura McGrath (Logan: Utah State University Press, 2011), 279–80. http://ccdigitalpress.org/cad/Ch10_Sayers.pdf.

5. Sayers, "Tinker-centric Pedagogy," 287.

6. Lindsay Thomas and Dana Solomon, "Active Users: Project Development and Digital Humanities Pedagogy," *CEA Critic* 76 (2014): 213.

7. Sarah Morris, "The Digital Humanities Summer Scholarship: A Model for Library-Led Undergraduate Digital Scholarship," *College and Undergraduate Libraries* 24, no. 2–4 (2017): 533. https://doi.org/10.1080/10691316.2017.1338978.

8. Lisa Spiro, "This is Why We Fight: Defining the Values of the Digital Humanities," in *Debates in the Digital Humanities*, ed. Matthew Gold and Lauren F. Klein (Minneapolis: University of Minnesota Press, 2012), 18–20.

9. "Digital Humanities Summer Scholars," Lafayette College, accessed October 22, 2017, https://sites.lafayette.edu/dhss/.

10. Mapping Media Freedom website, Index on Censorship, accessed February 3, 2018, https://mappingmediafreedom.org/.

11. Two examples are The Migrants' Files website, coordinated by Journalism++, accessed June 5, 2018, http://www.themigrantsfiles.com/; and the Mapping Texts website, partnered with the Chronicling America project, accessed June 5, 2018, http://mappingtexts.org/.

12. John Unsworth, "What's 'Digital Humanities' and How Did It Get Here?" in *Debates in the Digital Humanities 2015*, ed. Matthew K. Gold and Lauren F. Klein (Minneapolis: University of Minnesota Press, 2015), http://dhdebates.gc.cuny.edu/.

13. AntConc is free text-analysis software available online from Laurence Anthony at http://www.laurenceanthony.net/software/antconc/, and Voyant Tools are free web-based applications available at https://voyant-tools.org/.

14. Sayers, "Tinker-centric Pedagogy," 281.

Bibliography

Davidson, Cathy N. "Collaborative Learning for the Digital Age." *Chronicle of Higher Education*, August 26, 2011. http://www.chronicle.com/article/Collaborative-Learning-for-the/128789.

Gold, Matthew K., and Lauren F. Klein, eds. *Debates in the Digital Humanities 2015*. Minneapolis: University of Minnesota Press, 2015. http://dhdebates.gc.cuny.edu/.

Kapur, Manu. "Productive Failure." *Cognition and Instruction* 26, no. 3 (2008): 379–424. https://doi.org/10.1080/07370000802212669.

Lafayette College. Digital Humanities Summer Scholars webpage. Accessed October 22, 2017. https://sites.lafayette.edu/dhss/.

Mapping Media Freedom website. Index on Censorship. Accessed February 3, 2018. https://mappingmediafreedom.org/.

Mapping Texts website. University of North Texas and Stanford University. Accessed June 5, 2018. http://mappingtexts.org/.

Migrants' Files website. Coordinated by Journalism++. Accessed June 5, 2018. http://www.themigrantsfiles.com/.

Morris, Sarah. "The Digital Humanities Summer Scholars: A Model for Library-Led Undergraduate Digital Scholarship." *College and Undergraduate Libraries* 24, no. 2–4 (2017): 532–44. https://doi.org/10.1080/10691316.2017.1338978.

Ramsay, Stephen. "The Hermeneutics of Screwing Around; or What You Do with a Million Books." In *Pastplay: Teaching and Learning History with Technology*. Edited by Kevin Kee, 111–20. Ann Arbor: University of Michigan Press, 2014.

Sayers, Jentery. "Tinker-centric Pedagogy in Literature and Language Classrooms." In *Collaborative Approaches to the Digital in English Studies*. Edited by Laura Mc-Grath, 279–300. Logan: Utah State University Press, 2011. http://ccdigitalpress.org/cad/Ch10_Sayers.pdf.

Spiro, Lisa. "This Is Why We Fight: Defining the Values of the Digital Humanities." In *Debates in the Digital Humanities*, edited by Matthew Gold and Lauren F. Klein, 16–34. Minneapolis: University of Minnesota Press, 2012.

Thomas, Lindsay, and Dana Soloman. "Active Users: Project Development and Digital Humanities Pedagogy." *CEA Critic* 76 (2014): 211–20.

Unsworth, John. "What's 'Digital Humanities' and How Did It Get Here?" In *Debates in the Digital Humanities 2015*. Edited by Matthew K. Gold and Lauren F. Klein. Minneapolis: University of Minnesota Press, 2015). http://dhdebates.gc.cuny.edu/.

CHAPTER 5

Students as Lab Leaders

The Role of Master Builders in the build IT Makerspace @ San Diego State University Library

Jenny Wong-Welch, Charles Joseph Casabar, Rita Ghazala, and Lindsay White

Introduction

San Diego State University (SDSU) is a large, public institution and the southernmost campus of the twenty-three institutions that make up the California State University system. To fully understand the mission of SDSU, it is important to understand the Donahoe Higher Education Act in the California Education Code, which states that within the State of California there will be three public segments of higher education: the University of California system, the California State University system, and the California Community College system. Each segment has a unique educational purpose. For example, while the University of California was designated as the primary research institution, the California State University was designated as the primary teaching and learning institution.[1] The importance of this role of teaching and learning informs everything that happens on the SDSU campus.

Striving to be an influencer of teaching and learning activities on campus, the SDSU Library leveraged the university's strategic plan, specifically the call to "expand opportunities for undergraduate scholarship through innovative courses, experiences, and engagement,"[2] and applied for a university grant to create a makerspace. In 2015, the STEM Librarian, Jenny Wong-Welch, was awarded $11,713 to start the build IT makerspace @ SDSU Library. The library's justification for developing the makerspace consisted of three parts. First, while similar spaces, like the Engineering Machine Shop and the Art Studio, existed on campus, there wasn't a single location that allowed students from any major to access technology and equipment used for making. The library saw an opportunity to be a nexus providing all SDSU students an opportunity for hands-on experimentation, prototyping, problem-solving, and design thinking through access to emerging technology such as 3-D printers, robotics, programmable circuits, and augmentation and virtual reality equipment. Second, the goals for the library's makerspace emphasized its ability to foster a culture of engaged and active learning for all students. The philosophy of the new space was one in which small-group discussion; collaboration; participatory, project-based, and peer-to-peer learning; as well as experimentation, inquiry, curiosity, and play were encouraged. Third, to prove the impact of the grant, the library committed to assessing the new space, which included evaluating the types of learning it inspired, and tracking data on user demographics as well as the number of interdisciplinary projects that resulted from access to the space.

Jenny Wong-Welch—Designing the build IT Makerspace and Beginning the Master Builder Program

From the beginning, the mission of build IT was to be a student-run makerspace designed to foster creativity and innovation:

> By providing an infrastructure for the DIY learning of technology, build IT assists anyone in their mission of bringing their ideas to life. The build IT space provides a physical location where anyone can gather to explore, build, and learn through sharing resources and knowledge, working on projects, and networking. With its central location in the SDSU Library, access to build IT is available to anyone on campus regardless of their discipline or expertise.[3]

This goal was influenced by other maker literature that highlights how makerspaces, specifically library ones, help democratize access to making tools and equipment and welcome everyone into the experiential learning that happens inside, which ultimately builds a unique community of users and supporters.[4] It was a long implementation process to achieve this lofty goal. The makerspace started in a small, 120 square foot space located in the SDSU Library's 24/7 area with one 3-D printer. Over the next two years, it grew into a 1,200 square foot space with multiple 3-D printers, scheduled K–12 outreach events, a detailed training program, and various new services. While build IT has become an established space on campus, it will continuously evolve along with advancing technologies and the changing needs of the SDSU community.

During the early stages of the implementation process, I singularly focused on how to democratize access to emerging technology such as 3-D printers and programmable electronics. Initially, I thought that purchasing the technology and putting it in a shared space would cause it to become available to anyone on the SDSU campus and thus meet my goal. However, after opening the build IT makerspace, I came to realize that only individuals with previous experience with the technology were using it. So, to fully democratize access, I would need to create some sort of assistance service where anyone could learn the concepts behind the technology, how to effectively use it to make something, and its advantages and limitations. My revelation was that access is not only the ability to touch and use, but includes the ability to understand how to utilize something in an effective manner. If I wanted to design a space where students are acting as producers of creative or scholarly works, then I needed to support them not only by providing access to the tools, but also by supporting them in learning how to utilize the tools. It was this realization that led to the creation of the Master Builder program.

The Master Builder program was established as a student volunteer-run service. One reason for this approach was to have an assistance model that would not necessitate a staffing budget, but it has evolved into something much more focused on influencing a student's education through the experience of providing peer-assisted learning. Based on similar peer-based assistance programs such as the Prototyping Instructor (PI) program at the Georgia Tech Invention Studio,[5] the Master Builder program seeks students who agree to volunteer three hours every week to help staff the build IT makerspace and assist others with utilizing and applying its technology to their ideas and projects. At the start of each semester, I hold open enrollment where I recruit any student who has an interest in technology, enjoys helping others, and is willing to volunteer. Other than these stipulations, I do not require students to have any particular skill or experience. By keeping the requirements minimal, I hope to encourage students from various backgrounds to join. Throughout the build IT makerspace's two years of existence, over 100 students have signed on to be Master Builders. While the majority of the students are engineering majors, there still is a diverse subject background among them, as seen in figure 5.1.

FIGURE 5.1
Majors of Master Builders from January 2015 to May 2017

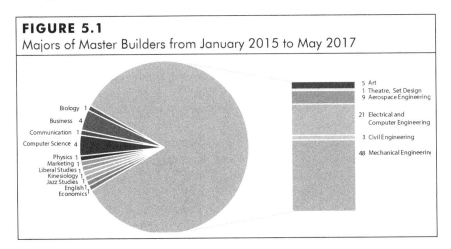

As mentioned, since the students are not required to have any experience before starting as Master Builders, they somehow need to learn the technology before they can teach it. To help with a Master Builder's development as well as standardize what is taught, I created a training program that includes multiple activities that individually cover a specific piece of technology. An activity is designed to teach a student the general purpose of the technology, how it works, how to use it, and other basic information. At the end of the activity, each student is required to complete a task that utilizes the technology to make a specific product. For example, at the end of the 3-D modeling/3-D printing activity, each student is asked to 3-D model a name-tag design and 3-D print it. Also, as a librarian, I like to intertwine information literacy concepts with the activities. For instance, within the 3-D printing activity, students learn the rationale behind open-source hardware and intellectual rights associated with it.

When I started the Master Builder program, I realized many of the students never got the chance to meet the other Master Builders because their schedules did not regularly overlap. To build community among the volunteers, I implemented weekly Master Builder meetings. While these meetings were not required, they were strongly encouraged. The meetings served as a forum for everyone to discuss and provide feedback on what was observed in the space. Typically, I would start by providing a discussion topic based on what I had seen, such as making sure the students acknowledge in a timely manner anyone who enters the space. Then, since I truly believe in making sure the students feel invested in the space, I would ask about their experiences and listen to their feedback. Also, since Master Builders are not required to have prior experience, the meetings allowed me to train everyone at the same time. For instance, each training activity was assigned during these meetings. I would develop a general lecture that covered the purpose of the technology and how it works. Then I would walk through using the technology, which students would immediately practice by completing a task. It was expected that once students completed the ending task, they should be comfortable assisting others with the technology. For instance, since not every Master Builder was able to attend the meetings, it was expected that those who did attend would review the material with those who were unable to attend. So far, there are eight activities within the training program covering technology such as 3-D printers, computer numerical control (CNC) machines, embroidery machines, Arduinos, and virtual reality equipment.

Library as Laboratory

While I initially created the build IT makerspace to serve as a platform for democratizing access to technology, I discovered that it could also be a place where the library can be seen as a stakeholder in shaping the teaching and learning process at SDSU, in effect acting as a lab where new approaches can be taught and learned. Since build IT opened its doors, numerous students, faculty, and staff have been able to learn how to successfully utilize the technology to complete a project through processes of active learning that include experimentation and discussion. However, it is often difficult to capture their learning progress because their completed projects are typically turned in for a grade, implemented in a lab or art show, or given as a gift. But another way to examine learning in such a space is through the development of the student volunteers who support it. While the assessment of other types of learning within build IT is something I hope to explore in the future, this chapter will focus on the teaching and learning process that has been captured through the experience of the Master Builders.

Master Builders and the Role of Experiential Learning

The build IT makerspace is distinctive because it gives students experiential learning opportunities that cannot be found elsewhere on campus. The first experiential learning opportunity is a Master Builder's ability to gain work experience while staying on campus and working between classes. For the majority of students, their role as a Master Builder is their first formal work experience. Typically, there are about thirty-five students serving as Master

Builders during one semester. To manage everyone, I start by individually reviewing expectations and responsibilities with each student. As the students serve as Master Builders, they learn and develop skills like customer service skills, teamwork, skills in people management and communication, confidence, leadership, and commitment. While I can see the students developing these skills, they often don't recognize the value of what they have learned. For instance, there was a mechanical engineering student who would refer to his time in build IT as simply a place where he goofed around with 3-D printers. However, once he graduated and obtained a job based on his Master Builder experience, he came to realize there was significant value in his time working on 3-D printers, dealing with patrons, and learning how to teach others.

To help reinforce to students that they are learning important skills, I will often spend time observing them as they work. Based on my observations, I will take them aside to have them reflect on their actions, while I will provide guidance and feedback. Finally, many students have told me that their Master Builder experience has led to getting a job or internship in their desired industry. These anecdotes provide evidence of the value of the Master Builder program in providing students with real-world work experience combined with the convenience of working on campus.

One of the most impactful experiential learning opportunities that build IT provides is the ability for students to work on projects that are subsequently implemented in the library. Something that I find valuable about libraries is their ability to serve as a safe platform for implementing new experimental projects; in a way, I see a library as a type of a research and development laboratory. When I was a pre-professional graduate assistant at the Grainger Engineering Library Information Center at the University of Illinois, Urbana-Champaign, I began to see how a library could be a place for individuals to test new ideas in practice and gain feedback to improve them. I would work on special projects that were often assigned by the librarian and that were meant to be put to use in the library. Once a project was completed, it was empowering to see it put into practice. I was also able to propose my own ideas as a project, which empowered me to trust myself to develop an idea, execute it, and reevaluate it. During my time there, I created many projects, such as an instructional workshop series, numerous webpages, and new services. My experience truly gave me the perspective that all libraries can be a place for learners to research, develop, and test their ideas. This background informed my thinking about the Master Building program. I wanted student volunteers working in the build IT space to have that same satisfaction of testing ideas and seeing some succeed as programs or services.

But I first had some challenges to address. I was finding it difficult to keep the Master Builders invested after they completed all training activities.

While the training activities provide each student with a foundational understanding of technology, they are not designed to be comprehensive. I thought that the Master Builders would benefit from additional challenges that would keep them enthused about working in the space. Also, it became evident as they progressed through the activities, a student's interests would often gravitate toward certain pieces of technology. How could I keep students invested, encourage them to deepen their learning in an area of interest, and engage them with projects?

To emphasize this idea of the library as a laboratory for the Master Builder, I decided to provide the students with dedicated time to master their craft by requiring that one of their three volunteer work hours be spent on their training activities. Once a Master Builder completed all of the training activities, I met with that student to discuss his or her interests. Based on our discussion, I then gave the student various opportunities to work on specialized projects that combined personal interests and career goals with a library need. These projects have varied from constructing simple 3-D printed tool holders to creating directional signage and even designing a complex time clock system.

While these special projects are meant to create a product that benefits the library, they actually benefit the Master Builders much more by giving them the opportunity to lead and control their own learning. They provide an opportunity for students to learn material outside their coursework in a formal setting without the fear of failure. I truly encourage students to dream of new ideas and propose their own projects. Once a student suggests something, I will mentor the student through understanding the feasibility of the idea, discuss any costs associated with it, who benefits, the longevity of the project, and its time frame. Since students are involved in the proposal stage, they develop a better understanding of the project. For instance, students are often given an assignment in class without an understanding of the context or the reason for completing it. By working for an actual client, the library, and working to understand the library's goals and purposes, they are able to design better products and services. Another advantage of these projects compared to a course assignment is that they are iterative. Because the project is not tied to a specific course, there isn't an end date. Since the library is consistent throughout a student's college career, students can continue their project from one semester to the next. Many projects are also iterative or even recursive, and repeated work on an idea for a design or service allows students the opportunity to improve upon a prototype as they make another iteration. Finally, this type of process creates a means for the students to transfer skills gained from one project to another project, which makes them hone these skills further.

The least tangible experiential learning opportunity in build IT is its ability to help students personally develop and grow through their interactions with others. Technology transverses all subject areas. For instance, a 3-D printer can be used to manufacture an art sculpture and a modified lab device. With the focus on technology as a cross-disciplinary tool in build IT, it has become a gathering place where anyone who is interested in technology feels comfortable sharing how they have used it for specific projects while learning from others whose experiences may be very different. With an average of seventy-five visitors every day, the traffic of so many different people through the space provides the Master Builders with numerous opportunities to learn from people of diverse interests. As each student interacts with everyone who wanders into the space, they learn skills such as responsibility, commitment, patience, empathy, compassion, understanding, honesty, integrity, self-reliance, and confidence. Ultimately, the experience of meeting a diverse population of people allows the Master Builders to develop a personal understanding of how technology can affect everyone's life.

Another aspect of learning through interactions comes from the relationships between the Masters Builders themselves. Many of the students who have served as Master Builders for build IT continue to volunteer in part because of the friendships that they have developed with the other Master Builders. As seen in figure 5.2, based on a recent survey, most students who are currently Master Builders plan to return for another semester.

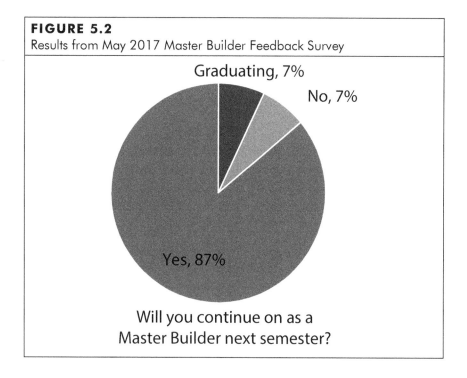

FIGURE 5.2
Results from May 2017 Master Builder Feedback Survey

Graduating, 7%

No, 7%

Yes, 87%

Will you continue on as a
Master Builder next semester?

This type of learning and growth is illustrated by a quote from one of the Master Builders:

> Since I did not live in the dorms, build IT is the first time I have made friendships that are not dependent on a class/major and have lasted consistently throughout semesters. The build IT makerspace fosters a sense of community I have not been able to find in other clubs, and I feel like it has helped me flourish and find my place on campus.

This student's feedback is reflective of daily experience in build IT. For instance, all too frequently, an off-shift Master Builder will continue to hang out in the space because it feels like home to that student. To help build a supportive culture among the Master Builders, I have them work on projects together. It is not uncommon to see other Master Builders become interested in a project that one Master Builder has started. It is very rewarding to see that as the Master Builders develop their own skills, others will turn to them for guidance because the Master Builders respect each other as experts as well as friends.

Students' Experiences as Lab Leaders: Learning from the Master Builders

The following sections are written by Master Builders of the build IT makerspace @SDSU Library and are meant to provide additional evidence of their learning. Each includes a short biography, an example of a specific project, and finally reflections on the overall experience of working as a Master Builder in build IT.

Charles Joseph Casabar

I am an electrical engineering student at San Diego State University (SDSU). I am also working toward a minor in computer science. After I finish my undergraduate program at SDSU, I intend to pursue a graduate degree in electrical engineering. My eventual goal is to work on designing electronics to help power things like electric vehicles.

I first heard about the build IT makerspace when my friend mentioned that the library was trying to start a new space focused on technology. I heard that the library was creating a space to teach people about 3-D printing and was looking for volunteers to help with running the space, managing the 3-D printers, and assisting others with learning about the technology. I was fortunate enough to have some prior experience with 3-D printers; in fact, I had recently built one from scratch. My experience helped me secure a position as a Master Builder, a student volunteer who helps out in build IT. Originally, I expected to work specifically with 3-D printing only, but as build IT grew, so did my work experiences.

Being a Master Builder has been a great learning opportunity. The exposure from volunteering has given me various new opportunities on campus. I get to meet others with similar interests from different backgrounds. Unlike lab courses, which are directed at students within a specific department or major, students who use the services in build IT have different backgrounds and areas of interest, which adds diversity to the experience. There is much more freedom in the topics and projects that are available to me to work on in build IT compared to typical classroom settings. This freedom is good because it broadens the scope of learning available in the space.

As mentioned, in build IT, Master Builders are able to work on special projects that relate to our interests. For example, one of the projects that I worked on as a Master Builder was designing a system to help count people as they entered and left the space, known as a Door Sensor/Counter. The data generated from this device is an important statistic for tracking usage of the space to provide evidence to a stakeholder of its value. The goal of the system was to detect when people walked through the main doorway and transmit the time and count to an online service for storing and analyzing. Beam-based person-counting systems were already being utilized elsewhere in the library, but they lacked wireless data logging capabilities. After researching online how other custom systems had been implemented, a prototype was made.

The first version served as a proof of concept and utilized some technology already present in build IT. This included a littleBits cloudBit, a Wi-Fi module that provided internet connectivity, a light sensor, and a modified laser pointer. Because the laser beam was directed across the doorway to a light sensor, the sensor could detect whenever someone or something passed through the doorway and interrupted the beam, and this was used to trigger the logging action to an online spreadsheet via the cloudBit. Using the littleBits modules proved to be a good initial prototype due to the ease of construction, and it also eliminated the need to buy parts that might not be used in later versions. While this version worked, I learned it had issues with reliability. I was also concerned with the safety of a laser pointer, as well as issues keeping the laser beam aligned with the sensor. Finally, the cloudBit module, which was a majority of the system's cost, also introduced a significant amount of delay, which made counting inaccurate.

After proving the feasibility of the initial concept, I constructed a second version. To eliminate the issues with the laser pointer and light sensor, an infrared-based distance sensor was used to detect motion through the doorway. The self-contained sensor unit did not have issues with safety since the light used was infrared, and it did not have alignment issues like before. The cloudBit was replaced with a cheaper, open-source Wi-Fi module that could be programmed with more functionality. This eliminated the most expensive component of the first version while increasing the capabilities of the system. The new Wi-Fi module also reduced the amount of time taken to log each person, allowing for more accurate counting. I used the Arduino environment to program the Wi-Fi module. I used Autodesk Inventor to design a magnetic bracket for holding the infrared distance sensor that could be 3-D printed. The online portion of the data logging system utilized Google spreadsheets and scripts to total the number of sensor events per day and back up the data from each day automatically.

When I reflect on doing the project, I have realized that designing and building the system in two stages was very useful. The first version using the littleBits module was easy to prototype. It also helped to expose flaws in the online logging system, as well as test the speed required to accurately detect multiple people moving in and out quickly. This guided the design process and made the second version much more effective. Also, while I already had most of the skills needed to complete this project, like soldering wires, programming with Arduino, and 3-D modeling in Autodesk Inventor, I was able to gain new experience with interfacing hardware and software with cloud-based systems, as well as logging data from real-world events. I have realized that although the programming and construction of the hardware were not new to me, this project did allow me to practice my skills on a real-world problem.

Finally, I chose to volunteer at build IT because I wanted to be able to share my 3-D printing knowledge with others and to help educate them about the exciting aspects of this technology. I started as a Master Builder when build IT was first launched. It has been great to see how it has grown to include other technologies like various electronics kits, 3-D scanning, and computer-controlled sewing, milling, and cutting. Being a Master Builder has allowed me to learn about each of these technologies through teaching them to others. Many of the topics I learned in build IT aren't available in standard electrical engineering curriculum. For instance, the mechanical aspects of machines fall outside of the scope of an electrical engineering program. The best part of build IT is the collaborative learning experience that comes from working with the other Master Builders, which differs from a standard classroom setting.

Rita Ghazala

I am majoring in art with an emphasis in multimedia at San Diego State University (SDSU). My career goal is to become a 3-D animator. When I came to SDSU as a freshman, I wanted to join various organizations to be more involved on campus. One of the organizations that became interesting to me was build IT. I remember learning about the organization from Jenny during my new student orientation. At first, I thought it was like a student club, where we had to meet once a week and plan events. However, when I came around and asked about it, I found out that I had to volunteer certain hours. I did not mind volunteering because I really wanted to learn something new and felt it was worth my time. Ultimately, I ended up joining build IT because it created an opportunity for me to learn something new, like 3-D printing, that I wouldn't have been able to learn anywhere else. Also, I joined because I saw it as an opportunity to help me gain experience with 3-D animation. When I first joined, I expected to learn only about 3-D printers. However, after a couple weeks, I discovered build IT was a place where I could also learn about other technology. Also, I discovered how it became a place where I could see people from other majors than mine, which allowed me to learn a lot of things from talking to them and to get new ideas.

After completing my training activities in build IT, I have learned a lot of new technologies and their applications. I have been able to apply what I've learned to my coursework as well as my own personal projects. After being a Master Builder for two semesters, I got the chance to work on a Master Builder project with Jenny, which was to create a new library map.

The project involved making a map for the library that detailed the layout of the group study rooms, the book stack call numbers, and other spaces on each floor. The goal was to make it easier for the librarians to direct the students to each floor. The previous library maps were so old that they often were to too difficult to read and misdirected students. So I was to work on making the maps somehow easier to read and understand.

To start the project, I first met with Jenny. She shared the old maps with me and explained what she was looking for with the new ones. After finalizing what should be done, we then discussed what tools to use. Jenny had experience with Adobe Illustrator and Photoshop, and she knew that I wanted to learn them. So she taught me some of the basics on how to use them. Then she left the project in my hands. Once I got started, I realized that I needed to know some more about how to do specific functions like change the perspective of each library floor. To learn how to do this, I researched YouTube videos and watched what they did. I then took what I learned and applied it to the library maps.

From doing the library maps, I have learned how to use Adobe Illustrator and Photoshop, how to draw a map, and how to render it with 3-D effects. I felt proud after completing the project. Not only did I create something after having never used the software before, but I was able to create something that the whole library uses on a daily basis. Also, I have been able to share my new skills with other Master Builders. They have seen the work that I did on the library maps and asked if I could work with them to create something. For instance, one time, a Master Builder, Dany, said he wanted to make a flyer for his new student organization, Extra Life. I helped choose a Creative Commons design and work in Illustrator to create his promotion event flyer. Another Master Builder, Eli, was interested in making a poster for his residence hall. I ended up teaching him the basics of Illustrator, and then he was able to make his own poster. Finally, last semester, I took an art class on Adobe Illustrator, Photoshop, and InDesign for my major. Since I already knew the basics from working on the library maps and teaching the other Master Builders, I did not struggle with the class and felt it was much easier for me to understand. Also, it has been great sharing with Jenny what I have learned from my class.

When I first came into build IT, I thought that I would mostly learn how to use the 3-D printers. However, I have learned so much more. I have been involved in build IT for two years. I plan to stay involved because I learn things in build IT that I would not learn anywhere else and this continues with each new semester. I believe that my experiences in build IT will help me in the future. I can see getting more job offers because they will see that I have knowledge and experience with more than just my art background. Also, I can use my new skills to work as a for-hire artist to make flyers and cards for other people who need them. Finally, build IT is a special place on campus because it accepts any type of person of any major and it connects those people. It is a place where people can come together to learn new things.

Being a Master Builder, I have learned things that I would not have learned from my coursework. For example, I have learned how to print 3-D objects and fix the 3-D printer when it jams. I would have never learned this in any of my classes because most are about art, and 3-D printing involves more engineering. As an art major, I had found that most of my friends were either art or business majors. Being a Master Builder gives me the opportunity to interact with people who are majoring in engineering or math. Even if I had friends who were majoring in engineering, we would never talk about engineering concepts. By being a Master Builder in build IT, I have a place where I can talk and share with other people. I inspire other Master Builders about creativity, and they inspire me about doing technology topics.

Lindsay White

I am an undergraduate student studying electrical engineering as a major with computer science as a minor. Upon graduation, I intend to pursue a graduate degree in electrical engineering and computer science (EECS), and then I hope to work in research of some sort; I have always told people that my goal was to work at a better-funded NASA. I would like to work somewhere on developing circuits or programs that will aid in scientific discoveries.

I first became involved in build IT because of my interest in 3-D printing. I was working in the SDSU Library's Media Center, where my boss knew that I had built a 3-D printer in high school, so he forwarded me the email that Jenny sent to the library staff asking for interested student volunteers for build IT. I went to the informational meeting, not knowing what to expect, and decided that I might as well try volunteering and seeing where it went—I had no idea what was going to happen in the space. I really like being involved in build IT because I can teach people new skills and help people with their projects. I do enjoy being able to work on projects and learning from them, but my primary purpose at build IT is to help other people learn, and I enjoy that.

I started as a Master Builder right as build IT began. It has been great to see the evolution of the space and its services. Jenny has always asked for our opinions on how things are going. I feel that she has given me lots of opportunities to give input into how things are conducted in build IT. For example, Jenny knew of my previous experience with 3-D printing and teaching people technology through my work as a mentor for a high school robotics team. To build upon those experiences, she included me in creating the training material for the 3-D printers. There have been many more instances where I have been included in what happens in build IT, like helping create the activities and programming for an outreach event for middle school girls.

Every year, there is a week in February that is designated "Engineer's Week," with the idea that doing projects and fairs and other outreach activities will drive young students to be interested in STEM. The Thursday of Engineer's Week is "Girls' Day," which focuses specifically on fostering young girls' interest in STEM. At SDSU, the MESA (Mathematics Engineering Science Achievement) program organized an event for Girls' Day in both 2016 and 2017, where they brought about forty middle school girls to campus for a variety of activities; build IT was one of their stops. Jenny first met with the MESA program director to discuss the specifics of the day. After that, she met with me, and we decided that we wanted to 3-D print bracelets for the middle school girls. I first had to investigate a feasible design for the 3-D printed bracelets. There were many limitations, such as print time limits, size, and best structural design. I began by drawing the basic design on build IT's whiteboard. Many Master Builders became interested in my work and started giving feedback on the design and what they thought worked best. After a little bit more discussion and further research, I decided to create solar system bracelets out of flexible filament, which is plastic that can be 3-D printed. My plan was to 3-D print the bracelets before the girls arrived, and on the day of the event we would give the girls a brief lecture-style overview of the solar system and have them paint the bracelets to take home.

After finalizing the bracelet design, I 3-D modeled the bracelets in Autodesk Inventor. I chose this software because I had previous experience with it from designing personal projects that I have 3-D printed. In creating the solar system design, I had to research how big each planet is and their celestial order. At first, I wanted to make the design an exact scaled version of the solar system, but it made the bracelets too large to print. Another challenge I had with making the bracelets was that I had no idea how long to make them so that they would fit around a middle schooler's wrist. I attempted to solve this problem by researching how big average wrist sizes are at different ages, and I also measured the wrists of people around campus and averaged them to find an ideal bracelet length. Finally, I faced a challenge with trying to use a flexible filament, a type of 3-D printed material that was new to us, on a printer that was not quite suited for it. To solve this issue, I researched on various blog feeds to determine what other people did that created the best results, and I also used a trial-and-error method to determine how to best print with the material.

For the most part, the skills that I needed for this project, Autodesk Inventor and 3-D printing, were skills that I already possessed from my various personal projects, but I did learn a lot of new things. For instance, I learned a lot from trying to 3-D print with the new flexible filament. I also had the opportunity to help lead the instruction session when the girls were in build IT. This event allowed me to learn how to teach and interact with middle schoolers. For this project, I got to practice my skills of 3-D modeling and 3-D printing, as well as conduct a scientific experiment about wrist sizes. At the end of the project, I wrote up a blog post for the build IT website to provide an example of how build IT interacts with the community around us.[6] It highlights how we work with a program on campus to help inspire an interest in STEM in local middle school girls. Finally, it has been great to reuse the skills and knowledge I have gained from this project on many of my other projects.

My experience in build IT has been lots of fun. When I joined, I did not have any concrete expectations of what I would get out of the experience. I have found it to be an enjoyable experience where I can learn skills that are directly related to the engineering field. For example, I have worked on other projects that involve a lot of computer programming, which is directly connected to my computer science minor. These programming projects give me experience that many of my classmates do not have the opportunity to get at this stage in our academic careers. I believe that being involved at build IT has given me an opportunity to gain experience that will ultimately help my future career. Also, as a commuter, being involved has given me somewhere to both make friends and to be when I am not in class. I do not know very many people on campus besides a few classmates from my major. The build IT makerspace allows me to make friends that I otherwise may not have found. There is a strong sense of community among those involved that I am grateful to have found and to be a part of.

Conclusion

The build IT makerspace @SDSU Library was started with a goal of democratizing access to technology, but it has evolved into a true powerhouse on campus for providing students with an experiential learning opportunity. The Master Builder program was created to help student participants not only master technologies and their applications, but to encourage others to learn to use these resources for their own projects. An unexpected benefit resulted from the program's ability to give any student numerous opportunities to engage in experiential learning. By volunteering in build IT, students can gain essential work experience to help prepare them for the workforce. Through training activities that teach each student the basics of using technology, students are able to explore and identify what interests them most. Building upon their training and interests, students have the opportunity to further develop their skills and gain new knowledge by working on special projects that are utilized in the library. Finally, the Master Builder program helps build a social network on the SDSU campus around technology. The students are able to make new friends and personally develop by learning from the connections that they make.

Notes

1. "The Donahoe Higher Education Act," University of California Office of the President, February 25, 2010, http://www.ucop.edu/acadinit/mastplan/donahoe.htm.
2. *Building on Excellence: A Strategic Plan for San Diego State University 2013–2018* (San Diego: San Diego State University, 2013), 6, http://go.sdsu.edu/strategicplan/images/finalstrategicplanbooklet.pdf.
3. "About," build IT website, San Diego State University Library, accessed June 1, 2017, http://buildit.sdsu.edu.
4. Kimberly Sheridan et al., "Learning in the Making: A Comparative Case Study of Three Makerspaces," *Harvard Educational Review* 84, no. 4 (2014): 505–31, https://doi.org/10.17763/haer.84.4.brr34733723j648u; John J. Burke, *Makerspaces* (Lanham, MD: Rowman and Littlefield, 2014), 1–32.

5.   Craig R. Forest et al., "The Invention Studio: A University Maker Space and Culture," *Advances in Engineering Education* 4, no. 2 (Summer 2014): 10–12, https://eric.ed.gov/?id=EJ1076126.

6.   Lindsay White, "Solar System Bracelets," build IT website, San Diego State University Library, accessed June 1, 2017, http://buildit.sdsu.edu/solar-system-bracelets.

Bibliography

Burke, John J. *Makerspaces: A Practical Guide for Librarians*. Lanham, MD: Rowman and Littlefield, 2014.

Forest, Craig R., Roxanne A. Moore, Amit S. Jariwala, Barbara Burks Fasse, Julie Linsey, Wendy Newstetter, Peter Ngo, and Christopher Quintero. "The Invention Studio: A University Maker Space and Culture." *Advances in Engineering Education* 4, no. 2 (Summer 2014): 1–32. https://eric.ed.gov/?id=EJ1076126.

San Diego State University. *Building on Excellence: A Strategic Plan for San Diego State University 2013–2018*. San Diego: San Diego State University, 2013. http://go.sdsu.edu/strategicplan/images/finalstrategicplanbooklet.pdf.

San Diego State University Library. "About." build IT website. Accessed June 1, 2017. http://buildit.sdsu.edu.

Sheridan, Kimberly, Erica Rosenfeld Halverson, Breanne Litts, Lisa Brahms, Lynette Jacobs-Priebe, and Trevor Owens. "Learning in the Making: A Comparative Case Study of Three Makerspaces." *Harvard Educational Review* 84, no. 4 (2014): 505–31. https://doi.org/10.17763/haer.84.4.brr34733723j648u.

University of California Office of the President. "The Donahoe Higher Education Act." February 25, 2010. http://www.ucop.edu/acadinit/mastplan/donahoe.htm.

White, Lindsay. "Solar System Bracelets." build IT website, San Diego State University Library. Accessed June 1, 2017. http://buildit.sdsu.edu/solar-system-bracelets.

CHAPTER 6

Testing the Edge of Scholarship

Supporting Student Research in the Ruppert Commons for Research, Technology, and Collaboration

Brittany Wofford and Liz Milewicz

Introduction

Laboratories are commonly understood as places for experimentation, where failure and success equally inform and improve research. Innovation works hand-in-hand with observation and assessment, helping to turn intellectual risk taking into constructive, collective knowledge. If we want our libraries to serve as laboratories, librarians themselves must be willing to take risks and learn from failure. Duke University Libraries embraced this vision in 2015 when we designed and launched The Edge: The Ruppert Commons for Research, Technology, and Collaboration with a mission to meet the needs of interdisciplinary, team-based, data-driven, and digitally reliant research.

Using this research commons as a case study, our chapter illustrates how intentional and context-driven design of spaces, policies, and services can encourage students and faculty to experiment and to reflect on processes and learning, all while helping to showcase and make more visible interdisciplinary, team-based projects. This case study is presented chronologically, following the phases of our research commons development (assessment, design, implementation, and assessment again) and focusing on our processes, experiments, and learning in each phase. We end with a recognition and exhortation that understanding how to support collaborative, innovative research requires that we ourselves engage in that work.

Developing a library laboratory begins with intentional design, informed by campus needs and interests. At Duke, this took the form of an environmental scan, interviews with campus stakeholders, and a visioning workshop. To support the kinds of team-based, interdisciplinary, vertically integrated, digital research emerging on campus, we needed to provide a resource-rich environment with easily accessible spaces and tools—one that could foster discovery, serendipity, and interdisciplinary collaboration while maintaining flexibility for future changes and continued experimentation. A cross-departmental management team regularly assesses how we are meeting the goals inspired by this vision. A range of projects, programs, and campus partnerships formed since The Edge's launch in January 2015 demonstrate how we implemented our vision, particularly students' involvement. We also share examples of our efforts to experiment and learn within this new space and to encourage that same experimental mind-set among researchers.

Assessment: Gauging Researcher Needs, Desires, and Gaps

Before designing The Edge, Duke University Libraries' staff engaged in activities intended to surface the needs of our users and identify ways those needs might be met. In addition to analyzing consultation statistics, we interviewed researchers, administrators, and staff across the university so that we would have a full sense of resources already available to faculty and students, what they lacked and needed, and what the libraries were in a good position to provide. Once we identified the need for a commons space, we conducted a visioning workshop with these same stakeholder groups in order to define the purpose and character of this space.

Changing User Behavior and Needs

Our exploration began with several observations within our libraries about user expectations and needs for library services, which had changed dramatically since the early 2000s. Face-to-face traffic at the main library service desk had fallen, while traffic to instant messaging rapidly increased. Though the total number of general reference consultations was declining, individual research consultations were getting longer, especially for more specialized assistance: for instance, the Data and GIS Lab saw more traffic and many repeat customers, with users seeking expert advice throughout a project. This department was also fielding more questions about data management plans, much of this driven by new requirements for National Science Foundation grant proposals.

We also noted increased interest in other areas of digitally reliant and interdisciplinary scholarship. More users were requesting scanning help, including for in-depth assistance with complex digitization projects. Digital humanities projects were increasing on campus, with more on the horizon following the Andrew W. Mellon Foundation's funding of Duke's five-year Humanities Writ Large proposal. A number of Humanities Writ Large programs focused deliberately on encouraging undergraduate engagement in research, from programs training students in humanities research methods to those providing opportunities for students to undertake research projects.[1] Other components, notably the Humanities Labs, brought faculty and graduate students into research collaborations with undergraduates (i.e., *vertical integration*) by building courses around interdisciplinary research projects.

Changing Research Environment

The libraries gained additional insight into campus needs by participating in the e-Science Institute, an initiative offered by the Association of Research Libraries and the Digital Library Federation to help libraries strategically assess and plan support for e-research across and among disciplines. As part of this program, we interviewed key stakeholders in e-research at Duke—faculty, institute directors, and administrators. These interviews were used to identify existing strengths and weaknesses in e-research support as well as opportunities and challenges.

While this institute prioritized high-level e-research, the exercise revealed needs relevant to multiple research communities at Duke, including student researchers. Researchers desired more assistance in working with data, help visualizing and analyzing data, creating data management plans, managing restricted data sets, and licensing content. There was also a desire for assistance selecting tools for conducting digital research and for collecting and publishing digital content.

Duke University Libraries had already begun taking measures to address some these needs, primarily through new hires and technology, but there was clearly an opportunity to take on a larger role. Because members of the Duke community often were not aware of existing services and resources, they would also benefit from a centralized, discipline-neutral space where one could locate assistance, consult with experts, and work with others. Among the recommendations in our e-Science Institute report was adapting libraries facilities to incorporate a research commons, where computational tools, information, expertise, and services could all be co-located.

Design: Creating and Developing the Vision

Designing Duke University Libraries' research commons was a multiphased process. It began with exploring other research commons environments to get a sense of the range of spaces and uses and the work involved in constructing and maintaining them. A campus-wide visioning workshop elicited the principles that would guide architectural and programmatic development of the space. Finally, architects and libraries personnel talked through the realities of location, time, money, and maintenance in order to draft an architectural plan that could support the collective vision for a research commons.

Surveying Spaces at Other Institutions

The Research Commons Exploratory Committee (RCEC), a working group composed of library personnel from multiple departments, was charged with exploring commons spaces and services at other institutions in order to determine which models could meet our needs. Research commons programs at other libraries have sought, variously, to support the research needs of upper-level undergraduates, graduate students, and faculty by providing technology-focused services, resources, and spaces for collaborative work and by providing training, consultation, implementation, and project support. Studying other commons programs helped us better understand organizational and cultural preconditions for supporting these spaces and their instruction and consultation services. RCEC members visited the University of Virginia Scholars' Lab and the Research Commons at Emory University and spoke with staff from similar operations at New York University, University of Illinois, University of Washington, and Columbia University. In addition, the group referenced white papers and other guides to library-based commons environments.[2] In its final report the RCEC recommended organizational changes and service developments to begin implementing immediately. It also recommended creating a physical commons in the libraries where faculty and students working on digital projects could access expert assistance and a wide range of resources in one location.

Conducting a Visioning Workshop with Campus Stakeholders

In fall 2012, Shepley Bulfinch, the architects who would design and develop our research commons, facilitated a visioning workshop attended by university administrators, faculty, graduate and undergraduate students, and library staff. Workshop activities challenged participants to imagine the future of research and scholarship at Duke. For instance, all participants responded to the prompt to "Look into your crystal ball …considering interdisciplinarity, globalization, MOOCs, digital scholarship, the pace of change, etc., describe key aspects of the research and learning environment at Duke five years from now."[3]

Several themes emerged as significant factors in the design of the research commons. In particular, the admonishment to "take risks" encompassed a number of campus needs and desires that the libraries could fulfill:[4]

- provide a broad range of spaces, services, and materials as catalysts for innovation;
- foster a community for experimentation through leadership and partnership;
- observe researcher behavior, identify new directions, and reinforce and expand services to support them; and
- utilize pilots to determine what services are needed and how to make them successful.[5]

Other themes that drove development decisions were to "host interdisciplinary and transdisciplinary collaborations," "expand role of library staff as partners, scholars, and teachers," "celebrate intellectual life and discovery," and "make research visible."[6] Later, the research commons planning team translated these aspirations into actionable policies and services.

Drafting an Architectural and Organizational Plan

We approached development of a research commons as a renovation project since we already had ideal space in one of our newer buildings, Bostock Library. As a renovation project, though, we needed to create a space that would visually and physically articulate the principles developed during the visioning process—a space that would clearly and instantly communicate its purpose to support team-based, digitally driven research projects. Involving student and faculty voices early in the process meant that we had buy-in from the beginning and that we centered their needs and vision in the process. Even so, designing the physical space of The Edge—a place accessible, welcoming, and encouraging exploration and risk—would be a challenge.

With the architects, we designed the physical space with an eye to ensuring openness to different kinds of use (e.g., minimizing locked or restricted-use areas; selecting lightweight, mobile, and reconfigurable furniture). We also attended carefully to the physical layout and materials (e.g., wide hallways with writeable walls; large and open work areas; glassed-in rooms) to make research visible and to help users easily discover and use the resources and expertise available to them. The Data and GIS department (later renamed Data and Visualization) would relocate to this space, providing an anchor for the kinds of research The Edge would support. We also carved out space for a new digital scholarship lab, in order to provide consultation and work space for the kinds of digitally inflected teaching and research encouraged by Humanities Writ Large, Bass Connections, and other campus initiatives.

We see the design phase as akin to building a house. Surveying the landscape and talking with stakeholders helped us to draw up the blueprints for this new kind of library space. This preparation helped us agree on the kind of presence and purpose a research commons would have on campus, not just physically but academically. We constructed the actual framework as we crafted policies, pursued partnerships, developed programs, and hired and trained staff. Obviously, such development also involved actual renovation of the first floor of Bostock Library. Beyond this architectural work, however, lay a number of organizational tasks. They can all be summed up in one question: *How would our current staffing, services, policies, and resources need to change in order to better facilitate the kinds of collaborative, experimental, and interdisciplinary scholarship this new space would support?*

The research commons planning team brought a cross-disciplinary, cross-professional perspective to this question. Consisting of IT staff as well as department heads of Digital Scholarship Services, Data and Visualization Services (formerly Data and GIS), and Research and Instructional Services, the RC planning team represented those departments responsible for the services that this new space would offer. Members of this team served on or oversaw subgroups formed to address emerging questions related to staffing, services, and policies (for instance, policies for reserving project rooms). Several members of the research commons planning team had also been part of the RCEC, as well as the eResearch Institute, and went on to form the Edge management team. As a result, they were deeply familiar with the needs and aspirations for this new space. This shared sense of purpose was critical, given the tensions inherent in circumscribing use of a high-visibility, high-demand space. Even before The Edge opened, we had many students, staff, and other members of the campus community who were interested in using the space in ways that didn't align with our mission. Our goal in crafting use policies and planning programming was to walk the line between opening space for use while encouraging a certain community and way of use.

Students played an integral role in shaping The Edge during the development process and after launch. Much of the early guidance came from our library's three student advisory boards: First-Year Advisory Board, Undergraduate Advisory Board, and Graduate and Professional School Library Board. The Undergraduate Advisory Board and the Graduate and Professional School Library Board were especially vocal in giving feedback as we planned for services and facilities policies, since they are based on West Campus, where The Edge is located. As part of the development phase, we worked with these student groups to address a number of issues that either reflected students' research needs or that would rely on students' input and involvement in order to resolve.

Making Space for Collaborative Research

Space as service is one of the most integral parts of The Edge. From the beginning, we wanted the physical space and its features to encourage the type of collaborative work that formed the mission of The Edge. We intended the project rooms—nine rooms of varying size with flat-screen displays, A/V hookups, and lockable storage—to serve as a focal point for team-based research activities. These spaces would be distinct from library study rooms, which are used for a variety of purposes, some unrelated to research. With these rooms and The Edge in general, we've continually found tension between setting policies around a high-visibility space and leaving enough freedom for frequent use. To successfully walk this line, we've relied on assessment and student feedback to let us know when we need to tweak our policies or make our processes more user-friendly.

The design process helped us envision the ideal use and users for project rooms: meeting and workspace for interdisciplinary, project-based research teams, primarily composed of students. In order to develop appropriate access policies for project rooms, we had to consider how these teams typically functioned and what type of access would best serve them. Offering varying levels of access gave us the flexibility to accommodate the needs of different project teams. For instance, some rooms were dedicated for just one project team's use so that those team members could have access whenever they liked, store research materials there, and keep notes and materials out until their project was completed. Other rooms were scheduled for recurring use by multiple teams, almost like a time-share. Teams received this kind of privileged access by submitting proposals demonstrating their project's fit with the mission of The Edge.

Any rooms not dedicated to a single team or not currently scheduled would be *grab-able*, meaning that they would be available for instant reservation and any students could use them as available and needed. The reservation process was facilitated by a surplus of iPad 1s left over from a departmental project. We built power into the walls between project rooms to mount iPads installed with scheduling software. This allowed students standing outside a room to view its schedule, up to a week in advance, and reserve it if it were available. This feature, among many others, was inspired by feedback from the library's student advisory groups.

During The Edge's development phase, the libraries' student advisory groups gave useful feedback on space design and policies, helping us to ensure that this would be a welcoming and accessible place. Students' ideas and input continue to inform the implementation process as we plan events and programming and continue to refine The Edge.

Fostering Community and Catalyzing Innovation

How to staff and program use of this high-traffic, high-visibility space was an early concern, especially given our goal of supporting collaborative work and encouraging intellectual risk taking. Developing and implementing a program of activities would help to communicate the purpose and potential of The Edge spaces and resources. Some spaces required additional staffing, so we hired students to fill these needs. These students have been critical to The Edge's mission, helping to direct use of the spaces and technology and, in some cases, demonstrating the value of cross-disciplinary and cross-professional partnerships.

The Brandaleone Data and Visualization Lab (formerly Data and GIS) already had computing resources and a staffing model for its public services, including graduate student assistants who assisted with use of the Bloomberg terminals. However, relocation to the highly visible first floor of Bostock Library would likely increase use that was not necessarily in line with The Edge's mission. We determined that, in addition to updating policies for lab use, we could help communicate intended use of this space and also encourage new approaches to research by displaying students' winning posters from the campus data visualization contest.

Both student workers and staff with the Research and Instructional Services department would need training and reskilling in order to staff the space, assist researchers in using services and resources, and work more closely with project teams. To address this, training was developed for undergraduate students who would staff The Edge Help Desk in order to build their familiarity with the resources available as well as with the libraries' service philosophy. Situated at the open entrance to The Edge, students staffing the Help Desk were the first point of contact for visitors and the first line of assistance for using this space.

The newly created Digital Studio (see figure 6.1) would be overseen by the Digital Scholarship Services (DSS) department, whose two staff members were regularly involved in collaborative digital project work. We developed a staffing model for this space based mostly around graduate student interns, who gain consultation experience through shadowing the DSS staff and working with them on digital projects. Additionally, we created a graduate student internship dedicated to programming and promoting events in the Digital Studio and The Edge. This individual would play a critical role in making digital scholarship more accessible through talks by teams and researchers and through training sessions in digital tools and methods.

FIGURE 6.1
Digital scholarship workshop in the Digital Studio

While libraries-based graduate-student internships are not new, these Edge-based experiences pushed both students and staff members to work and learn collaboratively. Staff members introduced students to different disciplinary questions and digital challenges through involving them on projects. Students working on digital projects developed skills and specialized knowledge that often established them as the resident experts. They then transferred these insights to others through talks and programs, as well as through one-on-one consultations. Much like the vertical integration found elsewhere on campus, these projects connected and helped to level otherwise hierarchical or professionally distinct groups, while simultaneously demonstrating the cross-disciplinary and collaborative approach to research and risk taking promoted by The Edge.

Implementation: Testing, Reflecting, Revising

Our collective goal was to create a space to support data-driven, digitally reliant, interdisciplinary, team-based research (figure 6.2). This mission helped to clarify our focus as we moved into the implementation phase, which as was marked by tremendous activity, as users and librarians alike worked in this new space and tested its potential. Implementation was (and is) a period marked by iterative adaptation of space, staffing, policy, processes, and resources in response to regular assessment of how The Edge supports its mission. We've experienced surprise successes and constructive failures, both of which we see as part of this ongoing learning and improvement process.

FIGURE 6.2
Team-based research

Rethinking Research

The question of how and why project teams used project rooms (figure 6.3) developed into a source of tension early on. From the beginning, we had envisioned the teams that would need dedicated space in The Edge as faculty-led and vertically integrated project teams. We used the terms *interdisciplinary, digitally reliant, data-driven*, and *research-based* to help us identify acceptable projects. Yet as we began vetting projects, we struggled to define which projects met these criteria. How many distinct disciplines must be involved for a project to be considered interdisciplinary? How digitally reliant or data-heavy do projects need to be? How many people must be involved in order to constitute a team? Is a team vertically integrated if only a few students are working with a faculty group member? If the research is being done for course credit, does it still count?

FIGURE 6.3
Project Room

We found that the teams involving faculty and those that were student-led or that had student-only membership were sometimes very different in nature and needed to be assessed differently. Faculty-led teams often grew out of a course, lab, or other effort, and their projects tended to fit neatly into the definition of project that we had in mind. In contrast, many student groups had more nebulous definitions for their projects, which also didn't always have a neatly scoped end goal. Or, if they did, it sometimes changed throughout the semester as they worked through their project. We were surprised that student-led research didn't always look like the research we were familiar with. We learned of projects in which students were offering volunteer consulting work with classmates, designing models, or teaching themselves visualization software. Their work was much more practical and came to us at a different point in the research cycle. Meeting the needs of these groups and working with them has both required that we redefine the primacy of academic research in student work outside of the classroom and that we, as librarians and library staff, realize that materials in our collections and our expertise are valuable outside of the classroom. Connecting with one of the many design teams in The Edge, for instance, allowed the Engineering Librarian to connect with students in the Engineering School, a program that had not previously sought out library services and resources.

We also received requests that we had never imagined: artists-in-residence who wanted a room for stone-carving; students who wanted to install a 3-D printer in a room; a new student-led online journal that needed incubation space. Some of these projects were far out of the scope of what we had envisioned but were still projects that we felt should be housed in The Edge. Additionally, we had to defend decisions about space use to applicants who thought their projects fit the definition of collaborative, interdisciplinary research projects when our opinion differed. Due to the volume of applications, it was important to The Edge management team that we closely aligned the projects we accepted to our mission while taking a generous interpretation of what those projects might be. In the case that a project application was not accepted for a long-term reservation, we also wanted to offer feedback and explain why.

We were selective with project teams because we imagined offering them additional library support and services. We matched each project team with a library staff member who was experienced in their area of work. While partnering with teams involved a very different type of work than we typically undertake as subject librarians, our colleagues in Data and Visualization Services were familiar with this approach and able to offer suggestions. We learned that subject expertise was not as important as our ability to manage projects, organize information, and communicate effectively. Novice researchers, especially those working on a team project, need to learn how to standardize file names and formats, use version control, share notes, and document work so that other team members can use it. Such management training seemed equally necessary to teaching research skills. In many ways, this prompted those of us who work in Research and Instructional Services to think about how and where we market our services and how we can work in a team with colleagues in other departments.

Rethinking Training and Hiring to Meet Changing Needs

We expected that students needing expert assistance in the digital humanities and with data analysis would swarm our halls upon opening. Although this expectation was not entirely borne out, we did find that some library services, such as data analysis and visualization, became even more popular due to a new location, while needs that we had not anticipated, such as space and event management, required staff support.

With the exception of The Edge coordinator and the graduate and undergraduate student staff, all other positions and departments predated The Edge and experienced changes as a result of relocating their services to The Edge. The Data and Visualization Services department had been previously located in the hinterlands of government documents, a location that confounded many students. To support the influx of users brought by their new location and changing needs on campus, the staff in Data and Visualization Services carefully tracked the types of questions and consultation requests they received. Their data justified hiring new staff with expertise in two expanding consulting areas: GIS and data visualization.

Planning and implementing new positions has also required a great deal of attention to users' needs. Because we anticipated advanced questions, we initially focused student training on making excellent referrals to library and campus services around digital humanities and data services. After reviewing reference statistics from the first month and a half of operation, we discovered that the questions from our patrons at this service point were similar to the questions we received at our main service desk. This meant that we could utilize the same training plan at this service point that we used for other library service desks, which allowed our student training to be more consistent and efficient.

Yet perhaps the greatest challenge (and opportunity) posed by The Edge was the way it forced rethinking of librarians' work. While it is difficult to predict the technical needs of a research project, we recognized that all projects, regardless of discipline, would benefit from guidance in team development and project management. If we wanted librarians to become partners in team-based research, we needed to understand and develop skills related to collaborative projects. One way that we have addressed this is to follow the project-based learning model pioneered by other programs and libraries, notably Columbia University Library's Developing Librarian Project.[7] Librarians in Research and Instructional Services have sought to put this into practice by embarking on a digital project of their own, documenting student activism at Duke during the 1930s through the 1950s. In the course of this project, librarians gained valuable skills and knowledge, such as project management and scoping, as well as those more specific to working on digital projects, such as using copyrighted materials and working with particular software packages. While this project began after our new research space had already opened, the need for such project-based training was identified during the prelaunch development process for The Edge.

Thoughtfully Expanding Partnerships and Programming

In addition to working cross-departmentally in the libraries, The Edge gave us the opportunity to partner with departments and schools across the university. These collaborations ranged from joint work with a single project team to the establishment of multiday programming with significant involvement from library staff members. These programs have solidified existing relationships or built bridges between departments where none existed previously. We've found these new relationships to be essential to supporting student work, as they so often surpass the bounds of campus entities in their research or work.

One example of this type of collaboration occurred when a student project team interested in 3-D printing requested space that could support printing for their project. Due to space constraints, we were unable to offer a space for their actual printing, but we connected them with the Innovation Co-Lab, a space on campus that housed a set of 3-D printers and offered design classes. This team used its space in The Edge to design and plan its work and the Innovation Co-Lab for the actual printing.

Working with our colleagues in the Innovation Co-Lab to serve this team spurred additional collaborations. We planned joint programming to showcase student research and work in both The Edge and the Innovation Co-Lab, including an exhibition of student-designed and -printed materials, such as a model human heart. Students participating in this program were especially interested in learning about the work of their peers. Other collaborative programming has included a large-scale DataFest, involving staff members from the department of Statistical Science and members of the library's Data and Visualization Services department, pitching panels about the productive use of software for an IT series hosted in The Edge, with library staff participants for an external audience. Many of these programs have been successful, aligning with The Edge's mission and drawing attendees who were interested in learning about the types of services that The Edge provides. We also learned early on that not every invitation to collaborate is one that we should accept. For example, we partnered with a campus arts organization for an event highlighting the arts on campus, and then realized that the event was not a good match for our mission. Given the need for space on campus, it is important to us to stick to collaborations that are in keeping with the mission of The Edge, which helps us avoid overuse of the space and preserve our mental health and staff resources.

Student involvement has been essential to our programming, particularly in envisioning activities that bring together students and different levels of scholarship. One event that immediately came to mind was a revamping of the library's End-of-Semester Study Break. This event involved library staff and students' parents baking goods to give out to students during one evening of exams. The event was incredibly popular, and the food was always completely picked over after twenty minutes. However, this event did nothing to address challenges that we heard from students at the end of the semester: that they were stressed, were overwhelmed, and didn't know where to find help. We wanted to use this event to market library and other campus resources to students at their point of need. Thus, the Duke version of Long Night against Procrastination (LNAP) was born.

The Long Night against Procrastination (LNAP) was already a success at other schools, having made its way to the United States of America after beginning in Germany. This event typically takes the form of an all-night study session, with the addition of workshops tutorials and fun events like desk yoga and dance parties. Many schools use this event to kick off finals week and to encourage students to begin work early.[8] Our version incorporated feedback from our two undergraduate student advisory groups. They reviewed a tentative program description that outlined possible activities, including flash dance parties, yoga sessions, crafting tables, and movie screenings as well as tentative campus partners. They cut almost every "fun" activity, focusing on those that provided academic support. While this certainly took our planning in a different direction, it meant that the resulting event was authentic to Duke's student culture and that it took into account their serious study habits.

Students on the advisory boards also provided important feedback about the services they saw as critical within this new research-intensive space. Students named the Thompson Writing Studio (TWS) as an important campus partner. The Thompson Writing Studio offers writing consultations that are so popular students often can't get an appointment during high-volume times, like midterms and the end of the semester. As a result of joining the LNAP event, TWS condensed its typical hour-long consultation session to a twenty-minute session that focused on a main question the student had about his or her work. This meant that many more students were able to be served in a set amount of time and that writing consultation was, by far, the most popular service offered at LNAP. This successful partnership with the Writing Studio has opened doors to other types of programming around writing in the library. Even during the spring semester, when LNAP is not offered, the Writing Studio has considered holding additional programming and offering different models of support for students as a result of the success it found during this event.

The feedback we got from planning the Long Night against Procrastination was also helpful in thinking about additional programming for students by students. In particular, we wanted to highlight the research that groups were already conducting in The Edge. In surveying the campus landscape, we realized that there were already many opportunities for graduate students to present their work. In contrast, undergraduates often have no opportunity to present outside of class. We wanted to create a program that would give the students an opportunity to reflect on their work in a low-pressure environment, while making the event formal enough to include on a résumé.

To attach status to the event and encourage student participation, we intentionally planned the event to be fairly formal—we hosted a reception following the event, held it in one of the nicest spaces in the library, and printed programs crediting the student presenters. In contrast, the event needed to be as low-maintenance as possible for the students, especially because it was scheduled for the end of the semester. We asked each group of students to give a lightning talk (five to eight minutes) that reflected on their work for the semester and how they completed that work—their research question, their process, and any roadblocks that they encountered. In essence, they didn't need to have a finished product to present, they just had to be willing to talk about what they were already doing.

We especially wanted to encourage students to talk freely about the process of their work, examining failures and what they learned from them. It is worth emphasizing that many of the collaborative projects the students engaged with during their time in The Edge were of the type that researcher Manu Kapur defines as "ill-structured,"[9] in this case as a result of researching and working on real-world questions, not a carefully planned classroom exercise. As Kapur demonstrated, groups working with these types of complex problems often fail or require additional assistance when attempting to solve the initial problem, but the gap they encounter in the process allows them to build additional problem-solving skills that do not occur when they are faced only with neatly structured problems.[10] Although these student projects were not necessarily formed with Kapur's research in mind, both the project leaders and the staff in The Edge have been united in emphasizing process over product. During The Edge Research Talks, guiding students with a set of open-ended questions about their research project gave them the opportunity to discuss how they overcame these obstacles and collaborated with their project team without the need for a finished product to display.

We scheduled several practice sessions beforehand, where students could rehearse their presentation in the event space and get feedback on their slides or talking points, and developed a quick info sheet about the presentation and dress code (whatever you feel comfortable in). Typically, ten to fifteen students participate in each event. The most successful presentations came from groups that had either worked directly with library staff or that were advised by faculty or graduate instructors who valued the library. Having a relationship in place or a faculty ally helped prioritize the presentation and meant that the students took it seriously.

In the future, we are interested in planning more student-centered programming, including student-led workshops and courses. Many student employees of The Edge are developing programming or advanced research skills, and we want to provide a platform for them to share these skills. We also want to expand programming around student works to incorporate research taking place on campus, not just the in libraries. We hope to use the space as a nexus for student researchers to meet and learn from each other and to present their work to a larger audience.

Assessment (Again): Learning from The Edge

When The Edge opened in January 2015, we already had a multipage assessment plan in place. Our library's Assessment and Users Services department had worked closely with The Edge management team to determine which aspects of the space and services were measurable and should be assessed: technology use, occupancy, the website, traffic flow, questions asked and answered, and more. They also helped us brainstorm ways to get direct feedback from our users, such as a web form linked from our homepage and an anonymous comment box on the desk. We began to analyze findings from our assessment a month into operation and were able to course-correct on a number of issues, from making AV cords more available to changing a truly terrible room-reservation interface. We found, though, that we had more information than we knew what to do with. We didn't have a way of setting high-level, unified goals for the entirety of The Edge that we could assess.

Redefining Metrics for Success

As much as we have relied on assessment to help us develop staffing models and to direct programming, we have also struggled to define specific, measurable goals for The Edge itself. The staff, services, and facilities in The Edge fit together like a mosaic and do not always overlap in terms of users and services. Because our services are so varied, we've found that cross-departmental programming is the most fruitful result of library assessment activities. From student surveys, we can see which services and resources are in demand or need to be highlighted. Additionally, these programs are excellent points for getting feedback from users, either from informal conversation after a session or from more formal program feedback forms.

We've also found that the individual departments that make up The Edge are the best at assessing their own activities. For instance, Digital Scholarship

Services meets on a weekly basis to discuss consultations, programming, and current projects. These meetings serve as a way for students and full-time staff to reflect on difficulties they've faced in their work in a supportive team environment, where failure is intended as a springboard for reflection and learning. Data and Visualization Services also meets on a regular basis as a department to discuss the lab and directions for programming and workshops. Decisions from these meetings are reported at The Edge management team's meetings, but individual departments have a great deal of autonomy in how they manage their individual areas.

How we define success for student projects in The Edge, or even just for The Edge itself, is something we think about a great deal. Should we have goals for the student projects and The Edge that are divorced entirely from traditional tangible products? Should we think more about engagement and community building, and what would success or effectiveness look like with those goals? For ourselves and for our students, we want to build a greater appreciation for the process of research, particularly for how failures (and not merely successes) can help us improve our research. Yet given the high premium placed on finished products and successful outcomes, how can we convince students to talk about the messy and less glamorous aspects of research-in-progress?

These questions point to the fact that The Edge is a very different space—both physically and programmatically. Its openness and flexibility have helped us to witness, and in turn respond to, the ways students work. By actively inviting and supporting project teams, we gain insight into the questions they're taking on and what kinds of resources and services can support them in this process. Approaching a project as beginners, especially alongside students, allows librarians to experience firsthand the knowledge and skill gaps that produce anxiety but can also lead to creative solutions. Such empathy is invaluable on its own, for allowing us to better understand what researchers need and to help them (and ourselves) work productively through uncertainty. As our libraries become laboratories, and as librarians become partners in research, we are learning by doing: joining team-based research projects, engaging with unfamiliar problems, and thus building our own capacity to embrace and model learning-from-failure and reflective practice.

Notes

1. Trinity College of Arts and Sciences, "Undergraduate Research," Humanities Writ Large, Duke University, 2017, http://humanitieswritlarge.duke.edu/funding/undergraduate-research.
2. Shepley Bulfinch, "Library Planning Study: Research Commons, Bostock Library," unpublished manuscript, Duke University Libraries, February 23, 2013.
3. Shepley Bulfinch, "Library Planning Study."

4. Shepley Bulfinch, "Library Planning Study."
5. Shepley Bulfinch, "Library Planning Study."
6. Craig Gibson's "Overview of Research Commons in Academic Libraries: A White Paper" (unpublished internal report, Ohio State University Libraries, 2012) was a timely and useful summary for our group (though apparently no longer available online). Members of our committee were also familiar with research on commons developments in libraries, notably Charles Forrest and Martin Halbert, *A Field Guide to the Information Commons* (Lanham, MD: Scarecrow Press, 2009), as well as Tim Bryson et al., *Digital Humanities: SPEC Kit 326* (Washington, DC: Association of Research Libraries, 2011), http://publications.arl.org/Digital-Humanities-SPEC-Kit-326/, both of which provided a broad perspective on the variety of ways academic libraries have adapted their spaces, services, resources, and staffing in order to meet changing research needs.
7. More information on the Developing Librarian Project can be found at Breaking the Code: The Developing Librarian Project website, accessed June 6, 2018, https://devlib.library.columbia.edu/.
8. Ilka Datig and Luise Herkner, "Get Ready for a Long Night: Collaborating with the Writing Center to Combat Student Procrastination," *College and Research Libraries News* 75, no. 3 (March 2014): 128–31, http://crln.acrl.org/index.php/crlnews/article/view/9086/9960.
9. Manu Kapur, "Productive Failure," *Cognition and Instruction* 26, no. 3 (2008): 379–424, https://doi.org/10.1080/07370000802212669.
10. Kapur, "Productive Failure."

Bibliography

Bryson, Tim, Miriam Posner, Alaine St. Pierre, and Stewart Varner. *Digital Humanities: SPEC Kit 326*. Washington, DC: Association of Research Libraries, 2011. http://publications.arl.org/Digital-Humanities-SPEC-Kit-326/.

Datig, Ilka, and Luise Herkner. "Get Ready for a Long Night: Collaborating with the Writing Center to Combat Student Procrastination." *College and Research Libraries News* 75, no. 3 (March 2014): 128–31. http://crln.acrl.org/index.php/crlnews/article/view/9086/9960.

Forrest, Charles, and Martin Halbert. *A Field Guide to the Information Commons*. Lanham, MD: Scarecrow Press, 2009.

Gibson, Craig. "Overview of Research Commons in Academic Libraries: A White Paper." Unpublished internal report. Ohio State University Libraries, 2012.

Kapur, Manu. "Productive Failure." *Cognition and Instruction* 26, no. 3 (2008): 379–424. https://doi.org/10.1080/07370000802212669.

Richardson, Shepley Bulfinch. "Library Planning Study: Research Commons, Bostock Library." Unpublished manuscript. Duke University Libraries, February 23, 2013.

Trinity College of Arts and Sciences. "Undergraduate Research." Humanities Writ Large, Duke University, 2017. http://humanitieswritlarge.duke.edu/funding/undergraduate-research.

CHAPTER 7

North Carolina State University Spotlight

Part 1, Fulfilling the Promise— and the Inspiration—of High-Tech Spaces

Jason Evans Groth

North Carolina State University's (NCSU) mission to "Think and Do" has empowered the NCSU Libraries to be a leader in connecting theory to practice, coursework to careers, and personal passions to global engagement. Additional information about how this mission informs the work of the NCSU Libraries is provided in the chapter "Preparing Students to 'Think and Do': Promoting the Value of Student Work," which appears in the Articulating the Value of Student Work section of the book.

This chapter discusses the student projects that have been realized through the use of inspirational high-tech spaces in the James B. Hunt Library. Opened in 2013, Hunt has been hailed as the Library of the Future, where "North Carolina's thinkers, dreamers and doers come together to seek solutions to the great challenges facing this world."[1] Projects that connect the library's innovative spaces and services to student passion have been transformative for students, for the NCSU community, and for the way the NCSU Libraries are understood. This is not by chance. We have designed, organized, and promoted library tools, spaces, and expertise to intentionally connect our students to both their current communities and their future selves.

One of the most striking features of the James B. Hunt Jr. Library, which opened to the NCSU community in January 2013, is the proliferation of very large high-definition screens, made with technology called Christie Microtiles. One greets you as you pass through the gates (the Art Wall; see figure 7.1); one is tucked into a very visible theater space just beyond the service desk and is close enough to touch and large enough to immerse the viewer (the Immersion Theater; see figure 7.2); one is mounted inside of a space called the Game Lab and is as tall and wide as the Immersion Theater (20' × 5'), but is also a touch screen; one is positioned above the staircase from the third floor modular study area to the fourth floor digital media enclave (the Commons Wall); and one is chopped into ribbons, each of which is several feet tall, and is mounted outside of the 270 degree visualization lab (the Viz Wall). The prominence of these screens means they are intended for more than wayfinding or event promotion (although they are certainly used as such)—they are also canvasses that are modular, approachable, and perfect for showcasing student work.

FIGURE 7.1
Art Wall

FIGURE 7.2
Immersion Theater

Another powerful design feature is the use of glass—especially windows—in the building. Thanks to the automated collection storage and retrieval system known as the BookBot, the collaborative space of the library was increased by 40 percent. The windows brighten the space, connect the user with the outside, and—since there are only a fraction of the 1.5 million books contained in the BookBot on open shelving—do not contribute actively to the degradation of materials. In addition, many of the rooms in the library are outfitted with frameless glass, including the study rooms and the digital media–making spaces—the Music Rooms and the Media Production Studios. This design was meant to help the NCSU Libraries show equipment or spaces without a user having to seek it out; it allows others to see creativity in progress, to be inspired by the work of peers; and it provokes curiosity. There was clear potential to use these prominent canvasses and studios to feature student work, but partnerships between librarians, students, and faculty were required.

As a NCSU Libraries Fellow, I began working with film studies professor Marsha Gordon in spring 2014 to fulfill the promise of such a collaboration. Professor Gordon, who was teaching a five-person graduate seminar on war documentaries, and I devised a project that would be student-led, would promote student use of library technology, and would be featured on one of the prominent screens as an exhibit. The collected projects would be used to exemplify both the power of the work and the potential of the space to show it. In essence, the students were asked to take work that would typically be shared with a specialized audience of film studies scholars and publish it in a public space.

What transpired was Shooting Wars: Documentary Images of American Military Conflicts,[2] a project that debuted in the Game Lab in April 2014. The students, Professor Gordon, and I enhanced the original assignment to move beyond a static exhibit and to become interactive. The NCSU Libraries provided support for research, help with curation of project materials (war documentary footage, audio files, etc.), and assistance with editing. Each student artist created three videos. Two were constructed using public-domain footage of a particular conflict with which America was involved, focusing on images of technology and death. The third was an interpretation of what the two other videos might mean for the viewer and creator. The artist then timed the three pieces to the same length and added a fourth component—a soundtrack—to be played during all the videos. The videos were then merged so they showed simultaneously on the Game Lab's 20-foot-wide wall, with the soundtrack. A menu allowed viewers to isolate the tracks. The class created artist statements, participated in an opening program, and then served as docents for the duration of the exhibit.

It was the first time the Game Lab was used in such a way, and over 150 people visited the exhibit over the course of the week it was presented. All of those involved were thrilled with the results. Professor Gordon said the project made her "think about how to use these spaces to create and disseminate knowledge in new ways and to talk to each other in ways that are maybe more open and more performative than I certainly have in my classes in the past."[3] For student Jason Buel, this way of publicizing research was novel: "I've never really thought of the library as a space for exhibition and distribution of these kinds of works."[4] Student Brian Robertson added that the product of their work felt more impactful "knowing that people were going see it outside of that class, that it was for more than a grade, that it might affect someone outside of what can feel like a pretty insular world."[5] The project now exists as a demonstration that is regularly shown to students and visitors to illustrate how the Game Lab can serve as a venue for publishing scholarly and creative projects.

The project was meaningful for the library and for Professor Gordon, who said, "Just think about the potential for this as the kind of project that can really give meaning to a twenty-first-century library and to a twenty-first-century classroom."[6] Based on this success, Gordon partnered with me to try a similar scenario with her English/Communications 364 undergraduate class "Film History to 1940." The goal, again, was to encourage digital media–making alongside research, with the result being an exhibit that be shown on the Hunt Library canvas. Students were asked to watch several early Thomas Edison Co. films and then remake one of their choosing. These films were mostly one-shot scenarios, and the students were asked to recreate the framing and the timing, ideally using HD devices they could borrow from technology lending at the library. My role was to pair these student creations with the original film, placing both on the canvas of the Immersion Theater.

The feedback was phenomenal. Students loved seeing their work on one of the public screens. The Immersion Theater displays a rotating program of data visualization, web projects, scientific posters, and similar works (see figure 7.3–7.5), but this was the first student media research project to get regular rotation. The thirty-two students who participated had a public opening, talked about the challenges of the project, and stared in awe as their work came to life. The project has now been repeated over three semesters, with both Professor Gordon and Professor Timothy Holland, and each semester's work has been retained and continues to be viewable through a touch-screen menu in the theater. The project combines entertainment and history and offers a powerful testimony for harnessing library technology and digital media studios. Other projects soon followed. The Immersion Theater has provided time in the spotlight to other student projects as well. One class produced an exhibition on female directors and their work in Hollywood. Another project concerned early Hollywood celebrity magazines. Students researched their topics using primary sources at NCSU or obtained via interlibrary loan services, ultimately producing a compelling display on the glamorization of celebrities through magazine culture.

FIGURE 7.3

Works in Immersion

FIGURE 7.4
Works in Immersion

FIGURE 7.5
Works in Immersion

The Music Rooms—four audio production suites in the Hunt Library—were some of the most anticipated spaces in the library. They did not open when the rest of the library did as their complexity was a little too great, but the potential of this space to provide students with a means of enhancing their multimedia communications skills was evident. After months of planning, the Music Rooms opened in the fall of 2013. Many in the NCSU community were eager to use this new space, evidenced by the waiting list of over fifty individuals who asked to be notified as soon as it became available. For this reason, I immediately began working with course instructors to find ways to incorporate the Music Rooms into class projects.

One example of this was my work with English rhetoric classes, in which the students were asked to recreate their favorite podcasts using the equipment in the rooms. This led to an ongoing recording/podcast workshop that has been offered to over 500 patrons. Similar projects are now regularly assigned, and the technology consultation program in the libraries helps students learn how to successfully navigate the audio production equipment and programs.

The rooms have also become a focus for a History of Hip-Hop class taught by Professor Will Boone. I have worked with Boone to create a beatmaking workshop that leads students through the steps an early hip-hop producer would use to choose a sample and the steps a modern hip-hop producer uses to create a beat. Students dig through crates of records, listen to them, find a sample, and digitize it. They then use Ableton Live, a very popular music production program, to manipulate the sample and create a "beat" out of it—a piece of music that can be repeated and modularized as the backing track for a hip-hop production. Three semesters of students have gone through the class and produced original music, and the workshop itself is now offered to all patrons. A third project focused on sharing the work done in the music rooms. The rooms are very visible and are featured on most library tours, but we wanted to move beyond showing the space to sharing the work that students used the space to create.

In the spring of 2017, digital media student Timothy Mensa and I began a music meet-up series. Students who have participated in the classes mentioned above, or who use the audio production spaces for personal projects, or who are simply interested in sharing their work, meet at the library once a week for a show-and-tell and a lightly moderated experts forum. They learn from one another using library spaces and have started a shared Google Drive folder of the work they are creating weekly. Providing students and other stakeholders with studio space in which to successfully fail, with staff assistance and consultation, and with a peer community, has been imperative to the growth of our high-tech spaces programming and to the cultivation of community of creators we so value on our campus.

I have also begun work on a new model for sharing all of the audio being produced by the creative community with a project called State of Sound. The idea is to replicate what the screens of Hunt Library did for public spaces, serving as an easy and attractive canvas for student work in an easy-to-find place on the libraries website. In effect, this would be a repository of NC State audio production work—from classes to home—that shows the diversity of production, serves as a promotional tool for original works, and captures a snapshot of an otherwise somewhat ephemeral making culture that is often not recognized or shared. Students hired as media consultants have already collaborated with me to create the mechanisms to receive the work, have devised ways to share it back through third-party existing online music-sharing apps, and have begun internally promoting the idea through the media-making spaces and workshops. By asking students to share their work and then sharing it back, the way libraries do, the spaces get promoted, the services get highlighted, and the work is revealed and exhibited in a way that audio oftentimes cannot be. This project may serve as a catalyst for future student sharing with digital media, and especially audio, within and beyond the classroom.

Conclusion

The high-tech spaces in the James B. Hunt Jr. Library can be astonishing and overwhelming; working with students and faculty to unleash the library's promise as a living, malleable workspace rather than a showcase of cutting-edge displays is less challenging and more rewarding than it may seem. What is required is honest development of content and the sincere commitment to collecting, sharing, and exhibiting the work of students and other community members. Once this principle is in place, harnessing the technology follows.

Rather than designing a space or purchasing technology for a singular, focused purpose, we have found success in rethinking the intent of spaces and services. Each new project allows us to add another example—a "recipe"—to our repertoire of projects. This in turn offers examples and starting points to inspire new faculty or student partners. Opening up the library as a canvas for the campus community has created an enhanced sense of investment and import for those who have created work in these spaces. Showing student and faculty work in context with a universe of knowledge conveys the value of contributions from emerging and experienced scholars and creators. This also helps to instill in scholars and creators an understanding of the importance of a library—and librarians—in any community.

Keeping up with continuous technological change is important to maintaining these spaces, but manuals and service agreements assist with that. The more significant undertaking is to connect with potential users, craft experiences and projects to engage them, support the sharing of the resultant work, and then create open and transparent project documentation to sustain the creative life cycle. The documentation is particularly important to student employee–supported projects since the personnel or tools associated with a project will change over time.

The power of high-tech displays or beautiful spaces is realized only when they are used to attract new audiences and community to work done by students and faculty. Ultimately, we use them to inspire collaboration and innovation, whether that's across a class of graduate students, between a librarian and a faculty member, or between a student worker and a group of students who just want to learn how to make a beat in a music studio. The Libraries offer help every step of the way, open doors to understanding how technological canvasses connect, and provide the space to showcase new knowledge and unbridled creativity.

Notes

1.   North Carolina State University, "The Library of the Future," online video, 2:36, April 3, 2013, https://www.ncsu.edu/huntlibrary/watch/.

2.   Jason Evans Groth et al., "Shooting Wars Summary," Shooting Wars: New Spaces Give Old Media New Meaning, produced by NCSU Libraries, online video. 2:23, 2017, http://www.lib.ncsu.edu/stories/shooting-wars.
3.   Evans Groth et al., "Shooting Wars Summary."
4.   Evans Groth et al., "Shooting Wars Summary."
5.   Evans Groth et al., "Shooting Wars Summary."
6.   Evans Groth et al., "Shooting Wars Summary."

Bibliography

Evans Groth, Jason, Marsha Gordon, Brent Brafford, and Wes Woody. "Shooting Wars Summary." Shooting Wars: New Spaces Give Old Media New Meaning. Produced by NCSU Libraries. Online video. 2:23, 2017. http://www.lib.ncsu.edu/stories/shooting-wars.

North Carolina State University. "The Library of the Future." Online video, 2:36. April 3, 2013. https://www.ncsu.edu/huntlibrary/watch/.

Section II
Library as Forum

CHAPTER 8

The Library as a Forum for Student Work

Amy S. Jackson, Cindy Pierard, and Suzanne M. Schadl

This section explores forums—defined as physical and digital spaces in which individuals and groups assemble and share experiences, ideas, and learning in community. Chapters present integrative and collaborative library or archival projects that bring together students, staff, and faculty, as well as families and the public. These groups gather around different examples of research, competition, composition, and performance. Diverse subjects surface in these chapters, ranging from expected issues like pedagogy and critical media literacy to unforeseen topics like surviving the zombie apocalypse, video disc jockeys or veejays, singing through grief, and adapting do-it-yourself (DIY) philosophies to collection development and archival instruction. As in other sections, the voices here include librarians (Apata, Fragola, Radcliff, Ross, Thomas) and students (Apata and Cain) as well as archivists (Cruces) and benefactors (Ross). A couple of these individuals report hybrid or dual identities as librarian/student and librarian/benefactor. Apata describes the challenges and opportunities between identities, articulating the educational value of what some scholars call "zones of development." Gutiérrez, Baquedano-López, and Tejeda identify these spaces as openings for transforming conflict "into rich zones of collaboration and learning."[1]

Fragola's spotlight chapter from NCSU (chapter 13) describes libraries as a "third place" between classrooms and living rooms. The theorist who coined the slightly different but similar term *third space* suggests that multidirectional exchanges among different communities just outside of their comfort zones challenge preconceived ideas and expectations.[2] He defines this third space as contested and negotiated, and because of its place between defined others, Bhabha suggests it can invoke instructive "disturbance(s) of direction" through "moment(s) of transit," sometimes described by others as "zones of proximal development."[3] Each chapter in this section depicts movement across spaces, formats, and communities. As a result, these chapters expand the focus of this book to include individuals unaffiliated with colleges and universities. Acting as partners in third space learning enables a broad spectrum of the community to generate and thus sustain scholarship and, perhaps more importantly, to create opportunities for serendipitous multicultural learning. If we "can't know what we don't know," we need mutually productive relationships to learn. Third space learning can occur organically through libraries because of their interdisciplinarity and simultaneous engagement of tradition and innovation. Without some provocation, however, library resources are typically limited to those "in the know." Bringing new researchers and partners to them requires active engagement.

By adding an emphasis on learning within communities, this section highlights additional opportunities for more engagement and inclusion. The success of the University of Iowa's "Show What You Know" event among foreign students indicates the socioeducational advantages of welcoming differing interests, cultures, languages, and racial identities into library spaces. Thomas (chapter 9) cogently warns that space is not enough and that "innovative and collaborative work comes from embracing the benefits of unpredictable learning environment that naturally lends itself to collaborating, experimenting, failing, and letting go." In his call to action, Derek Bruff suggests the standard expectations for professorial expertise and student naiveté impede transformational learning. As he explains, this dependency enables students to anticipate their professors' prior knowledge and avoid grappling with difficulty on the professors' behalf. It also allows instructors to control outcomes and circumvent uncertainties in the classroom. From another vantage point, Freire observes a similar challenge in his critique of the banking model of education. This ineffective paradigm, as Freire notes, authorizes the supremacy of teachers who deposit their mastery into presumably passive and empty student minds.[4] In critical librarianship, Elmborg acknowledges the profoundly impenetrable underpinnings of such expectations and calls on educators to intentionally resist these hierarchies and develop alternative models.[5] This book is an effort to do just that.

As forums, libraries facilitate exploration and experimentation. From this perspective, failure and success go together. Examples of projects that succeed in some ways and present challenges in others abound in this section. Apata (chapter 11), for instance, acknowledges feeling uneasy at the Friday

Night Sing Ins she organized when participants' conversations gravitated away from historical and impartial references "toward current events and the ways in which they could actively resist efforts to normalize prejudice via musical protest." The political may have seemed too personal or biased while the academic seemed impartial. Thomas (chapter 9) describes a similar response to an exhibit at the University of Iowa. In efforts to engage a larger discussion about violence in popular media and veterans' experiences of war, the library collaborated with the Veterans Association to host a Call of Duty tournament. Complaints ensued, and the library took the installation down early. The following year, librarians enlisted the Iowa Center for Teaching in a collaborative effort with veterans to host the same event, but this time with better facilitated conversations. Apata articulates plans to do the same for future Sing Ins.

In his call to action, Bruff cites failure as a productive space for producing knowledge and developing confidence. The authors contributing to this section acknowledge lessons they have learned in failure. In so doing, they demonstrate the multidirectional efficacy of authentic learning in forums. Thomas (chapter 9) illustrates the trial, error, and opportunity in learning through the process and evolving educational alliances that leverage transliteracy—defined as multiple intersecting literacies including but not limited to media, visual, and multimodel examples. As she states: "This framework gives the libraries room to examine space from varying perspectives and forces library staff and users to think differently together about knowledge production and dissemination as communal activities rather than the one-sided 'transmission(s) of information from masters to pupils' or from librarians to patrons." Radcliff, Ross, and Cain (chapter 10) also reflect on experimentation, failure, and correction when they discuss outreach to faculty and parents in addition to students. Fragola (chapter 13) notes opportunities for NCSU to expand community engagement with its Student Short Film Showcase. Apata (chapter 11) acknowledges lessons related to timing, scale, and inclusiveness. Likewise, Cruces (chapter 12) demonstrates radical openness with a community collecting strategy that brings zinesters into the archives as teachers and trainers. In each of these cases, efforts to learn in community underscore this focus on forum. They also highlight this book's emphasis on recognizing or—more pointedly—legitimizing students and community members as producers as well as consumers of information.

By their nature, forums wrestle with culturally and personally sensitive issues. The chapters in this section illustrate opportunities in social tension for collaboration and learning. Apata (chapter 11) states that "voice-building is collaborative" and "through a constant, chaotic conversation" people "find both the platform and what to say." Each chapter in this section engages information, politics, democracy, or citizenship. Radcliff and Ross (chapter 10) make direct ties between research and citizenship, and Ross suggests that the public stage on which students share their work constitutes vital participation in "an informed citizenry and a healthy democracy." Cain, the student working with Radcliff and Ross, identifies research as a form of social protest, noting that "activism and academics are not mutually exclusive; the university can foster scholarship and activism simultaneously." Her research is a direct challenge to structural racism and academic assumptions that tend to discredit young men of color. Cruces (chapter 12) is also critical of systemic elitism and offers community-partnered zine collecting as an intervention that preserves Chicana and LGBTQ voices. Apata (chapter 11) challenges perceptions of the library as quiet, neutral, and individualist, while sharing her efforts to bring community together in song and history after the 2016 elections.

Each of the authors featured in this section grapples with how to advocate for social justice while securing safe and respectful environments. They tend to settle in a space between collections, people, and empathy. Apata (chapter 11), for example, recommends "embracing ...collections through our programming and outreach efforts and listening to our constituents." Cruces notes that "when students create documentation that represents themselves, and add it to the archives, they fill their zines and the archives with their experiences and interests." Fragola (chapter 13) argues that providing space for students to interact with audiences of students, faculty, and community members sets NCSU's Short Film Showcase apart. One student highlights cross-generational connections between content and creative inspiration: "One time, after seeing a particularly appealing animation, I was given the opportunity to talk to the creator after the show and make an acquaintance! When my work was shown this semester, an inspired and excited middle schooler came up to me and it was a nice experience to have been able to be in both sets of shoes."

The connection between people, content, and scholarship has sustained libraries for centuries. Some predict the same for the future: "Librarians in 2050 will be doing the same thing we are doing now—making content accessible to our users."[6] On the contrary the "Academic Library Autopsy Report, 2050" foretells the tragic obsolescence of book collections, library instruction, and ultimately academic librarians.[7] Neither of these forecasts makes the important link between information, creativity, people, and learning. The ACRL *Framework* "Scholarship as Conversation" frame suggests that the brick and mortar of learning is people linked together with and through information in forums or communities.[8] The good news for the future of education and libraries is that students embrace the idea and carry it forward. Cain (chapter 10), for example, affirms "we must be conscientious about the sources we choose and mindful of how our scholarship affects others. Finally, we must integrate empathy into the work we do and understand research as the platform for fostering understanding of experiences and positionalities different from our own." Apata (chapter 11) argues that "librarians, like musicians, are trained to listen creatively…. Beyond the reference desk, we can listen creatively for marginalized voices by recognizing lacunae in our collections and filling the gaps with works by authors from underrepresented groups. Creative listening hears perceived, rather than expressly stated needs."

If libraries are listening creatively, they will invest in people and build forums into their physical and digital spaces. Social engagement offers opportunities for the public "to communicate with [libraries] and each other; …add[ing] value to existing library data by tagging, commenting, rating, reviewing, text correcting; and …creat[ing] and upload[ing] content to add to our collections."[9] These contributions give us access to what and whom we do not know. Physical and digital spaces that assemble communities so they can share experiences enable important conversations and acquaintances. In doing so, they make diverse subjects accessible to multiple audiences, creating a freer flow of each through "zones of development." Libraries have always provided opportunities for students to engage with established disciplinary work. Facilitating disciplinary practice in library spaces is the logical next step for promoting active and social learning.

Simply put, lifelong learning cannot occur in the absence of third spaces that leverage the power of community. Radically open community partnerships that improve communication, empathy, and access to the lifeblood of scholarship—defined here as conversation between human resources and their material culture—are the future of education. Library spaces must therefore lend themselves to student success by welcoming emerging scholars and the public to share their ideas and research in forums. By creating alternative environments rich in human resources and scholarly or creative content, libraries resist the false dichotomy between technology and tradition. They also give students opportunities to practice scholarship.

Notes

1. Kris D. Gutiérrez, Patricia Baquedano-López, and Carlos Tejeda, "Rethinking Diversity: Hybridity and Hybrid Language Practices in the Third Space," *Mind, Culture, and Activity* 6, no. 4 (1999): 287.

2. Homi K. Bhabha, *The Location of Culture* (New York: Routledge, 1994), 1–2.

3. Lev Vygotsky, "Interaction between Learning and Development," *Readings on the Development of Children* 23, no. 3 (1978): 34–41.

4. Paulo Freire, *Pedagogy of the Oppressed*, trans. Myra Bergman Ramos (New York: Continuum, 1970), 65–80.

5. James Elmborg, "Critical Information Literacy: Implications for Instructional

Practice," *Journal of Academic Librarianship* 32, no. 2 (2006): 192–99.

6. Patricia T. Tully, "The Library's End? A Long Way Off," *Chronicle of Higher Education*, January 23, 2011, *Expanded Academic ASAP*, EBSCOhost. 00095982.

7. Brian T. Sullivan "Academic Library Autopsy Report, 2050" *Chronicle of Higher Education*, January 2, 2011, https://www.chronicle.com/article/Academic-Library-Autopsy/125767.

8. Association of College and Research Libraries, *Framework for Information Literacy for Higher Education* (Chicago: Association of College and Research Libraries, 2016), http://www.ala.org/acrl/standards/ilframework.

9. Rose Holley, "Crowdsourcing: How and Why Should Libraries Do It?" *D-Lib Magazine* 16, no. 3/4 (March/April 2010), https://doi.org/10.1045/march2010-holley.

Bibliography

Association of College and Research Libraries, *Framework for Information Literacy for Higher Education*. Chicago: Association of College and Research Libraries, 2016. http://www.ala.org/acrl/standards/ilframework.

Bhabha, Homi K. *The Location of Culture*. New York: Routledge, 1994.

Elmborg, James. "Critical Information Literacy: Implications for Instructional Practice." *Journal of Academic Librarianship* 32, no. 2 (2006): 192–99.

Freire, Paulo. *Pedagogy of the Oppressed*. Translated by Myra Bergman Ramos. New York: Continuum, 1970.

Gutiérrez, Kris D., Patricia Baquedano-López, and Carlos Tejeda. "Rethinking Diversity: Hybridity and Hybrid Language Practices in the Third Space." *Mind, Culture, and Activity* 6, no. 4 (1999): 286–303.

Holley, Rose. "Crowdsourcing: How and Why Should Libraries Do It?" *D-Lib Magazine* 16, no. 3/4 (March/April 2010). https://doi.org/10.1045/march2010-holley.

Sullivan, Brian T. "Academic Library Autopsy Report, 2050." *Chronicle of Higher Education*, January 2, 2011. https://www.chronicle.com/article/Academic-Library-Autopsy/125767.

Tully, Patricia T. "The Library's End? A Long Way Off." *Chronicle of Higher Education*, January 23, 2011, *Expanded Academic ASAP*, EBSCOhost. 00095982.

Vygotsky, Lev. "Interaction between Learning and Development." *Readings on the Development of Children* 23, no. 3 (1978): 34–41.

CHAPTER 9

Students Exposed
What Happens When Student Work Ends Up in the Learning Commons

Brittney Thomas

Introduction

Over the past few decades, fast-changing technologies have forced academic libraries to navigate wave after wave of change. As home-based internet connections have multiplied, libraries have transferred attention from building collections to developing a broader array of user-oriented services, spaces, and resources. Designating prime library real estate for active learning space has enabled many academic libraries to align their efforts with other institutional goals for supporting increased student success.

Lessons learned at the University of Iowa Libraries' Learning Commons illuminate shifting perceptions of the way library spaces can be transformed from places for passive consumption of knowledge to dynamic environments in which knowledge creation parallels "the reorientation of knowledge in higher education" to more constructivist connections between experiences and ideas.[1] The transition highlighted in this chapter expands the library's list of what can happen in an environment that stimulates the broader academic community by connecting ideas and cultural differences through the active practices of sharing and learning in community.

Today, the University of Iowa Libraries' Learning Commons provides an active, dynamic and collaborative study space where librarians, students, teaching faculty, and other stakeholders can learn together. Originally envisioned as the "extension of the classroom, a place that fosters collaborative and interactive learning,"[2] the Learning Commons has evolved into something even more dynamic. This chapter delineates that evolution from three frameworks: the learning environment, educational alliances, and transliteracy. The idea is to illustrate a librarian's perspective on how the Learning Commons embodies a forum for educational alliances and transliteracy.

Learning Environment

Situating the learning space model within the more complex framework of the learning environment enables us to understand the value and complexities of learning commons as forums. As noted in *Learning Environments: Where Space, Technology, and Culture Converge*, this framework brings together "a multiplicity of players, forces, and systems interacting" with one another.[3] An environment is by nature dynamic and fluid, "changing in response to influences from outside or arising inside."[4] This emphasis on "the conditions and circumstances of learning" in an environment rather than a space underscores the importance of learning within and through a combination of technical and human resources in a "cultural backdrop against which learning takes place."[5]

Recognizing the complexities of learning spaces as composite environments "invites a wider range of participants: administrators of various levels and functions, faculty, guest experts, librarians, IT staff, instructional designers, and learning theorists and researchers."[6] This framework gives the libraries room to examine space from varying perspectives and forces library staff and users to think differently together about knowledge production and dissemination as communal activities rather than the one-sided "transmission(s) of information from masters to pupils" or from librarians to patrons.[7] This idea, also expressed in educational philosophy targeting the instructive qualities of life experience and sharing among adult learners, combines the roles of students and teachers to stimulate diversity and educational creativity.[8] Acknowledging that learning environments are complex, unpredictable, and influenced by all of the cultures and knowledges circulating within and through them bridges gaps between higher education and society at large. This more dynamic ecosystem presents new opportunities for the widest range of participants to identify, engage with, and practice sharing their knowledge as well as interests.

Library staff at the University of Iowa did not originally use the learning environment framework to help guide activities in the Learning Commons. After some reflection, however, they recognized its usefulness in reorienting perceptions of the impact of the variety of activities hosted in the

Learning Commons over the past several years. Many of the activities did not attract large audiences, but subtle trends emerged. The activities that were most successful were those that were directly connected to a class curriculum and extended to individual student interests. This realization quickly set the groundwork for the library as forum concept to emerge.

When the Learning Commons first opened, we assumed that it would be inherently dynamic and active. Despite the extreme physical makeover, the idea of what a library was in large part did not change for students, faculty, and staff. They used the Learning Commons the same way they would have used any other library, except in larger numbers. Students did not use the six open group areas as the collaborative work spaces as had been intended, so library staff invited instructors to use them as venues for student presentations, which previously had been confined to a private classroom. The instructors found that these spaces enriched their classes by raising expectations for effective public speaking. They noted that students performed better in the group spaces than they normally did in the classroom where they had spent the entire semester. The spaces in the Learning Commons provided opportunities for students to gain much-needed public speaking experience with audiences that were much larger, more diverse, and more unpredictable than their classmates. For the libraries, the class presentations brought an air of collaboration and discussion into the environment, making the place feel more collaborative, active, and dynamic.

With the introduction of class presentations, instructors began to see the Learning Commons as a place to innovate with their curriculum and interact differently with their students. In addition to accessing badly needed space, instructors were able to consult with library staff to integrate the Learning Commons community more seamlessly into their course curriculum. Introducing class presentations into the Learning Commons was our first opportunity to experience the Learning Commons as a forum, a place where students could share their ideas and thoughts with each other and with the community passing by, not to mention library staff. Partnering with instructors allowed us to maintain a small amount of control over what happened in the space since content was "vetted" via the traditional course model. Over time we would learn that the Learning Commons worked as a forum only when we handed over control to the students.

Looking at spaces such as the Learning Commons within the framework of the learning environment allows us to incorporate a wide range of learning models that intentionally play with interpersonal dynamics and unpredictability. A 2013 article by Hattwig and colleagues about the *ACRL Visual Literacy Competency Standards for Higher Education* states that "in an academic participatory culture, students are expected to make contributions to research, learning, and communication as knowledge producers."[9] Assuming the role of expert may be difficult for students, many of whom might feel like they are imposters, particularly those who are underrepresented in or new to the university setting. Using the Learning Commons as a forum can change the teacher-learner dynamic, flipping their roles around so students can occupy a position of focus and authority while faculty become part of the audience. This turnabout helps the students to see themselves as true academics, and it works in a public space like the Learning Commons, as opposed to a classroom, because instructors can maintain some form of ownership over a traditional classroom. In the classroom, instructors welcome students over the course of a semester, confirming their authority over the space. The Learning Commons is different because its larger and more diverse audience fuses the teacher into the commons. This process enables students to take the stage as knowledge creators, experts, and teachers, adding a modern twist to class presentations. The traditional safety of the classroom gives way to the vulnerability of a more public and unpredictable forum.

Our next lesson grew out of the class presentations. "Show What You Know" (see figures 9.1 and 9.2) was the brainchild of a rhetoric instructor known for his innovative use of digital media in the classroom. Our colleague wondered how we could use the group areas as a way for students to connect their new academic lives to their social experiences and begin building their identity as academics. The instructor, skilled in assignment design, drafted an assignment that could be used at the beginning of the semester as an icebreaker. Students created a short presentation about a topic they felt used their skills and

FIGURE 9.1
Spring, Show What You Know

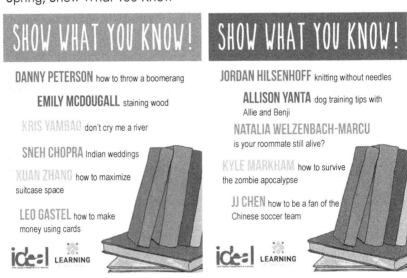

FIGURE 9.2
Fall, Show What You Know

could also inspire interest and learning in their peers. The assignment included a research portion so students could begin to identify how their chosen passions related to academic information. The class then voted on their favorite presentation, and the winning student was offered an opportunity to present in the Learning Commons at a reception the following week. It was amazing to see what students chose to as their areas of expertise, ranging from "How to Survive the Zombie Apocalypse" to "How to Swing Dance."[10] We have a lot of fun with this event, ordering cookies and punch and marketing it across campus. At the end of the event, participating students autographed an event poster, which was then given to the University Archives, leaving the students' marks on the libraries' archival collections and connecting their academic experience forever to the University of Iowa.[11] The "Show What You Know" event has been so successful that it has become a biyearly activity, happening at the beginning of every fall and spring semester.

Educational Alliances

The forum concept levels the playing field enough for students try on new, more authoritative roles, allowing them to employ educational alliances with each other and with their instructors. The educational alliance is a conceptual framework that mutually reinforces social bonds in the classroom because of its basis in mutual respect, shared responsibility for learning, effective communication and feedback, cooperation, and trust and security.[12] According to Baepler and Walker, the "focus on alliance is built on the general proposition that the social context in which teaching and learning takes place can affect, either positively or negatively, student academic or developmental outcomes."[13] What is to say that these types of alliances cannot be formed within environments such as the Learning Commons? In many ways this has already happened. When students present in the Learning Commons, they are exhibiting knowledge to more than just the instructor: their peers and the informal audience around them can take on a much larger role in the mind of the student. For example, we serendipitously discovered the perfect audience for the "Show What You Know" presentations when one of our librarians sent a flyer to the international services department and a large number of international students showed up eager to learn about the people and place in which they were living.

Bickford and Wright advocate for an educational community where "learners—including faculty—are enriched by *collective* meaning making, mentorship, encouragement and an understanding of the perspectives and unique qualities of an increasingly diverse membership."[14] By recognizing the educational alliances that are formed during these interactions, librarians gain an opportunity to integrate multicultural and inclusive awareness into our own practices, ultimately increasing participation and securing a environment for sharing diverse community perspectives. Learning within a community is very often how students approach new interests online, and work environments expect them to learn similarly. Bickford and Wright state that "building community enables the creation of spaces for learning …and conversely …creating learning-centered spaces can enhance our ability to build community," effectively adding to the complexity of the learning environment ecosystem.[15] The educational alliances that students and instructors foster within the Learning Commons enables a relatively equitable community that is integral to the sustenance and development of a forum.

During the fall 2014 semester, we explored an additional opportunity to reframe another traditional learning activity, further exploring the role of the Learning Commons as a forum. The Learning Commons partnered with Hancher Auditorium to host a pop-up museum called "Worth Fighting For."[16] The pop-up museum was a product of a semester long-campaign revolving around artist-in-residence Liz Lerman, a choreographer, writer, and thinker. Throughout the fall semester, Lerman visited a variety of classes, guiding them as they created interdisciplinary works on the topic of war and its effect on society, which was also the subject of her current work, "Healing Wars," a dance theater piece that explored the American Civil War with characters who migrate through history to contemporary wars.[17] Participating instructors designed assignments where students created artifacts that were shared with the public in a pop-up museum hosted by the Learning Commons.[18] Many students used unique research materials from the libraries' collections in preparation. Their finished products varied widely in content and format, including performance pieces, presentations, video installations, and fine art. The project also included an arts management course that planned every aspect of the museum, including exhibit locations, scheduling, marketing, volunteer management, and assessment.

The pop-up museum was a fantastic experience for the Learning Commons because it pushed the envelope of what is normally considered acceptable in a library. The exhibitors were loud, noisy, messy, and controversial, while at the same time reflective, thoughtful, and respectful. Looking back, the students seemed to understand the underlying currents of activity happening in the space, and they included those dynamics in the decisions they made. At the same time, students took risks that they might not have taken in the classroom. They were extremely creative in how they chose to use the spaces in the Learning Commons. Collaborations between classes occurred spontaneously, with many students incorporating each other's work into their own. For example, one class created a set of "Nine Cloth Printed Banners"

FIGURE 9.3
Nine Banners

(see figure 9.3), and another class incorporated those banners in a performance piece titled "The Mothers."[19] In the "Worth Fighting For" showcase, exhibitions, presentations, and performances made use of technology and physical and virtual spaces to facilitate community interaction, create and share knowledge within diverse groups, and foster learning, all the while allowing interaction to take place both inside and outside the formal classroom setting.[20]

The success of most of these activities lies not only in their connection to classroom outcomes but also in the fact that they connect these outcomes to informal learning opportunities, by placing them within the "spontaneous and informal interaction of campus life" and allowing what would be mere social alliances to evolve into educational alliances.[21] We can go even further to support these authentic learning experiences by singularly highlighting them within learning environments, priming students to recognize and reflect upon these experiences when they happen, even when they are not connected to the curriculum. Higher education can become even more valuable when connected to the ordinary concerns of life, particularly within the range of opportunities that technology provides for creating new kinds of learning activities and experiences. This, Sullivan tells us, is the "social dimension of learning."[22] In fact, we've found more success partnering with groups on campus that are known for supporting the social side of student life when hosting events with no direct curricular connection. Highlighting informal experiences on their own merit also further enhances library participation in the academic community as a forum.

Forums find authenticity in the fact that they expose and provide voice to experiences that are not considered traditionally "academic." Our most successful example of such informal learning experiences is the annual "Capture Iowa" exhibition. "Capture Iowa" is a campus photo project that showcases student life at the University of Iowa. The project focuses on the social side of academia and, in particular, on the first-year experience. First-year students are encouraged to submit pictures of their lives to a hashtag via Instagram. At the end of the year, images are juried, and selected photographs are showcased in an exhibition. In addition, the collection is also exhibited on a screen in the Learning Commons. We've begun exhibiting the most recent "Capture Iowa" collections at the beginning of the fall semester to introduce the new group of incoming students to the project and to help them get excited about experiences they will likely have over the coming years. The "Capture Iowa" project has given us the opportunity to connect the learning environment to students' social lives, which can be just as important to their growth and development as their academics. Bringing these experiences out into the open, in a traditionally academic setting, allows students to step back and to look at their personal and social lives as learning opportunities as well.

The University of Iowa has identified other ways to connect both informal and formal learning opportunities. One example of this is the Hawkeye Service Teams, a program that promotes "service learning, social justice, and community building."[24] During the spring semester, participating students take an academic course that introduces them to theoretical approaches in service learning. As a class, the students embark on a service learning trip over spring break. Upon returning they reflect on their experience and create a website that showcases what they experienced and learned. The website is presented to their peers during a reception at the end of the semester.[25] During the past semester, the Learning Commons partnered with the Center for Student Involvement and Leadership to host the Hawkeye Service Team reception, giving these students access to a larger and more varied audience.

Transliteracy

As part of a digital participatory culture, "students often share and create visual information through social media sites and work with images across academic and personal spaces," which should be reflected in the learning environments designed within the academic institution.[26] Even more students are already making this shift in their academic lives, becoming more than consumers, but participants who "create and remix content as part of [their] social networks that may include academic groups and activities."[27] In response, librarians have begun to focus on new forms of literacy that permeate the higher education landscape, particularly visual literacy, digital literacy, and media literacy. The term *transliteracy* strives to combine these new literacies into a cohesive unit recognizing the term's fluidity between each one. Marcum advocates for libraries to "recast the model of information literacy to embrace [these] multiple literacies."[28] Librarians have a ready tool in their arsenal with the complex learning environment and educational alliances within which they work to create discrete instructional processes that make use of these environments and, with their help, can be seamlessly interwoven into traditional academic curriculum. Librarians can accomplish this in a number of different ways, through "play, performance, simulation, appropriation, … distributed cognition, collective intelligence, judgment, …negotiation, transmedia navigation, …and networking."[29] At the University of Iowa, the Main Library Learning Commons has become the perfect place for students to interact with and find support for real-life transliteracy skills, and faculty can use the Learning Commons to incorporate transliteracy activities into the curriculum. The most common example of this in most learning commons is the introduction of various tutoring services, such as the writing center. These initiatives help faculty take the lead in higher education's efforts to teach and support transliteracy. The *ACRL Visual Literacy Competency Standards for Higher Education* provides a wonderful guide to identifying and mapping out transmedia learning outcomes.[30] Although their focus is on visual literacy, they state that their visual literacy guidelines are intentionally closely connected with the ACRL information literacy framework, making them a useful tool for transliteracy work.

Despite these examples of effective social learning in the Learning Commons, two years of data at the University of Iowa confirmed our suspicion that students weren't using the group areas for collaborative work. Additionally, feedback from instructors and students told us that two of the group areas were not very effective for social learning activities. We jumped on the opportunity to reimagine at least one of those areas into something completely different. We have had great success showcasing digital exhibitions on the large screens, and we have decided to turn one of the underutilized spaces into a formal digital exhibition space. The transformation has been slow, giving us time to experiment. We hope to eventually have a full semester lineup of exhibitions including student work, live streaming lectures across campus, events across the nation, and showcases of some of our digital collections. We also hope to find funding to make the exhibition space interactive. A dedicated exhibition space will allow us to connect meaningfully with an increasingly diverse student population as we apply "the fundamentals of visual language" to creating visual products across the disciplines.[31]

We advocate for students to learn about issues that affect their personal and professional lives, including privacy, ethics, copyright, and safety. Nonetheless, we have yet to identify a meaningful way to bring such ideas to a forum. Some believe the digital exhibition space will give librarians opportunity to discuss these issues with students and determine how to approach their value and relevancy in students' lives and academic pursuits. From a library perspective, it seems students have no stake in the game, and as a result, they remain unclear that their creation and distribution of "images and video online and via social networks, …form[s] an online identity with consequences for their academic and professional lives. They must consider the impact of the personal information images carry and demonstrate respect for others' privacy."[32] The exhibition space can provide a forum for librarians and students to interact around these issues, improving the approach in the libraries as well as students' understanding of the long-term importance of such issues. We can usher in this learning moment and identity transformation by creating discussions in seamless exhibition experiences that showcase student works alongside library collections and faculty research, equalizing responsibilities for privacy, ethics, copyright, and safety in publishing. The libraries can go even farther to level the playing field by integrating student work into the institutional repository alongside faculty research. Installing student work into its own digital collection allows students to see themselves as creators as well as consumers. It becomes an opportunity to discuss the concepts of open access and authorship in community. In the future we hope to expand upon our success with the "Show What You Know" event posters and create a digital collection that houses all of the student work that has been showcased in the Learning Commons.

Expectations for students to use and produce digital content have emerged throughout the higher education curriculum with no cohesive plan to support such production. At the University of Iowa, we have a comprehensive support network for faculty interested in designing active learning activities, but we lack direct support for students who are expected to complete these activities. This is where the Learning Commons can step in. Because the space is already known for integrating and connecting student support services that go beyond research and writing, we can continue to expand this network to include transliteracy. In the early 2000s, educators assumed that digital natives had the intellectual wherewithal to understand the cultural implications that come with creating media. We are learning increasingly that this assumption is incorrect. When left without the intervention of a learning environment where these issues reveal themselves practically, students interact with media in seemingly mindless ways. We must "equip a learner to understand and analyze the contextual, cultural, ethical, aesthetic, intellectual, and technical components involved in the production and use of visual materials."[33]

To some extent we have already begun to provide support for students, albeit in a piecemeal way. In 2015 we installed the One Button Studio in the Main Library. Designed by Penn State University, the One Button Studio is an open-source, "simplified video recording [studio] that can be used without any previous video production experience.... You only need to bring your flash drive with you and push a single button."[34] Our goal for the One Button Studio was to provide a space for students to practice presentations and make video recordings without having to know how to use a complicated camera, lights, and a microphone. With all the video equipment preset, students could focus on just the content. The One Button Studio mimics real life, with most students never needing more than their smartphone to record and publish any type of media content. Instead of focusing on how to teach students to use video equipment, faculty can focus class time on teaching students to reflect on the types of content they create and choose to incorporate into the public forum. Additionally, instructors have another tool at their disposal to integrate innovative learning opportunities into their curriculum. The One Button Studio is an easy entry into the digital media landscape, and faculty can use the studio to help their students engage with specific literacy skills.

As we continue to support students in their use of the Learning Commons for meaningful conversations and opportunities to showcase their work and interact with us, each other, and their instructors in a variety of new and innovative ways, we must also consider the ways in which we assist them and learn from those practices. Our experience suggests a primary concern is a requirement for help with digital media creation. Even with the use of the One Button Studio, many students, and even faculty, need help fitting the recording studio into the larger process of video production.

Some of our more controversial activities, and coincidently best learning opportunities, have come in the form of digital art exhibitions. We exhibited our first "Video Art Show" in the spring of 2014, using a monitor in one of the group spaces. Our primary goal was to show students what it looked like to use the monitors and to get students more excited about using the open group spaces. The art show was coordinated with help from a graduate student in media arts and was juried by staff from the Digital Public Arts and Humanities department. We opened the show for students at the university and hosted a reception for the selected artists where we provided popcorn and soda (a play on the movie theater) while they watched the show. The "Video Art Show" was extremely successful, and the next year we hosted two exhibitions. The first, "Small Bytes Microcinema," was connected to a new initiative the university was exploring, the Theme Semester. The Theme Semester is a year-long collaboration that "brings diverse perspectives to bear on a topic of importance to Iowa and the world.... Grounded in the educational mission of the university, the Theme Semester provides opportunities for teaching, engagement, and learning both on campus and throughout the state of Iowa."[35] That year's theme was "Food for Thought," and all submissions were to have something to do with food. The second video show, scheduled to be exhibited right after the first, was a repeat of the original "Video Art Show."

The subject matter students chose to highlight in their videos at both shows expanded on sensitive themes that were relevant to their lives, such as the body, gender identity, sexuality, violence, and mental health. We put up a whiteboard on which audience members could provide feedback in response to the mature nature of the content. The audience responded to the feedback board quite well, resulting in spontaneous dialogue. We were nervous about the reaction to the videos, but we were also hesitant to remove any of them, not only because that would be in direct conflict with our values as librarians, but also because these were topics that were important to students, topics that they needed to talk about. We wanted to hear what they had to say. We realized that it was important to provide a space for students to have these discussions, and what better space than the Learning Commons?

Not surprisingly, those discussions were very bumpy. During the "Worth Fighting For" exhibition, the Learning Commons encountered a few exhibits that engaged with sensitive issues, including an exhibit by the UI Veterans Association (UIVA) designed to help students get to know more about veterans on campus and to help students participate in a larger discussion about the effects of war and violence in popular media. To do this, the UIVA challenged audience members to a video game tournament using *Call of Duty*, a widely popular video game series in the US and one that is commonly played by active military personnel while overseas. Due to the extreme violence of the game, we received many complaints and decided that the UIVA would take the installation down early. We were not satisfied with that conclusion. We found great potential in the idea of facilitating conversations around controversial issues in the Learning Commons, especially if we could connect to course initiatives and do so in a safe, engaging, and inclusive way. Lessons from that experience prompted us to partner a year later with the Veterans Association and the Center for Teaching to host the same event for Veterans Day, as well as a tournament with a series of lectures on video games. We maintained communication with concerned parties and campus administrators and found compromises that addressed all concerns, most significantly, finding a space in the Learning Commons that wasn't connected to a major thoroughfare where we could host the tournament while still hosting the lectures in a public area. Higher education strives to address these issues in terms of service learning, leadership development, project-based learning, and all learning models where control over what is said can be exerted. The Learning Commons is an ideal space for practicing those conversations in a learning environment that engages diverse players and cultures in unpredictable ways, effectively minimizing faculty and staff control over the process.

Reframing the Learning Commons as a forum allows students to play with the concept of performance and display and what it can look like outside of formal spaces. In the Learning Commons, students can practice engaging in issues they find important in a low-stakes environment. Just like the class presentations, exhibitions are a useful tool for students to practice communicating through the objects they create. In this way, the exhibitions emulate students' real lives, particularly in the digital sphere. The Learning Commons can mimic how students process life events in their learning and ensure opportunity for reflection and learning by identifying curricular partnerships with faculty. By providing space for students to showcase work and to publicly interact with each other, learning commons can open up possibilities for inappropriate commentary and activities that aren't always well thought out, promoting experimentation in learning processes. We must consider carefully when deciding how the Learning Commons should address inappropriate behavior and commentary.

As a forum, the Learning Commons is a space that necessarily puts different peoples' values at odds with each other. Determining how to provide safe and welcoming space as well as advocacy for free speech and discussion of relevant, yet controversial, issues is tricky but increasingly important. What is our role as library facilitators and curators? How do we deal with inappropriate behavior? Is there anything to learn in how libraries have historically addressed controversial texts? We often walk a thin line when blurring these course-based collaborative experiences or research-indicative grappling encounters with students' study space. Allowing such activities to happen in the Learning Commons puts librarians in a difficult spot. No one knows what will happen until it does, and we wonder if the learning moments are worth the amount of control we relinquish. Despite these reservations, controversial conversations are opportunities for students and librarians to experience giving and receiving feedback, which can be directly associated with their lives online and with the importance of debate in academia.

A large part of transliteracy is citizenship. Using the Learning Commons as a model of social space (both digital and physical), we can reframe student interactions and original works with an understanding of what it means to be citizens, in both the traditional and digital sense. We can provide space and opportunities for students to understand where personal experiences and ownership begin and end and where group expression begins and ends, while also creating opportunities to advance diversity by highlighting common ground and differences among groups on campus, something that is sorely lacking in many higher education and social settings.

The learning environment, Warger and Dobbin argue, is an ecosystem where students can show not only "mastery but also imagination and creativity."[36] They can connect what they are learning to what is relevant in their lives. Warger and Dobbin also argue that "with minimally mediated access to large amounts of information and with a substantially enhanced social dimension available to students, the set of directions students can take in their learning is far larger and growing."[37] Warger and Dobbin may have been talking about the digital world, but that argument can be extended into a physical space as well through innovative technologies, realigning services, and so on. The magic of the learning commons is that it is an experimental microcosm of the "environmental changes brought by technology and a tipping of control in favor of students regardless of faculty intentions."[38] Faculty must intentionally let go of the reins in order to use the learning commons effectively. So too must library staff, administrators, and students. We must also be strategic in the amount of mediation and control we do try to exert in such spaces. Often such attempts at control fail spectacularly. However, without some attempt at mediation, we run the risk of not providing a safety net to students who do experiment and fail, who may not yet have the ability to understand and reflect upon their experiences, and who can place others at risk. We see our students attempting to interact with topics that influence their lives and are often controversial, and in those attempts, mistakes will be made. Like a true learning environment "intentions and design cannot account for everything that happens; some elements escape control or are at least unintended."[39]

As libraries continue to face declining budgets and increasing costs, it will become imperative to look for alternative funding sources and to automate as much of the exhibition process as possible. Currently, we have one full-time staff member dedicated to the entire Learning Commons and rely on partnerships from other library and campus departments. In that way, it truly resembles a community commons. Each group has different strengths and resources they bring to the table. To improve on what we've accomplished with the Learning Commons, we must get more participation and buy-in from university leadership as well as from the community. With the cost of higher education rising and budgets shrinking, we must keep in mind that in resource-scarce environments, leadership is under pressure to make wise decisions about which innovations to promote and to sustain. Part of knowing where the money is best spent is understanding the system of factors within the learning environment that improve student success and make use of the environment. Additionally, to successfully influence those decisions, the libraries must put forth a united vision that aligns with the university's mission and vision. By treating the Learning Commons as a dynamic and complex environment, we can realistically advocate for the resources and funding needed to make such environments sustainable. Without proper support and funding, many learning spaces disappear after a few years, when the technology and learning pedagogies those spaces embodied become obsolete. The University of Iowa Libraries proves an excellent example of this process, starting with the Information Commons in the early 90s, one of the first of its kind. Over two decades later, the Information Commons is gone, and the Learning Commons has taken its place. The learning environment accounts for these rapid changes and situates such spaces within even larger and more complex environments, where additional resources, policies, and technologies influence what happens within the smaller learning environment. When used during the planning and design stages of library renovations or new services, the learning environment model can provide a foundation for innovation in a sustainable way.

We must also consider the unintended consequences of our innovations. By providing a forum for students, we are pushing the learning commons farther towards the collaborative end of the spectrum at the cost of space for quiet reflection. The most common mistake in learning commons design is not providing any space whatsoever for quiet, individual study, getting rid of reading rooms and study carrels altogether instead of improving on them. Currently the Learning Commons acts as a pendulum, moving from one end of the learning spectrum to the other, depending on the needs of the students. The Learning Commons is often quiet, for example, reflecting the traditional reading room rather than a forum. To ensure that future renovations and innovations are successful, we must first acknowledge that sometimes the environment in the Learning Commons is not conducive to all types of learning. To some extent we have achieved a wary kind of success when we are able to do this. We must still consider reincorporating traditional learning spaces in future designs and consider how we can facilitate collaborative learning more effectively.

This pendulum reminds us that student learning has always been part of the academic library mission. In the pre-digital era, we provided a quality collection of information for teaching, learning, and research initiatives. That contribution to student success has produced some essential uses of the library that cannot be shunned. In many academic libraries the traditional reading room, where students congregated to study communally, has been completely replaced, whereas it could have simply been updated. We recognize the environment academic libraries are situated within by understanding that to move forward we must build strategically on what we have already created. Our past and future are inextricably combined in supporting student success with environments that include the reading room and the learning commons, quiet study and collaborative activity. The result of this combination is truly reflective of our users' needs.

Conclusion

The three frameworks described in this chapter, the learning environment, educational alliances, and transliteracy, create an ideal context in which to situate the Main Library Learning Commons at the University of Iowa and the experiences, actions, and beliefs of our academic community. We can use them to create a road map for where the libraries, and higher education, should go. Our course is set, and over the next few years the Learning Commons will continue to learn, innovate, and experiment as a forum for faculty and students to do the same in community with the libraries. As we move forward, we can use these frameworks to be more communicative with students and thoughtful in the services, resources, and spaces we provide. This environment will include opportunities for faculty to connect their curriculum to real-world experiences and continue to add value to the larger campus environment as a place where many come to innovate and connect. The most valuable lesson learned has been that providing space is not enough. Innovative and collaborative work comes from embracing the benefits of an unpredictable learning environment that naturally lends itself to collaborating, experimenting, failing, and letting go, essentially replicating the skills and actions that we want our students to learn.

Notes

1. Rebecca M. Sullivan, "Common Knowledge: Learning Spaces in Academic Libraries," *College and Undergraduate Libraries* 17, no. 2–3 (2010): 130, https://doi.org/10.1080/10691316.2010.481608.

2. Nancy L. Baker, Tom Rocklin, and Steve Fleagle, "Fostering Learning through Library Spaces: The University of Iowa Libraries," *Iowa Research Online* 1, no. 5. (2007), http://ir.uiowa.edu/lib_pubs/124/.

3. Tom Warger and Gregory Dobbin, *Learning Environments: Where Space, Technology, Culture Converge*, ELI Paper 1 (Louisville, CO: Educause Learning Initiative, October 2009), 6, https://library.educause.edu/~/media/files/library/2009/10/eli3021-pdf.pdf.

4. Warger and Dobbin, *Learning Environments*, 6.

5. Warger and Dobbin, *Learning Environments*, 3.

6. Warger and Dobbin, *Learning Environments*, 6.

7. Warger and Dobbin, *Learning Environments*, 9.

8. Paulo Freire, *Pedagogy of the Oppressed,* trans. Myra Bergman Ramos (New York: Seabury Press 1970).

9. Denise Hattwig et al., "Visual Literacy Standards in Higher Education: New Opportunities for Libraries and Student Learning," *portal: Libraries and the Academy* 13, no. 1 (January 2013): 81, https://doi.org/10.1353/pla.2013.0008; Association of College and Research Libraries, *ACRL Visual Literacy Competency Standards for Higher Education* (Chicago: Association of College and Research Libraries, 2011), http://www.ala.org/acrl/standards/visualliteracy.

10. Kyle Markham. "How to Survive the Zombie Apocalypse," Show What You Know event poster, 2015, "Records of the University Libraries," no. RG 21.0001.001, special Collections and University Archives, University of Iowa Libraries, Daniel Levitt, "How to Swing Dance," Show What You Know event poster, 2015, "Records of the University Libraries," no. RG 21.0001.001, Special Collections and University Archives, University of Iowa Libraries, accessed February 1, 2018.

11. Show What You Know Event Poster, 2015, "Records of the University Libraries," no. RG 21.0001.001, Special Collections and University Archives, University of Iowa Libraries, accessed February 1, 2018.

12. Richard G. Tiberius and Janet Mancini Billson, "The Social Context of Teaching and Learning," *New Directions for Teaching and Learning* 1991, no. 45 (Spring 1991): 67–86, https://doi.org/10.1002/tl.37219914509.

13. Paul Baepler and J. D. Walker, "Active Learning Classrooms and Educational Alliances: Changing Relationships to Improve Learning," *New Directions for Teaching and Learning* 2014, no. 137 (2014): 28, https://doi.org/10.1002/tl.20083.

14. Deborah J. Bickford and David J. Wright, "Community: The Hidden Context for Learning," chapter 4 in *Learning Spaces*, ed. Diana G. Oblinger (Louisville, CO: Educause, 2006), 4.2-4.3.

15. Bickford and Wright, "Community," 4–5.

16. Worth Fighting For webpage, Hancher, University of Iowa, accessed December 30, 2017, https://hancher.uiowa.edu/theme/fight.

17. "Healing Wars." created and directed by Liz Lerman, webpage, University of Iowa, accessed February 2, 2018, https://hancher.uiowa.edu/lerman.

18. Worth Fighting For Pop-Up Museum Opening Reception webpage, Hancher, University of Iowa, accessed February 2, 2018, https://hancher.uiowa.edu/worth-fighting-pop-museum-opening-reception.

19. "Nine Cloth Print Banners," in *Worth Fighting For Pop Up Museum,* exhibition catalog (Iowa City: Hancher, University of Iowa, 2014), 3, accessed February 2, 2018, https://hancher.uiowa.edu/sites/hancher.uiowa.edu/files/WFF_PopUpMuseum_Catalog.pdf; "The Mothers," in *Worth Fighting For Pop Up Museum,* exhibition catalog (Iowa City: Hancher, University of Iowa, 2014), 4, accessed February 2, 2018, https://hancher.uiowa.edu/sites/hancher.uiowa.edu/files/WFF_PopUpMuseum_Catalog.pdf.

20. Worth Fighting For Pop Up Museum Opening Reception webpage.

21. Sullivan, "Common Knowledge," 139–140.

22. Sullivan, "Common Knowledge," 139–140.

24. "Hawkeye Service Teams," University of Iowa, Leadership and Service Programs, accessed December 30, 2017, https://leadandserve.uiowa.edu/programs/service-teams/.

25. "2017 Alternative Spring Break," University of Iowa, Leadership and Service Programs, accessed June 5, 2017, https://leadandserve.uiowa.edu/programs/service-teams/2017/.

26. Hattwig et al., "Visual Literacy Standards inHigher Education," 65.

27. Hattwig et al., "Visual Literacy Standards in Higher Education," 65.

28. James Marcum, "Beyond Visual Culture: The Challenge of Visual Ecology," *portal: Libraries and the Academy* 2, no. 2 (2002): 202 https://doi.org/10.1353/pla.2002.0038.

29. Hattwig et al., "Visual Literacy Standards in Higher Education," 65.

30. Association of College and Research Libraries, *ACRL Visual Literacy Competency Standards.*

31. Hattwig et al., "Visual Literacy Standards in Higher Education," 81.

32. Hattwig et al., "Visual Literacy Standards in Higher Education," 83.

33. Association of College and Research Libraries, *ACRL Visual Literacy Competency Standards.*

34. One Button Studio website, Pennsylvania State University, accessed December 30, 2017, http://onebutton.psu.edu/.

35. "Theme Semester," Outreach and Engagement at Iowa, University of Iowa, accessed December 30, 2017, https://outreach.uiowa.edu/theme-Semester.

36. Warger and Dobbin, *Learning Environments,* 6.

37. Warger and Dobbin, *Learning Environments,* 6.

38. Warger and Dobbin, *Learning Environments,* 6.

39. Warger and Dobbin, *Learning Environments,* 6.

Bibliography

Association of College and Research Libraries. *ACRL Visual Literacy Competency Standards for Higher Education*. Chicago: Association of College and Research Libraries, 2011. http://www.ala.org/acrl/standards/visualliteracy.

Baepler, Paul, and J. D. Walker. "Active Learning Classrooms and Educational Alliances: Changing Relationships to Improve Learning." *New Directions for Teaching and Learning* 2014, no. 137 (2014): 27–40. https://doi.org/10.1002/tl.20083.

Baker, Nancy L., Tom Rocklin, and Steve Fleagle. "Fostering Learning through Library Spaces: The University of Iowa Libraries." *Iowa Research Online* 1, no. 5 (2007). http://ir.uiowa.edu/lib_pubs/124/.

Bickford, Deborah J., and David J. Wright. "Community: The Hidden Context for Learning." Chapter 4 in *Learning Spaces*. Edited by Diana G. Oblinger, 4.1–4.22. Louisville, CO: Educause, 2006.

Freire, Paulo. *Pedagogy of the Oppressed*. Translated by Myra Bergman Ramos. New York: Seabury Press, 1970.

Hancher. Worth Fighting For webpage. University of Iowa. Accessed December 30, 2017. https://hancher.uiowa.edu/theme/fight.

———. "Worth Fighting For Pop-Up Museum Opening Reception" webpage. University of Iowa. Accessed February 2, 2018. https://hancher.uiowa.edu/worth-fighting-pop-museum-opening-reception.

Hattwig, Denise, Kaila Bussert, Ann Medaille, and Joanna Burgess. "Visual Literacy Standards in Higher Education: New Opportunities for Libraries and Student Learning." *portal: Libraries and the Academy* 13, no. 1 (January 2013): 61–89. https://doi.org/10.1353/pla.2013.0008.

Levitt, Daniel. "How to Swing Dance," Show What You Know event poster, 2015. "Records of the University Libraries," no. RG 21.0001.001. Special Collections and University Archives, University of Iowa Libraries.

Marcum, James. "Beyond Visual Culture: The Challenge of Visual Ecology." *portal: Libraries and the Academy* 2, no. 2 (2002): 189–206. https://doi.org/10.1353/pla.2002.0038.

Markham, Kyle. "How to Survive the Zombie Apocalypse," Show What You Know event poster, 2015. "Records of the University Libraries," no. RG 21.0001.001. Special Collections and University Archives, University of Iowa Libraries.

Pennsylvania State University. One Button Studio website. Accessed December 30, 2017, http://onebutton.psu.edu/.

Sullivan, Rebecca M. "Common Knowledge: Learning Spaces in Academic Libraries." *College and Undergraduate Libraries* 17, no. 2–3 (2010): 130–48. https://doi.org/10.1080/10691316.2010.481608.

Tiberius, Richard G., and Janet Mancini Billson. "The Social Context of Teaching and Learning." *New Directions for Teaching and Learning* 1991, no. 45 (Spring 1991): 67–86. https://doi.org/10.1002/tl.37219914509.

University of Iowa. "Hawkeye Service Teams." Leadership and Service Programs. Accessed December 30, 2017. https://leadandserve.uiowa.edu/programs/service-teams/.

———. "Healing Wars," created and directed by Liz Lerman, webpage. Accessed February 2, 2018. https://hancher.uiowa.edu/lerman.

———. "The Mothers." In *Worth Fighting For Pop Up Museum*, 4. Iowa City: Hancher, University of Iowa, 2014. Accessed February 2, 2018. https://hancher.uiowa. edu/sites/hancher.uiowa.edu/files/WFF_PopUpMuseum_Catalog.pdf.

———. "Nine Cloth Printed Banners." In *Worth Fighting For Pop Up Museum*, 3. Iowa City: Hancher, University of Iowa, 2014. Exhibition catalog. Accessed February 2, 2018. https://hancher.uiowa.edu/sites/hancher.uiowa.edu/files/ WFF_PopUpMuseum_Catalog.pdf.

———. Show What You Know Event Poster, 2015. "Records of the University Libraries," no. RG 21.0001.001. Special Collections and University Archives, University of Iowa Libraries.

———. "Theme Semester." Outreach and Engagement at Iowa, University of Iowa. Accessed December 30, 2017. https://outreach.uiowa.edu/theme-Semester.

———. "2017 Alternative Spring Break." Leadership and Service Programs. Accessed June 5, 2017. https://leadandserve.uiowa.edu/programs/service-teams/2017/.

Warger, Tom, and Gregory Dobbin. *Learning Environments: Where Space, Technology, Culture Converge*. ELI Paper 1. Louisville, CO: Educause Learning Initiative, October 2009. https://library.educause.edu/~/media/files/library/2009/10/ eli3021-pdf.pdf.

CHAPTER 10

Celebrating Student Scholarship with an Undergraduate Research Prize

Kevin M. Ross, Carolyn Radcliff, and Talia Cain

It is easy to underestimate the power of research. As a student, I face huge pressures to achieve high scores, get good grades, and be involved in campus organizations. In trying to balance all of my academic assignments and extracurricular interests, I start to see my tasks and responsibilities belonging to separate columns on a to-do list. I focus on getting things done so I can move on to whatever is next. Until recently I seldom envisioned the university as a place capable of nurturing my passion and mind simultaneously.

I recently completed a research project entitled "Critical Media Literacy: Liberating the 'Criminal' and Empowering African American Males."[1] As an aspiring educator, I am troubled by the harmful deficit model that has been used in academic literature to explain the achievement gap between students belonging to the dominant group and students belonging to marginalized groups. The deficit model blames students of color or students with low socioeconomic statuses for their academic disparities and ignores the structural inequalities and systemic oppressions that contribute to the achievement gap.[2]

I began my project with the intention of using academic research to expose how specific forces in society might work against minority groups in school settings. I narrowed my focus to examine the educational experiences of African American males and developed a research question that asked how the media perpetuates stereotypes of African American males as criminals. I wondered what the psychological effects of such stereotyping was and how it could impact academic performance among African American males. Moreover, I explored the possibility of pedagogical tools that might combat these negative outcomes.

In doing this research, I engaged with many sources that challenged my previous assumptions about the media. I was inspired by the concept of critical media literacy, which involves developing students' abilities to critically examine media sources. This pedagogy empowers students by allowing them to interrogate the dynamics of power, privilege, and oppression involved in media representations. Critical media literacy marks a shift from the curriculum traditionally taught in school settings and serves to validate differing cultures, ways of life, diverse ethnic and racial identities, and a broad spectrum of experiences for students with different backgrounds.[3] This acknowledgment of diversity has the effect of leveling the educational playing field and making schools more equitable.

Research offered me the chance to construct a cohesive, credible, and well-supported argument in an incredibly important subject area. I absorbed the existing body of research related to my topic and synthesized my findings to advocate for social justice. However, I did not recognize the potential of research to influence how people view the world until after I had the opportunity to reflect on the process. Research is not merely a reflection of reality, but a construction. It shapes how we frame and understand issues, and thus has the power to play an active role in challenging the status quo. The Kevin and Tam Ross Leatherby Libraries Undergraduate Research Prize gave me this opportunity.

Talia Cain, Chapman University Student

* * *

The Leatherby Libraries at Chapman University started its research prize contest for undergraduate students in 2007. Having reached the tenth anniversary of the contest, we are well positioned to reflect on how the contest has changed in concert with new ways of inquiry and information creation and on its role in supporting and honoring student research. A decade of experience has taught us how to diversify the contest and reflect collectively on its merits. In this chapter, we present a case study of how the Kevin and Tam Ross Undergraduate Research Prize (URP) recognizes and honors student scholarship. We explain the goals and processes of the contest and discuss the partnership elements that make the URP contest successful. A student contestant and a contest benefactor coauthor this chapter, enabling a forum with rich and diverse perspectives on the benefits of the competition. The reflection by student Talia Cain, presented in part above, underscores how the process of conducting research has contributed to the development of her scholarly identity. Talia entered the contest because it offered a unique outlet to examine her responsibilities as a student researcher, deconstruct her research methods, and redefine her identity as an undergraduate scholar. As she explains cogently, "Throughout my years in the school system, I have learned what it takes to 'do school' well. I know how to complete my assignments and get good grades, but rarely do I consider the bigger picture and the implications of my work. The Undergraduate Research Prize contest allowed me to step out of my everyday role of being a student and assess my research abilities as both a consumer of information and producer of knowledge."[4]

Background and Goals

The URP is modeled on similar contests at other universities. While the library at University of California, Berkeley, was the first to establish such a contest, an Internet search reveals that today there are two dozen or more academic libraries that conduct research contests. This list includes Brown University, Indiana University South Bend, La Sierra University, Labette Community College, Loyola Marymount University, Ohio State University, Oregon State University, Radford University, Temple University, University of California Berkeley, University of Georgia, University of Nevada Las Vegas, University of Redlands, University of Toronto, University of Washington, Westminster College, and Wesleyan University.[5] One common purpose among the contests is the desire to recognize and reward excellence in the use of information sources. For some institutions, the research award process is a way for the library to demonstrate direct involvement in the research activities of students and to celebrate students as producers of information and contributors of knowledge. Talia Cain's contributions to this chapter demonstrate the achievement of this goal.

Chapman University is a private university with 6,300 undergraduate students and 2,000 graduate students. The university has ten colleges and schools that offer programs in arts, humanities, and social sciences; business and economics; communication studies; educational studies; film and me dia arts; health and behavioral sciences; law; performing arts; pharmacy; and science and technology. The Leatherby Libraries support all programs except for the law school, which has its own library. Liaison librarians assist faculty and students through collection development and management, information literacy instruction, reference services, and personalized research appointments.

The Leatherby Libraries, working with a generous donor, established the URP with three core goals in mind. First, we wanted to encourage and recognize excellent research and effective use of library resources by undergraduate students at Chapman University. This goal evolved partially in response to the proliferation of easy access to online information that varies substantially in quality and authority. We wanted to underscore the value the library brings to the academic enterprise through careful selection and acquisition of materials and by providing access to a wide range of scholarly, primary, and other authoritative materials. That said, applicants are not limited to using so-called library materials, that is, items identified or obtained only from the library. We recognize and appreciate that many scholarly and research materials exist outside the library system and that students' bibliographies often include additional sources that are at times integrated into library instructional materials. For example, the liaison librarian for history has added links to primary documents and archival repositories on history LibGuides, promoting awareness and visibility of these potentially useful resources during information literacy instruction.

The second goal of the URP was to cultivate information literacy. At the time the contest started, we had adopted the ACRL *Information Literacy Competency Standards for Higher Education* as the guiding document for our instructional program.[6] We created a multilevel curriculum map and developed specific learning objectives based on the *Standards*. The university's regional accrediting agency, Western Association of Schools and Colleges (WASC) Senior College and University Commission, had also identified information literacy as one of five core competencies.[7] With all of this as backdrop, the contest became a way to promote information literacy in a holistic manner. Consequently, the contest guidelines emphasized evaluation of information, thoughtful use of library services, and reflection on the process in addition to use of resources. When ACRL moved from the *Standards* to the *Framework for Information Literacy for Higher Education*,[8] we reviewed and revised the guidelines, essay requirements, and rubric to accommodate the shift to threshold concepts and a more active student-as-creator approach.

The third goal was strengthening the library's campus reputation and relationships, particularly with faculty. The library is well regarded on campus and scores well on annual internal faculty surveys of expectations and performance. The liaison librarian program fosters communication with all academic departments, and the number of requests for information literacy instruction grows most years. In this context, the URP contest is an opportunity to increase the recognition of the library as an important resource for students and of librarians as active participants in supporting and recognizing student scholarship. In our view, too often librarian contribution to student scholarship is short-lived and task-based. Librarians rarely have a role in evaluating student work. The contest is one way that librarians can stake a legitimate interest in the long view of student scholarship and information creation and partner with faculty to celebrate student research.

Why We Fund the Undergraduate Research Prize

by Kevin M. Ross

The decision to fund the Leatherby Libraries Undergraduate Research Prize (URP) was an easy one that my wife, Tam, and I based on three reasons. First, as a librarian and associate dean for the Leatherby Libraries, I realize that the library is the central repository of knowledge on a university campus and that it plays a crucial role in supporting student and faculty research. Therefore, sponsoring a research prize contest was a natural fit for my family. There is a university-wide initiative to support undergraduate student participation in research activities on campus, which culminates every year in a major research day event. Unfortunately, the library is not able to directly participate in this initiative because it does not confer degrees. The URP offers an opportunity for the Leatherby Libraries to participate in a meaningful manner and to promote the value of the library and the research process to undergraduate students.

The second reason is to provide continuity for this valuable initiative. A former public services librarian and colleague brought the idea of sponsoring a research prize for undergraduate students to my attention in 2006. I fully supported the idea and worked closely with this librarian to ensure that our URP both was concentrated on the research process and had a moderately rigorous submission process. From 2010 to 2013, a donor who had an affiliation with the library graciously supported the prize. Once that donor decided to direct her funds elsewhere, my wife and I stepped in to support our students and continue the sponsorship of this wonderful prize. Supporting student-led research; interacting with students, their friends, and family members; and watching our students grow in knowledge is very gratifying.

Third, librarianship is more than a career; it is a profession, one with a basic premise of service as its foundation. We decided that sponsoring the contest would be a rewarding way to give back to the library and institution that has treated us so well the past sixteen years. The cash is beneficial for students, but the contest also provides an environment for students to join in the academic conversation. By providing students with a public forum to share their research, the URP allows them to participate in public speaking, to thoughtfully summarize the major elements of their research, and to present their research to a variety of stakeholders including faculty, librarians, fellow students, and parents. This participation is vital for an informed citizenry and a healthy democracy. In the end, the main reason that we have agreed to name and continue to support this contest of undergraduate students across the many areas of study we offer here at Chapman University is that we respect and value our students.

The Contest

The contest is open to currently enrolled undergraduate students at Chapman University. Applicants submit an essay about their use of library resources, a summary of their research paper or project, a bibliography, and a faculty support form. The 600-to-800-word essay is the key document, and it describes students' selection, evaluation, and use of information resources for their research paper or project. The summary of research gives context for the essay and enlightens the judges about the subject matter. We ask for a summary instead of the full paper or project so that the faculty and librarian judges are not overwhelmed with reading material and so it is clear we are not evaluating the research itself. The bibliography serves as documentation of sources used and provides context. Finally, the faculty support letter is an opportunity for the judges to understand the perspective of the student's professor. These letters provide context in a different way, as the faculty member describes the student's scholarly work and accomplishments.

Kevin and Tam Ross Undergraduate Research Prize— Essay Requirements[9]

Judges will examine your use of library resources and what you have learned through the research process. All materials submitted with your application will be reviewed with this in mind but the 600–800–word essay you write will be the key document for providing judges information in these areas.

1. What types of information resources did you use at the Leatherby Libraries, online, or through other libraries and archives? Include a discussion of books, journal articles, databases (e.g., ERIC, PsycINFO, Academic Search Premier, etc.), archival material, websites, audiovisual materials, or other materials. If this doesn't apply to your research process, explain why.

2. What research processes and search techniques did you use to find the materials for your project? How did the keywords and limiters you used affect the results you retrieved? If this doesn't apply to your research process, explain why.

3. How did you critically evaluate the information sources you located? Specifically, how did you apply the criteria of timeliness, relevance, authority, accuracy and purpose (TRAAP)? If this doesn't apply to your research process, explain why.

4. How did assistance from a librarian, library staff member, or a library service (for example, library instruction session, one-on-one meeting with a librarian, visit to Special Collections and Archives, or interlibrary loan) affect your research process? If this doesn't apply to your research process, explain why.

5. What have you learned about the research process from conducting research for this paper/project? How will you use what you have learned in the future? How would your research be valuable to other scholars? If this doesn't apply to your research process, explain why.

Judges look for originality, depth, or sophistication in the use of library resources and information literacy as demonstrated in the essay and other application materials. The librarian members of the contest committee developed a detailed rubric for the judges to use when evaluating each applicant's responses to these questions. The rubric also provides guidance in evaluating the overall quality of writing in the essay and the overall quality of the application. We deliberately focused on evaluative qualities that would not intrinsically privilege some disciplines or types of projects. For example, if we evaluated the length and quality of the students' bibliographies, then students completing senior history capstone projects would likely receive high scores as their use of sources is quite extensive. The inclusive approach to evaluating entries opens the door to wide range of project types, from research posters to term papers to lab reports.

We award first, second, and third place prizes, adding an honorable mention in years when the number of outstanding entries is exceptionally high. Judges on the panel evaluate each application and submit their scores to one person for compiling. Judges are then presented with a compilation that shows the average score for each applicant, how many times an applicant was scored highest by a judge, and how many times an applicant was in a judge's top three. Sometimes these different ways of presenting the scoring data show the same three applicants in first, second, and third places. Sometimes the applicant's ranking moves around. This information serves as the central point of discussion during a face-to-face meeting of the judging panel. At the meeting, all judges are given an opportunity to talk about the applications and to make a case for which students should receive which awards. By the end of the meeting, consensus is reached. All students and their faculty members are notified of the outcome.

The winners of the URP are recognized at a spring student awards ceremony. Students are encouraged to invite family and friends to share the experience. Students, faculty members, the panel of judges, and other members of the university community come together to celebrate the students' achievements. We also use this as an opportunity to remind the audience of the importance of supporting student research, the meaning and value of information literacy, and the role that librarians play in undergraduate education. The students are invited to the podium to talk about their research, to discuss why they chose to enter the contest, and to acknowledge their faculty mentors. Students receive a certificate recognizing their ranking and contribution to the contest and a cash award. The ceremony concludes with photographs of the students with the contest cosponsor, faculty members, fellow students, family, and friends. Information about the students and their contest entries is preserved online in the university's digital commons, with the students' permission. This includes student major and faculty sponsor, description of the research project, and a summary of the essay. Students may submit their final research paper or project to the digital commons as well.[10]

Partnerships and Marketing as Keys to Success

One foundational approach we took to outreach while developing the URP contest was to establish relationships with others across campus to make it a successful program. In particular, we knew that we would have to connect to faculty, and we decided to do so in two distinct ways. The first was to build on the strong bonds between liaison librarians and classroom faculty. Librarians' liaison responsibilities involve every program, department, school, and college at Chapman University. Librarians can fortify their relationships with faculty by personally promoting the contest to them and asking them to encourage their students to participate. Librarians can also promote the URP both before and during information literacy sessions as a positive approach for students to promote their own university-level undergraduate research.

Secondly, we decided it would be wise to incorporate faculty into the judging process. We debated how best to involve faculty, knowing that their schedules are often challenging to work around, but after consideration we decided to aim for securing three faculty members from a variety of disciplines. Our initial outreach to faculty was successful, and we invited faculty members from the sciences, education, and the humanities to join three librarians on the panel of judges during our initial launch of the URP. Since then, disciplines represented on the panel include biological sciences, dance, English, and kinesiology, and two faculty members have been part of the program for more than ten years.

In order to maintain this relationship with faculty moving forward, we demonstrate our appreciation to the faculty judges in two ways. One, we invite them to attend the annual URP ceremony, where we recognize them for their participation in front of the students, family members, faculty, and community members in attendance. Two, we bring them up front immediately after the ceremony and present them with a token of our appreciation from the university gift shop. Though these are modest ways to recognize their contributions, the faculty members really seem to appreciate our efforts. We have been fortunate to work with several faculty members during the life of the contest, and all of them have been collaborative and collegial with the librarians throughout the process.

The success of the URP contest also relies on effective marketing. We take a comprehensive approach utilizing online and print promotional avenues to maximize our outreach efforts. The contest is promoted through library blog posts, on Facebook, and on the library's website, which features a rotating spotlight technique to highlight the URP and other events sponsored by the library. The spotlight is located on the homepage, the same place where students begin their library research. We create posters to display in the library and flyers to hand out at relevant library and university events, such as the annual book sale and undergraduate research and poster session days. Sometimes we advertise the contest on the jumbotron, a large screen located in the center of campus that is readily seen by students crossing campus.

We partner with other campus offices, including the office of strategic marketing and communications, whose staff provides artwork, designs, and valuable suggestions for reaching our target audience. The dean of students sends out one or two email blasts to all undergraduate students as well. All of these communications point to the contest details available at the URP page of the university's institutional repository, the Chapman Digital Commons. Using the digital commons as the launch point for the contest is a natural fit. Not only can students submit applications for the URP on the site, they can also view previous winners' entries and, if a winning student chose to submit it, past research papers or projects.

Every year we review the effectiveness of the marketing efforts and implement changes as appropriate. Timing is one of the most challenging aspects of marketing because we need to get the word out several weeks before the deadline. Publicizing the contest cannot begin until we determine the composition of the judging panel. This includes recruiting new faculty members if needed; reviewing and possibly revising the essay requirements and rubric; updating the application packet; creating a reasonable time line for judges to receive and evaluate the applications; setting application deadlines; and establishing the date for the awards ceremony shortly before the end of the spring semester. In a significant improvement, future marketing efforts will include accepting applications throughout most of the academic year. In this way, we will be able to reach students working on major projects during the fall semester instead of hoping those students will be willing to wait until spring to submit an application. We know that most students focus on the current term and the work they need to do in the moment. Asking or expecting students to go back to work from a previous semester is not realistic, particularly because the URP requires an essay and faculty support letter.

During the first couple of years of the contest, history students dominated. This was a challenge to us because it created a persistent perception that "history students always win," even years after other majors were well represented in the winners' circle. Through our comprehensive partnership and marketing efforts, we were able to dispel that notion, and we now have even more students entering from the arts, sciences, humanities, social sciences, and the professional schools. This breadth of participation is energizing and demonstrates the diversity of thought and the high caliber of our students throughout the various disciplines offered on campus.

Benefits to Students

The Kevin and Tam Ross URP contest adds value to the undergraduate student experience. Not surprisingly, winners of the contest accrue the most benefits, including the tangibles such as the cash prize and certificate, and intangible achievements such as pride and a sense of belonging within the scholarly community. Winning students are prepared to join the scholarly discussion, sharing their research in an academic venue with supportive friends, family, colleagues, and faculty. They earn the opportunity to coalesce their thoughts in a public forum through speaking about their scholarship and their process while the audience celebrates their work. Students who submit their work to the Chapman Digital Commons add to the scholarly conversation and establish themselves as members of the worldwide scholarly community. Since 2014, nine student research papers have been downloaded over 1,600 times from locations around the globe.

All students who enter the contest benefit from working through the application process, which emphasizes a metacognitive understanding of themselves as scholars. These students also work with faculty mentors who provide not just letters of support but also public acknowledgement of their belief in the quality of the student's work and in the student's realized potential as a researcher.

Participation in the URP contest is open to all undergraduate students. The Chapman University student population is generally well prepared academically, with a freshman-to-sophomore retention rate of 90 percent and a six-year graduation rate of 79 percent. The undergraduate body is about 60 percent women and 60 percent White, while 86 percent of undergraduates receive financial aid.

In an effort to solicit entries from a diverse student population, we have relied predominately on personal connections with faculty. We have also expanded the conceptualization of diversity to include not only standard demographic characteristics such as sex and ethnicity but also subject discipline and research topics, which can be considered as a manifestation of one's perspective. Faculty have the closest connections with students and are often seen by students as trustworthy sources. Through the development of personal relationships with those faculty, librarians initiate a trusted message of opportunity to participate in the contest. We have seen that the combination of widespread advertising and marketing strategies described earlier with individualized connections to faculty and students results in an array of diverse applicants, topics, and disciplines.

The majority of applicants and prize winners are women. In fact, women are somewhat overrepresented compared to their proportion in the undergraduate student body, comprising 67 percent of applicants and 86 percent of winners. We do not collect demographic data from applicants, so we do not know how the applicant pool compares to the student body as a whole. However, we continue to promote this contest with a goal of inclusiveness, providing a forum for the students to share their research and perspectives.

In terms of topic areas, the most recent four years of the contest have seen a diverse array of topics, including Japanese American identity and internment camps; PTSD in veterans; empowering African American males in the educational system; American Sign Language and Deaf identity; explorations of gender through theater; indigenous people of Peru; patient activation in diverse populations; and saving Czechoslovakian Jews during WWII. This breadth of topics exemplifies not only diversity in perspective but also deep understanding of the critical issues that impact populations based on identity, gender, disability, and ethnicity.

Looking at the majors or disciplines of study of our contestants, we see additional ranges of thought and perspective. Majors represented by the applicants have included anthropology, Asian studies, athletic training, biology, communication studies, dance, education, environmental studies, film studies, history, kinesiology, music, psychology, sociology, and theater. This spanning across disciplines demonstrates to us that the contest encourages students with varied interests to feel represented in a research process that crosses boundaries.

A Student Reflects

Like many research contests, the Kevin and Tam Ross Undergraduate Research Prize contest centers around the reflective essays written by students. The essays offer windows into the thought processes of undergraduate students as they develop and refine their research skills. As noted in a study examining submissions to the University of Michigan's undergraduate research award contest, students are enthusiastic in their pursuit of research and they use complex research methods.[11] This study describes students as having "the ability to use obstacles productively—students would hit a wall in their research, and, after a period of frustration and often despair, would find a new resource that sent them down a totally different path, opened their minds to a new way of thinking, and led them to a very different topic or research question than they initially thought they would pursue."[12] This description of perseverance evokes dispositions described in the *Framework for Information Literacy for Higher Education*.[13] In particular, it is a good representation of "productive persistence," as described by Hannon in his rhetorical analysis of the *Framework* dispositions.[14]

Like the researchers at the University of Michigan, we have been fortunate to learn directly from students themselves how they conduct research and how they see themselves as scholars. Talia Cain, the 2017 winner of the Kevin and Tam Ross URP, is a coauthor of this chapter. Talia is a sophomore double majoring in integrated educational studies and English literature. Here she explains how reflecting on her research affected her evolving identity as a researcher and contributor to the scholarly conversation.

Connecting Academics and Activism through Critical Research

by Talia Cain

Reflecting on the ways I found and evaluated sources, I recognize the value of information literacy in today's digital age. While it is easy to find information quickly on the Internet, it is imperative that students critically identify if a source is credible, question the purpose and intent of sources, and demonstrate expansive knowledge of library and Internet resources. Without these skills, research has little value and application. People nowadays have quick access to all sorts of information, but undergraduate scholars are in an especially privileged position. We have the opportunity to engage with primary texts, empirical studies, and peer-reviewed articles. We have access to information written by authorities on topics and published in credible scholarly journals. If we apply creativity and critical thinking within the research process, we too, as undergraduate scholars, may contribute something meaningful and impactful to the conversation.

In addition, by reflecting on my process, I began to understand how research inherently merges academics and activism. Some people view activism as distracting, and because of the large price tag attached to higher education, feel that students should invest themselves solely in their education and focus on doing well in school. This attitude creates a stigma around student activism, but in reality, student research is a form of social protest. Activism and academics are not mutually exclusive; the university can foster scholarship and activism simultaneously.

Asking nuanced questions and listening carefully to the preexisting scholarly conversations gives one the platform to construct new knowledge. In this construction of knowledge, one has the potential to influence people's attitudes and understandings and, ultimately, change society. We have the power to use research to promote social change if we can see how research is the bridge between our hearts and our minds. When we question the nature of reality and inquire toward new understandings, we can propose ways for people to change how they view or interact with the world.

In completing and reflecting on my research process, I have redefined my identity as a researcher. I now consider myself more than just a student or passive consumer of knowledge, but a social justice–oriented scholar who produces information. I am aware of the privilege I have in receiving a university education and aware of the responsibility I have for using this education to shape a better world. When we have the power to create new knowledge, we must commit ourselves to critical research—work that challenges the norms and biases of society and takes an active role in shaping a more equitable and just future. To do this, we must take intellectual risks and place ourselves outside of our comfort zones. We must be conscientious about the sources we choose and mindful of how our scholarship affects others. Finally, we must integrate empathy into the work we do and understand research as the platform for fostering understanding for experiences and positionalities different from our own.

Conclusion

The URP contest is a cost-effective way of achieving the goals of recognizing student scholarship, fostering information literacy, and strengthening library relationships and reputation. With the support of the faculty, the contest sponsors, the library administration, and librarians, we have been able to create treasured connections with undergraduate students. We are privileged to learn about their research processes, about their studies, and about them as emerging scholars. It is our honor to recognize and celebrate their work.

Notes

1. Talia Cain, "1st Place Content Entry: Critical Media Literacy: Liberating the 'Criminal' and Empowering African American Males," Kevin and Tam Ross Undergraduate Research Prize 17, Chapman University, April 17, 2017, http://digitalcommons. chapman.edu/cgi/viewcontent.cgi?article=1038&context=undergraduateresearchprize.

2. See Pedro A. Noguera, *The Trouble with Black Boys* (San Francisco: Jossey-Bass, 2008); Naliah Suad Nasir, Milbrey W. McLaughlin, and Amina Jones, "What Does It Mean to Be African American? Constructions of Race and Academic Identity in an Urban Public High School," *American Educational Research Journal* 46, no. 1 (March 2009): 73–114; Ernest Morrell, Rudy Duenas, and Veronica Garcia, *Critical Media Pedagogy* (New York: Teachers College Press, 2005); and Miles Anthony Irving and Cynthia Hudley, "Cultural Mistrust, Academic Outcome Expectations, and Outcome Values among African American Adolescent Men," *Urban Education* 40, no. 5 (2016): 476–96.

3. See Douglas Kellner and Jeff Share, "Critical Media Literacy: Crucial Policy Choices for a Twenty-first-Century Democracy," *Policy Futures in Education* 5, no. 1 (2016): 59–69; Elliot Gaines, *Media Literacy and Semiotics* (New York: Palgrave Macmillan, 2010).

4. Cain, "1st Place Contest Entry."

5. See Lynn Jones, "The Rewards of Research: Library Prizes for Undergraduate Research," *College and Research Libraries News* 70, no. 6 (2009): 339–42, as well as the following websites for respective library research awards, all accessed December 28, 2017: "Undergraduate Prize for Excellence in Library Research," Brown University Library, https://library.brown.edu/ugresearchprize/index.php; "Library Prize for Undergraduate Research," Indiana University South Bend Libraries, https:// library.iusb.edu/about-us/awards/libraryprize/index.html; "Library Undergraduate Research Prize (LURP)," La Sierra University Libraries, http://libguides.lasierra. edu/lurp; "Paper of the Year," Labette Community College, http://www.labette.edu/ library/paper.html; "Undergraduate Library Research Award," Loyola Marymount University, http://digitalcommons.lmu.edu/ulra/; "Undergraduate Research," Ohio State University—Lima, https://lima.osu.edu/research/undergraduate-research/; "Library Undergraduate Research Awards," Oregon State University, https://library. oregonstate.edu/awards/undergrad-research; "Winesett Awards for Library Research," Radford University, http://www.radford.edu/content/library/services/student-awards-and-contests/winesett-awards-for-library-research.html; "Livingstone Undergraduate Research Awards," Temple University, http://guides.temple.edu/ libraryprize; "Charlene Conrad Liebau Library Prize for Undergraduate Research," University of California, Berkeley, Library, http://www.lib.berkeley.edu/researchprize; "UGA Libraries' Undergraduate Research Awards," University of Georgia, Athens, http://www.libs.uga.edu/researchaward/; "The 2006 Winners of the Libraries' Award for Undergraduate Research Have Been Selected!" University of Nevada, Las Vegas, Libraries, https://www.library.unlv.edu/award/winners.html; "Armacost Library Undergraduate Research Award (ALURA)," University of Redlands, https://inspire.redlands.edu/alura/; "University of Toronto Libraries Undergraduate Research Prize," https://onesearch.library.utoronto.ca/undergrad-research-prize/ criteria; "Library Research Award for Undergraduates," University of Washington,

http://www.lib.washington.edu/researchaward; "Undergraduate Research Awards," Westminster College, https://www.westminstercollege.edu/about/resources/giovale-library/undergraduate-research-awards; "Friends of the Wesleyan Library Undergraduate Research Prize," Wesleyan University, https://www.wesleyan.edu/libr/friends/library_research_prize.html.

6. Association of College and Research Libraries, *Information Literacy Competency Standards for Higher Education* (Chicago: Association of College and Research Libraries, 2000), accessed June 5, 2017, http://www.ala.org/acrl/sites/ala.org.acrl/files/content/standards/standards.pdf (page discontinued).

7. WASC Senior College and University Commission, "Standard 2: Achieving Educational Objectives through Core Functions—Teaching and Learning," in *2013 Handbook of Accreditation, Revised* (Alameda, CA: Western Association of Schools and Colleges—Senior College and University Commission, 2013), http://www.wascsenior.org/content/2013-handbook-accreditation.

8. Association of College and Research Libraries, *Framework for Information Literacy for Higher Education* (Chicago: Association of College and Research Libraries, 2016), http://www.ala.org/acrl/standards/ilframework.

9. Chapman University, "Essay Requirements," Kevin and Tam Ross Undergraduate Research Prize, Chapman University Digital Commons, accessed September 8, 2017, http://digitalcommons.chapman.edu/undergraduateresearchprize/urp_essay_requirements.html.

10. Chapman University, "Essay Requirements."

11. Jennifer L. Bonnet et al., "The Apprentice Researcher: Using Undergraduate Researchers' Personal Essays to Shape Instruction and Services," *portal: Libraries and the Academy* 13, no. 1 (2013): 37–59.

12. Bonnet et al., "The Apprentice Researcher," 56.

13. Association of College and Research Libraries. *Framework for Information Literacy.*

14. Richard Hal Hannon, "Getting at the Dispositions," *Information Literacy Assessment* (blog), April 18, 2016, http://blog.informationliteracyassessment.com/?p=739.

Bibliography

Association of College and Research Libraries. *Framework for Information Literacy for Higher Education*. Chicago: Association of College and Research Libraries, 2016. http://www.ala.org/acrl/standards/ilframework.

Association of College and Research Libraries. *Information Literacy Competency Standards for Higher Education*. Chicago: Association of College and Research Libraries, 2000. Accessed June 5, 2017. http://www.ala.org/acrl/sites/ala.org.acrl/files/content/standards/standards.pdf (page discontinued).

Bonnet, Jennifer L., Sigrid Anderson Cordell, Jeffrey Cordell, Gabriel J. Duque, Pamela J. MacKintosh, and Amanda Peterset. "The Apprentice Researcher: Using Undergraduate Researchers' Personal Essays to Shape Instruction and Services." *portal: Libraries and the Academy* 13, no. 1 (2013): 37–59.

Brown University Library. "Undergraduate Prize for Excellence in Library Research." Accessed December 28, 2017. https://library.brown.edu/ugresearchprize/index.php.

Cain, Talia. "1st Place Contest Entry: Critical Media Literacy: Liberating the 'Criminal' and Empowering African American Males." Kevin and Tam Ross Undergraduate Research Prize 17, Chapman University, April 17, 2017. http://digitalcommons.chapman.edu/cgi/viewcontent.cgi?article=1038&context=undergraduateresearchprize.

Chapman University. "Essay Requirements." Kevin and Tam Ross Undergraduate Research Prize, Chapman University Digital Commons. Accessed September 8, 2017. http://digitalcommons.chapman.edu/undergraduateresearchprize/urp_essay_requirements.html.

Gaines, Elliot. *Media Literacy and Semiotics.* New York: Palgrave Macmillan, 2010.

Hannon, Richard Hal. "Getting at the Dispositions." *Information Literacy Assessment* (blog). April 18, 2016. http://blog.informationliteracyassessment.com/?p=739.

Indiana University South Bend Libraries. "Library Prize for Undergraduate Research." Accessed December 28, 2017. https://library.iusb.edu/about-us/awards/libraryprize/index.html.

Irving, Miles Anthony, and Cynthia Hudley. "Cultural Mistrust, Academic Outcome Expectations, and Outcome Values among African American Adolescent Men." *Urban Education* 40, no. 5 (2016): 476–96.

Jones, Lynn. "The Rewards of Research: Library Prizes for Undergraduate Research." *College and Research Libraries News* 70, no. 6 (2009): 339–42.

Kellner, Douglas, and Jeff Share. "Critical Media Literacy: Crucial Policy Choices for a Twenty-first-Century Democracy." *Policy Futures in Education* 5, no. 1 (2016): 59–69.

La Sierra University Libraries. "Library Undergraduate Research Prize (LURP)." Accessed December 28, 2017. http://libguides.lasierra.edu/lurp.

Labette Community College. "Paper of the Year." Accessed December 28, 2017. http://www.labette.edu/library/paper.html.

Loyola Marymount University. "Undergraduate Library Research Award." Accessed December 28, 2017. http://digitalcommons.lmu.edu/ulra/.

Morrell, Ernest, Rudy Duenas, and Veronica Garcia. *Critical Media Pedagogy: Teaching for Achievement in City Schools.* New York: Teachers College Press, 2005.

Noguera, Pedro A. *The Trouble with Black Boys: And Other Reflections on Race, Equity, and the Future of Public Education.* San Francisco Jossey-Bass, 2008.

Ohio State University—Lima. "Undergraduate Research." Accessed December 28, 2017. https://lima.osu.edu/research/undergraduate-research/.

Oregon State University. "Library Undergraduate Research Awards." Accessed December 28, 2017. https://library.oregonstate.edu/awards/undergrad-research.

Radford University. "Winesett Awards for Library Research." Accessed December 28, 2017. http://www.radford.edu/content/library/services/student-awards-and-contests/winesett-awards-for-library-research.html.

Suad Nasir, Naliah, Milbrey W. McLaughlin, and Amina Jones. "What Does It Mean to Be African American? Constructions of Race and Academic Identity in an Urban Public High School." *American Educational Research Journal* 46, no. 1 (March 2009): 73–114.

Temple University. "Livingstone Undergraduate Research Awards." Accessed December 28, 2017. http://guides.temple.edu/libraryprize.

University of California, Berkeley, Library. "Charlene Conrad Liebau Library Prize for Undergraduate Research." Accessed December 28, 2017. http://www.lib.berkeley.edu/researchprize.

University of Georgia, Athens. "UGA Libraries' Undergraduate Research Awards." Accessed December 28, 2017. http://www.libs.uga.edu/researchaward/.

University of Nevada, Las Vegas, Libraries. "The 2006 Winners of the Libraries' Award for Undergraduate Research Have Been Selected!" Accessed December 28, 2017. https://www.library.unlv.edu/award/winners.html.

University of Redlands. "Armacost Library Undergraduate Research Award (ALURA)." Accessed December 28, 2017. https://inspire.redlands.edu/alura/.

University of Toronto Libraries. "University of Toronto Libraries Undergraduate Research Prize." Accessed December 28, 2017. https://onesearch.library.utoronto.ca/undergrad-research-prize/criteria.

University of Washington. "Library Research Award for Undergraduates." Accessed December 28, 2017. http://www.lib.washington.edu/researchaward.

WASC Senior College and University Commission. "Standard 2: Achieving Educational Objectives through Core Functions—Teaching and Learning." In *2013 Handbook of Accreditation, Revised.* Alameda, CA: Western Association of Schools and Colleges—Senior College and University Commission, 2013. http://www.wascsenior.org/content/2013-handbook-accreditation.

Westminster College. "Undergraduate Research Awards." Accessed December 28, 2017. https://www.westminstercollege.edu/about/resources/giovale-library/undergraduate-research-awards.

Wesleyan University. "Friends of the Wesleyan Library Undergraduate Research Prize." Accessed December 28, 2017. https://www.wesleyan.edu/libr/friends/library_research_prize.html.

CHAPTER 11

Making Noise
Teaching Civil Rights Movement Music in the Dartmouth College Music Library

Memory Apata

While music is often embodied by sound and motion, the academic music library is perceived as a place of quiet and stillness. This chapter describes the Friday Night Sing-Ins at Dartmouth College's Paddock Music Library, which transformed the library from a quiet space for solitary scholarship into a collaborative destination for performance and critical conversation. I proposed the sing-ins in January 2017 as part of the month-long Martin Luther King Jr. Celebration sponsored by the Dartmouth Office of Institutional Diversity and Equity. Following a year of hate-filled campaign rhetoric, heightened racial tension, and mass protests, the sing-ins offered an opportunity to create a forum on campus for discussing these issues within the context of music, using protest songs as the objects of inquiry. Additionally, the project enabled the library to show that librarians were aware of the tensions on campus and able to support students through those tensions. Throughout the sing-ins, participants sang the songs of the Civil Rights Movement and examined the music's history and performance contexts at protests in the US and internationally. Participants explored the idea that performance itself could serve as a resource to which the library could provide access and that the music library can be a place where the music documented on shelves comes to life through community performances.

In this chapter, I connect themes from my graduate coursework in the music department to the library's goals for experiential learning, institutional collaboration, and resource marketing. I apply my experience as an ambassador for the library in the music classroom to argue against perceptions of the library as quiet, neutral, and individualist. The idea is to break from these biases and reimagine the music library as a forum for collaborative sound and critical reflections that support the continuation of creativity and performance-as-research in the library. An exercise in lateral thinking, the sing-ins evolved as the idea emerged and developed through participatory processes.[1] My dual perspectives as library staff member and graduate student in the master of arts in liberal studies program at Dartmouth helped shape my plan for the events and my ability to be flexible with the outcomes. In designing this event, I challenged the perception of the library (and librarians) as quiet and apolitical, which led to reflections on my own voice and agency within my institution as both staff member and graduate student. Multiple factors contributed to shaping the sing-ins, including advice from colleagues in the music library, serendipitous interdisciplinary collaborations with students and staff, and readings and input from undergraduate classmates in Dr. William Cheng's course titled "Changing the World with Music."[2]

In *Just Vibrations: The Purpose of Sounding Good*, William Cheng posits that it might be possible "that people who work with music for a living can lead by example in agendas of interpersonal care and communication."[3] Why? Because musicians and music scholars are uniquely trained in listening and performance. For many musicians and musicologists, sounding good is their livelihood, so they are well practiced in making both beautiful music and beautiful arguments, respectively. Cheng suggests that the ability to sound good, in both musical and scholarly situations, could also imply a responsibility to *do* good in those same arenas. The musical skills of listening and performing (sounding good) become the basis for what Cheng calls a reparative musicology. Reparative musicology can occur when situations present "opportunities for care and repair," both in the practice of music and in human interactions. The idea of "doing good" is applicable to all sorts of situations that require repair, from hypercompetitiveness in the professional academic arena to the systemic oppression of marginalized voices both in the classroom and the world. Once the opportunity for repair is identified through creative listening, musicians can position themselves to do or perform good. The musical skill of listening is imperative in recognizing these opportunities for repair because the voices of those most in need of a platform are not always easily heard. Listening means looking for the voice, which might not always be discernible through the din of a world oversaturated with the ideas of already privileged voices.

The idea of listening for the voice translates easily into the world of librarianship. Librarians, like musicians, are trained to listen creatively. A good reference interview doesn't merely answer the direct question asked by the patron. It attempts to perceive needs beyond the initial inquiry. For instance, the question, "Do you have sheet music here?" doesn't end with the answer, "Yes, it's over there." The librarian listens further and asks the patron, "For which instrument?" or "For performance or study?" Beyond the reference desk, we can listen creatively for marginalized voices by recognizing lacunae in our collections and filling the gaps with works by authors from under-represented groups. Creative listening hears perceived, rather than expressly stated needs, but it is not often applied beyond point-of-need interactions. Librarians are highly skilled in symptom-driven listening and problem solving, but listening should go one step further, beyond the stacks and into the broader community. This further step is accomplished by being attuned to the public, and not just in their direct requests. Listening means actively searching for ways to align the library's mission of service with the needs of its patrons. Krista Ratcliffe perfectly explains this type of listening in her code of cross-cultural conduct:

> Perhaps through listening we can avail ourselves with more possibilities for inventing arguments that bring differences together, for hearing differences as harmony or even as discordant notes.... Admittedly, we cannot hear everything at once ...yet we can listen to the harmony and/or discordant notes, knowing that more than meets the eye lies before us.[4]

During my simultaneous work on the sing-ins and in Cheng's class, it occurred to me that, being armed with listening skills in both the music and library realms, the music librarian is doubly prepared for the caring work of recognizing opportunities for repair via creative listening. I was lucky enough to have the opportunity to put this realization from my studies into practice in my work. I challenged myself in the several months following the presidential election of 2016 to make a practice of listening and noticing my listening habits, good and bad, musical and nonmusical, as a student and as a librarian. In the classroom, this was a straightforward practice. Listen to your classmates and contribute to the conversation. Learn when it's better to listen versus speak up ("sound good"). In the classroom, sounding good came naturally for me, while listening was more difficult. In the classroom generally, students can make mistakes, flesh out new ideas, and reflect on the literature as a group. The environment typically lends itself to passionate conversations about issues important to most members of the class. In my case, I found that passion occasionally caused me to tune out what my classmates were saying to formulate my next response. My instinct was to sound good, rather than to listen.

In the library, I found listening to be quite natural. Most of my work in access services centers around listening closely to questions and serving individual patrons. I'm never distracted by formulating a response because my focus is on the patron. But what about sounding good? First, there is really no reason to sound good in the library. Libraries are supposed to be quiet! The idea of sound itself in the library is a controversial one. Yes, libraries have been busily rebranding themselves in recent years, transforming their study carrels into noisier makerspaces or places for collaborative group study, but the fact remains that in the students' perception, libraries and librarians still uphold the stereotypical silent soundscape. For proof, I asked classmates in "Changing the World with Music" to share one word that they associated with the terms *library* and *librarian*. One of the most common responses was the word *quiet*. This likely comes as no surprise to anyone, let alone a librarian reading this book. Libraries are *supposed* to be quiet, right? In fact, quiet is an excellent marketing tool for libraries advertising their services on campus. Even as content migrates partly from the stacks to the web, we still need libraries! Where else would students study quietly? But is quiet all it's cracked up to be? What if we entertained the notion that the quiet stereotype actually *damages* the library and, more specifically, the librarian? Preconceptions of the library as quiet could lead to preconceptions that librarians themselves are quiet. Furthermore, librarians themselves might begin to believe that they are supposed to be quiet, maintaining order and following protocol even when they might want to change it. How are we to "sound good" if the world doesn't expect us to make noise at all? And to take it a step further, how are we to *do* good if we can't even recognize our own voices? If society sees librarians as quiet and compliant, we begin to see ourselves as voiceless. We might become aware of the systems of oppression that permeate every aspect of our culture but be unprepared to act in a concrete way to dismantle them.

As I began to ask myself these questions in the fall of 2016, I sought examples of librarians making real change (and real noise!) in the world. My struggle with the contradiction between public service and neutrality, two of the most basic tenets of library work, led me to search for instances of public and academic librarians actively resisting neutrality for social justice. How had librarians acted against systemic oppression while honoring neutrality? How had the stereotype of the quiet librarian been challenged? I found a wonderful role model within my own institution in Jill Baron, whose work to change the Library of Congress subject heading "Illegal Aliens" to "Undocumented Immigrants" continues to inspire me.[5] Beyond Dartmouth I was inspired by efforts of professors and librarians to create syllabi such as the #FergusonSyllabus, the Lemonade Syllabus, and the #Syllabus4Ham to address gaps in their institutions' courses.[6] As a graduate student with a budding interest in library science, I was new to most of the conversations circulating between library professionals on library blogs and in library publications addressing the topic of neutrality, inclusion, and activism. Some of the sources I encountered include books published by Library Juice Press, conversations tagged with #critlib on Twitter, and posts on the *Social Justice Librarian* blog.[7] The literature seemed prolific and intimidating. I felt I lacked the historical knowledge on these issues to adequately join the conversation. However, as a student who also happened to be a librarian, I thought I could be well positioned to reach out to student groups on my campus whose voices were not necessarily being answered. I wasn't sure how to go about searching for these voices, so I simply kept my ear to the ground, actively and creatively listening.

Listening for Opportunities for Repair

This vigilance bore strange fruit the day after the presidential election of 2016. Dartmouth's hometown of Hanover, New Hampshire, had overwhelmingly voted for the Democratic candidate, and the Republican candidate's election led to a scene of utter despair that was palpable in the library that morning. Several student employees called in sick. There were no early-morning studiers at the work tables, and during our regularly scheduled departmental staff meeting, we could scarcely begin to address the agenda items. It all seems melodramatic, but it truly felt as if the entire campus was frozen in disbelief. My supervisor addressed the mood with music library staff and kindly told us to take the time we needed that day to make ourselves right again. I sat at my desk, wondering how I could get through the day. I wanted to throw myself into my work and forget the election results. But, staring at my computer screen, I felt incredibly helpless and completely distracted. What could I, as a librarian in a supposedly "neutral" space, do to resist? At home, I would sing and dance, express my grief in movement and sound, and ideally with others. Sharing movement, music, and pain in a group is restorative. In the library I wanted to create a musical community with which to share what was bubbling up within me—pieces by Nina Simone, including "Mississippi Goddamn" and "The King of Love Is Dead," or a rare arrangement of "In Zion."[8] My mind kept repeating the lyrics: "While still here, there is work to be done: the good news to share with each one." These words were a reminder that individual interactions were important at this time, and I was determined to share hope, as well as grief, with my coworkers and students that day.

Before my next meeting, I stopped by the library café for a pick-me-up. In the main entryway, a group of students had hung handwritten posters with statements of support for marginalized groups on campus on that difficult morning (see figure 11.1). To my surprise, a library staff member walked straight up to these signs and began to take them down. Not knowing what to say, I asked, "Oh, is that what we're doing?" The staff member shrugged and continued to remove the signs. Meanwhile, a different librarian had posted

FIGURE 11.1
Handmade signs in the Dartmouth Library. Source: Laura Braunstein, "Untitled," digital photograph, Dartmouth College Library Facebook page, November 9, 2016, <https://www.facebook.com/pg/dartmouth.college.library/photos/ >.

photos of these posters on the Dartmouth College Library Facebook page, aligning the library with the message of the posters. The entire morning, I had been thinking about the issue of library neutrality; the fact that as terrible as I was feeling, I still needed to welcome and serve all members of the Dartmouth community, regardless of my feelings about their political beliefs. But here was my conundrum incarnate. I couldn't speak for the motivations behind either staff member's actions, but it seemed to me that one staff member saw these signs as uninviting and intolerant of a locally unpopular political stance, while the other saw them as inviting, tolerant, and in line with the library's mission statement "that each user of the library is unique and important."[9]

Although I disagreed with the action, I tried to understand the motivation for taking down the signs. How could these messages, which were so full of love from my perspective, be considered offensive? I thought back to a demonstration earlier that year, when students marched through the library chanting, "Black Lives Matter," and "If we can't study, you can't study."[10] The protest evoked discomfort in a place that many (though not all) students felt very comfortable—the library. It called attention to the fact that comfort is not a given for all members of the campus community; that even places that seem benign and neutral can embody systems that oppress many. To the detriment of the protesters' message, reports by numerous media sources not present at the protest (including conservative news outlet Breitbart) reported that students studying in the library had been harassed if they refused to join the protesters.[11] According to a statement by the college, these complaints were never supported by videographic evidence of violence, but the events left many patrons and library staff feeling unsafe in the library.[12] In part, the goal of the protest was to point out that institutional spaces, like the library, are *not* safe for everyone, especially those for whom such spaces represent a system that ignores, forgets, or quiets them. In response to the protest, the Dean of Libraries stated in an email:

> Disruptive events have and will occur in the Libraries, and safety should be our highest priority. While we do not have any reports of a staff member being threatened during the protest, we would like to reiterate our full support in Library staff protecting both themselves and others, and to call Safety and Security and/or 911 if at all concerned about any incident.[13]

I mention the Black Lives Matter protest, not to defend, justify, or condemn the actions of the library staff member who removed the signs the day after the election. I mention the protest to recognize that acts that point out the embedded bias and inherent political nature of the library complicate efforts to carry out mission statements such as "each user of the Library is unique and important" or "we will work to ensure that our community conveys a message of inclusion to every student—no matter their gender, race, orientation, or socioeconomic background."[14] The Black Lives Matter protest in the library was an attempt to break the silence in a place of constructed quiet. The removal of the posters in front of the library the day after the presidential election was an act to rebuild this quiet and supposed comfort. The problem with restoring quiet (also known as silencing) is that it is the opposite of listening. Libraries and librarians are trained to listen. With that training comes the responsibility not just to listen, but to respond by doing good, *sounding* good—out loud. Here was an opportunity for us to do that good; to listen and respond in kind.

After the incident in the café, I walked across campus back to my office. A group of students, including one of my quieter supervisees from the music library, had begun to assemble on the Dartmouth Green with sleeping bags and handmade signs. My mind buzzed as I descended into the basement of the performing arts center where the music library is located completely hidden from view. I ran into another student employee, a non-US citizen who told me that she hadn't slept the night before because she was worried about what might happen to her and her family. A student worker who had shown up for her shift was dismally conversing with friend across the circulation desk. Determined to do something, *anything*, to help, I skimmed a few library blogs, many of which suggested workshops on recognizing fake news. But I work in a *music* library, I thought. That's just not what we do. Later that day a group of nearly 300 students, staff, and faculty gathered for a spontaneous "walk for love and justice." In footage of the event, participants chatted and chanted together as they marched through downtown Hanover. I was heartened by the march, but in coverage of the event, I noticed an absence of protest music.[15] My immediate thought was that I could teach protest music in the library. Again, a nagging voice told me to slow down—teaching protest music isn't really the place of the librarian. It is definitely *not* neutral. Could I gather people in the music library to sing and listen to music of the Black Lives Matter movement?! Still feeling bound to the idea of neutrality, I thought the safer bet would be to situate protest songs in historical contexts, creating an exhibit on the music of the Civil Rights Movement. Since I wanted to address issues of racial tension, I thought that the songs of the Civil Rights Movement could be a good medium for starting a conversation about current events with students, staff, faculty, and community members. I pitched the idea to my supervisor as an exhibit accompanied by a singing workshop. In my pitch, I made a point that we each have a duty to help one another through immense pain and should be prepared to seize opportunities for making change if the occasion arises. That's when I understood that the sing-ins were my way to carry on as a private citizen, entitled to my opinions, *and* as a librarian, sharing information and professional experience. Although the music library had never hosted an event before, she agreed to the idea. I formulated the following "desired outcomes" for future reference as they emerged throughout the planning and implementation of the sing-ins in concert with participants (no pun intended).

The Friday Night Sing-Ins would

- Offer a musical means for the Dartmouth community, including patrons and staff, to critically reflect during a period of immense emotional hardship.
- Initiate relationships with library patrons outside of the Dartmouth music community.
- Collaborate with campus departments and groups committed to diversity.
- Showcase the music library as a musical makerspace and destination for creative student research on campus.
- Inspire patrons to creatively utilize library resources, including monographs, LPs, and scores for historical research and performance.
- Open a conversation about the role of music, the music library, and the individual in efforts for social justice at Dartmouth.

Finding Partners

Armed with little more than the idea of singing and conversing together, I began looking for collaborators on campus. It was at this early point in the planning process that I realized how uncomfortable I was leading a discussion on the topic of race. I knew I was musically prepared to lead a group in singing simple harmonies, but who did I think I was to be leading a conversation about race? To begin with, I'm white. I have no way of understanding the lived experience of people across racial differences. I was also concerned that by teaching the music myself, I would be putting myself at risk professionally if I didn't include all perspectives on the issue of civil rights. The American Library Association (ALA) *Bill of Rights* states that "Libraries should provide materials and information presenting all points of view on current and historical issues," so if I led the sing-ins, would I also need to make sure that our collections included segregationist music in equal measure?[16] Would I need to ensure that this music was exhibited equally both aurally and visually without framing the segregationist music as being on the wrong side of history? Furthermore, I didn't even know many black students or staff members with whom to collaborate, a fact about which I was incredibly ashamed.

Unpacking that feeling of shame is important to me because it taught me a significant lesson. Shame is uncomfortable. It can paralyze us and cause us to shrink away from opportunity when things get difficult. But it is our job, if we wish to create an inviting environment for every single patron, to face that discomfort and not just learn from our mistakes but do something with our newfound awareness. In retrospect, I realize that instead of coming to black student groups on campus with an idea of my own, asking the groups to help facilitate it, I should have asked what the community actually needed and responded with their feedback in mind. This mistake of asking for advice only within my own little library bubble affected the turnout and conversation at the sing-ins. In the end, based on the advice from my (mostly white) colleagues, I went ahead with the sing-ins and sought to cofacilitate them with a black student.

I started by getting in touch with OPAL, the Office of Pluralism and Development. I knew about the department because I had attended an information session about their Intergroup Dialogue program, which "uses co-facilitated discussions to engage students in authentic conversations about difficult topics across social identity groups."[17] This department employs staff representatives for many minority groups on campus, and I got in touch with the Dean of Black Students, Kari Cooke. In our meeting, she expressed support for the sing-in idea, but brought several challenges to my attention, namely that students *do* want programming that supports movements for social justice but that even when they ask for specific programming, students don't always attend the events due to the rigorous academic calendar at Dartmouth. Dean Cooke advised spreading the word as widely as possible, but didn't give me false hope that this would be a hit event. Dean Cooke also recommended a student leader, Tyné Freeman, a senior music major with a strong interest in healing through music, as a potential music director. Tyné became the most valuable collaborator for the sing-ins, bringing to the table both an exceptional musical talent and an open, kind, and patient attitude to her role.

The Dartmouth College Office of Institutional Diversity and Equity (IDE) facilitates an annual Martin Luther King Jr. Celebration. This consists of a month of programming on the topic of civil rights throughout the month of January. The IDE's mission statement aligns closely with the library's as this office "creates partnerships with offices and individuals across the institution to provide resources that promote access, respect, and community for all."[18] Although it was never my intent to create programming that would coincide with this celebration, the timing was fortuitous and the IDE offered to market our events, providing some financial help for printing programs and posters for the sing-ins.

Time and Place

Tyné and I met several times during the weeks prior to the sing-ins to discuss the format and repertoire for the events. One goal of the sing-ins was to bring musical inquiry to the locus of musical information on campus, so we planned to use the library's study lounge for the event. This was one of the first major challenges for the planning process because it shook up the misconception that libraries are inherently quiet spaces. Tucked away in the basement of the performing arts center, the Dartmouth Music Library is known as one of the best-kept secret study spots on campus. Contrary to its reputation, the music library is not an officially designated quiet space. Knowing there might be some resistance to noise in the library, we proposed a time outside of normal library hours so that regular study would not be disrupted and gave verbal notice to students near the end of regular hours that a musical event would be taking place. In order to accommodate the library schedule and to maximize student attendance, we chose to have the sing-ins on Friday evenings at 5 p.m. Since the library closes at five o'clock, we wouldn't be disturbing patrons who were there to study, and because Dartmouth's weekend activities don't begin until later in the evening, we would be able to catch students in the window between their final Friday classes and their evening extracurriculars. The events were advertised on the music library's social media outlets, via Listservs for the music and African and African American studies departments, in the daily campus-wide newsletter, and on the college events website. A film and media studies student who had received news about the events via departmental Listserv created a promotional video using footage from the first week's sing-in.[19]

Repertoire

I suggested many songs I had learned growing up in the Southern Baptist church, which I knew had been adapted by the Civil Rights Movement. Being from Little Rock, Arkansas, the home of Central High School and the Little Rock Nine, I was familiar with the music of the Civil Rights Movement, as the story of the first integrated high school had been told to me throughout my life. Tyné knew many of these pieces but not all of them and was graciously open to my suggestions and to learning pieces that she associated neither with faith traditions nor with the Civil Rights Movement. She also began composing an original piece, "Bridges," which would reflect on the songs we planned to teach and the current political moment.[20] We agreed on a core group of songs to be taught over the course of four sessions including

- This Little Light of Mine

- We Shall Overcome
- Lift Every Voice and Sing
- Ain't Gonna Let Nobody Turn Me 'Round
- Keep Your Eyes on the Prize
- Wade in the Water
- We Shall Not Be Moved
- Woke Up This Morning with My Mind on Freedom

Materials

Our attendees would include Dartmouth students, staff, faculty, and the wider non-Dartmouth community. We expected a range of musical abilities, from undergraduate music majors who could read music to community members who would need to learn by rote memorization. In order to teach the pieces to those with informal musical backgrounds, Tyné would sing through each piece once and then invite participants to join in. For those attendees able to read music, I originally planned to distribute copies of the Student Nonviolent Coordination Committee (SNCC) songbook, *We Shall Overcome*.[21] However, I found that the melodies and rhythms transcribed in the songbook were often inconsistent with reference recordings.[22] Furthermore, although the distribution of such copies would fall under the domain of fair use of copyrighted material, I thought it best to transcribe the melodies myself, rather than using the SNCC songbook. Unfortunately, I did not have the foresight at the time to document the exact reference recordings I used. In many cases, I transcribed the more familiar melodies from memory. I used the notation software Sibelius for the transcriptions so that the key could easily and quickly be changed if the range was unsuitable for the group of singers. Although most of the songs could have been learned a cappella, we asked for permission to borrow an upright piano from a nearby music department practice room for accompaniment. Tyné was tasked with accompanying, supported by another library staff member, David Bowden, on guitar. David's desire to attend the events, although he didn't plan to sing, inspired the inclusion of chord charts in the musical program so that musicians who are not singers would still be able to participate in the sing-ins. The program included the following instructions for use:

> This program includes chord symbols, lyrics, and the melody of some of the best-known songs of the Civil Rights Movement. If you are unfamiliar with reading music, simply follow along with the lyrics and join the group when you become comfortable with the tune. If you can read music,

you are welcome to sing the melody as written. Because of the improvisatory nature of the recordings upon which the tunes are based, you might notice an unfamiliar note or two in the notated melody. Don't worry! Just sing what feels right to you. If you are an instrumentalist, you may sing and/or play. There might be opportunities for instrumental solos.

The transcriptions are based on songbooks written by Guy Carawan and Pete Seeger, traditional hymnals, and recordings of singing protesters in Washington D.C. and Albany, Georgia in the 1960s. [Peter Blood and Annie Patterson, eds., *Rise Up Singing*, 15th anniversary ed. (Bethlehem, PA: Sing Out Corporation, 2004).] Historically, these songs were learned by ear, without notated music. However, one purpose of the sing-ins is to inspire the creation of new and singable music for social justice. Therefore, we have transcribed a simplified melody, not only for the purposes of learning the tunes, but as a reference for participants inspired to compose after the event.

Most of the tunes are adaptations of traditional spirituals whose lyrics were changed to suit the cause of civil rights. The lyrics we have chosen to include are an amalgam of both the secular protest lyrics and the original faith-based texts. We invite participants of all creeds to join in the singing of all verses, with the knowledge that the singer does not have to be Christian to understand their full effect.

Teaching Strategy

Tyné and I shared a background in jazz performance, and the teaching format we planned reflected this experience. We created mock set lists, interspersed with built-in moments for dialogue about the pieces. The dialogue would be fairly free-form, but we planned to offer prompts such as, "What is your past experience with this piece?" and "What was it like to sing this song together, distanced from its historical context?" In some instances we would offer historical information about the pieces, and in others we would allow the music to speak for itself. Discussion would include topics such as participatory versus performative music in protest settings, singing alone versus in a group, historical background of the songs, and the relevance or irrelevance of the Civil Rights Movement song repertoire in the current political moment.

The format outlined above quickly disintegrated as participants took control of their own learning. Most participants joined in the singing immediately if they were already familiar with the tune, rather than waiting for Tyné to sing through the piece completely. Many attendees offered their individual perspectives intermittently, rather than during the scheduled moments for discussion. Instead of adhering to the predetermined set list, this improvisation by the participants prompted the facilitators to stray from the lesson plan proper and to "read the room" before playing the next tune.

Discussion of participants' past experiences with the pieces led to unexpected musical contributions as well. Incorporating creative contributions from the attendees built a sense of fellowship and community over the course of the month. For instance, we learned that "We Shall Overcome" had been adopted by many international human rights movements. One participant had originally heard the piece in India, and following interest from the group, shared a verse in Hindi at the next week's sing-in. Following the buzz from one of the first sing-ins, a Dartmouth professor emeritus contacted us and offered to give a short lesson on a song not listed in our program, "Oh, Wallace," which he had learned during the march on Selma. I was also able to incorporate much of what I was learning in the "Changing the World with Music" class, which Tyné chose to audit as well. One of our assignments was to attend the keynote address and performance by Reverend Sekou and Jay Marie Hill for the Martin Luther King Jr. Celebration at Dartmouth. At the performance, Tyné and I learned several contemporary protest songs, including "I Can't Breathe," which we taught the following Friday at the sing-in.[23]

Listening for the will of the group allowed the facilitators to share agency and ownership with the attendees throughout the process. The downside of allowing this much room for improvisation was that many discussions were left unframed by historical background. I felt it was important not to interrupt the flow of the event by steering the conversation back toward a discussion of library resources. Conversations about the history of the songs and the resources available for study remained a major fixture in the discussion portions of the events, but participants' conversations gravitated toward current events and the ways in which they could actively resist efforts to normalize prejudice via musical protest.

Participants

The event drew staff and faculty participants from many non-library groups across campus including the Tucker Center, the Student Wellness Center, the Office of Institutional Diversity and Equity, East Wheelock House, and the academic departments of history, philosophy, sociology, visual arts, and math. Most undergraduates in attendance were regular patrons of the music library or were affiliated with the music department or campus a cappella groups. The majority of attendees were community members from Hanover and Lebanon, New Hampshire. Many community and Dartmouth staff members brought their children, some as young as five years. All attendees participated in music-making, and the majority of attendees participated in the conversation guided by the facilitators. Some participants attended just once, but many came back multiple times over the course of the month. An estimated fifty unique patrons attended over the course of the month. The highest attendance was during the week of Martin Luther King Jr. Day, which coincided with the week of the 2017 presidential inauguration and the Women's March on Washington.

Despite our unexpectedly large turnout for the sing-ins, our group was not particularly diverse. The majority of attendees were white community members over the age of forty. For the first couple of weeks I was discouraged by this fact, as I felt the discussions would have greatly benefited from a broader variety of perspectives and experiences. It's very difficult to have a discussion about race when one race is overrepresented in the conversation. I eventually accepted that we would simply have to meet people where they were and come up with better ways to attract a more diverse audience next year.

Takeaways

The impact of an event like the sing-ins is difficult to measure quantitatively. For several reasons, we did not offer a survey to participants to determine what each patron learned from the experience. This was the first event ever hosted at the music library. The large turnout was unexpected and the response was overwhelming. Each of the five events over the course of the month was unique, teaching different repertoire to groups whose musical skills varied from week to week. The main idea was to offer the library as a space for music and discussion, and this goal was certainly met. The feedback given verbally during the sing-ins and afterward via emails from participants was overwhelmingly positive.

* * *

We so enjoyed your singalong on Friday.... Thank you for your part in spreading hope through music! –Rosemary Brown, Hanover, NH

* * *

Congratulations on your wonderful idea for the sing-in sessions at the music library. We appreciated the information about the history of the songs and the opportunity to gather to sing them this week and today in particular. As you mentioned, it would be nice if they were purely historical and not needed again but it is heartening and strengthening to sing them now. Our gratitude to everyone that had a hand in the activity and a special hand, with much appreciation, for Tyné, her accompaniment and her "Bridges" song.

Sincerely,

Myrna and Samuel Vélez

* * *

Tyné and Memory,

Just a short note to thank you for organizing the sing-along on Friday evening. I wish that I had been able to attend for multiple sessions, but unfortunately I was not able to do so. I will treasure the experience that I did have; I was singing and humming "to love is to build a bridge" all weekend. Tyné, you have a very special gift; thank you for sharing it with us.

Best,

Esther C. H. Walker, Dartmouth College General Counsel

* * *

Dear Memory,

It was such a gift to participate in last Friday's "sing-in." It was especially kind of you and Tyné to allow me to present "my" freedom song and to sing it with the group.

One thing I noticed very quickly: the entire session was infused with a democratic spirit and had the feeling of a "beloved community." A remarkable achievement!

Again, many thanks!

Anonymous

The popularity of the event was recognized by the Martin Luther King Jr. Celebration Committee, who have discussed the possibility of the sing-ins as an annual event. The positive buzz following the sing-ins was greatly appreciated. However, the events were far from perfect as we experimented each week with new ways of teaching the music, facilitating the discussion, and inviting contributions from participants. Allowing the space to make mistakes and try things that might not work set the stage for creating successful future musical events pertaining to social justice in the library.

First, we learned that more time is needed for planning an event of this scale. A month was insufficient time to research the pieces, transcribe them, find cofacilitators, and advertise the events. If the work had been spaced out over the course of three or four months, there would have been more time to target our marketing efforts on social media and at other college events. Planning several months in advance would also allow enough time to request specific materials for reference and display in the music library collection. Second, Tyné was responsible for teaching the music for all five events. In the future, it would be more practical to have a roster of artists teaching one sing-in each. In a subsequent event in the music library, I recruited one of Dartmouth's a cappella groups to facilitate with good results. If an a cappella group was to be used as a core group of teachers, not every member of the group would need to be present for all of the events. Third, funding must be secured for honoraria for the teachers. Tyné volunteered an estimated fifteen hours of her time preparing for and teaching the sing-ins, not including time spent on her original composition. Fourth, the next series of sing-ins should be recorded for the purposes of marketing in subsequent years and as a reference for repertoire and discussion topics. Fifth, the repertoire could be much more diverse, pulling not only from the Civil Rights Movement in the 1960s, but from contemporary artists who have written singable songs pertaining to the struggle for racial equality in the United States. Sixth, it would have been helpful to have a representative from the Office of Pluralism and Development, whose specialty is intergroup dialogue, at the events to help facilitate discussion. Library employees planning similar events might consider taking training courses in mediation and consensus building if they plan to facilitate alone. Lastly, a more visible connection must be made between the sing-in and its potential as a starting point for research. Library collections could be displayed more prominently and accompanied by explanatory text. Greater efforts should be made to make explicit the connection between the library resources and the practice of creating and performing music.

Conclusions

Joining Professor Cheng's class as a student, rather than a library teacher, offered a new way of listening for me. In the classroom, I was a peer to the students I serve in the library, not an authority figure. This position gave me the opportunity to listen jointly as a student and as a librarian to learn which musical topics really excited them. Dartmouth students were genuinely interested in music as it pertains to social justice. Of course, the topic of "Changing the World with Music" naturally led to conversations about protest and music, but enrollments in similar courses through the women, gender, and sexuality studies and African American and African studies departments would suggest that this interest was not isolated to this particular music class.

As noted in the 2017 ACRL *Environmental Scan*, "To say that racial and social justice issues have been prominent in national life in the past few years would be an understatement."[24] As students continue to pursue research interests in social justice, libraries must respond. Despite the silencing effect of neutrality on librarians, librarians have powerful voices within institutions of higher education. We have the agency to include or exclude information from our collections and to grant or deny access to that information. Whether or not we choose to be inclusive and balanced in our work, the power to make those decisions of access still lies with us. But using this powerful voice takes practice. During the sing-ins, I often fell silent during those moments in which the conversation veered away from the "lesson plan." I worried that, as a representative of the library, I should remain neutral. As an outgoing and opinionated student, I felt that I had a right to join in the conversation, but as a library employee I felt voiceless. We must work against the sort of fear I felt in speaking out and take ownership of our voices to empower ourselves and our patrons.

Additionally, we should acknowledge that although our voices are complicated by issues of visibility, value, and neutrality, the library is part of the system that silences or neutralizes (!) marginalized voices. As many of my colleagues at Dartmouth have pointed out, some students may come to us with little or no experience in a library setting, with no prior knowledge of how to find a book in the stacks, how to find materials in the catalog, or how to acclimate themselves to the culture of quiet in libraries. We may believe that libraries are already trusted entities within the campus community, but this is not an assumption that we can afford to make. Not every student sees the library as a welcoming or neutral place. Librarians can call the library neutral because for us, it is our comfort zone. As much as we would like to see ourselves as open-minded mediators of campus culture, we must recognize that our supposed neutrality is based in our own experiences and we don't even begin to understand that which we don't already see.

From a student's perspective, neutrality often fails to acknowledge the needs of patrons whose backgrounds require a different kind of public service. In short, neutrality embraces neither multiculturalism nor critical theories of race, gender, and sexuality. We as librarians must actively create opportunities for dialogue around these issues. If we are to "sound good," libraries and librarians need to recognize and cultivate their own powerful voices. For me, voice-building is the cumulative process of listening, experimentation, and reflection that draws upon our entire experience as humans, not just our roles in the workplace or in the classroom. Voice-building has no beginning, middle, or end. It has no goal, no mission statement. Voice-building is collaborative. It is through a constant chaotic conversation with one's internal truths and the experiences shared by the people around us that we find both the platform and what to say. But selectors can't go on silently building collections of works by marginalized authors without speaking up for them in public. The most visible way to do this in the academic library is by embracing these collections through our programming and outreach efforts and listening to our constituents.

Notes

1. Edward De Bono, *Lateral Thinking* (New York: Harper and Row, 1970).
2. William Cheng, "Changing the World with Music" (course presented at Dartmouth College, Hanover, NH, January 2017).
3. William Cheng, *Just Vibrations* (Ann Arbor: University of Michigan Press, 2016), chap.1, https://doi.org/10.3998/mpub.9293551.
4. Krista Ratcliffe, "Rhetorical Listening: A Trope for Interpretive Invention and a 'Code of Cross-Cultural Conduct.'" *College Composition and Communication* 51, no. 2 (1999): 203, https://doi.org/10.2307/359039.
5. Lisa Peet, "Library of Congress Drops Illegal Alien Subject Heading, Provokes Backlash Legislation," *Library Journal,* June 13, 2016, http://lj.libraryjournal.com/2016/06/legislation/library-of-congress-drops-illegal-alien-subject-heading-provokes-backlash-legislation/#_.
6. Sociologists for Justice, "Ferguson Syllabus," accessed May 6, 2017, https://sociologistsforjustice.org/ferguson-syllabus/; Candice Benbow, "Lemonade Syllabus," Candice Marie Benbow website, accessed May 6, 2017, https://issuu.com/candice-benbow/docs/lemonade_syllabus_2016; Trevor Boffone, "#Syllabus4Ham: The

HAMILTON Syllabus," Trevor Boffone, Ph.D. website, June 2, 2016, https://trevor-boffone.com/2016/06/02/syllabus4ham-the-hamilton-syllabus/.

7.   See Library Juice Press website, http://libraryjuicepress.com/books.php, and *Social Justice Librarian* blog, https://sjlibrarian.wordpress.com/.

8.   The Cathedral Singers–Topic, "In Zion," YouTube video, 4:12, posted January 28, 2017, https://www.youtube.com/watch?v=t62qRqSfxjQ.

9.   Dartmouth College Library, "Library Mission and Goals," 2011, accessed April 1, 2017, https://www.dartmouth.edu/~library/home/about/mission.html (page discontinued).

10. Campus Reform, "Dartmouth College #BlackLivesMatter Protest," YouTube video, 1:37, filmed November 12, 2015, posted November 14, 2015, accessed February 20, 2017, https://www.youtube.com/watch?v=OJAuVQlLxD0.

11. Breitbart Tech, "No Punishment for Black Lives Matter Protesters Harassing Dartmouth Students," Breitbart, May 31, 2016, http://www.breitbart.com/tech/2016/05/31/no-punishment-for-black-lives-matter-protesters-harrassing-dartmouth-students/.

12. "Statement Regarding Student Protest in Baker-Berry Library," news release, Dartmouth College website, November 16, 2015, http://www.dartmouth.edu/press-releases/statement-regarding-student-protest.html.

13. Jeffrey Horrell, "Last Thursday's Protest in the Library," email to Library Group, November 17, 2015.

14. Philip Hanlon, "The President's Plan," Dartmouth College Office of the President, accessed April 1, 2017, https://www.dartmouth.edu/~president/forward/plan.html.

15. *The Dartmouth Review*, "Trump's Election Triggers Protest at Dartmouth," filmed November 9, 2016, YouTube video, 2:57, posted November 10, 2016, https://www.youtube.com/watch?v=QFqPIlkpw0U.

16. American Library Association, *Library Bill of Rights*, (Chicago, American Library Association, 1939; last updated January 23, 1980), http://www.ala.org/advocacy/intfreedom/librarybill.

17. Dartmouth Office of Pluralism and Leadership, "Education/Training," accessed May 2, 2017, http://www.dartmouth.edu/~opal/programs/edutrain/ (page discontinued).

18. Office of Institutional Diversity and Equity website, Dartmouth College, accessed April 1, 2017, http://www.dartmouth.edu/~ide/.

19. Chinedum Nwaigwe, "Dartmouth Music Library Hosts Civil Rights Movement Sing-In," filmed January 6, 2017, YouTube video, 2:02, https://www.youtube.com/watch?v=973BS-qCNIo.

20. Tyné Angela Freeman, "Bridges," audio recording, 5:34, September 22, 2017, Bridges https://open.spotify.com/album/3flR19mCSf78PSkSvRTDOS (requires login).

21. Guy Carawan and Candie Carawan, comps., *We Shall Overcome! Songs of the Southern Freedom Movement* (New York: Oak Publications, 1963).

22. See Carl Benkert, recorder, *Freedom Songs: Selma, Alabama*, Folkways Records, 1965, accessed via Spotify, https://open.spotify.com/album/08cePtysaicbmd03f-wTbQ9?si=FjdSGe1eQ-e895tPszj3hw>; Guy Carawan, recorder and producer, *Sing for Freedom: The Story of the Civil Rights Movement through Its Songs*, Smithso-

nian Folkways Recordings, 1990, accessed via Spotify, https://open.spotify.com/album/1zpgiafncHNnCWAZ32QJOM?si=CCMRGgkHQGeWu8j7jeCeqQ

23. Dartmouth College, "2017 MLK Jr. Keynote Performance with Rev. Osagyefo Sekou," filmed January 16, 2017, YouTube video, 1:42:17, https://youtu.be/ViqqZA-OK8_0.

24. ACRL Research Planning and Review Committee, *Environmental Scan 2017* (Chicago: Association of College and Research Libraries, March 2017), 36, http://www.ala.org/acrl/sites/ala.org.acrl/files/content/publications/whitepapers/EnvironmentalScan2017.pdf.

Bibliography

ACRL Research Planning and Review Committee. *Environmental Scan 2017*. Chicago: Association of College and Research Libraries. March 2017. http://www.ala.org/acrl/sites/ala.org.acrl/files/content/publications/whitepapers/EnvironmentalScan2017.pdf.

American Library Association. *Library Bill of Rights*. Chicago: American Library Association, 1939; last updated January 23, 1980. http://www.ala.org/advocacy/intfreedom/librarybill.

Benbow, Candice. "Lemonade Syllabus." Candice Marie Benbow website. Accessed May 6, 2017. https://issuu.com/candicebenbow/docs/lemonade_syllabus_2016.

Benkert, Carl, recorder. *Freedom Songs: Selma, Alabama*. Folkways Records, 1965. https://open.spotify.com/album/08cePtysaicbmd03fwTbQ9?si=FjdS-GeleQ-e895tPszj3hw.

Blood, Peter, and Annie Patterson, eds. *Rise Up Singing: The Group Singing Songbook*, 15th anniversary ed. Bethlehem, PA: Sing Out Corporation, 2004.

Boffone, Trevor. "#Syllabus4Ham: The HAMILTON Syllabus." Trevor Boffone, Ph.D. website, June 2, 2016. https://trevorboffone.com/2016/06/02/syllabus4ham-the-hamilton-syllabus/.

Braunstein, Laura. "Untitled." Digital photograph. Dartmouth College Library Facebook page. November 9, 2016. https://www.facebook.com/pg/dartmouth.college.library/photos/.

Breitbart Tech. "No Punishment for Black Lives Matter Protesters Harassing Dartmouth Students." Breitbart, May 31, 2016. http://www.breitbart.com/tech/2016/05/31/no-punishment-for-black-lives-matter-protesters-harrassing-dartmouth-students/.

Campus Reform. "Dartmouth College #BlackLivesMatter Protest." YouTube video, 1:37. Filmed November 12, 2015. Posted November 14, 2015. https://www.youtube.com/watch?v=OJAuVQlLxD0.

Carawan, Guy, recorder and producer. *Sing for Freedom: The Story of the Civil Rights Movement through Its Songs*. Smithsonian Folkways Recordings, 1990. Accessed via Spotify, <URL>.

Carawan, Guy, and Candie Carawan, comps. *We Shall Overcome! Songs of the Southern Freedom Movement*. New York: Oak Publications, 1963.

Cathedral Singers–Topic. "In Zion." YouTube video, 4:12. Posted January 28, 2017.

https://www.youtube.com/watch?v=t62qRqSfxjQ.

Cheng, William. "Changing the World with Music." Course presented at Dartmouth College, Hanover, NH, January 2017.

———. *Just Vibrations: The Purpose of Sounding Good.* Ann Arbor: University of Michigan Press, 2016. https://doi.org/10.3998/mpub.9293551.

Dartmouth College. "Statement Regarding Student Protest in Baker-Berry Library." News release, November 16, 2015. http://www.dartmouth.edu/press-releases/statement-regarding-student-protest.html.

———. "2017 MLK Jr. Keynote Performance with Rev. Osagyefo Sekou." Filmed January 16, 2017. YouTube video, 1:42:17. https://youtu.be/ViqqZAOK8_0.

Dartmouth College Library. "Library Mission and Goals." 2011. Accessed April 1, 2017. https://www.dartmouth.edu/~library/home/about/mission.html (page discontinued).

Dartmouth Office of Pluralism and Leadership. "Education/Training." Accessed May 2, 2017. http://www.dartmouth.edu/~opal/programs/edutrain/ (page discontinued).

Dartmouth Review. "Trump's Election Triggers Protest at Dartmouth." Filmed November 9, 2016. YouTube video, 2:57, posted November 10, 2016. https://www.youtube.com/watch?v=QFqPIlkpw0U.

De Bono, Edward. *Lateral Thinking: Creativity Step by Step.* New York: Harper and Row, 1970.

Freeman, Tyné Angela. "Bridges." Audio recording, 5:34, September 22, 2017. Bridges. https://open.spotify.com/album/3flR19mCSf78PSkSvRTDOS (requires login).

Hanlon, Philip. "The President's Plan." Dartmouth College Office of the President. Accessed April 1, 2017. https://www.dartmouth.edu/~president/forward/plan.html.

Horrell, Jeffrey. "Last Thursday's Protest in the Library." Email to Library Group, November 17, 2015.

Nwaigwe, Chinedum. "Dartmouth Music Library Hosts Civil Rights Movement Sing-In." Filmed January 6, 2017. YouTube video, 2:02. https://www.youtube.com/watch?v=973BS-qCNIo.

Office of Institutional Diversity and Equity website. Dartmouth College. Accessed April 1, 2017. http://www.dartmouth.edu/~ide/.

Peet, Lisa. "Library of Congress Drops Illegal Alien Subject Heading, Provokes Backlash Legislation." *Library Journal*, June 13, 2016. http://lj.libraryjournal.com/2016/06/legislation/library-of-congress-drops-illegal-alien-subject-heading-provokes-backlash-legislation/#_.

Ratcliffe, Krista. "Rhetorical Listening: A Trope for Interpretive Invention and a 'Code of Cross-cultural Conduct.'" *College Composition and Communication* 51, no. 2 (1999): 195–224. https://doi.org/10.2307/359039.

Sociologists for Justice. "Ferguson Syllabus." Accessed May 6, 2017. https://sociologistsforjustice.org/ferguson-syllabus/.

CHAPTER 12

DIY Archives
Zine Collections in Houston

Lisa Cruces

> "Our goal is to share our stories, including the ones from
> mujeres who don't consider themselves writers, artists,
> or poets. We want to share the stories we don't tell, but
> other mujeres need to hear. We want to encourage other
> mujeres to express themselves. We are a space for gente
> who identify as mujer, in any way they choose to. Mujer is
> queer, mujer is straight, it's political, it's flaca, it's gordita,
> it's a grito, it's a mouthed curse, it's a walk alone at night.
> Mujer is a million things and so are you."
>
> —Natasha Hernandez, co-founder and editor of St. Sucia[1]

With strong roots in the hippie and punk rock movements of the late twentieth century, the DIY (do-it yourself) ethos has expanded to queer and feminist studies, incorporating counter-narratives and physical installations into
the informational milieu through a variety of self-produced artifacts, ranging from fanzines and photographs to recordings, music labels, and public
forums, which challenge dominant sociocultural ideologies.[2] Some writers
describe the production that has emerged as youth-centered, self-empowered,
and improvised, while others recognize the long-lasting and fluid influences
over the past fifty years, especially in regard to the impact of bottom-up approaches to preservation and dissemination in the DIY culture.[3] This ethos
has gained increased attention recently in archives and cultural heritage work
because some scholars and communities are criticizing libraries, archives, and

museums (LAM) for their lack of inclusivity and the silences they create or perpetuate. While some archiving projects, like the Louisville Underground Music Archives (LUMA), engage local communities in the identification of materials, and literary archivists use social media to connect with donors and advances in self-archiving digitally born literature,[4] communities previously seen as peripheral—people of color (POC) and LGBTQ—have responded to silences in the historical record by practicing do-it-yourself archiving. Less frequently, these communities build partnerships with "activist archivists."[5]

As Danielle Cooper puts it, the archives of marginalized communities, specifically those of LGBTQ individuals, "matter to archival studies because these archives provide compelling cases of how marginalized communities develop information organizations that are relevant to community information needs."[6] In short, when combined together in one place such as an archive, in an organizer's home, at a community center, or at an institution, like a university library or archive, self-published politically charged interventions with dominant culture underscore the value of forums. They contribute to a deeper understanding of individuals and communities because their ground-up approach emanates from the community at large into those institutions that honor and value differing approaches.

This chapter explores a DIY archives project centered on POC and LGBTQ zines at the University of Houston (UH). Its focus on archival and community partnerships as well as social and instructional engagement reverses the authority in archival collections and outreach to makers of zines (zinesters) who engage students in production that is later incorporated into the archives. As Jeena Freedman at Barnard College argues, zine preservation in active library spaces give young women's voices "a home on library shelves."[7] The project at UH takes this idea one step farther by creating a space for local LGBTQ artists and people of color to share their work as well as their experiences with student makers, whose self-publications are beginning to find homes in archival boxes alongside those of community members.

"Short for magazine or fanzine in the archives and special collections, zines are self-publications, motivated by a desire for self-expression, not for profit."[8] They have a variety of characteristics and are often handmade or photocopied. Most historians suggest that zines first emerged in the 1930s and 1940s, and they were frequently exchanged among science fiction fans, hence "fanzines." Increasingly easy to duplicate and distribute thanks to innovations in mimeographs and photocopiers, zines have fluctuated in their popularity but remained into the digital age. No two zines are alike, but almost every zine creates a special connection and intimacy between the creator and the reader. In the 1990s, the genre had major resurgence fueled by the Riot grrrl movement led by young white women who challenged sexism in the punk scene. To some extent this sentiment remains in contemporary feminist discussion. As Elke Zobl notes, the Riot grrrl movement enlivened "thousands of young women—mostly middle- and upper-middle class or college-educated white women in their late teens and early twenties" to produce feminist zines, which "lacked a reflection on white privilege and continued the hegemonic narrative."[9] Zinesters of color, Bianca Ortiz and Piepzna-Samarasinha see the history through a different lens as "equally birthed 'out of the self-publication methods utilized by Chicana, Latina, Black, Indigenous and APA [Asian Pacific American] artists, poets and writers during the '60s and '70s."[10] By all accounts, self-publishing in the format of zines carried forth the mission of self-empowerment by building on DIY values and practices.

With the expansion of feminism into the mainstream and the added layers of intersectionality and identity politics, zines have persisted as a medium accessible to most and not constrained by the limitations of publishing, editing, or other institutional strictures. As Jenna Freedman notes, they enable marginalized women of color to share their ideas, "build community and assert their existence with more confidence."[11] Modern-day zines continue to come in all shapes and forms, ranging from anarchist manifestos to quirky personal narratives. Increasingly their subject matter delves into the intersection of class, race, sexual orientation, and political ideology. For example, the zine RAIX, the fruit of a collaboration the Texas Freedom Education Fund and activists in the Texas Rio Grande Valley, addresses the intersectionality of queerness, gender, and reproductive justice specific to communities along the US-Mexico border. On the other hand, the zine series produced by St. Sucia (see figure 12.1), a zine press base in San Antonio, Texas, is a perfect example of the modern zine's ability to speak to different communities all at once. As founders Latinx feminists Isabel Castro and Natasha Hernandez put it, "St. Sucia is a megaphone gritando NO ESTAS SOLA!"[12] These examples resonate among the area studies archivists and librarians at UH who see them as outlets in which emerging Latinx scholars, artists, activists, and poets voice their feelings and thoughts on recent political topics such as immigration, encroachments on women's access to health services, and race.

Reaching out to these communities is important at UH, as descriptions of student life suggest in their praise for institutional efforts to promote "diversity by recruiting students and hiring faculty from minority groups actively" alongside work to cultivate "an environment where there is confident interaction between different groups."[13] UH has a student body of approximately 40,000 students and is the second most ethnically diverse major research university in the United States with students from more than 137 nations. Nearly 64 percent of the undergraduate students are POC, including 31.5 percent identifying as Hispanic or Latino, 22.2 percent as Asian, and 10.5 percent as African or African American. Almost 47 percent of the faculty also reflect this diversity, with 18.2 percent identifying as African or African

FIGURE 12.1
"ST. SUCIA XI: LEER, REVISAR, RESPONDER", courtesy of St. Sucia

American, 16.4 percent as Hispanic or Latino and 12.1 percent as Asian.[14] Many UH students also identify as first-generation college students and have no prior knowledge of archives and special collections, much less the perception of these spaces as prospective resources for their research or personal interests, to say nothing of repositories for their creative works or cultural heritage. Getting students in the door is a challenge, and those who do cross the threshold often do so because their instructors have required them to visit. Once inside, however, students often voice awe at the rich materials they experience during visits to the archives (rare books, maps, and manuscripts). This sort of cultural production is rarely immediately reflective of students' own identities and personal experiences.

UH Special Collections and Archives has striven to build hip-hop collections, LGBTQ collections, performing arts collections, and women's archives that reflect Houston's unique history and communities while simultaneously piquing the interests of diverse researchers, including students and community members. These precedents and openness to collecting materials produced from different experiences and forms of knowledge have had a significant impact on the conditions that enable a forum around zines at UH. Other precedents for DIY Zine archives have also helped with proven models for launching a zine archives at UH. Chief among them was the Zine Library at Barnard College.[15] Established in 2003 with a modest budget of $500, the Barnard Collection demonstrated how self-published works could be incorporated into traditional library spaces and complement existing resources. The curator at Barnard notes that these works "unmediated by editors and publishers" or by "authors uncredentialled by educational degrees or professional accomplishments" are tools for challenging libraries to hear and preserve criticism from communities they tend to marginalize like "young mothers of color."[16] These critical works also enhance strong collecting area within women's studies and support more inclusive library instruction. The Fanzine Collections at University of Iowa's Special Collections also provided guidance and logistical details on how to make zines available in an archival setting.[17]

The projects at Barnard and Iowa exemplify the important considerations at UH for establishing the zine archives. First and foremost, the collecting scope had to fit within the structure of the archives in its alignment with existing collecting areas for Special Collections. In the case of UH, those areas were Texas; women, gender, and sexuality studies; Hispanic studies; performing arts; and university history. The zines would also have to be actively utilized as teaching and outreach tools, and ideally as a means for building community into collections, underscoring a commitment to forum in the archives. These considerations have been key in influencing decisions regarding the handling of zines and the types of activities for which they are used. Faculty engagement with these collections has been essential as well. Thankfully, a member of the Art School faculty, Dr. Roberto Tejada, a specialist in artist books and poetry, was an early supporter of the zine collections at UH and a contributor to the collection. He was keenly interested in zines as a substitute and supplement for much more expensive artist books. Similar to artists books, zines are frequently included in special collections because they are interesting art objects that are simultaneously cheap and immediate modes of communication.[18] Zines also often visually and kinetically engage makers and readers, which makes them important for community engagement. They are a preferred medium for self-publishing because their fabrication through a variety of methods in inherently inclusive and widely accessible.

These external arguments for zine collections as more inclusive community forums and the internal request to provide this kind of material as a supplement to more expensive and exclusive artists' books enabled UH Special Collections to hasten its zine acquisition and solicitations for donations from zinesters around the city and surrounding area. From the onset, an important goal was to develop distinctive collections reflecting Houston's unique DIY arts communities and UH's diverse student body in an affordable and accessible way. The secondary objective was to introduce special collections as places telling students' stories in a community that might otherwise feel excluded from Special Collections. A zine archive replete with items produced in greater Houston as well as works by UH students emerged as a low-cost, student-focused community collecting strategy that also lent itself to collaborations with groups on and off campus.

With no designated funds and a limited familiarity with the genre, UH archivists approached local zine organizers and community members to collaborate and learn together while developing the breadth of the collection and acquisition sources. In line with DIY culture, zines can be hard to acquire because small, independent, or underground presses or individuals produce them in opposition to standardized publishing and archival practices.[19] Zine Fest Houston has proved an impactful partner in this process. Founded in 2004, but with roots going back to 1990s DIY culture, Zine Fest Houston started out as an annual event dedicated to promoting zines, mini-comics, and other forms of small-press, alternative, and underground DIY media and art. Today in its thirteenth year, Zine Fest Houston has expanded through year-round programming at different venues around the city and sometimes at zine fests across the country. Organizers have been eager to partner with UH Special Collections for the preservation of their archive and for the opportunity to introduce students to the empowering process of zine-making and sharing.

In January of 2017, Zine Fest Houston deposited thirteen banker's boxes of zines, comics, and ephemera related to the annual festival, much of it acquired through the personal curation of zinester Shane Patrick Boyle. All of the organizers repeatedly voiced their excitement about seeing their work gathered up and preserved for posterity. Zine Fest Houston organizers Sarah Welch and Maria-Elisa Heg noted in personal correspondence that they agreed to donate the Zine Fest Houston Archive to UH because they wanted to share and celebrate the history of the organization and the zines that have been produced by the artists, creators, and activists of South Texas from the early 1990s through today with the entire Houston community and with students, visiting scholars, and professors at the university. Additionally, they saw UH as a good fit in terms of location and archive storage facilities. They stated that they couldn't be happier with the partnership that has formed and look forward to adding to the collection throughout the years. The relationship was key to quickly building the bulk of the zine collections, and more importantly for legitimizing the university's collecting efforts in the Houston zine community and providing an outreach partner for community forums with students.

Along with agreeing to make annual deposits of zines collected by Zine Fest Houston, the group agreed to welcome a UH Special Collections table at different events sponsored by the group. They also agreed to collaborate with librarians and archivists to lead a panel and workshop themed around health topics such as reproductive rights, sex education, and mental health where students could work with local zinesters to make and, if they were so inclined, to deposit their zines into the UH archives. In a short while, this collaboration has resulted in nineteen students from a variety of disciplines producing and depositing their zines on curanderismo, gender identity, environmental justice, mental health, feminism, and nutrition. In effect, their voices on these important contemporary issues have found their way into the archival fabric at UH, ensuring that the celebrated diversity of the student body alongside that of the community is preserved within the archives and disseminated on campus and in the community. This presence at Zine Fest Houston events facilitated a small exhibit of the Zine Fest Houston Records and solicitation for additional donations to the archives. Among the outcomes of working with students and Zine Fest Houston organizers are increased awareness of UH's zine collections and the annual fest as well as more deposits by UH students. When students create documentation that represents themselves and add it to the archives, they fill their zines and the archives with their experiences and interests. This process helps create a forum in which community, students, and archives teach one another.

Since their first deposit, Zine Fest Houston has partnered with UH librarians for several tabling events on and off campus introducing UH students and faculty to the festival each fall. They have also collaborated on a panel and zine-making workshop for UH students cosponsored by Women, Gender, and Sexuality Studies, as well as the reproductive rights organization and the Lilith Fund—expanding outreach in an organic way. This arrangement is beneficial for all parties involved: while UH collections grow at little cost to the institution, zines gain legitimacy and prominence among a wider audience, inclusive of community makers, university scholars, and emerging student zinesters. The presence of zines in UH Special Collections creates opportunities for the archives to emulate inclusive practices and reserve space for student work and time for collaborative community partnerships in collection development. Years after graduating, the students who are involved can visit the archive, look back, and see themselves documented. Community members might also see themselves in these archives and, by extension, as part of the UH population.

It is important to note that zines are productive references in classrooms. In feminist studies, for example, they stand out as tools for challenging the perceived irrelevance of feminism. Teaching with zines lends itself to the feminist pedagogy of participatory learning, validation of personal experience, and the development of critical-thinking skills.[20] Inherently personal, either because of their content, their production, or both, zines are often the products of individuals' or groups' desire to express themselves without the restrictions of publishing, editing, or other institutional strictures like course requirements or university affiliated status. As Creasap states, "Zines share commonalities with independent media of earlier women's movements, such as scrapbooks, pamphlets, and manifestos."[21] Along with lending themselves to integration in Women, Gender, and Sexuality Studies coursework, zines provide a tactile introduction to a variety of formats found in Special Collections. Because of their physical nature, zines are easy to handle, and people can often acquire multiples. Soon after the acquisition of its first zines, UH Special Collections began to incorporate zines into instruction sessions with faculty in Women, Gender, and Sexuality Studies. Often the students' questions and areas of interest shift to the experiences of queer women and communities of color. This feedback helps to further refine the collecting scope of the zines UH collects, ensuring they are more inclusive of LGBTQ communities and people of color. As Honma puts it, "Because of their do-it-yourself ethos, zines are often embraced by those from marginalized background because of their freedom to experiment with different modes of writing, expression, and presentation."[22]

UH Faculty members have expressed interest in having zine workshops incorporated into course assignments, and this work is currently in the developmental stage. This planning touches on one of the challenges involved in building collections of student work; it can be labor-intensive, and budgets for specialized services are limited. Currently one archivist at UH manages all outreach and instruction related to zines, and it has been challenging to scale out this work. While LibGuides are being developed to help manage user needs, hands-on work requires face-to-face time and follow-up. These important projects are typically labors of love for the formats and the communities served, and they remain under-recognized in archival planning for using the structure to leverage the archives' power to "mak[e] and legitimiz[e] forms of knowledge and cultural production that neoliberal restructuring otherwise renders untenable."[23] Future plans for the zine collections at UH are ambitious despite these barriers. UH Libraries are exploring an oral history component and an Omeka digital exhibit to further raise the visibility of the zine collections. Continuing efforts are in place to develop student-curated exhibits and student-created zine collections through cosponsored workshops.

This desire to create oral histories has emerged directly from the UH/ Zine Fest Houston partnership in response to the recent passing of Zine Fest Houston founder Shane Patrick Boyle. The idea is to engage another campus partner, the Center for Public History, in assigning students to projects involving interviews and transcription. This involvement further employs students in the collecting efforts of archives and libraries. As long as there are individuals in need of a forum in which their personal passions, interests, and voices can be heard and shared in community, zines will persist, maybe even expanding their reach across campus to document a broader range of student experiences and collaboration in cocurated exhibits between student organizations and courses in Hispanic studies, creative writing, and art. Often zines are identified with political messages and counterculture movements, but much of our campus's interest has been in zines pertaining to the Latinx experience, immigration, borders, and writing. Here again, students influence the archive. In a time when much of a student's output is digital and fleeting, zines provide a physical form of self-expression and voice.

Notes

1. Natasha Hernandez, "About," St. Sucia website, accessed March 27, 2018, http:// stsucia.bigcartel.com/about.

2. Rosa Reitsamer and Elke Zobl, "Alternative Media Production, Feminism, and Citizenship Practices," in *DIY Citizenship: Critical Making and Social Media*, ed. Matt Ratto and Meghan Boler (Cambridge, MA: MIT Press, 2014), 329–342.

3. George McKay, *Senseless Acts of Beauty* (New York: Verso, 1996); Sarah Baker and Alison Huber, "Notes towards a Typology of the DIY Institution: Identifying Do-It-Yourself Places of Popular Music Preservation," *European Journal of Cultural Studies* 16, no. 5 (2013): 513–30.

4. Caroline Daniels et al., "Saving All the Freaks on the Life Raft: Blending Documentation Strategy with Community Engagement to Build a Local Music Archives," *American Archivist* 78, no. 1 (2015): 238–61.

5. Wendy M. Duff et al., "Social Justice Impact of Archives: A Preliminary Investigation," *Archival Science* 13, no. 4 (2013): 317–48.

6. Danielle Cooper, "House Proud: An Ethnography of the BC Gay and Lesbian Archives," *Archival Science* 16, no. 3 (2016): 265.

7. Jenna Freedman, "Grrrl Sines in the Library," *Signs* 35, no. 1 (2009): 52.

8. "Zines: Definition," Barnard College, accessed March 27, 2018, https://zines.barnard.edu/definition.

9. Elke Zobl, "Cultural Production, Transnational Networking, and Critical Reflec-

tion in Feminist Zines," *Signs* 35, no. 1 (September 2009):3.

10. Leah Lakshmi Piepzna-Samarasinha, "Brown Star Kids: Zinemakers of Colour Shake Things Up," *Broken Pencil*, no. 24 (2004): 25–26.

11. Freedman, "Grrrl Sines in the Library," 57.

12. Hernandez, "About."

13. "University of Houston Diversity: How Good Is It?" College Factual, accessed March 27, 2018, https://www.collegefactual.com/colleges/university-of-houston/student-life/diversity/.

14. "University of Houston Diversity."

15. "Zines: Definition."

16. Freedman, "Grrrl Zines in the Library," 52.

17. "Guide to the Zines Collection," University of Iowa Special Collections, accessed March 27, 2018, http://collguides.lib.uiowa.edu/?MSC0331.

18. Susan E. Thomas, "Value and Validity of Art Zines as an Art Form," *Art Documentation: Journal of Art Libraries Society of North America* 28, no. 2 (2009): 28.

19. Rowena Koh, "Alternative Literature in Libraries: The Unseen Zine," *Collection Building* 27, no. 2 (2008): 48.

20. Kimberly Creasap, "Zine-Making as Feminist Pedagogy," *Feminist Teacher* 24, no. 3 (2014): 155–68.

21. Creasap, "Zine-Making," 157.

22. Todd Honma, "From Archives to Action: Zines, Participatory Culture, and Community Engagement in Asian America," *Radical Teacher*, no. 105 (Summer 2016): 34.

23. Kate Eichhorn, quoted in Joanna Gardner-Hugget, review of *The Archival Turn in Feminism: Outrage in Order*, *Afterimage* 42, no. 2 (2014): 33.

Bibliography

Baker, Sarah, and Alison Huber. "Notes towards a Typology of the DIY Institution: Identifying Do-It-Yourself Places of Popular Music Preservation." *European Journal of Cultural Studies* 16, no. 5 (2013): 513–30.

Barnard College. "Zines: Definition." Accessed March 27, 2018. https://zines.barnard.edu/definition.

College Factual. "University of Houston Diversity: How Good Is It?" Accessed March 27, 2018. https://www.collegefactual.com/colleges/university-of-houston/student-life/diversity/.

Cooper, Danielle. "House Proud: An Ethnography of the BC Gay and Lesbian Archives." *Archival Science* 16, no. 3 (2016): 261–88.

Creasap, Kimberly. "Zine-Making as Feminist Pedagogy." *Feminist Teacher* 24, no. 3 (2014): 155–68.

Daniels, Caroline, Heather Fox, Sarah-Jane Poindexter, and Elizabeth Reilly. "Saving All the Freaks on the Life Raft: Blending Documentation Strategy with Community Engagement to Build a Local Music Archives." *American Archivist* 78, no. 1 (2015): 238–61.

Duff, Wendy M., Andrew Flinn, Karen Emily Suurtamm, and David A. Wallace. "Social Justice Impact of Archives: A Preliminary Investigation." *Archival Science* 13, no. 4 (2013): 317–48.

Freedman, Jenna. "Grrrl Sines in the Library." *Signs* 35, no. 1 (2009): 52–59.

Gardner-Hugget, Joanna. Review of *The Archival Turn in Feminism: Outrage in Order*, by Kate Eichhorn. *Afterimage* 42, no. 2 (2014): 33.

Hernandez, Natasha. "About." St. Sucia website. Accessed March 27, 2018. http://stsucia.bigcartel.com/about.

Honma, Todd. "From Archives to Action: Zines, Participatory Culture, and Community Engagement in Asian America." *Radical Teacher*, no. 105 (Summer 2016): 33–43.

Koh, Rowena. "Alternative Literature in Libraries: the Unseen Zine." *Collection Building* 27, no. 2 (2008): 48–51.

McKay, George. *Senseless Acts of Beauty: Cultures of Resistance since the Sixties*. New York: Verso, 1996.

Piepzna-Samarasinha, Leah Lakshmi. "Brown Star Kids: Zinemakers of Colour Shake Things Up." *Broken Pencil*, no. 24 (2004):25–26.

Reitsamer, Rosa, and Elke Zobl. "Alternative Media Production, Feminism, and Citizenship Practices." In *DIY Citizenship: Critical Making and Social Media*. Edited by Matt Ratto and Meghan Boler, 329-342. Cambridge, MA: MIT Press, 2014.

Thomas, Susan E. "Value and Validity of Art Zines as an Art Form." *Art Documentation: Journal of Art Libraries Society of North America* 28, no. 2 (2009): 27–38.

University of Iowa Special Collections. "Guide to the Zines Collection." Accessed March 27, 2018. http://collguides.lib.uiowa.edu/?MSC0331.

Zobl, Elke. "Cultural Production, Transnational Networking, and Critical Reflection in Feminist Zines." *Signs* 35, no. 1 (September 2009): 1–12.

CHAPTER 13

North Carolina State University Spotlight

Part 2, Showcasing Student Work through Public Programs

Marian Fragola

North Carolina State University's (NCSU) mission to "Think and Do" has empowered the NCSU Libraries to be a leader in connecting theory to practice, coursework to careers, and personal passions to global engagement. Additional information about how this mission informs work in the NCSU Libraries is provided in the chapter "Preparing Students to 'Think and Do': Promoting the Value of Student Work," which appears in the Articulating the Value of Student Work section of the book.

The NCSU Libraries places a special emphasis on showcasing student work through public programming. This emphasis helps shape the Libraries' overall suite of programs, branded as "NCSU Libraries Presents." Over the past several years, "NCSU Libraries Presents" has systematically and strategically grown to include approximately 100 separate programs during the academic year, with annual attendance of nearly 9,000. The opening of the Hunt Library in 2013 has played a part in that growth. This destination venue offers unique physical spaces that lend themselves to creative programming, curated by library staff, as extensions of existing series or explorations of something new.

The principle that informs this programmatic focus on student work is that students are producers as well as consumers of knowledge. As such, they are tasked throughout their college careers to engage with the intellectual life and scholarship offered at the university and to produce tangible or actionable results through that scholarship. At the NCSU Libraries, we provide opportunities to continually practice research skills and participate in a community of scholars by sharing discoveries, failures, and findings. This is particularly important because students have few opportunities outside of the classroom to share the concepts they are learning and to demonstrate the ways in which they are contributing to their fields of study. The NCSU Libraries position as a "third place" on campus—neither classroom nor living space, but a hub of intellectual activity—positions it to serve both as a forum and amplifier for student work.[1]

One example of this type of programming is the Student Short Film Showcase. Since its inception in 2011, this program has provided a venue for students to show and discuss their creative work in a public forum. The program began when librarians approached faculty in the College of Design and the College of Humanities and Social Sciences with the idea of showcasing student pieces created in a film class, a digital video production class, and an animation studio. These student projects use different media and support different learning objectives and skill building, but they all require an enormous amount of work for students. While students share work in class with their peers, there was no campus setting to screen these works for a wider audience.

Our faculty partners all eagerly agreed to participate, remarking upon the dearth of opportunities for students to share their work beyond the immediate classroom. In his filmed introduction that precedes the Student Short Film Showcase, digital production professor Jim Alchediak says, "It's a really nice opportunity for students to showcase their work and, of course, it's increasingly rare for students to have an opportunity to see their work play in front of a live audience like this."[2] Beginning in the spring of 2011, faculty selected the best of the student projects developed in their classes to be featured in a showcase performance. The Libraries organized the event, providing the venue, the technical support to screen the pieces, the event coordination, the marketing, and the branding and collateral, including printed programs. Librarians also served as video DJs—or "veejays"—and emcees, introducing each piece and leading the discussion with student creators after the screening.

The campus responded positively to the showcase, suggesting that there was a demand for this type of program. Attendance doubled in the program's second year, with a standing-room-only crowd of more than 100. We have continued to include the showcase in our regular suite of programs, increasing it from a once-a-year to a once-a-semester offering, attended by hundreds of people every year.

Every semester, the student film work itself is consistently strong and inspiring: some pieces are moving, some experimental, some humorous. Students are thrilled to see their work presented on a large screen with high-quality audio. What sets the showcase apart and deepens its impact is the interaction. The students talk with the audience of other NC State students, faculty, and members of the Raleigh community who come specifically to see student work and share the experience of making their films and learning through the process (see figure 13.1). As one student told us in a questionnaire emailed to student presenters, "There is a special sense of validation for the effort I went through when [my work] is shown in front of an audience outside of the class I worked in."

Student filmmakers explain to the audience their newfound appreciation for working with actual 16 mm film stock, which is expensive and necessitates extensive preplanning not required by digital formats. Students also discuss their creative inspirations, their cinematic influences, and their understanding of how to incorporate elements such as natural light and amplified sound.

Student animators talk about the technical intricacies of different styles of animation—2-D, 3-D, stop-action, and rotoscope. They tell of the countless hours of tedious work and the frustrations (and unexpected benefits) of having to scale the ideas they had in their heads to a vision that could be

FIGURE 13.1
Students discuss their work from the stage during the Student Short Film Showcase.

accomplished within the parameters of their skill set and the time frame for the assignment.

In addition to giving the students a chance to share what they have learned before a wider audience, the showcase has also inspired attendees. Students often bring family and friends, and members of the community attend, some year after year. Audience feedback, particularly from current students, indicates that this program that makes them feel proud of other students and inspires them to attempt similar creative works. Some students have specifically discussed how they were motivated to sign up for a course after seeing student work produced for that course at a library program. One student's experiences, shared with us in a questionnaire sent to student presenters, highlight the inspirational role of the program:

> As a Freshman coming to the Student Short Film Showcase through the Scholars Forum, I was exposed to what was created in the Intro to Animation class that is offered for my major. It was exciting to see finished products of peers and upperclassmen, and is the reason I took Intro to Animation as soon as my schedule permitted. One time, after seeing a particularly appealing animation, I was given the opportunity to talk to the creator after the show and make an acquaintance! When my work was shown this semester, an inspired and excited middle schooler came up to me and it was a nice experience to have been able to be in both sets of shoes.

Other libraries programs reflect NC State's emphasis on cross-disciplinarity by featuring student work across a variety of departments within the same event. For example, in 2017, the NCSU Libraries piloted a new student-focused program: the Undergraduate Research Slams (see figure 13.2). To help us learn about student research projects from many disciplines and to maximize the program's reach across several of NC State's twelve colleges, we partnered with the Office of Undergraduate Research and with the Undergraduate Research Student Advisory Council. As a result of that collaboration, the topics we were able to feature ranged from quantum chemistry, to animal science, to film studies.

We recruited undergraduate students who had worked on a significant research project and the Libraries held two public events where each student had five minutes and five slides to communicate his or her research. Branding these events as slams helped convey that substantive exposure to student research can still be fun and fast-paced.

FIGURE 13.2
Students have five minutes and five slides to present their research in the Undergraduate Research Slams.

The Undergraduate Research Slams had an audience of more than one hundred attendees in total and were well received. Attendees enjoyed hearing about a wide range of topics; sample feedback responses from evaluation forms included

- "I was surprised by how much undergraduate research is going on, both in the sciences, business related fields, and film."
- "I am just starting to write an undergraduate research proposal so this was a great event to see final projects and how they all turned out."
- "I am an Engineering student currently looking to participate in research, so it was interesting to see what projects are currently being studied."

From the Libraries' perspective, we believe it is important to curate presentations of student work at the same level as other Libraries programs. Events must be well coordinated, aggressively marketed, and expertly executed. Keeping to this standard demonstrates to students that we value their work and their time and helps us maintain our "NCSU Libraries Presents" brand.

Working with students is rewarding. In our experience, students are extremely appreciative and excited about the opportunity to present their work to a broad audience outside of their classroom. At the same time, planning programs with students can be difficult because of their busy schedules. Some students who have not presented at the Libraries before may not realize that our expectations of them are high, and they do not practice their presentations ahead of time, follow instructions about how to format the work that we need, or submit it in a timely way, despite email instructions and reminders from library staff. These challenges, while sometimes frustrating, are themselves learning opportunities for the students and do not diminish the sense of reward that we as librarians get from working with them.

We emphasize quality by asking faculty to suggest or even select those students who have produced excellent work or who would be good at talking about their work, or both. Even with this selection mechanism in place, however, quality sometimes varies. Still, we know from evaluation forms that people who attend programs featuring student work are interested in hearing about what students learned from the projects or pieces they present and that students benefit from the presentation process even their product or presentation is less than perfect. In fact, sometimes student work that may not appear polished or complex has an interesting story behind it—after hearing students describe the challenges they faced or what they learned from a particular assignment or project, attendees may come away with an appreciation of the learning process that makes how polished the work is or how poised the student is in his or her presentation less important.

Presenting student work is also an excellent way for the Libraries to initiate and foster relationships with faculty. In our experience, faculty rarely have the resources or expertise to plan and especially market public programs. Most programs and colloquia hosted by departments feature visiting faculty from other institutions or well-known speakers, scholars, and authors, rather than student scholars or producers. When departments feature student work, they rarely attempt to garner an audience wider than the department or college itself, though as the university continues to emphasize the importance of cross-disciplinary collaboration this may change. At this point, faculty welcome and appreciate the Libraries' expertise in programming, marketing, event coordination, and execution. Faculty have also used student presentations as opportunities to invite department heads and deans to see the type of work that students are doing in their classes, helping to reinforce the Libraries as a center for scholarship. And, the Libraries is able to capitalize on the role as a valued partner and collaborator.

In addition to our work with departments, we have also recently begun to work directly with the students themselves to brainstorm and develop programming ideas. One example of this is a recent collaboration with a graduate student to feature a panel discussion on women in the field of data science. The Libraries provided guidance and support, but the student successfully led the planning and implementation of this event. We would like to continue to explore and expand student-directed programming, which would give students program planning and outreach experience, as well as allowing us to tap directly into student interests on student time.

A future goal is to develop more systematic ways to convey the benefits of providing a forum for student work to upper-level campus administration, our Friends of the Library supporters, and other campus groups. Currently, we actively promote "NCSU Libraries Presents" programs, which include those featuring student work, to our Friends of the Library members, but have not, to date, developed more systematic ways to convey the benefits of providing a forum for student work to upper-level campus administration, our Friends of the Library supporters, and other campus groups.

Conclusion

Academic libraries can create public programming from a limitless well of inspiration—the creative work, classroom projects, and research being conducted by their students year after year. By providing a forum for presenting student work, and by supporting it with expertise in planning, marketing, and coordination, the academic library has an opportunity to play a unique role on campus—that of a convener and hub of intellectual activity that can cross and combine disciplines. Additionally, by presenting student works, we as librarians can better understand what students are learning and producing in their classes. This in turn makes us better able to adapt to their needs and support them with other library resources.

Notes

1. Ray Oldenburg, *The Great Good Place* (New York: Marlowe, 1999).
2. NCSU Libraries, "Student Short Film Showcase Screens Thursday," February 12, 2018, https://www.lib.ncsu.edu/news/student-short-film-showcase-screens-thursday.

Bibliography

NCSU Libraries. "Student Short Film Showcase Screens Thursday." https://www.lib.ncsu.edu/news/student-short-film-showcase-screens-thursday. Raleigh, NC: 2018.

Oldenburg, Ray. *The Great Good Place: Cafés, Coffee Shops, Bookstores, Bars, Hair Salons, and Other Hangouts at the Heart of a Community.* New York: Marlowe, 1999.

Section III
Library as Archive

CHAPTER 14

The Library as an Archive of Student Works

Amy S. Jackson, Cindy Pierard, and Suzanne M. Schadl

This section addresses student scholarship as a high-impact practice, the library's role in the student-centered scholarly communications cycles, and the intellectual property issues surrounding this work. Chapters in this section present case studies of student learning in high-impact activities such as capstone projects (Clemons and Fierke, chapter 16), writing-intensive courses, and products submitted to student writing journals (Biswas, Schlanger, and Gauder, chapter 15). They also present ideas to strengthen student buy-in and participation in open culture (Rigling, chapter 18) and to address copyright and intellectual property challenges faced by scholars (Myers, chapter 17). Voices include those of librarians (Clemons, Gauder, Schlangen, Myers, and Rigling), subject faculty (Fierke and Biswas), and a director of a writing program (Biswas). These chapters provide concrete examples of how the library can archive products of high-impact practices and encourage openness while respecting the intellectual property of our scholars. Interestingly, this section has more citations to other scholarly articles than other sections in this book, perhaps because archiving is not new to our profession and several other writers have already written extensively about its value. We hope the contributions in this section provide inspiration for other libraries seeking to archive student-produced works and support authentic learning experiences on their campuses.

Bruff's call to action, from the introduction to this book, asks those involved in all aspects of higher education to support student-created content and authentic learning experiences. The chapters in this section reflect responses to this call. Authors provide examples of libraries making student work available to the general public through different online platforms. These opportunities help students and professors transform the problem of "busywork" assignments not seen outside of the classroom into authentic scholarly work accessible through library resources. Biswas, Schlanger, and Gauder, for example, illustrate how an undergraduate writing journal coordinated by the English department and published in the library's institutional repository (IR) gives students hands-on experience writing, editing, and managing workflow. In this case, students gain professional training and credit for writing, publishing, and management of knowledge production. As Bruff notes, students tend to respond to these kinds of authentic assignments with enthusiasm and a greater sense of accomplishment. Clemons and Fierke also use the IR to archive student projects, which leads to students viewing themselves as "beginning scholars." Through the public dissemination of their work, these assignments move from classroom work into an authentic, publically accessible work.

When we refer to "the library as an archive" in this book, our intention is to convey the idea of the library acting as a repository of works created by students, published or unpublished, in a physical or digital form. Consequently, this section does not focus on the physical spaces of libraries and archives, which are addressed in the other sections, nor does it address curatorial activities, another significant activity that generally takes place in archives. While the Society of American Archivists defines archives as a place "where people go to find information,"[1] often in the form of primary source, unique, or unpublished documents, libraries are also places where people to go find information in published forms. Some of the published student-produced work addressed in this section includes assignment-based projects, capstone projects, or works created independently from courses. In each case, students are treated as part of the scholarly communications cycle—which the ALA defines as an "ecosystem" within the "dynamic digital environment of contemporary scholarship."[2]

George Kuh and the Association of American Colleges and Universities state that every student should participate in at least two high-impact activities during his or her undergraduate program in order to increase rates of student retention and student engagement.[3] These activities include writing-intensive courses, undergraduate research, capstone courses or projects, first-year seminars and experiences, common intellectual experiences (core courses), learning communities, collaborative assignments and projects, diversity or global learning, service learning or community-based learning, and internships. Products created during the course of these activities can be archived in the library, but may not currently be sought out by liaison librarians. Writing-intensive courses, undergraduate research, and capstone courses or projects are obvious starting points to look for writing-intensive assignments for potential archiving, and creative assignments in the other activities may also yield archivable student products. Liaison librarians should work with faculty designing courses to determine appropriate products that can be archived by the library.

Traditionally, libraries privilege text-based information produced by established scholars and writers. The idea of supporting emerging scholars and allowing them into our collections, while not entirely new to our profession if we consider the long-standing tradition of archiving doctoral dissertations and masters' theses, has been evolving alongside emerging scholarship. The chapters in this section demonstrate expanded efforts to include new kinds of scholarship like undergraduate journals and capstone project findings. This kind of archiving enables libraries to support university-backed high-impact activities that invite students to participate more directly in the scholarly communications cycle. In doing so, libraries demonstrate to university administrators the value of the library in multiple educational processes—illustrating libraries' flexibility in providing students with increased opportunities for success.

Much of the scholarly communications cycle happens outside of the library. However, libraries participate in this cycle when we archive or publish this work, and when scholars come to libraries to find and apply such works. Emerging scholars who are participating in this process without the burden of seeking tenure understand the disruptive power of making information freely available and may eventually become strong supporters of the open-access system. It is through these scholars that we may be able to move away from the traditional system based on closed access journals.

Archiving student work in the library can take many forms. Libraries first ventured into this role through archiving physical theses and dissertations, and then through archiving digital versions. This role has continued to evolve, especially as digital resources alleviate physical space requirements, and many librarians consider capstone projects and other student work as candidates for the IR. One can also imagine other electronic works, not limited to text, in the IR, physical materials in the archives, and physical artifacts on display or archived in the library for future exhibits. Students who contribute to projects represented in this section feel a sense of participating in the scholarly communications cycle as their work is read and experienced by others, in many cases outside of the institution. Their work also provides examples and inspiration for future students. These are examples of high-impact, library-supported activities providing additional value to the student and proving the value of the library to the campus learning environment.

However, libraries do not have unlimited resources to find and recruit student work, and the NCSU spotlight chapter on open cultures (Rigling) brings attention to the fact that "the libraries do not have the capacity to be, nor should they be the sole keeper of student works, but we can help students embrace their own roles as prospective producers, publishers, and distributors of their work." This is especially relevant to students after graduation when they may no longer have access to the university library. NCSU libraries demonstrate the power and utility of open-source software and Creative Commons–licensed works for both creators and others who may wish to reuse or improve previously created works. In 2017 the library hosted a program advocating use of open materials, marketed as OpenCon2017, providing, as Rigling states, "an opportunity for students to learn more about how to share their work, cultivate their professional identity, and learn advocacy skills." Additionally, open culture advocacy was incorporated into makerspace instruction through use of open-access and Creative Commons–licensed materials.

While libraries may not have unlimited resources, library student employees are often an untapped resource for help with library projects.[4] Although we use students to keep buildings open, they often have expertise in their areas, which we are unaware of, that may be helpful for digital archiving projects. For example, library student employees may be good candidates for board members for writing journals, writing awards, and other sources for recognizing emerging scholarship. By valuing students for their knowledge and not just the number of hours they can work, we can find additional expertise to help us run these types of projects.

Students creating work for activities outside the classroom may feel a stronger sense of ownership and investment in the products, due to the voluntary nature of the work and its disconnection from the traditional classroom grading structure. They may take pride in their work and be happy to see its impact on other students and community members. Biswas, Schlanger, and Gauder reflect on this phenomena in their exploration of an undergraduate student writing journal supported outside of the traditional classroom structure through a collaboration between the English department and the library. Although a student's classroom assignments are completed with the submission of a final paper, with the option of submitting it to the writing journal, the next steps are beyond classroom learning. Students serving as editorial board members submit and edit their work and the work of others without receiving classroom credit. These students are furthering their role in the scholarly communications cycle and participating in authentic learning projects that reach a broader audience than they originally envisioned.

Institutional repositories are a natural fit for archiving electronic works of emerging scholars. Many libraries host institutional repositories intended for faculty works, and marginally for student work that is considered scholarly, such as theses and dissertations. These repositories support archiving and preservation of the intellectual output of an institution (including faculty publications) through an online platform. Institutions hosting a repository take the responsibility of providing long-term preservation, access, and dissemination of documents deposited there. Academic institutions and their libraries are ideal organizations to take this role, due to their long-term sustainability and altruistic support of the community (local and academic). Libraries also do not have commercial interests in sustaining their resources and view students and faculty as their stakeholders. Established scholars and emerging scholars can assume that all work curated by the library will continue to be discoverable and usable, even as platforms change and technology evolves. But what would happen if libraries used their institutional repository as a tool to archive any type of student work, beyond theses and dissertations? Clemons and Fierke write about a capstone class project deposited in the institutional repository. By writing for others beyond their classes, students experience a greater motivation to create high-quality work, and students can view examples of other student projects. By adding their projects to the cumulative knowledge gained by all class participants, they are participating in a scholarly communications cycle with students in the past and future.

While providing students with the tools for archiving their work in an online platform, we also need to provide training and education on copyright and intellectual property so that students understand their rights as well as the rights of others. As Myers says, "When asked about copyright law, students are often able to articulate the ways in which common acts of infringement are carried out (e.g., illegal file sharing of songs and films online). However, when asked about how they manage the copyright in works they have created or reuse works of others in compliance with the law, students are often left speechless." Myers provides an in-depth introduction to copyright and rights management, bringing into focus the importance of respecting intellectual property rights of all types of creators represented in the library.

In addition to copyright and intellectual property, another challenge faced when archiving student works is curation of these works. Institutional archivists and data curators, for example, consider how long libraries should retain data. As curators of a different type of data—student scholarship—librarians should also be aware of this question. Should student works be deaccessioned? If so, which ones and when? What happens if there is a request to remove the work by the author or another interested party, now or in the future? While there are no standard answers to these questions, each library and each collection added, physical or digital, must address these questions individually, and librarians should be aware of these issues when recruiting student work. Other student-produced materials may require special considerations due to culturally sensitive subjects, inflammatory subjects, or personally identifiable information, and may not be suitable for sharing, especially without context. These issues should be thought through beforehand and arrangements should be made in consultation with the student creator to avoid conflicts and misunderstandings. Possible alternatives include redacting information, keeping surrogate records with contact information for the author, or determining that sharing without any context is not realistic.

Archiving student-produced work in the library has many benefits for both students and the library. Students who plan on advancing in academia will gain a greater understanding of the scholarly communications cycle by participating directly within it. Sharing their work produces authentic experience that replicates opportunities outside of the classroom. The library gains acknowledgement as an active participant in high-impact student activities, increasing engagement with the library by students, and general student retention on campus. As we continue to network across campus communities, our definition of the types of resources available in the library should continue to evolve. With broad archiving of student-produced work, libraries can emerge as the cultural center of campus and true partners in the educational experience of our students.

Notes

1. Society of American Archivists, *What Is an Archives?* (Chicago: Society of American Archivists, 2007), http://files.archivists.org/advocacy/AAM/WhatIsAnArchives.pdf.
2. Association of College and Research Libraries Working Group on Intersections of Scholarly Communication and Information Literacy, *Intersections of Scholarly Communication and Information Literacy* (Chicago: Association of College and Research Libraries, 2013), 2, http://acrl.ala.org/intersections.
3. George D. Kuh, *High-Impact Educational Practices* (Washington, DC: Association of American Colleges and Universities, 2008).
4. Amanda Melilli, Rosan Mitola, and Amy Hunsaker, "Contributing to the Library Student Employee Experience: Perceptions of a Student Development Program," *Journal of Academic Librarianship* 42, no. 4 (2016): 430–37.

Bibliography

Association of College and Research Libraries Working Group on Intersections of Scholarly Communication and Information Literacy. *Intersections of Scholarly Communication and Information Literacy: Creating Strategic Collaborations for a Changing Academic Environment*. Chicago: Association of College and Research Libraries, 2013. http://acrl.ala.org/intersections.

Kuh, George D. *High-Impact Educational Practices: What They Are, Who Has Access to Them, and Why They Matter.* Washington, DC: Association of American Colleges and Universities, 2008.

Melilli, Amanda, Rosan Mitola, and Amy Hunsaker. "Contributing to the Library Student Employee Experience: Perceptions of a Student Development Program." *Journal of Academic Librarianship* 42, no. 4 (2016): 430–37.

Society of American Archivists. *What Is an Archives?* Chicago: Society of American Archivists, 2007. http://files.archivists.org/advocacy/AAM/WhatIsAnArchives.pdf.

CHAPTER 15

A Student Journal to Celebrate, Preserve, and Improve Beginning Undergraduate Writing

Ann E. Biswas, Maureen Schlangen, and Heidi Gauder

At the end of each semester, composition instructors at the University of Dayton (UD) collected portfolios of student writing for the annual program assessment, encouraging their students to return the following semester to pick up their folders of work. However, the stacks of unclaimed portfolios that piled up in faculty offices each year was an indication that students cared little about what they had written, perhaps believing no one beyond their instructor was interested in reading their writing now or in the future. Nevertheless, academic scholars have recognized that student writing improves—as do a sense of ownership and pride in one's writing—when students know their work will be shared with authentic audiences in wider public spaces.[1] As a result, many institutions have created journals of outstanding undergraduate research. Today, the Council on Undergraduate Research lists well over 200 journals, the majority of which include work from advanced students' disciplinary research; however, few journals exist to celebrate the work of *beginning* student writers. In 2014, *Line by Line: A Journal of Beginning Student Writing* (https://ecommons.udayton.edu/lxl/) was created, in part, to provide undergraduates with an authentic audience and to celebrate the wide variety of writing emerging from first- and second-year composition courses. *Line by Line* is an open-access online journal published twice a year by the UD English department and hosted by the university library. If their work is selected for publication, students know it will be shared not only with their peers but also with a wider public audience. Likewise, the archival repository that hosts the journal serves as an important record of what students are writing and thinking about during their formative years as academic writers. Importantly, the journal highlights the value of collaboration between an English department and a university library to promote and preserve undergraduate scholarship.

This chapter presents a case study of *Line by Line*, describing key steps in its development, major decisions and challenges as the journal took shape, and project outcomes for the journal's first three years. We begin with a review of the scholarship that has emerged regarding student writing in institutional repositories and the importance of student journals for providing authentic writing experiences. We conclude with a discussion of the potential for library archives as sites to preserve undergraduate writing and research of all kinds. It is hoped that the information that follows will allow individuals to replicate a journal of this kind at their home institutions.

Review of Literature

Recent literature has revealed that the publishing and archiving of undergraduate work can influence writing and teaching methods, elicit greater commitment from students, and help students see themselves as authors and scholars who can contribute to academic discourse. Exline acknowledged reservations that faculty, librarians, and even students can have about placing undergraduate work in the persistent public realm—the obvious ones being quality and colocation with the work of established scholars.[2] She highlighted ways archiving in a repository can benefit students as well as institutions. For example, a repository can cultivate a network of students, scholars, and researchers to support all stages of the research cycle. Undergraduates can share and build upon their research during the undergraduate years and beyond, and students can learn about copyright. Moreover, repositories can provide model papers for future students' reference and to help support recruitment.[3]

In 2013, an Association of College and Research Libraries working group on scholarly communication and information literacy contended that academic libraries must facilitate open scholarship to "transform student learning, pedagogy, and instructional practices through creative and innovative collaborations." In its report, the group suggested that librarians and faculty examine the economics of scholarly publishing and begin to see publishing as pedagogy. Working together, librarians and teaching faculty can incorporate digital literacies into the curriculum and educate students on ownership, authorship, and copyright in the advancing information environment.[4]

An assessment by Weiner and Watkinson of an undergraduate journal started at Purdue University in 2011 revealed that an academic library can be a natural publishing partner for academic departments wishing to incorporate undergraduate publishing into their curricula. The article described administrative processes, purposes and expected benefits of the journal, and competencies gained from contributing to it.[5]

In looking for ways to get her writing students more engaged with their assignments, Putnam realized that though students in composition courses spend weeks drafting and revising their papers, their instructor is often the only one who reads what they write, reinforcing students' belief that writing assignments are meaningless tasks that must be "gotten through" in order to pass a required course. "Students were writing simply because I asked them to write," she explained. "They had no particular reason to care about what filled the blank computer screen or pages in front of them except the grade that I was to give them."[6] When students write to this nebulous teacher/reader, they may view their work as a "private communication" between the student and the instructor, "a work with no future and an audience of one."[7] Having students write to a broader audience, such as to readers of an online student journal, can improve the perceived purpose and authenticity of the writing task involved.[8] In their article on producing a student journal of political science research, Barrios and Weber found that "a student journal, both as a production process and as a tangible product of that process, provides students with work that has a future and reach far beyond an audience of one."[9]

Yet some have argued that after a decade or more of schooling in which they write only for a teacher, students can encounter great difficulty writing to a broader academic audience. In his seminal work "Inventing the University," Bartholomae deconstructed this dynamic, describing the immense challenges placed on students to appropriate the conventions and language of a specialized academic discourse "as though they were easily or comfortably one with their audience."[10] In other words, students don't come to higher education knowing how to write like scholars to scholarly readers; they need to go through a kind of socialization process whereby they gradually "learn to speak our language."[11]

Likewise, some students might question their ability to add to the scholarly conversation, seeing themselves as far less authoritative than their source authors. In an effort to understand why some writing students resort to cheating, Ritter found that composition students often don't see themselves as real authors. In her course-wide survey of first-year composition students' opinions of what characterizes an author, she discovered that "only a third of the students considered themselves authors, even though all were in the process of writing an 'academic' paper for English 101."[12] Thus, placing students in the challenging role of trying to sound scholarly and adopt the conventions of academic discourse may lead some students to plagiarize—or worse, purchase papers online.

Ní Uigín and colleagues argued that an online student journal can help ease students' transition into this academic authorial mind-set. They described the outcomes of an online student journal for students in an MA program on Irish language at the University of Galway. They wrote, "[The journal] was a practical attempt to enhance the students' identity as scholars who rightfully hold a place in the Academy" and to provide students with "an initiation into the discourse of their area of study."[13] In this manner, shifting from writing to "disembodied audiences" to ensuring "students write for real audiences and purposes, not just the teacher in response to generic prompts" may ease students' appropriation of academic literacy and authorial identity.[14] With a stronger authorial mind-set, students nurture a sense of ownership of their writing—something Leekley and colleagues noted can "provide an incentive for students to work to improve their writing."[15] Rather than viewing their assignments as having little worth, students see meaning, purpose, and value in the process of producing writing intended for publication in an online undergraduate journal as their work becomes situated in a broader academic community.

Efforts to engage beginning student writers, along with publishing and archiving student work, connect well with the Association of American Colleges and Universities (AAC&U) high-impact educational practices, which are shown to increase rates of student retention and student engagement. These practices include first-year seminars and experiences, the best of which "place a strong emphasis on critical inquiry, frequent writing, information literacy, collaborative learning, and other skills that develop students' intellectual and practical competencies."[16] Writing-intensive courses at all levels and across the curriculum are also identified as a high-impact educational practice. Likewise, effective first-year seminars and writing-intensive courses rely on engaging writing approaches, including discussions about scholarly communication.

Case Study of *Line by Line*

Founded in 1850, the University of Dayton is a top-tier Catholic research institution with approximately 8,000 full-time undergraduate students, 2,500
graduate and law students, and seventy-five academic majors for undergraduates in arts and sciences, business, education, and engineering. Approximately 90 percent of UD's undergraduates live on campus or in the student
neighborhood, which allows the university to incorporate a robust residential
curriculum that stresses cultural, leadership, professional, and personal development. UD's commitment to community acknowledges the dignity of every person and promotes solidarity and the common good. With an average
ACT composite score of 26.1 and 86 percent coming from the top half of their
high school class, first-year students arrive at UD well prepared academically;
still, like most college students, they must undergo a formidable transition to
academic research and writing.

To help in this transition, the UD English department typically offers
about 200 sections of composition courses per year. Most students take a two-
year sequence of courses to fulfill their writing requirement: ENG 100 the
first year and ENG 200 the second. Higher-performing incoming students
can complete this requirement by taking one course, ENG 200H, their first
year. Finally, students in an integrated, interdisciplinary program called Core
complete their composition requirement in a series of collaboratively taught
courses that combine English, history, philosophy, and religious studies. All
of these courses are part of the university's general education program, called
the Common Academic Program (CAP). CAP was designed around seven
overarching student learning outcomes, the first of which, scholarship, is described as follows:

> All undergraduates will develop and demonstrate advanced
> habits of academic inquiry and creativity through the pro-
> duction of a body of artistic, scholarly, or community-based
> work intended for public presentation and defense.[17]

Although yearly assessment results found that beginning composition
students were clearly developing these important habits of inquiry and creativity, in 2013 there were few if any opportunities for public presentation of
their work and no permanent space for preserving it. Although the university
offered a unique daylong symposium of student research presentations, the
event happened just once a year, and nearly all of the English presentations
came from upper-division courses. UD's English department also presented
an award each year to recognize exemplary writing from any English course,
but almost exclusively the entrants came from upper-level English literature

courses. Although winners received recognition, including their name on a plaque and a $100 prize, their writing was not published, posted, or archived. Similarly, a student-led art and literary journal, supported by the department, provided excellent opportunities for students to share their work publicly; however, the publication was exclusively for creative and artistic work such as poetry, photography, and short stories—not work from the composition courses.

A confluence of events occurred in the fall of 2013 that paved the way for the creation of an online journal of undergraduate writing that would support the university's scholarship outcome, providing composition students with an opportunity to demonstrate academic inquiry through the production of writing intended for public presentation. In particular, the university joined bepress Digital Commons, an online institutional repository system. The library began actively seeking department and faculty interest in creating journals, hosting conferences, and archiving faculty scholarship in the repository, which was named eCommons. The library hosted several information sessions for faculty and staff about the capabilities, versatility, and functions of the institutional repository. Importantly for the English department, the library was offering this institutional resource as well as support for journal development at no cost to departments. Using this electronic publishing platform was a logical choice for the new undergraduate writing journal as it allowed the English department to bypass the costly, time-consuming process of designing, programming, and branding its own journal website or, perhaps even more costly, designing, printing, and distributing a printed journal. Thus, eCommons provided a ready-made, open-access space for the new journal and its archives. The university retains complete institutional ownership of the content, regardless of whether the relationship with the repository host continues.

Around this same time, a new Writing Program Administrator (WPA) was beginning her four-year appointment and looking for a project to showcase the wide variety of writing that students were producing in the composition courses. Hearing of the library's new online platform, she wrote a proposal to the department chair, asking for support to create a new undergraduate composition journal. In addition to showing how the journal would support the CAP scholarship outcome in an innovative and engaging way, the proposal argued that the journal would fill a department need by offering beginning college writers who produce exemplary work the chance to have that work publicly recognized, shared, and preserved.

The chair and the department faculty approved the proposal, and work began in early 2014 to launch the first issue. Student journals often have a staff to handle the production management and review process; however, *Line by Line* had to be run on a shoestring budget with an all-volunteer board and the WPA, who would oversee and coordinate the journal review and editorial production process. Consequently, the journal needed to develop on an efficient, streamlined scale that would be sustainable. With the constraints of the budget in mind and volunteer members' limited time available, the project unfolded in a number of key of steps: (1) develop an editorial board; (2) create the journal's main policies and procedures; (3) design the journal website; (4) determine the submission, review, and final selection process; and (5) advertise the journal and solicit student work.

The first step involved recruiting an editorial board, which would make the initial decisions on how the new journal would be structured and managed. It was important that the board included students as well as cross-disciplinary partners, specifically those from the university library. A call went out to the English department faculty and library instructional staff for interest in serving on the new editorial board, and the responses were numerous. The initial board included the following members:

1. university library instructional staff
2. tenured and tenure-line English faculty members
3. full-time, non-tenure-track English faculty members
4. graduate English students
5. undergraduate English students
6. the director of the university writing center
7. the WPA (serving as chair)

The board agreed that each member (other than the WPA and undergraduates) would serve for a two-year term. The WPA would serve for the duration of his or her appointment as WPA, and the undergraduate board members would serve a one- or two-year term, depending on their year in school. Over the first three years, interest in serving on the board remained high, and membership remained consistent with few exceptions. One non-tenure-track member stepped down after serving two years, but two others joined the board, as did an adjunct instructor. Several of the students graduated, but each year, new ones quickly took their places, and in year three, several student board member applicants had to be turned away. As *Line by Line* approached its third anniversary, the editorial board had fourteen members.

Initially, the board set out to define the basic policies regarding the journal, such as the schedule for soliciting and reviewing submissions, the types of writing that would be accepted, and how best to facilitate journal production. In addition, the board made decisions regarding how to advertise and market the site. During this initial period, the library was an invaluable partner providing expertise in formulating journal policies and explaining issues related to copyright and open-access publishing.

In addition, during a one-and-one-half-hour webinar training session with bepress consultants, the WPA and the library's director of information systems and digital access learned how to use the journal's administrative site tools to configure and manage the editorial workflow. Working together, the WPA and library staff customized some of the tools to simplify the process so it could be handled by fewer individuals and involve fewer steps. Because the platform would enable a variety of electronic submissions, it was agreed that a range of digital formats would be accepted in addition to traditional text-based essays (e.g., websites, videos, PowerPoint files, and Prezi links). During the months leading up to the first issue's publication, the WPA trained individual board members on the editorial management process, which was entirely handled via email. Being able to communicate in this manner has been extremely beneficial. Because the board is large, we have been able to get by with minimal in-person meetings. Virtually all editorial tasks, including review, selection, and copyediting, are handled online.

Once the fundamentals of the site operation were well in hand, the board wrote a template syllabus statement for English faculty to use to let students know about the journal (see appendix 15A). Likewise, to generate interest and excitement among faculty about the journal, the editorial board brainstormed a list of eight possible journal titles. They prepared a SurveyMonkey questionnaire for faculty, asking them to rate how they felt about each one. The winning entry became the title: *Line by Line: A Journal of Beginning Student Writing.*

From the beginning, it was agreed that, in addition to being a place to exhibit outstanding student writing, the journal should provide experiential learning opportunities for students on the editorial board as well as those enrolled in the English department's production, design, and web publishing courses. For example, student board members could assist with managing the production workflow and editorial process as part of project-based learning experiences. Students in upper-level professional and technical writing courses could be called upon for help with design and wording issues. One of the original graduate student board members, a double major in English and art and design, created a series of logo options, one of which was adopted for the journal.

Plans called for *Line by Line* to be published twice a year, once in the fall and once in the spring. Each issue included work from the prior semester's courses. The first issue was planned for midterm of the fall 2014 semester and would include work from spring 2014 composition courses. Any student enrolled in one of the composition courses could submit his or her work during a call for submissions period, which extended from approximately mid-semester through two weeks after the end of the semester. The board anticipated that we would publish about ten submissions in each issue, depending on the number of submissions received.

Considerable time was also spent discussing the extent of instructor involvement in the submission process (e.g., Should the instructor submit the student work, or should the student? Should instructors have to approve student submissions?). Initially, it was thought that instructors should submit their best students' work; however, the decision was made to put the submission process squarely on the shoulders of the students. This was done for two reasons. First, self-submission would replicate what happens when a scholar submits a paper to a journal, giving students the experience of submitting their own work to an academic publication. Secondly, board members were mindful that adding submission as a responsibility for instructors might reduce the likelihood of submissions and potentially undercut the success of the journal. Therefore, the board decided not to give instructors any responsibility for their students' submissions. Instructors could recommend that students submit their work, but the final decision rested with the students, who would be encouraged to polish their drafts before submission by asking instructors for suggestions, visiting the university writing center for peer assistance, or talking with reference librarians to improve their research.

Another difficult decision over which the board deliberated had to do with the manuscript selection process and the amount of editorial work that would be done. Because of the lack of staff and the limited time board members had available, we agreed not to include a revise and resubmit process as one might typically have with an academic journal. Each submission would be read by two board members who were faculty, library staff, or graduate student members. The main criterion for preliminary acceptance was whether, in the individual board member's opinion, the work merited an A-plus for the course in which it was written. If both board members agreed that the writing was outstanding, the submission was accepted and moved into a pool of semifinalists. If the first two readers' decisions did not match, an undergraduate board member would review the submission and determine whether it should be accepted for the semifinalist pool.

After all submissions were reviewed, the semifinalists' works were posted to a Google site. All board members then read the semifinalists' projects and, using a Google Form, gave each entry a score from 1 to 10 (10 was the highest level of achievement). Those with the highest tallies became finalists.

Once the finalists were selected, the student board members and other board member volunteers did minimal copyediting to correct typographical errors and obvious wording errors. After much deliberation, the board decided it would be best to let the student writing stand as written; that is, editors should not revise student writing to make it fit anyone's expectations for correctness. This was particularly important when board members discussed how to handle English language learners' submissions. It was agreed that a journal of outstanding *beginning* student writing—not necessarily error-free student writing—was what was being sought.

In addition, because learning the process of writing is a central focus of all the composition courses, the editorial board decided that along with their final projects, each student author would write a brief reflection, which would be published alongside his or her final project. In this reflection, students would explain their writing process, including how they approached the particular assignment and what steps they took to improve each draft. It was thought this information would be helpful for two reasons. First, it encouraged student authors to use higher-order metacognition to more deeply reflect on how they write. Likewise, current composition students visiting the site could get a better sense of what is involved in writing an exemplary text for their course.

The board members hoped that students would be drawn to the site and would want to submit their work to achieve recognition. However, we knew that an added incentive in the form of prize money might help build interest, and the English department agreed to fund awards for each issue. The top award, for the most outstanding writing in an issue, was named for a highly respected department lecturer who taught in the composition program for more than thirty years. This $200 award was presented to the writer whose work represented the highest standards of the course for which the project was written. Additionally, two $100 awards were presented in each issue for best writing in a particular genre (e.g., research, critique, literacy narrative, multimodal composition). It was agreed that the monetary awards might provide added motivation for students to submit their best work. Board members would select award winners for each issue, a decision that for the first six issues has been based on the semifinalists' ratings.

Outcomes and Measures

In the journal's first three years (six issues from August 2014 to May 2017), *Line by Line* published 25 percent of works submitted—47 out of 188 submissions. In that time, articles were downloaded just under 6,400 times (see figure 15.1). Readership has been worldwide, with 61 percent of downloads from the United States and the remaining 39 percent coming from 100 other countries. A significant majority of downloads (85 percent) came from educational institutions—representing almost 600 of the 836 download sites worldwide. The remaining 15 percent of readers came from corporations, libraries, nonprofit organizations, government agencies, and military installations. One article, Grant A. Johnson's "The Gender Pay Gap; Continually Hurting Women," published in the first issue, had been downloaded more than 1,100 times by May 2017;[18] it is among the 20 most-downloaded items in the university's repository, which includes more than 25,000 items.

FIGURE 15.1
Line by Line readership downloads.

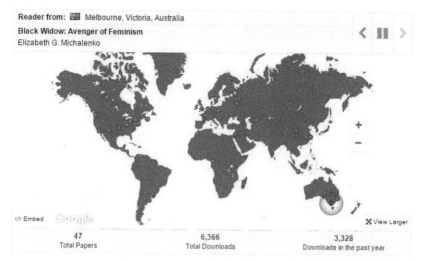

Benefits of a Student Composition
========

Benefits of a Student Composition Journal

Publishing an undergraduate composition journal has brought about all of the benefits its creators expected as well as some additional ones for students, faculty and staff, the library, and the university. For students, the following benefits have been the most significant:

- The journal provides an authentic audience and a purpose on which to focus. Writing with these key concepts in mind helps affirm what students are learning in their courses about rhetoric and the writing process. Students who prepare their assignments with the belief that their writing might be shared approach the task with a higher level of engagement and a renewed sense of agency.
- The journal provides college students with professional experience and credit for having their work published, which are assets for both résumés and graduate school applications. One student whose work received the award for best writing of the issue told us, "I've always considered myself more of a math and science person and never really thought of myself as a great writer. Winning this publication really challenged the narrative I have of myself and helped me to see myself and my academic career in a different light."

- Once an issue is published, student authors receive monthly reports from the repository, letting them know the number of times their work has been downloaded and from where those downloads originated. Of this process, one student author told us the monthly report "serves as a reminder, especially on rough days, that my hard work does mean something. It is also nice to know that my work is relevant." Thus, being selected for publication in the journal helps build for students a sense of membership in an academic community.
- Students experience the sense of accomplishment and pride that comes from having one's work acknowledged and published for public access. Students have told us the process of being selected instilled confidence and motivated them to continue improving their writing after their work was published. Said one student, "Having my writing published in *Line by Line* during my first semester of college gave me a boost of confidence in my writing abilities and an extra drive to push myself further in all of my writing assignments."
- For undergraduate and graduate students serving on the editorial board, the site provides professional training and experience in publication management and editing, all important additions to résumés and graduate school applications.

Teaching faculty and the campus administration have also benefited from the journal's presence, as it provides an opportunity to showcase departmental work, highlight cross-campus collaboration, and serve as a pedagogical tool.

- The English department is able to showcase the exceptional work being produced in composition courses. The value of this extends beyond the English department to other university faculty, administrators, parents, alumni, and students. The journal provides evidence of quality in beginning composition courses to prospective students and English majors and minors. Likewise, the publication helps make visible to a variety of stakeholders how writing in these courses helps support the scholarship outcomes in the university's Common Academic Program. As one English professor told us, "By engaging beginning students in the research process—which includes publication—we signal our ongoing commitment to research at all levels of the curriculum."
- With several volumes archived in the repository, the journal provides models of excellent writing for instructors to use in their courses. For example, students can analyze and critique select student essays as well as use them as examples of ways to approach specific assignment genres. As one faculty member notes, "In some ways, my pedagogy depends on helping students understand what

certain rhetorical genres are and do, the purpose of writing them, and how to adapt writing to different audiences and circumstances. So, I am constantly reinforcing rhetorical situations of assignments with students, and [*Line by Line*] essays provide models of how to write within certain rhetorical situations."

- The department chair noted, "The presence of [*Line by Line*] in the library collection signals our commitment to dissemination of knowledge." Thus, the journal symbolizes and validates the importance the English department and library place on information literacy and writing as a process that has value and should be shared and preserved.

- Likewise, the quality of the editorial work in *Line by Line* reinforces the impact of interdisciplinary collaboration among the library, the writing center, and the English department.

In hosting *Line by Line* in the institutional repository, the library has reinforced its role as a supportive partner in advancing student learning, supporting scholarship, and delivering on the educational mission of the university. The journal's success has brought attention to the repository from faculty, who then see it as a strong mechanism for promoting their own scholarly work. Other benefits the library has noted:

- As members of the editorial board, librarians have the opportunity to see the end product of a process in which they take part. The instruction team routinely provides research support and library instruction to the English department's writing program and across the university; however, the librarians rarely see the final product. Reviewing manuscripts not only allows librarians to understand how beginning student writers employ research skills, but also helps inform future library instruction for the writing program. It is also worth noting that in this case, serving on the editorial board is considered service and outreach to the campus community, which is a job requirement for many librarians.

- The repository platform provides a permanent, stable, discoverable home for undergraduate student scholarship, the content of which provides cultural context—a historical record of what students valued and were thinking and writing about at the time it was published.

- Library staff use *Line by Line* in live demonstrations of the repository to illustrate the platform's versatility in organizing and sharing research.

- Readership metrics for *Line by Line* illustrate that the repository, which is indexed in Google and Google Scholar, is a reliable and effective medium for scholarly communication. The readership and discoverability have prompted other departments and scholars to start journals as well. Since *Line by Line* began publishing, the library has helped to launch a new peer-reviewed education journal and acquired backfiles and publishing rights for a reputable communication journal, both of which have recorded strong readership and submissions in their initial issues on the platform.

The establishment of *Line by Line*, especially so early on in the development of the university's institutional repository, has been very positive for the journal's stakeholders. Just as important, the university benefits as well. The works in *Line by Line* are evidence that University of Dayton students are well prepared to write as scholars and professionals.

Challenges of a Student Composition Journal

Developing and publishing *Line by Line* presented a variety of challenges, some of which were anticipated, others not. Worth noting for those looking to replicate a journal such as this, however, is that the challenges faced have been primarily logistical and those related to faculty and board member engagement. There have been few technical or system-related challenges to overcome.

When submissions open for each issue, the WPA sends a Call for Submissions flyer to faculty via email, asking them to forward it to their higher performing students. Likewise, instructors are encouraged to staple the flyer to papers receiving A-plus grades. What began as a positive trend in the number of submissions changed with the sixth issue. As shown in table 15.1, submissions increased from thirteen for the fall 2014 issue to forty-six for the fall 2016 issue. However, submissions fell sharply in the spring of 2017. This might be an indication that faculty are beginning to decrease their diligence in encouraging submissions.

TABLE 15.1
Submissions by Issue

Issue	No. of Submissions	No. of Submissions Published
Fall 2014	13	7
Spring 2015	25	10
Fall 2015	18	7
Spring 2016	35	9
Fall 2016	46	7
Spring 2017	26	7

In addition, although thirty-one out of approximately forty composition instructors have had their students submit work to the first six issues, most of the submissions have come from eight instructors' courses. Consequently, sustaining faculty engagement and excitement about the journal has been a challenge. It is hoped that as the journal continues to become familiar on campus, to students, and in the broader community, faculty buy-in will improve.

The distribution of student contributions has been an area of concern. As shown in table 15.2, the bulk of student submissions—77 percent—come from our three first-year courses. The remainder—23 percent—come from ENG 200, the second-year course in the two-year sequence. It is interesting to note that the largest percentage of contributions come from ENG 200H, which supports higher-performing first-year students. Although submissions from this course make up the highest percentage of submissions, far fewer sections of ENG 200H are offered than the other courses, so these contributions are disproportionately represented. This likely speaks to higher-performing students' confidence in their skills as beginning writers, but it might also reinforce the need to encourage student writers from all of the program's courses to submit their work.

TABLE 15.2
Submissions by Course in the First Six Issues

COURSE	No. of Submissions	Percentage of Total	No. of Submissions Published
ASI 110/120 (first-year CORE course)	11	7%	5
ENG 100 (first year)	49	30%	16
ENG 200H (first year)	66	40%	23
ENG 200 (second year)	37	23%	3
TOTAL submissions	163	100%	47

Another challenge has been to keep on top of the busy editorial schedule. Because the journal is published around midterm each semester, the work of reviewing submissions happens more or less continuously. In other words, in the summer, the board reviews submissions from the spring semester for publication the next fall, and in the break between semesters during the holidays, the board reviews work from the previous fall for publication in the spring. This, combined with the copyediting and issue preparation steps, takes up significant time. To complicate matters, most of the faculty board members are off contract during the summer, and student board members are working, on vacation, or studying abroad. Considering everyone is volunteering for this work, it has been a struggle to meet deadlines.

In addition, as noted earlier, the board decided it was best to avoid correcting students' writing during the copyediting phase of production. Nevertheless, when reviewing each submission, board members needed to make a judgment call regarding how many writing errors could be overlooked to still merit "A-plus work" for the course (the only qualification for selection as a semifinalist). Might board members have differing views of what constitutes A-plus work? Consequently, one of the most unexpected complications arose when it became clear that the undergraduate student board members, who review a submission only if the first two readers disagree, were making a good portion of the decisions on the semifinalists. Figure 15.2 illustrates the number of submissions received for each issue and how many of those submissions went to an undergraduate reader for the tiebreaker.

What this indicates is that faculty, library staff, and graduate students have disagreed a large percentage of the time on what constitutes an A-plus paper for a particular course. In fact, as shown in table 15.3, in five out of the first six issues, more than 40 percent of submissions were decided by a third reader, and in the spring 2015 issue, more than half were. Writing studies scholars have noted for many years the discrepancy that can exist in writing assessment; clearly, this is an issue the board should research if this trend continues.

FIGURE 15.2

Third-reviewer semifinalist decisions by issue

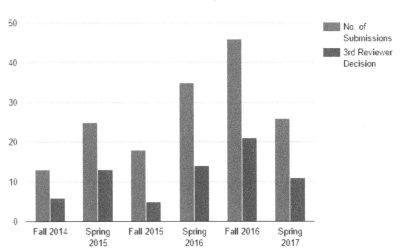

TABLE 15.3
Semifinalists Decided by Undergraduate Third Reviewer

Issue	No. of Submissions	Decision by 3rd Reviewer	Percentage Decided by 3rd Reviewer	No. of Submissions Published
Fall 2014	13	6	46%	7
Spring 2015	25	13	52%	10
Fall 2015	18	5	28%	7
Spring 2016	35	14	40%	9
Fall 2016	46	21	46%	7
Spring 2017	26	11	42%	7

Potential of Library Archives and Institutional Repositories

At UD, each time a new issue of *Line by Line* is announced, it provides an opportunity for faculty to consider archiving for themselves and their own students. For example, a collection called the Dunbar Music Archive (https://ecommons.udayton.edu/dunbar/) features a music faculty member's curated collection of musical settings for texts by the famous Dayton poet Paul Laurence Dunbar; the collection also contains spoken-word performances of Dunbar's poetry by a poet and English faculty member. In addition, a collection called the Writers' Room (https://ecommons.udayton.edu/writersroom/, launched in 2017, is an archive of an audio drama podcast series written, performed, and recorded by undergraduates in an upper-level English course. As publications and collections such as *Line by Line* and others bring more readership to repositories, libraries can expect to field more inquiries about conventional and unconventional ways to archive undergraduate work.

Line by Line and other library-supported open-access publishing endeavors also have opened the door to important conversations with undergraduates—some of whom will pursue academic careers—about copyright, authors' rights, information literacy, and scholarly communication. As Riehle and Hensley write:

> Publishing student work in open access institutional repositories, for example, can be an excellent opportunity for students, but dialogue about the process and implications is important.... Their lack of understanding about [authors'

rights, copyright, discoverability, and scholarly communication] leads one to ask: If they do not learn about these topics and issues as undergraduate students, when will they do so?[19]

Conclusion

Publications such as *Line by Line* position the library as a publisher, a role that more academic libraries are embracing.[20] The University of Dayton Libraries' open-access publishing platform includes journals, conference proceedings, undergraduate honors theses, faculty publications, and more, discoverable to scholars and researchers primarily through its indexing in Google and Google Scholar. This library-as-publisher model provides an opportunity for beginning student writers to model academic writing for publication; in doing so, libraries can amplify new voices and draw attention to novice writers. *Line by Line* and other undergraduate journals reaffirm the concept of the library as a cultural center of the university, collecting and curating as well as publishing new works and ideas. While university presses historically have promoted faculty scholarship, the library-as-publisher approach includes space for a variety of campus constituents.

Various librarian and staff positions contribute to the success of *Line by Line* throughout the publishing process. At UD, this includes the scholarly communications manager, the director of information systems and digital access, and the coordinator of research and instruction. On other campuses, a journal of beginning student writing might also involve metadata librarians, first-year librarians, marketing staff, and other positions that connect first- and second-year writers with library publishing.

Much of the work for *Line by Line*, as a journal of beginning student writing, is done by students, staff, and faculty associated with the English department: instructors who teach in the first- and second-year writing program encourage students to submit their work; students in their courses submit manuscripts; the department's WPA is the journal's lead editor; and department-affiliated students, faculty, and staff make up the lion's share of the editorial board. However, librarians also play an active role, not only as editorial board members and reviewers during the submission process, but also as instruction librarians, providing research support to all students in the writing program, regardless of whether they submit their work to *Line by Line*.

With *Line by Line* and other library-supported publishing opportunities, undergraduates can receive significant practical experience in, for example, academic writing for an authentic audience, research methods, peer review, and the journal submission process. They also can receive the satisfaction of knowing others are reading their work. *Line by Line* has shown that these experiences early in an undergraduate career can help students build confidence in their writing as they add publications to their résumés. Some may even come to view writing as a career option. As one student wrote, "After having my writing published, I reevaluated my academic path. I am a business major; however, I have always enjoyed English and am an avid reader. I definitely reconsidered my major and thought about English as an academic path and as a future career."

Although Walkington has noted, "The impact of undergraduate research journals on student learning has not been systematically evaluated,"[21] *Line by Line* and other undergraduate journals anecdotally demonstrate their value in providing experiences that support the cultivation of a new generation of scholars well prepared to create, share, and advance knowledge. As one UD faculty member put it, "Besides serving as an incentive to do good work and as a reward for having done good work, *Line by Line* encourages students to think about the possibility of being published in the future." For many a writer, that is its own reward.

Appendix 15A. The *Line by Line* Syllabus Boilerplate Statement

Publish Your Writing in *Line by Line*

Published each fall and spring semester, *Line by Line: A Journal of Beginning Student Writing* showcases outstanding student work from ENG 100, 200, 200H, ASI 110, and ASI 120. Any writing or digital project created for an assignment in this course is eligible for publication in the journal's next issue. Awards are given for the most outstanding student writing in each issue. Work selected for publication will demonstrate clear writing, critical thinking, and, if applicable, creative presentation. Please talk to me if you are interested in submitting your work in this course for publication. To learn more about *Line by Line*, visit http://ecommons.udayton.edu/lxl.

Notes

1. Sharon A. Barrios and Lori M. Weber, "Beyond the Audience of One: Producing a Student Journal of Politics," *PS: Political Science and Politics* 39, no. 1 (2006): 107, https://doi.org/10.1017/S1049096506060227; Dorothy Ní Uigín, Noelle Higgins, and Belinda McHale, "The Benefits of Student-Led, Peer-Reviewed Journals in Enhancing Students' Engagement with the Academy," *Research in Education* 93, no. 1 (May 2015): 62–63, https://doi.org/10.7227/RIE.0010; Dawn Putnam, "Authentic Writing Using Online Resources: Selling Our Words in the Community," *English Journal* 90, no. 5 (May 2001): 102–6, http://www.jstor.org/stable/821862.

2. Eleta Exline, "Extending the Institutional Repository to Include Undergraduate Research," *College and Undergraduate Libraries* 23, no. 1 (2016): 18–19, https://doi.org/10.1080/10691316.2014.950782.

3. Exline, "Extending the Institutional Repository," 25–26.

4. Association of College and Research Libraries Working Group on Intersections of Scholarly Communication and Information Literacy, *Intersections of Scholarly Communication and Information Literacy* (Chicago: Association of College and Research Libraries, 2013): 6–10, http://acrl.ala.org/intersections.

5. Sharon A. Weiner and Charles Watkinson, "What Do Students Learn from Participation in an Undergraduate Research Journal? Results of an Assessment," *Journal of Librarianship and Scholarly Communication* 2, no. 2 (March 2014): 2–11, https://doi.org/10.7710/2162-3309.1125.

6. Putnam, "Authentic Writing," 102.

7. Barrios and Weber, "Beyond the Audience of One," 107.

8. William Rifkin et al., "Students Publishing in New Media: Eight Hypotheses—A House of Cards?" *International Journal of Innovation in Science and Mathematics Education* 18, no. 1 (2010): 43–54.

9. Barrios and Weber, "Beyond the Audience of One," 110.

10. David Bartholomae, "Inventing the University," *Journal of Basic Writing* 5, no. 1 (1986): 9.

11. Bartholomae, "Inventing the University," 5.

12. Kelly Ritter, "The Economics of Authorship: Online Paper Mills, Student Writers, and First-Year Composition," *College Composition and Communication* 56, no. 4 (2005): 610, http://www.jstor.org/stable/30037888.

13. Ní Uigín, Higgins, and McHale, "The Benefits of Student-Led, Peer-Reviewed Journals," 63.

14. Grant Wiggins, "EJ in Focus: Real-World Writing: Making Purpose and Audience Matter," *English Journal* 98, no. 5 (May 2009): 30–31, http://www.jstor.org/stable/40503292.

15. Robert M. Leekley, Stephanie Davis-Kahl, and Michael C. Seeborg, "Undergraduate Economics Journals: Learning by Doing," *Journal of College Teaching and Learning* 10, no. 2 (2013): 106.

16. Association of American Colleges and Universities, "High-Impact Educational Practices: A Brief Overview," excerpt from George D. Kuh, *High-Impact Educational Practices: What They Are, Who Has Access to Them, and Why They Matter*

(Washington, DC: Association of American Colleges and Universities, 2008), accessed May 25, 2017, https://www.aacu.org/leap/hips.

17. University of Dayton, "Common Academic Program Learning Outcomes," Undergraduate Catalog, 2016–17 Academic Year, accessed May 31, 2017, http://catalog.udayton.edu/undergraduate/cap/learningoutcomes/ (page discontinued).

18. Grant A. Johnson, "The Gender Pay Gap: Continually Hurting Women," *Line by Line: A Journal of Beginning Student Writing* 1, no. 1 (2014), article 7, http://ecommons.udayton.edu/lxl/vol1/iss1/7.

19. Catherine Fraser Riehle and Merinda Kaye Hensley, "What Do Undergraduate Students Know about Scholarly Communication? A Mixed Methods Study," *portal: Libraries and the Academy* 17, no. 1 (2017): 172, https://muse.jhu.edu/article/645357.

20. Charlene N. Simser, Marcia G. Stockham, and Elizabeth Turtle, "Libraries as Publishers: A Winning Combination," *OCLC Systems and Services: International Digital Library Perspectives* 31, no. 2 (2015): 69–75, https://doi.org/10.1108/OCLC-01-2014-0006.

21. Helen Walkington, "Developing Dialogic Learning Space: The Case of Online Undergraduate Research Journals," *Journal of Geography in Higher Education* 36, no. 4 (2012): 549, https://doi.org/10.1080/03098265.2012.692072.

Bibliography

Association of American Colleges and Universities. "High-Impact Educational Practices: A Brief Overview." Excerpt from *High-Impact Educational Practices: What They Are, Who Has Access to Them, and Why They Matter*, by George D. Kuh (AAC&U, 2008). Accessed May 25, 2017. https://www.aacu.org/leap/hips.

Association of College and Research Libraries Working Group on Intersections of Scholarly Communication and Information Literacy. *Intersections of Scholarly Communication and Information Literacy: Creating Strategic Collaborations for a Changing Academic Environment*. Chicago: Association of College and Research Libraries, 2013. http://acrl.ala.org/intersections.

Barrios, Sharon A., and Lori M. Weber. "Beyond the Audience of One: Producing a Student Journal of Politics." *PS: Political Science and Politics* 39, no. 1 (2006): 107–10. https://doi.org/10.1017/S1049096506060227.

Bartholomae, David. "Inventing the University." *Journal of Basic Writing* 5, no. 1 (1986): 4–23.

Exline, Eleta. "Extending the Institutional Repository to Include Undergraduate Research." *College and Undergraduate Libraries* 23, no. 1 (2016): 16–27. https://doi.org/10.1080/10691316.2014.950782.

Johnson, Grant A. "The Gender Pay Gap: Continually Hurting Women." *Line by Line: A Journal of Beginning Student Writing* 1, no. 1 (2014). http://ecommons.udayton.edu/lxl/vol1/iss1/7.

Leekley, Robert M., Stephanie Davis-Kahl, and Michael C. Seeborg. "Undergraduate Economics Journals: Learning by Doing." *Journal of College Teaching and Learning* 10, no. 2 (2013): 105–12.

Ní Uigín, Dorothy, Noelle Higgins, and Belinda McHale. "The Benefits of Student-Led, Peer-Reviewed Journals in Enhancing Students' Engagement with the

Academy." *Research in Education* 93, no. 1 (May 2015): 60–65. https://doi. org/10.7227/RIE.0010.

Putnam, Dawn. "Authentic Writing Using Online Resources: Selling Our Words in the Community." *English Journal* 90, no. 5 (May 2001): 102–6. http://www.jstor. org/stable/821862.

Riehle, Catherine Fraser, and Merinda Kaye Hensley. "What Do Undergraduate Students Know about Scholarly Communication? A Mixed Methods Study." *portal: Libraries and the Academy* 17, no. 1 (2017): 145–78. https://muse.jhu. edu/article/645357.

Rifkin, William, Nancy Longnecker, Joan Leach, Lloyd Davis, and Lindy Orthia. "Students Publishing in New Media: Eight Hypotheses—A House of Cards?" *International Journal of Innovation in Science and Mathematics Education* 18, no 1 (2010): 43–54.

Ritter, Kelly. "The Economics of Authorship: Online Paper Mills, Student Writers, and First-Year Composition." *College Composition and Communication* 56, no. 4 (2005): 601–31. https://www.jstor.org/stable/30037888.

Simser, Charlene N., Marcia G. Stockham, and Elizabeth Turtle. "Libraries as Publishers: A Winning Combination." *OCLC Systems and Services: International Digital Library Perspectives* 31, no. 2 (2015): 69–75, https://doi.org/10.1108/ OCLC-01-2014-0006.

University of Dayton. "Common Academic Program Learning Outcomes." Undergraduate Catalog, 2016–17 Academic Year. Accessed May 31, 2017. http://catalog. udayton.edu/undergraduate/cap/learningoutcomes/ (page discontinued).

University of Dayton Libraries Digital Collections/eCommons. *Line by Line: A Journal of Beginning Student Writing.* Accessed June 22, 2018. http://ecommons. udayton.edu/lxl/.

Walkington, Helen. "Developing Dialogic Learning Space: The Case of Online Undergraduate Research Journals." *Journal of Geography in Higher Education* 36, no. 4 (2012): 547–62. https://doi.org/10.1080/03098265.2012.692072.

Weiner, Sharon A., and Charles Watkinson. "What Do Students Learn from Participation in an Undergraduate Research Journal? Results of an Assessment." *Journal of Librarianship and Scholarly Communication* 2, no. 2 (March 2014): 1–31. https://doi.org/10.7710/2162-3309.1125.

Wiggins, Grant. "EJ in Focus: Real-World Writing: Making Purpose and Audience Matter." *English Journal* 98, no. 5 (May 2009): 29–37. http://www.jstor.org/ stable/40503292.

CHAPTER 16

Students as Content Creators

Empowering Students to See Themselves as Part of Institutional Scholarship

Jessica Clemons and Melissa Fierke

Introduction

"Who thinks it is a little weird to have a librarian on a remote field station with you?" About two-thirds of the class of sixty-five students in the State University of New York College of Environmental Science and Forestry summer field course at Cranberry Lake Biological Station raise their hands. Admittedly, it is a little out of the ordinary to take students on a boat christened *The Forester*, across a lake, to stay in rustic cabins for three weeks and integrate classroom learning with intensive field research. Teaching information literacy in the dining hall, while perhaps a little unorthodox, is a perfect example of the embedded librarian. There is no excuse for ignoring the literature for these students, but it is not just the appropriate incorporation of the literature into a research project, but the holistic approach to scholarship, from creation to dissemination, that is powerful and distinctive. Student work researched, created, and presented on the field station is now archived and disseminated through Digital Commons @ ESF, an institutional repository (IR) of the F. Franklin Moon Library for the State University of New York (SUNY) College of Environmental Science and Forestry (ESF).

223

The experience is very rich for the undergraduate students and utilizes high-impact practices to help students learn new skills and apply them directly and at a faster pace than in the traditional fifteen-week, three-credit course. Having instruction just in time, with a specific outcome, and receiving designated time to implement and utilize the information presented creates a robust learning experience and increases the quality of research completed on the station. Our approach is consistent with other literature where the librarian has a specific integration into a course.[1] Librarians have a uniquely broad perspective on campus, working across communities from students to faculty, and they have a deep understanding of the user groups they serve.[2] With this knowledge, librarians also contribute to high-impact practices through their work.

In *High-Impact Educational Practices*, George Kuh identifies ten practices designed to help undergraduate learning and retention.[3] Three of those practices, collaborative assignments and projects, undergraduate research, and capstone courses and projects, have clear connections with information literacy components and tend to create outputs that can be captured electronically. Presenting student work in the institutional repository lends the air of authority due to the application of institutional distinction and branding. It also celebrates the student as a scholar and brings high-impact practices, or rather the output from high-impact practices, into the spotlight.

Librarians can play a critical role in high-impact practices through embedded librarianship. Embedded librarianship comes from the concept of embedded journalism, where proximity, and timing are important. Embedded librarians typically have extensive subject expertise and have regular, deep communications with the students, faculty, and staff within the departments.[4] The traditional role of the liaison librarian is certainly at the heart of the Cranberry Lake Field Station examples.

In recent scholarly conversations, some librarians and information professionals contend that institutional repositories have been used as a digital version of the archaic stacks, minus the dust, and have not lived up to their expectations of really effecting change in the scholarly publishing life cycle.[5] Items are placed neatly in the collection and either used or not used, just as in print collections. IRs have failed to be the transformative publishing alternatives originally intended. But in a different light, if IRs are not used as alternative publishing options, but more straightforwardly as platforms to elevate the visibility of the institution, then there are real ways to integrate the service of an IR throughout the mission of the institution.

This chapter focuses on a fully embedded information literacy session as a core part of a required course. It is important to recognize that not many schools have this intensive summer experience. We highlight the role the library plays to celebrate students as content creators and students as scholars, particularly undergraduate students. Work from these individuals, as well as other student-produced work in our institutional repository, demonstrates the breadth and depth of the ESF curriculum and celebrates the work of our early scholars.

Growing the F. Franklin Moon Library Institutional Repository: Digital Commons @ ESF

Conversations about implementing a robust IR began in early 2013 with an emphasis on faculty work. As these exchanges grew deeper and were more meaningful, it was clear that faculty work was not the only contribution that would be included in the planned service. There was also great interest in nonjournal article content, and discussions about the flexibility and adaptability of this new service began to grow. The repository collections were set up to group as many items together as possible, including a broad collection of faculty scholarship and a general collection for student scholarship. More specialized collections were developed as needed. As noted by Hertenstein, a variety of student-created content, from formal works, such as electronic theses and dissertations (ETDs), to informal works, such as class projects, are already present in IRs and deserve consideration for inclusion in any campus IR.[6] Furthermore, Hertenstein states that faculty support and student willingness to contribute content are critical for successful implementation of these types of collections—the statement "if you build it, they will come" is false when it comes to IR implementation.

There are several undergraduate student collections in F. Franklin Moon Library's Digital Commons @ ESF. Each of these collections has a different model of creation, population, metadata entry, and content type. Students' intellectual property is respected in these collections, as it should be in all types of electronic distribution of works. Items in the repository follow the Digital Commons @ ESF Guidelines and Policies.[7] As with faculty research and other authored pieces, if any student has an issue with sharing his or her item or content, we remove it from the collection. This is part of the institution's policies and guidelines and is standard in IRs and across open-access policies. These collections came into existence because of a persistent enthusiasm for encouraging opportunities for librarians and the services we offer to partner with faculty in highlighting scholarship with a broad range of value. Additionally, recruiting these types of collections is an example of the entrepreneurial spirit required of an embedded librarian in a research context.[8] There are more formal types of student work collections, such as undergraduate journals, and their contributions are being reviewed in relation to student learning and faculty collaboration.[9] Other collections may have similar connections and therefore have additional value outside of the end products that are deposited.

A Case Study: Cranberry Lake Biological Station
Going Far beyond "Just" Populating the IR

The main campus of ESF sits on twelve acres in Syracuse, New York, and has an additional 25,000 acres of regional campuses and research forests throughout Central New York and the Adirondack State Park. The ESF student body consists of approximately 1,650 undergraduate students and 600 graduate students, many of whom reside on the Syracuse campus. Environmental and Forest Biology (EFB) is the largest department on campus and hosts seven undergraduate majors: aquatic and fisheries science, biotechnology, conservation biology, environmental biology, environmental education and interpretation, forest health, and wildlife science. In the mid-1990s, key faculty developed a field-work-intensive required course, Ecological Monitoring and Biodiversity Assessment (EFB 202), at Cranberry Lake Biological Station (CLBS) to incorporate real-world problem solving as part of a required field course, rather than artificial problem solving in the laboratory.[10]

This course was developed before internet availability at the station, and the availability of print library materials on the station was extremely limited. Shortly after, in 2012, a new librarian was added to the library faculty as the library liaison to EFB, and she was invited to teach information literacy at CLBS. Faculty in the program felt students were not appropriately carrying out literature reviews and thus were not incorporating peer-reviewed research and ecological theory in their final projects. Working closely with the faculty, we developed an information literacy component as part of the class that served to elevate the undergraduate research performed on site.

The first summer was an experience of deep transition in the F. Franklin Moon Library, as we were building a new digital library. Initially, library resources could not be accessed digitally due to lack of resources and poor bandwidth; access to peer-reviewed literature was extremely limited. The next summer, in 2013, students took a boat to another satellite campus, the Ranger School, to access digital resources, which resulted in improved access and stronger projects. During year three, a robust internet system was installed at CLBS that could handle basic types of computing required for literature reviews, citation management, and presentation development.

Students who enroll in this immersive course live at CLBS for three weeks. During the first two weeks of the course, students study a wide variety of taxonomic groups of organisms (e.g., aquatics, entomology, mycology), and faculty introduce them to a broad range of field, laboratory, and analytical methods (e.g., orienteering, sampling techniques, statistics). Students then complete a group research project during the third and final week of the course. Research projects require proficiency in field sampling methods, basic experimental design, and statistical analysis and the ability to cooperatively troubleshoot and solve problems with a grounding in the literature. The course culminates in a daylong research symposium during which groups present their findings to their peers and a panel of judges. Final projects are uploaded to the IR. As the keystone course in EFB curriculum, EFB 202 is a core experience of students as content creators and represents complete integration of information literacy throughout the research process, from observations, to hypothesis and methods development, data analysis and creation, and dissemination of a polished presentation as the culminating product of the group research project.

Teaching the Students/Course Development/ Pedagogy

Initially, the information literacy component of the course was built around the *Information Literacy Competency Standards for Higher Education,* which is suitable for the types of information-seeking needs and behaviors of the students.[11] In the first iteration of the component, this was realistically all we could focus on: identifying needs, accessing information, evaluating sources, and accomplishing a specific stated goal. The fifth standard, understanding the ethical and economic factors surrounding information, was not within the scope of the curriculum, nor could it be incorporated effectively in the half-day session. The learning outcomes for the course were built simplistically around these concepts of helping students find articles to inform their hypotheses and methods development. There was, at that time, no existing service to incorporate past projects into the teaching, learning, and research at the station.

The *Framework for Information Literacy for Higher Education,* adopted in 2016, is consistent with the final and most recent iteration of this course, clearly articulating the value of student work.[12] The course culminates in a final group project. The assignment is straightforward and integrates two weeks of field-based experiences into a student-designed, intensive group research experience. Two high-impact practices identified by Kuh, collaborative assignments and projects and undergraduate research, are woven through the core experience.[13] Adapting the course to the *Framework* helped to create the story arc of the information sessions—that is, to tie all the pieces together. What seems to be most compelling here is not the educational theory, but that students start to see themselves as beginning scholars. They move through the research process at an accelerated pace and at a different scale than scientists who produced the formal journal articles they read, but the students are present in similar spaces and on similar journeys in that they make observations, read the literature, generate hypotheses, and then carry out field sampling and data analysis to understand what their research means in the larger context of the science that underpins their topic. Adding the last component of publishing their findings brings them even further into the sphere of science, as their findings are published in a way that others can access and build upon.

Each student group of three to five students produces the same product: a formal abstract and a twenty-minute presentation that they deliver on the last day of class. Four judges are present and evaluate the group presentations. Two judges focus on scientific merit, one evaluates the overall group presentation, and the fourth judge focuses on individual style and presence. Because there is limited time for review of the student presentations, and to highlight exemplary research projects, the judges and the EFB 202 course coordinator select exemplars for first, second, and third place for the presentations. The winners receive the William Shields Award. Typically, there are fifteen to twenty presentations as part of the research symposium, and all abstracts as well as the presentations of the Shields awardees are added to the IR with appropriate metadata. The Shields Award, created in honor of an active emeritus faculty member who played a strong role in the department for decades, celebrates outstanding student research.

Establishing the connection of students as creators of scholarship, rather than just consumers of information, is the final cog in the scholarly communication cycle for this course. The final presentations, or at least the presentations that receive honors, are lightly reviewed by the graduate teaching assistant and converted from PowerPoint to PDFs so they are more compatible and accessible for the future users. A few simple stylistic elements are added to the symposium proceedings, including a group photograph if possible, and then everything is published through our IR as an effective way to capture the breadth of ideas and topics, which can be used as a teaching tool in the following sections of the class and in subsequent years.

The practice of using previous students' work to share with the next year's cohort not only helps students understand the expectations of the course, but also helps accelerate research project development. This is not a new practice in this course, as faculty members who taught at the station previously used to save presentations in a very informal, ad hoc way. This new development, of formally including student content in the IR, reduces the burden on the course coordinator and other faculty on the station and extends well beyond the summer classroom. During the first-year seminar for all EFB students in the fall semester, the librarian shares these student collections as part of the library welcome to help new students get excited and understand what their future academic career at ESF will look like.

Information Literacy Teaching and Learning Theory

Teaching the information literacy component of the CLBS experience is very iterative and based on progressive teaching and learning theory. The foundation of the teaching experience is very closely aligned with Char Booth's excellent work, *Reflective Teaching, Effective Learning*.[14] Booth uses her understanding of instructional design to outline the USER method: Understand, Structure, Engage, and Reflect, which is a deliberate design method to help instructors be more aware of their teaching and develop specific objectives throughout the learning process. To understand, the first phase, it is critical to identify the problems learners need to overcome and ask how, as an instructor, we can help them with that task. It is at this point during the information literacy session where we go through the assignment together to develop a clear understanding of the task the learners are preparing to undertake. We ask and answer these questions: Do students have a clear understanding of what they have been asked to do? Where does information literacy apply in the many pieces of the research project? These questions should be answered very early in the process, and the instructor must develop steps to accomplish this goal.

The instructor organizes sessions around the objectives and creates clear outcomes during the structure part of the process. This just-in-time instruction is beneficial for students as it identifies specific targets, even if they are somewhat arbitrary. The teaching faculty, librarian, and judges expect students to cite several appropriate scholarly items. Students are encouraged to find and save ten journal articles, in addition to *scholarly* internet resources, which tend to be state government environmental resources, or highly credible documents that do not follow the journal article peer-review process. This figure is somewhat arbitrary, but we have discovered that giving students a specific goal for what they need to collect helps to keep them on task and engaged. They may not cite all articles and resources in their projects, but as they work through statistics and gather data, they may need to shift from their initial thinking about what is important to their topic or system. It is helpful for students to have access to a breadth of scientific articles so they can think broadly when it comes to comparable research done on similar topics. Students have the final project looming, and they are regularly reminded that group work time is to help them cultivate interpersonal skills, develop a more informed hypothesis, learn how to communicate in a scholarly way, and learn how to deliver an effective presentation.

To engage is to develop the discrete teaching materials and deliver instruction to the students. Throughout this information literacy session, students are regularly reminded of the final presentation they will develop and deliver in just seven days. It is essential they know this is a critical step to developing an effective research agenda and final project, and thus plan accordingly. Students observe the components of a scientific journal article (the introduction, methods, results, and discussion), which helps them differentiate journal articles from other database content and prepare them for the steps in the scientific discussion that their final presentation must follow. Students see themselves as content creators especially when they are reminded of elements of a good presentation (logical flow, inline citations, inclusion of statistical values, readable text, etc.). Instructors use every opportunity to model good presentation style and delivery and remind them to think about the information literacy presentation: What did they find effective and engaging, and where did it fall short? The information literacy instruction provides examples of how to cite the references embedded within the presentation. Many students have asked about references and find them awkward or difficult to incorporate into the verbal presentation pieces. Imagery as a storytelling tool is emphasized as an especially compelling way to deliver ideas. Students are reminded to take pictures during their field work, and the instructor demonstrates searches for online images, as well as proper citations for images. Photography is encouraged, specifically images of field sites and the students in action (smartphone technology has made this process easy and ubiquitous), and the instructors recommend that the students include these images in their presentations. Students need to cite themselves appropriately, which provides a connection between the research they create and the larger community. Because citation is such a critical part of the pedagogy, a citation manager is taught in about ten minutes for those students who are ambitious enough to try using it.

The four-hour instruction period is structured in a series of short lectures, question-and-answer sessions, and group work with individual consultations. The students have clear goals in mind and are expected to leave with seven to ten references that they characterize as highly relevant, with the expectation that they will incorporate most of the resources they use in their presentation, the minimum being five references. The difference in numbers of citations that students find versus what they cite helps to drive a conversation about the research process. What they read and learn may help them decide to adjust their hypothesis or their methodology. As a result, some references may cease to be useful or relevant and do not truly contribute to the final product. Given the compressed nature of the experience, we urge students to err on the side of caution and gather as many relevant citations as they can find and then move forward in the research process. This admittedly arbitrary expectation about the number of citations is more direct that the typical answer, which tends to be "as many as it takes." The small goal-setting expectation encourages students to leave the session with new or refreshed skills, which serve them for the rest of their time at CLBS and at ESF.

In 2016, there were formal student presentations to use as exemplars for the first time. In previous years, individual faculty may have had student examples to share to give a general idea of what a final project might look like. Providing previous students' research and presentations for new students, presented formally through the IR, helps students move more quickly past the ideation phase of their presentation so that they can more quickly adapt or disregard other processes. Using these examples demonstrates effective executions and real examples of the applications of the information literacy session from students in prior years.

The fourth phase is reflection, where the evidence of learning is assessed, and students prepare for the next opportunity by revising or reusing the content in future courses. Because the information literacy experience is so directly related and integrated into the curriculum, reflection is key to its sustained success and directly implemented in subsequent sections and the next year. Assessment of the information literacy component of the program has been essential for the iteration of the instruction. Specific feedback from students is gathered to improve the experience from session to session and year to year via a simple analog handout, completed at the end of each session by all students. Students understand the feedback will be used specifically to address future iterations of the session. Every cohort of students is different, and there will typically be conflicting preferences. Looking for general trends in student comments and feedback helped the instructors avoid spending too much time on topics that are well understood and allowed for more focused time on areas of weakness. This type of informal feedback is mentioned at the beginning of classes, where students hear about the various iterations of the course, and why, based on previous students' feedback, certain pieces are included or excluded and how topics that are more specifically relevant to the task at hand are included. At the end of the class, students are encouraged to provide similar feedback. The questions are as follows:

Library skills evaluation

1. What is the most useful thing you learned about during this presentation?
2. Was any information not helpful? If so, why not?
3. Are you now more likely to consult library resources for your research? Any other relevant comments?

4. On a scale of 1 (not helpful) to 5 (very helpful) how would you rate the library session as part of your Cranberry Lake experience?

5. On a scale of 1 (not comfortable) to 5 (very comfortable) how comfortable do you feel searching for information on your topic?

6. On a scale of 1 (not comfortable) to 5 (very comfortable) how comfortable do you feel integrating sources into your paper?

7. Anything else you would like to share?

Because students enrolled in the program at different class years, from the end of their freshman year to super seniors (EFB 202 being the last class they need to graduate), their varying skill levels are acknowledged and appreciated. It is highly unusual for students to be disengaged because they need to fully utilize their time to stay on track with their research project over the next six days. There is no formal assessment of student learning outcomes in relation to the information literacy component yet. However, faculty facilitating group projects and the judges have noted a higher quality and an increased expectation with the students' projects since integrating the information literacy component. For now, that is enough for us to continue the program and the relationship, including the IR collection.

Most students who take the course return to the main campus for the fall, and anecdotally, spending time with students as the library liaison in summer brings about more contact and a willingness for students to initiate fruitful conversations to aid them in other courses. During the first-year seminar (for freshmen and new transfers), there is a library introduction component during the first few weeks of the semester, and being a part of the Cranberry Lake field experience has become a highlight that helps librarians to engage students in their curriculum while helping them understand what a modern academic library can offer.

Future Steps

Part of the success of the Cranberry Lake IR project, and the other undergraduate collections, is that the repository is discussed and woven throughout the process. Students and faculty see full participation in the IR as a requirement for their class and field work. It is treated essentially as a teaching and learning tool for undergraduate students to see themselves as emerging full members of the scholarly community as they finish their degrees at ESF.

Implementing and executing the IR, from the experience at ESF, is consistent with much of the literature on IRs. Simply building an IR will not be enough magic to make items appear. What we view as the success of ESF's library as an archive project for student work is that there is a real, high-profile connection from consumer to producer. It closes the scholarly communication loop for our students so they experience all of the pieces in a compressed time frame. It also uses the IR as a platform to celebrate the student scholar. Finally, it generates support and use of our IR, Digital Commons @ ESF, with dynamic content not found anywhere else.

There have been many ongoing conversations with a variety of faculty across departments at ESF to include student work in the IR. From simple class projects that connect the curriculum to the public (information brochures, for example) to central capstone research projects, the common vein is a fear of exposure. Exposing work that is potentially subpar is a hurdle that can prevent collections from going online. Typically, there is little context associated with the end products, including learning outcomes, expectations, skills that were utilized, and student reflections. As these conversations develop, partners should expect to have rich conversations about levels of permission for different collections, specific embargo dates, and desired shared outcomes for meaningful contributions to the IR.

What is especially meaningful about using the IR to host student work is that it unveils work that is too often hidden in the classroom, whatever and wherever that may be. Placing items in the IR gives the credibility of institutional branding, which helps to begin the creation of a professional identity for our emerging scholars, according to some faculty.[15] While the Cranberry Lake experience is likely to continue long into the future as it is core to the curriculum, several of the other collections may also continue to grow while others stagnate. Even those collections that are small and static remain as testaments to the students, the curriculum, and the education from the institution.

Strong interpersonal relationships were a cornerstone to the successful startup information literacy program at the field station and correlating collection of student work in our institutional repository. In addition to acting as the liaison to the department of environmental forest and biology, the librarian also served as the institutional repository manager. In most institutions, especially most large institutions, it will be unlikely that the subject specialist would serve the additional duty of IR manager. In those instances, it will be critically important to have strong relationships between library employees to ensure that the collection has the support it needs to launch and be successful.

ESF's institutional repository is fully indexed in our discovery service and is discoverable via major internet search engines. In contrast to having no collections or being "housed" on the college website, these full-text items are readily findable and accessible. Digital Commons has the functionality to be search-engine-optimized, which helps to surface the collections more effectively, but that feature has not been implemented in any collection at the time of this writing because it was not part of the initial rollout of the service. That feature may be phased in later. As the collections develop and mature, annual reports will become more meaningful in terms of assessing the impact and metrics. We can use this information to share with departments across campus, inform library practices as they relate to IR management, and help our students share their excellent work.

Acknowledgements

The authors wish to thank Dr. Gregory McGee, who initiated the partnership between the library and Cranberry Lake Biological Station, and Dr. Donald Leopold, who supported the idea and creation of the Shields Award for outstanding research projects.

Notes

1. Henry M. Walker and Kevin R. Engel, "Research Exercises: A Sequenced Approach to Just-in-Time Information Literacy Instruction," *Research Strategies* 19, no. 2 (2003): 135–47, https://doi.org/10.1016/j.resstr.2004.03.003.

2. Barbara I. Dewey, "The Embedded Librarian," *Resource Sharing and Information Networks* 17, no. 1–2 (2004): 5–17, https://doi.org/10.1300/J121v17n01_02.

3. George D. Kuh, *High-Impact Educational Practices* (Washington, DC: Association of American Colleges and Universities, 2008).

4. Kathy Drewes and Nadine Hoffman, "Academic Embedded Librarianship: An Introduction," *Public Services Quarterly* 116 no. 2–3 (2010): 75–82, https://doi.org/10.1080/15228959.2010.498773.

5. Clifford Lynch, "Institutional Repository Strategies: What We Learned at the Executive Roundtables," audio recording, 52:41, CNI: Coalition for Networked Information, March 29, 2017, https://www.cni.org/topics/repositories/institutional-repository-strategies-what-we-learned-at-the-executive-roundtables.

6. Elizabeth Hertenstein, "Student Scholarship in Institutional Repositories," *Journal of Librarianship and Scholarly Communication* 2, no. 3 (2014), http://doi.org/10.7710/2162-3309.1135.

7. SUNY College of Environmental Science and Forestry, "Digital Commons @ ESF Guidelines and Policies," accessed May 15, 2017. http://digitalcommons.esf.edu/policiesandguidelines.html.

8. Jake Carlson and Ruth Kneale, "Embedded Librarianship in the Research Context: Navigating New Waters," *College and Research Libraries News* 72, no. 3: (2011). 167–70.

9. Mack Mariani et al., "Promoting Student Learning and Scholarship through Un-

dergraduate Research Journals," *PS: Political Science and Politics* 46, no. 4 (2013): 830–35, https://doi.org/10.1017/S1049096513001133; Char Miller, "Riding the Wave: Open Access, Digital Publishing, and the Undergraduate Thesis" (keynote address, United States Electronic Thesis and Dissertation Association [USETDA] 2013 Conference, Claremont, CA, July 24–26, 2013), http://scholarship.claremont.edu/pomona_fac_pub/377.

10. Dudley Raynal et al., "Problem Solving in Conservation Biology and Management: Exercises for Class, Field, and Laboratory," in *Ecological Surveys: The Basis for Natural Area Management*, ed. J. P. Gibbs, M. L. Hunter, Jr., and E. J. Sterling (Malden, MA: Blackwell Science, 1998), 141–60.

11. Association of College and Research Libraries, *Information Literacy Competency Standards for Higher Education* (Chicago: Association of College and Research Libraries, 2000), http://www.ala.org/acrl/standards/informationliteracycompetency.

12. Association of College and Research Libraries, *Framework for Information Literacy for Higher Education* (Chicago: Association of College and Research Libraries, 2016), http://www.ala.org/acrl/standards/ilframework.

13. George D. Kuh, High-Impact Educational Practices (Washington, DC: Association of American Colleges and Universities, 2008).

14. Char Booth, *Reflective Teaching, Effective Learning* (Chicago: American Library Association, 2011).

15. Susan Dieterlen, Research Assistant Professor in the School of Architecture at Syracuse University, personal communication to J. Clemons, February 10, 2015.

Bibliography

Association of College and Research Libraries. *Framework for Information Literacy for Higher Education*. Chicago: Association of College and Research Libraries, 2016. http://www.ala.org/acrl/standards/ilframework.

Association of College and Research Libraries. *Information Literacy Competency Standards for Higher Education*. Chicago: Association of College and Research Libraries (ACRL), 2000. http://www.ala.org/acrl/standards/informationliteracycompetency.

Booth, Char. *Reflective Teaching, Effective Learning: Instructional Literacy for Library Educators*. Chicago: American Library Association, 2011.

Carlson, Jake, and Ruth Kneale. "Embedded Librarianship in the Research Context: Navigating New Waters." *College and Research Libraries News* 72, no. 3 (2011): 167–70.

Dewey, Barbara I. "The Embedded Librarian." *Resource Sharing and Information Networks* 17, no. 1–2 (2004): 5–17. https://doi.org/10.1300/J121v17n01_02.

Dieterlen, Susan. Email message to author. February 10, 2015.

Drewes, Kathy, and Nadine Hoffman. "Academic Embedded Librarianship: An Introduction." *Public Services Quarterly* 116 no. 2–3 (2010): 75–82. https://doi.org/10.1080/15228959.2010.498773.

Hertenstein, Elizabeth. "Student Scholarship in Institutional Repositories." *Journal of Librarianship and Scholarly Communication* 2, no. 3 (2014). http://doi.

org/10.7710/2162-3309.1135.

Kuh, George D. *High-Impact Educational Practices: What They Are, Who Has Access to Them, and Why They Matter.* Washington, DC: Association of American Colleges and Universities, 2008.

Lynch, Clifford. "Institutional Repository Strategies: What We Learned at the Executive Roundtables." Audio recording, 52:41. CNI: Coalition for Networked Information, March 29, 2017. https://www.cni.org/topics/repositories/institutional-repository-strategies-what-we-learned-at-the-executive-roundtables.

Mariani, Mack, Fiona Buckley, Theresa Reidy, and Richard Witmer. "Promoting Student Learning and Scholarship through Undergraduate Research Journals." *PS: Political Science and Politics* 46, no. 4 (2013): 830–35. https://doi.org/10.1017/S1049096513001133.

Miller, Char. "Riding the Wave: Open Access, Digital Publishing, and the Undergraduate Thesis." Keynote address, United States Electronic Thesis and Dissertation Association (USETDA) 2013 Conference, Claremont, CA, July 24–26, 2013. http://scholarship.claremont.edu/pomona_fac_pub/377.

Raynal, Dudley, James Gibbs, Neil Ringler and Donald Leopold. "Problem Solving in Conservation Biology and Management: Exercises for Class, Field, and Laboratory." In *Ecological Surveys: The Basis for Natural Area Management.* Edited by J. P. Gibbs, M. L. Hunter, Jr., and E. J. Sterling, 141–60. Malden, MA: Blackwell Science, 1998.

SUNY College of Environmental Science and Forestry. "Digital Commons @ ESF Guidelines and Policies." Accessed May 5, 2017. http://digitalcommons.esf.edu/policiesandguidelines.html.

Walker, Henry M., and Kevin R Engel. "Research Exercises: A Sequenced Approach to Just-in-Time Information Literacy Instruction." *Research Strategies* 19, no. 2 (2003): 135–47. https://doi.org/10.1016/j.resstr.2004.03.003.

CHAPTER 17

Copyright Considerations
Creation and Sharing

Carla S. Myers

The works students create are no longer limited to research papers. Today students are responsible for creating a wide variety of scholarship in both print and digital formats, including, but not limited to, manuscripts, PowerPoint presentations, photographs, graphics and art, music, and video recordings. US copyright law impacts almost every aspect of this creation process, from the reuse of third-party works in the new works student are creating to the copyright they hold in the works they have created. By learning about copyright, students empower themselves to make more informed choices when reusing third-party works and in managing the copyright they hold in the works they create.

Many students are familiar with the concept of intellectual property rights but do not possess the knowledge needed to make thoughtful applications of the law. When asked about copyright law, students are often able to articulate the ways in which common acts of infringement are carried out (e.g., illegal file sharing of songs and films online). However, when asked about how they manage the copyright in works they have created or reuse works of others in compliance with the law, students are often left speechless. The first step students can take to better understand US copyright law is to study the foundational provisions that identify how copyright is secured, the types of works eligible for copyright protection, copyright ownership, and the scope of protection provided under the law.

Copyright Basics
Securing Copyright

Copyright protection instantly vests "in original works of authorship fixed in any tangible medium of expression."[1] This means that students automatically secure copyright protection as soon as their original thoughts and expressions are captured in a physical medium or a digital format.

The types of works that are eligible for copyright protection include:

1. literary works;
2. musical works, including any accompanying words;
3. dramatic works, including any accompanying music;
4. pantomimes and choreographic works;
5. pictorial, graphic, and sculptural works;
6. motion pictures and other audiovisual works;
7. sound recordings; and
8. architectural works.[2]

Students' ability to secure copyright is limited only by their imagination and a medium available to them. Examples of this concept include

- a haiku written in a notebook
- a poster for an upcoming event saved in Publisher, or an architectural design saved in AutoCAD
- a diagram sketched on the back of a napkin
- a mural painted on a wall
- a sculpture crafted from rocks and clay gathered during a nature walk
- a model printed on a 3-D printer
- a picture captured on a digital camera
- choreography sketched out on a sheet of paper
- a video recording of their dog playing in fallen leaves captured on their smartphone
- a musical composition written on sheet music paper

Works Not Eligible for Copyright Protection

Certain types of works are not eligible for copyright protection. These works are identified in Section 102(b) of US copyright law and include but are not limited to facts, ideas, names, short phrases and slogans, procedures and processes, and discoveries. These types of works were specifically deemed by Congress to be ineligible for copyright protection to help "promote the progress of science and useful arts,"[3] which is the purpose of copyright outlined by the framers of the Constitution in Article I, Section 8, Clause 8. The fact that these types of works cannot be copyrighted can be alarming to students who are interested in gaining intellectual property protection for them, especially when it comes to new and unique ideas they may have; however, students may be able to pursue patent protection or trademark protection for some of these types of works.

Copyright Ownership

Generally, the person who creates the work holds the copyright in it. If two or more students work together to create a copyrightable work "with the intention that their contributions be merged into inseparable or interdependent parts of a unitary whole,"[4] then that work may be considered a work of "joint authorship" and all the creators would share the copyright equally. When "a work [is] prepared by an employee within the scope of his or her employment or a work [is] specially ordered or commissioned for use as a contribution to a collective work,"[5] it may be considered a "work made for hire." US copyright law states that "In the case of a work made for hire, the employer or other person for whom the work was prepared is considered the author …and, unless the parties have expressly agreed otherwise in a written instrument signed by them, owns all of the rights comprised in the copyright."[6] Students may sometimes find themselves in work-made-for-hire situations. Examples include but are not limited to works created as part of a job or an internship or institution-sponsored grant work they perform with a faculty member. Talented students may be commissioned to create works that are eligible for copyright protection, for example:

- A music student is asked to compose a short piece of music to play in the background of an informational video.
- An art student is hired by a business owner to paint a mural in the entryway of her restaurant.
- A photography student is asked to take photographs at a wedding.
- An English major is asked by a family friend who works for the Chamber of Commerce to serve as the editor of a new visitor's guide being prepared by the city.

If a student thinks that a work he or she is creating may fall into a work-made-for-hire situation, the student should speak with the person or organization employing him or her to obtain clarification on who will own the copyright in the work.

Scope of Copyright Protection

For those works that are eligible for copyright protection, US copyright law grants to the creators the right "to do and to authorize any of the following:"[7]

1. to make copies of the work in a physical or digital format;
2. to prepare alternate versions of the work, called "derivatives" (examples could include a sound recording of a poem they have written or a translation of a manuscript);
3. to distribute copies of the work to others;
4. "in the case of literary, musical, dramatic, and choreographic works, pantomimes, and motion pictures and other audiovisual works, to perform the copyrighted work publicly;"
5. "in the case of literary, musical, dramatic, and choreographic works, pantomimes, and pictorial, graphic, or sculptural works, including the individual images of a motion picture or other audiovisual work, to display the copyrighted work publicly; and"
6. "in the case of sound recordings, to perform the copyrighted work publicly by means of a digital audio transmission."[8]

Duration of Copyright

Copyrightable works created by an individual are protected for the life of the author plus seventy years. Works of joint authorship are protected for seventy years after the passing of the last surviving author. "In the case of an anonymous work, a pseudonymous work, or a work made for hire, the copyright endures for a term of 95 years from the year of its first publication, or a term of 120 years from the year of its creation, whichever expires first."[9]

Rights Management

Once students understand how copyright is secured in works they create and the rights granted to them under the law, they can then think more carefully about how to manage these rights. One of the first steps in the rights management process should be identifying themselves as the copyright holder of the work. While creators are not required by law to place a notice of copyright on a work to secure copyright protection, including a notice will help users readily identify who the rightsholder is should they need to obtain permission to reuse the work or if they are interested in contacting the creator to pass along comments about it or discuss the work in more depth. The copyright notice should include

- the word *copyright*
- the copyright symbol ©
- the year of creation
- the creator's/rightsholder's name

For example: Copyright © 2017 Carla Myers

Normally the year included in the notice is the year when the work is first published. For unpublished works, the year the work was created should be used. Recently, some creators have also begun to include their email address in the copyright notice so that users can readily identify how to contact them. Should students decide to do this, they should be sure to include an email address that they check regularly.

Creators are also not required to register works with the US Copyright Office (USCO) to secure protection. However, registering a copyright with the USCO does provide some distinct benefits, including establishing a public record of ownership. The USCO has recently (2017) updated a circular it publishes on registration of copyrights that "provides guidelines for submitting a complete, accurate copyright claim" and that explores options for "completing online and paper applications, submitting a filing fee, preparing a deposit copy, communicating with the Office, [and] determining when [a] registration takes effect."[10] The circular can be found online at https://www.copyright.gov/circs/circ02.pdf and can serve as a useful guide for students looking to register with works.

Transfer of Rights

Under US copyright law, "the ownership of a copyright may be transferred in whole or in part" to another.[11] Stim states, "If a copyright owner transfers all of his rights unconditionally, it is generally termed an *assignment*. When only some of the rights associated with the copyright are transferred, it is known as a *license*."[12]

If students are approached with a request for a copyright assignment, they should seek help from reputable resource, which could include an attorney or copyright librarian, for assistance with the process. More often, though, students are looking to share their works with others in a way that does not involve a full transfer of rights. In these situations, the use of licenses may be the best way to communicate this intent to the person looking to reuse the work or in identifying the ways in which they, as the rightsholders, are comfortable with others reusing their work.

Creative Commons Licensing

While students could technically write the license themselves or hire an attorney to do so, a series of readily available licenses have been made available through the Creative Commons (CC), which "is a nonprofit organization that works to increase the body of work (cultural, educational, and scientific content) that is available to the public for free and legal sharing, use, repurposing, and remixing."[13] The CC offers various types of licenses that allow students to authorize others to reuse their work under a set of predetermined conditions. These licenses include those shown in tables 17.1–17.4:

TABLE 17.1
Creative Commons Attribution License

	Attribution (CC BY)	https://creativecommons.org/licenses/by/4.0/
This license requires that the person reusing the work "must give appropriate credit [to the creator], provide a link to the license, and indicate if changes were made. [They] may do so in any reasonable manner, but not in any way that suggests the licensor endorses [them] or [their] use."		
Source: "Attribution 4.0 International (CC BY 4.0)," creativecommons.org, accessed May 2017, https://creativecommons.org/licenses/by/4.0/.		

TABLE 17.2
Creative Commons ShareAlike License

	ShareAlike (SA)	https://creativecommons.org/licenses/by-sa/4.0/
In addition to providing attribution, as outlined above, "if [users] remix, transform, or build upon the material, [they] must distribute [their] contributions under the same license as the original."		
Source: "Attribution-ShareAlike 4.0 International (CC BY-SA 4.0)," creativecommons.org, accessed May 2017, https://creativecommons.org/licenses/by-sa/4.0/.		

TABLE 17.3
Creative Commons NonCommercial License

	NonCommercial (NC)	https://creativecommons.org/licenses/by-nc/4.0/
Under this license, the user must provide attribution to the original creator, and their reuse of the work may not be for commercial purposes, which the CC defines as "not primarily intended for or directed towards commercial advantage or monetary compensation"		
Source: "Attribution-NonCommercial 4.0 International (CC BY-NC 4.0)," creativecommons.org, accessed May 2017, https://creativecommons.org/licenses/by-nc/4.0/.		

TABLE 17.4
Creative Commons NoDerivatives License

	NoDerivatives (ND)	https://creativecommons.org/licenses/by-nd/4.0/
This license requires that users provide attribution to the original creator and, if they "remix, transform, or build upon the material, [they] ...not distribute the modified material."		
Source: "Attribution-NoDerivatives 4.0 International (CC BY-ND 4.0)," creativecommons.org, accessed May 2017, https://creativecommons.org/licenses/by-nd/4.0/.		

All CC licenses require Attribution (CC-BY). The other licenses can be used in conjunction with the CC BY license (e.g., Attribution-NonCommercial, or Attribution-NonCommercial-NoDerivatives) to specify reuse rights.

Restricting Reuse

Sometimes students wish to merely share their works with others by posting them online, but are not comfortable with anyone reusing the work in any capacity or without their express permission. In these situations, students should be sure to include a copyright notice on their work, followed by the phrase "All rights reserved." While including this phrase will not negate any third-party reuse options found within the law (e.g., the fair use exemption found in Section 107 of US copyright law), it can serve as a helpful reminder for users that the rightsholder wishes to retain control over uses of the work.

Reuse Rights

US copyright law provides allowances, known as "exceptions," for certain uses of copyrighted works by individuals who are not the rightsholder. Students should be aware of these exceptions as they can benefit from them, especially when looking to reuse copyrighted works created by others as part of works they are creating. While there are numerous exceptions written into the law (see 17 USC §§ 107–122), the exception best-known and most flexible is the fair use exception found in Section 107 of US copyright law. It states:

> The fair use of a copyrighted work, including such use by reproduction in copies ...for purposes such as criticism, comment, news reporting, teaching (including multiple copies for classroom use), scholarship, or research, is not an infringement of copyright. In determining whether the use

made of a work in any particular case is a fair use the factors to be considered shall include—

1. the purpose and character of the use, including whether such use is of a commercial nature or is for nonprofit educational purposes;
2. the nature of the copyrighted work;
3. the amount and substantiality of the portion used in relation to the copyrighted work as a whole; and
4. the effect of the use upon the potential market for or value of the copyrighted work.

The fact that a work is unpublished shall not itself bar a finding of fair use if such finding is made upon consideration of all the above factors.[14]

When making a fair use determination about reusing the copyrighted work of another, students must work carefully through the four factors found in the statute to determine if their reuse of a work might be considered fair or infringing. Tools and resources are available to help students work through a fair use decision, including

- *The Fair Use Evaluator* (http://librarycopyright.net/resources/fairuse/index.php). Developed by Michael Brewer and the Copyright Advisory Subcommittee of the ALA Office for Information Technology Policy (OITP), this tool is intended to help users "understand how to determine the 'fairness' of a use" as well as "collect, organize & archive the information [they] might need to support a fair use evaluation."[15]
- *Thinking Through Fair Use* (https://www.lib.umn.edu/copyright/fairthoughts). Based on Columbia University Libraries Copyright Advisory Office Fair Use Checklist (https://copyright.columbia.edu/basics/fair-use/fair-use-checklist.html), this tool, developed by the University of Minnesota's Copyright Services, "helps [users] structure [their] own reflections about the fair use factors, and provides a record that [they] did consider relevant issues."[16]

Other Reuse Options

If the reuse of a copyrighted work does not fall within the scope of fair use or one of the other exceptions found in US copyright law, other options students can consider include the following.

Obtaining Permission to Reuse a Work

If the reuse of a work does not fall within the scope of fair use or one of the other exceptions found in US copyright law, the person wishing to reuse the work can reach out to the copyright holder and ask for permission to use the work. Both the permissions request and agreement should be done in writing or through email so there is documentation of the agreed-upon terms. Information on how to draft permissions requests and sample letters can be found on the website of the Columbia Copyright Advisory Office (https://copyright.columbia.edu/basics/permissions-and-licensing.html).

Obtaining a License to Reuse a Work

Sometimes when students reach out to rightsholders to inquire about permission to reuse a work, the rightsholder will agree, but only if the student pays a fee and agrees to very specific terms, which could include reuse in certain capacities (e.g., print or digital) and for a specific duration of time. In these situations, students will have to decide if the terms being extended are a good fit for their intended reuse and if they are amenable to paying the requested fee. If they enter into a license agreement with the rightsholder, they should require that all terms be set forth in writing and be signed by both parties.

Some publishers will require that license requests be submitted through their website using a standard form. Contact information will usually be made available on publishers' permissions websites that students can use to ask for assistance in framing their request or seeking clarification regarding license terms.

Using Creative Commons or Open-Access Works

Students themselves can reuse CC-licensed works in new works they are creating so long as they follow the terms of the license as identified by the rightsholder. The CC provides a useful search interface through which users can narrow search results based on format type and license type (https://search.creativecommons.org/).

Open-access (OA) publications provide another option for students looking to reuse the works of others. The Scholarly Publishing and Academic Resources Coalition (SPARC) defines OA as "the free, immediate, online availability of research articles combined with the rights to use these articles fully in the digital environment."[17] In addition to making their scholarly research freely available online, authors who publish OA works allows users to reuse their works for various purposes. Some OA works are published under CC licenses while others are published under license terms crafted by the author or the journal the work is published in. Users should read these licenses carefully and ensure they are complying with any terms set forth by the author or publisher.

Using Public Domain Works

Public domain works do not have copyright protection and therefore can be used without fear of infringement. According to the USCO, "A work of authorship is in the 'public domain' if it is no longer under copyright protection or if it failed to meet the requirements for copyright protection."[18] Copyright has expired in works published or copyrighted before 1923 in the United States. Crews tells us that "the copyright to works published before 1989 may also have expired due to [the rightsholders'] failure to comply with formalities that copyright law once required."[19] The chart "Copyright Term and the Public Domain in the United States" developed by Peter Hirtle (https://copyright.cornell.edu/publicdomain) can be used by students looking to determine the copyright status of a work.

Section 105 of US copyright law states that any work created by an employee of the US government as part of his or her job responsibilities is also in the public domain. Examples include but are not limited to photographs taken by National Aeronautics and Space Administration, publications put out by the National Parks Service, and the Congressional reports.

Works may also be in the public domain if they consist primarily of facts. Examples include height charts, a ruler, and a multiplication table.

Citing Sources

If a student is reusing a Creative Commons work, then citing the source by providing attribution to the original creator is part of the license requirements. Providing attribution to the original creator of a work is not just tied to the reuse of CC works, though. Attribution is not required by law when reusing works under the fair use exception or when reusing public domain works. However, students should remember to accurately cite sources or provide credit to the original creators when reusing the works of others in order to avoid claims of plagiarism. Alternately, it is a common misconception that so long as a source is cited properly the user does not have to consider how copyright might apply to the situation. This is untrue. Merely citing a source does not negate claims of copyright infringement. Essentially, this means when reusing the works of others, students have two decisions to make: first, can they reuse the work in a way that is compliant with US copyright law, and, if yes, how can they properly cite the work or provide credit to the original creator in order to avoid claims of plagiarism? Students can learn more about plagiarism and strategies for avoiding it through the Purdue Online Writing Lab (OWL) website (https://owl.english.purdue.edu/owl/resource/589/1/).

Finding Answers to Copyright Questions

Having a knowledge of the basics of US copyright law and the fair use exception will empower students to make more thoughtful decisions when it comes to managing the copyright in works they have created or reusing the works of others. There will be times when this knowledge is not enough to answer very specific questions regarding the law. In these situations, students can look to reputable resources and identify partners who can help them in finding answers to their questions.

Reputable Resources

Unfortunately, much of the information on US copyright law provided online is incorrect or misleading. The list below includes reputable resources through which students can find fact-based information on the law.

- *Copyright Law of the United States* (https://www.copyright.gov/title17/). Here students will find the full text of the law itself.
- *The website of the United States Copyright Office* (https://www.copyright.gov/). Here users can find a wide variety of tools and resources that can help them in understanding the law and guide them through the process of registering works.
- *The Stanford Copyright and Fair Use website* (https://fairuse.stanford.edu/). This resource, which is developed and maintained by the Stanford University Libraries, provides users with information about "copyright issues especially relevant to the education and library community, including examples of fair use and policies. Useful copyright charts and tools are continually added to help users evaluate copyright status and best practices."[20]
- *The Copyright Advisory Network* (http://librarycopyright.net/). Developed and maintained by members of the OITP, this website provides tools and resources on copyright as well as a forum where users can post questions about copyright that will be answered by librarians who have a specialized knowledge of US copyright law.

Partnerships

Libraries may have a designated staff member serving as a "copyright librarian" who can help students work through copyright questions or find quality resources that can assist them in interpreting the law. Students can reach out to their local public or academic library to see if it has a librarian who provides copyright consultations and how they can get in contact with that person. Student can also reach out to a local chapter of the American Bar Association (ABA;   https://www.americanbar.org/directories/lawyer-referral-directory. html) to see if it hosts any events or programming through which members of the public can receive free (pro bono) or reduced-cost consultations with an attorney who specializes in intellectual property law.

Other Intellectual Property Considerations

Students are not limited to securing copyright protection for works they create. Other types of intellectual property rights they can pursue include patents, trademarks, and servicemarks.

Patents

The United States Patent and Trademark Office (USPTO) defines patents as "the grant of a property right to the inventor, issued by the United States Patent and Trademark Office,"[21] and it identifies types of patents available that include, but are not limited to

1. **Utility patents** [that] may be granted to anyone who invents or discovers any new and useful process, machine, article of manufacture, or composition of matter, or any new and useful improvement thereof;

2. **Design patents** [that] may be granted to anyone who invents a new, original, and ornamental design for an article of manufacture.[22]

Generally, in order to have patent protection, the new work must

- have some usefulness (utility), no matter how trivial
- be novel (that is, be different from all previous inventions in some important way)
- be nonobvious (a surprising and significant development) to somebody who understands the technical field of the invention.[23]

Trademarks and Servicemarks

Entrepreneurial students may be interested in starting their own business or developing a brand around a product or service they offer; this could be as simple as a tutoring service, or it could be a complex business venture. Other forms of intellectual property, trademarks and servicemarks, can help them in these endeavors. According to the USPTO, "A trademark is a word, name, symbol, or device that is used in trade with goods to indicate the source of the goods and to distinguish them from the goods of others, [and] a servicemark is the same as a trademark except that it identifies and distinguishes the source of a service rather than a product."[24]

Securing Patent and Trademark Protection

Unlike copyright, which is instantly granted, patents must be applied for and granted by the USPTO. Trademark and servicemark protection can exist without registration, but the benefits and protections are limited. As a result, if students are serious about protecting a brand they develop, they should consider registering their marks with the USPTO. While students can submit patent, trademark, and servicemark applications through the USPTO website (https://www.uspto.gov/), the process for doing so is somewhat more complex than registering a copyright with the USCO. Students looking to file applications may wish to engage the assistance of an attorney or use a legal website such as LegalZoom (https://www.legalzoom.com/index-b.html), both of which will require that students spend money, but which could turn out to be a worthwhile investment if their brand or business gains traction with consumers. Students struggling with start-up costs may wish to see if their local Bar Association or an ABA-certified law school located nearby offers these services pro bono or at a reduced cost.

Putting It All Together

Students should feel empowered and excited to share their creations with others and, as rightsholders, feel comfortable in taking advantage of the rights granted to creators under US copyright law. Students should also feel confident in their ability to use exceptions found in US copyright law when wanting to reuse the copyrighted works of others and, out of respect to their fellow rightsholders, do so in a responsible way. Creative Commons licensing provides students with convenient and easy-to-understand options for allowing others to use their work while ensuring they receive credit for its creation. In addition to copyright, students should also consider other areas of intellectual property, including patent, trademark, and tradeservice law, that they can utilize to protect their creations. When students find themselves uncertain about certain applications of the law, they should seek partnerships with trusted individuals such as librarians, who they know can help them locate quality information about the law.

Notes

1. 17 United States Code, § 102(a).
2. 17 United States Code, § 102(a).
3. United States Constitution, Article I, Section 8, Clause 8.
4. 17 United States Code § 101.
5. 17 United States Code § 101.
6. 17 United States Code § 201(b).
7. 17 United States Code § 106.
8. 17 United States Code § 106.
9. 17 United States Code § 302(C).
10. US Copyright Office, *Copyright Registration*, Circular 2 (Washington, DC: Library or Congress, September 2017), 1, https://www.copyright.gov/circs/circ02.pdf.
11. 17 United States Code § 201(d)(1).
12. Richard Stim, "Copyright Ownership: Who Owns What?" Stanford University Libraries Copyright and Fair Use, accessed May 2017, https://fairuse.stanford.edu/overview/faqs/copyright-ownership/.
13. "What Is the Creative Commons?" Creative Commons Wiki, accessed May 2017, https://wiki.creativecommons.org/images/3/35/Creativecommons-what-is-creative-commons_eng.pdf (page discontinued).
14. 17 United States Code § 107.
15. "Fair Use Evaluator," Copyright Advisory Network, American Library Association Office for Information Technology Policy, accessed October 31, 2017, http://library-copyright.net/resources/fairuse/index.php.
16. "Thinking Through Fair Use," University of Minnesota Libraries Copyright Services, accessed October 31, 2017, https://www.lib.umn.edu/copyright/fairthoughts.
17. "Open Access," Scholarly Publishing and Academic Resources Coalition (SPARC), accessed May 2017, https://sparcopen.org/open-access/.
18. US Copyright Office, "Definitions," accessed May 2017, https://www.copyright.gov/help/faq-definitions.html.
19. Kenneth D. Crews, *Copyright Law for Librarians and Educators*, 3rd ed. (Chicago: American Library Association, 2012), p. 19.
20. "About the Stanford Copyright and Fair Use Website," Stanford University Libraries Copyright and Fair Use, accessed October 30, 2017, https://fairuse.stanford.edu/about/.
21. US Patent and Trademark Office, "General Information Concerning Patents," October 2015, https://www.uspto.gov/patents-getting-started/general-information-concerning-patents.

22. US Patent and Trademark Office, "General Information Concerning Patents."
23. "Qualifying for a Patent FAQ," Nolo, accessed October 31, 2017, https://www.nolo.com/legal-encyclopedia/qualifying-patent-faq.html.
24. US Patent and Trademark Office, "General Information Concerning Patents."

Bibliography

Copyright Advisory Network. "Fair Use Evaluator." American Library Association Office for Information Technology Policy. Accessed October 31, 2017. http://librarycopyright.net/resources/fairuse/index.php.

Creative Commons. "Attribution 4.0 International (CC BY 4.0)." Accessed May 2017. https://creativecommons.org/licenses/by/4.0/.

———. "Attribution-NoDerivatives 4.0 International (CC BY-ND 4.0)." Accessed May 2017. https://creativecommons.org/licenses/by-nd/4.0/.

———. "Attribution-NonCommercial 4.0 International (CC BY-NC 4.0)." Accessed May 2017. https://creativecommons.org/licenses/by-nc/4.0/.

———. "Attribution-ShareAlike 4.0 International (CC BY-SA 4.0)." Accessed May 2017. https://creativecommons.org/licenses/by-sa/4.0/.

Creative Commons Wiki. "What Is the Creative Commons?" Accessed May 2017. https://wiki.creativecommons.org/images/3/35/Creativecommons-what-is-creative-commons_eng.pdf (page discontinued).

Crews, Kenneth D. *Copyright Law for Librarians and Educators: Creative Strategies and Practical Solutions*, 3rd ed. Chicago: American Library Association 2012.

Nolo. "Qualifying for a Patent FAQs." Accessed October 31, 2017. https://www.nolo.com/legal-encyclopedia/qualifying-patent-faq.html.

Scholarly Publishing and Academic Resources Coalition (SPARC). "Open Access." Accessed May 2017. https://sparcopen.org/open-access/.

Stanford University Libraries. "About the Stanford Copyright and Fair Use Website." Copyright and Fair Use. Accessed October 30, 2017. https://fairuse.stanford.edu/about/.

Stim, Richard. "Copyright Ownership: Who Owns What?" Stanford University Libraries Copyright and Fair Use. Accessed May 2017. https://fairuse.stanford.edu/overview/faqs/copyright-ownership/.

University of Minnesota Libraries. "Thinking Through Fair Use." Copyright Services. Accessed October 31, 2017. https://www.lib.umn.edu/copyright/fairthoughts.

US Copyright Office. "Definitions." Accessed May 2017: https://www.copyright.gov/help/faq-definitions.html.

US Copyright Office. *Copyright Registration*. Circular 2. Washington, DC: Library of Congress, September 2017. https://www.copyright.gov/circs/circ02.pdf.

US Patent and Trademark Office. "General Information Concerning Patents." October 2015. https://www.uspto.gov/patents-getting-started/general-information-concerning-patents.

CHAPTER 18

North Carolina State University Spotlight

Part 3, The Power of Open: Tools and Practices for Opening Up Student Work

Lillian Rigling

North Carolina State University's (NCSU) mission to "Think and Do" has empowered the NCSU Libraries to be a leader in connecting theory to practice, coursework to careers, and personal passions to global engagement. Additional information about how this mission informs the work of the NCSU Libraries is provided in the chapter "Preparing Students to 'Think and Do': Promoting the Value of Student Work," which appears in the Articulating the Value of Student Work section of the book.

This chapter presents a set of case studies focusing on our public engagement in the context of the movement to create a more open, transparent, and sharing culture through open access to research products. The NCSU Libraries' work is grounded in open culture and programs that introduce students to open tools and practice have been a powerful way to help students learn to work collaboratively and transparently, as well as prepare a portfolio of their accomplishments. The ways we have designed, organized, and promoted library tools, spaces, and expertise connect our students with the communities where they live today and the lives they will build going forward, whether they choose a career in academia, industry, or the arts. These projects are just a few components of a broader series of programming designed to demonstrate the commitment the NCSU Libraries bring to supporting students as producers, the challenges inherent to this work, and the ways in which the Libraries can support and articulate the value of student creations. While actively exploring and engaging in this space, we do not purport to have the answers and are still investigating how best to provide emerging scholars and creative students with the tools, spaces, and resources to share, save, and disseminate their work.

Though the libraries strive to provide venues for students to disseminate and showcase their works, we also recognize the value of empowering students to develop and share their work independently. The libraries do not have the capacity to be, nor should they be, the sole keeper of student works, but we can help students embrace their own roles as prospective producers, publishers, and distributors of their work. In the NCSU Libraries, we have created multiple programming opportunities to help students understand and take advantage of their roles with content creation and distribution, whether the work they are sharing is a scholarly paper, artwork, code, or specific forms of made products such as designs.

In particular, we have focused on introducing students to open tools such as open-source software and Creative Commons–licensed resources. David Wiley defines open content as any work that is "licensed in a manner that provides users with free and perpetual permission to engage in the 5R activities." The Rs are

1. Retain—the right to make, own, and control copies of the content
2. Reuse—the right to use the content in a wide range of ways
3. Revise—the right to adapt, adjust, modify, or alter the content itself
4. Remix—the right to combine the original or revised content with other material to create something new
5. Redistribute—the right to share copies of the original content, your revisions, or your remixes with others[1]

In an attempt to connect with motivated students across multiple disciplines and departments, we hosted a full-day student-oriented conference on open culture and open creation. With the support of the Scholarly Publishing and Academic Resources Coalition (SPARC) and the Right to Research Coalition (R2RC) we applied to host an OpenCon Satellite Event—a local meeting that leverages the momentum of the international OpenCon meeting, designed with the mission of "Empowering the Next Generation to Advance Open Access, Open Education and Open Data." Through our satellite event, we aimed to tailor content from the international OpenCon meeting to our local context, with a goal of reaching undergraduate and graduate students at our university and other local universities or colleges.[2]

This event, called OpenCon 2017: North Carolina Student Leaders, was marketed as an opportunity for students to learn more about how to share their work, cultivate their professional identity, and learn advocacy skills. Students submitted a brief application to attend, which assessed their knowledge of and interest in open scholarship, and asked students to tell us a little about what they were hoping to get out of the day. With the permission of the global OpenCon organizers, we incentivized participation by providing acceptance emails so participants could include a line on their résumé or CV indicating they were an OpenCon North Carolina Student Leader.

This event engaged with undergraduate and graduate students from the sciences, social sciences, and humanities to explain the power of openness and open licensing in retaining control of their early work while simultaneously engaging with a broader community of scholars and practitioners. Throughout the day, students learned about facets of openness through hands-on tool-based sessions, workshops, and talks with advocates of open sharing and access. Students received a brief introduction to the concept of openness in scholarship and practice and learned about licensing their own work and using openly licensed works through hands-on sessions. Students then had the opportunity to make their own online portfolio using GitHub pages where they could share a résumé as well as examples of work they had created at NC State.

Students also had the opportunity to meet a local open-source advocate—Tom Callaway, University Outreach Team Lead at Red Hat—who has made a career working with open tools and openly licensing his own work. In his keynote address, he told his own story of working in the open in his early career and the doors that it opened for him. He also discussed how he values visibility and openness of a candidate's work when hiring new professionals. Our students perked up at the opportunity to hear from a real potential employer; it demonstrated that not only do students feel pride in their work, but others, including prospective employers, value this work as well. Finally, students participated in advocacy training, where they learned how to demonstrate the value of open to key stakeholders, including employers, professors, or administrators.

OpenCon provided our students who had a pre-existing interest in sharing their work with an opportunity to engage deeply with open practices, but we recognize that not all students are willing to devote a full day to learn about sharing their work. We wanted to offer meaningful and actionable instruction about sharing work with a community. As a university with an active makerspace community that regularly engages with open-source software, open hardware, and openly licensed materials, we chose to integrate this content into pre-existing makerspace instruction.

We integrated instruction about intellectual property, copyright, open licensing, and the life cycle of information into two pre-existing tool-training workshops: Developing Arduino Projects and Developing 3-D Printed Projects. The first workshops were offered during Open Access Week 2016 for a mini-workshop series titled Power of Open. The content was designed in a partnership between librarians with tool expertise from the NCSU Libraries' makerspace and librarians from the NCSU Libraries' Copyright and Digital Scholarship Center with knowledge of copyright, licensing, and the scholarly life cycle. These workshops began with a primer on ownership and licensing, and then delved deeply into hands-on tool training. We taught students how their individual making activity is shaped by a larger community of makers who are actively engaged in sharing their work openly.

After the success of the Power of Open miniseries, it was clear that this content could be more than just a special addition for Open Access Week; it had the potential to be core to our students' experience of making. We redesigned the workshops to include content about copyright, licensing, and sharing throughout, and offered them as basic introductory Arduino and 3-D Printing and Design workshops. The new content wove hands-on work with the tools together with conversations about how to participate in a broader making community through sharing. For example, in the 3-D Printing and Design workshops, after a basic primer on Creative Commons licensing, students were asked to download a CC-licensed remixable file from Thingiverse, an online repository where users can share digital design files. They then worked to remix and print this openly licensed file , and finally, we discussed what their rights to the remixed file were and how they might upload or share their altered file or their original design to Thingiverse or a similar repository of openly licensed files.

Workshop evaluations (see figures 18.1 and 18.2) indicated that embedding this discussion into this making environment was valued by our students. Multiple students reported that the most useful thing about these workshops was the information about licensing or copyright.

FIGURE 18.1
Course evaluation 1

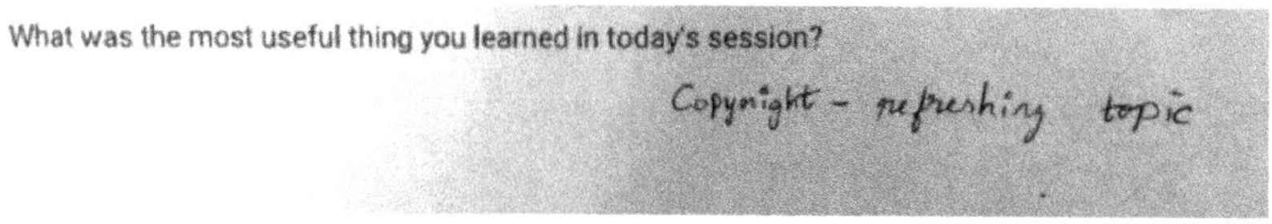

What was the most useful thing you learned in today's session?

Copyright - refreshing topic

FIGURE 18.2
Course evaluation 2

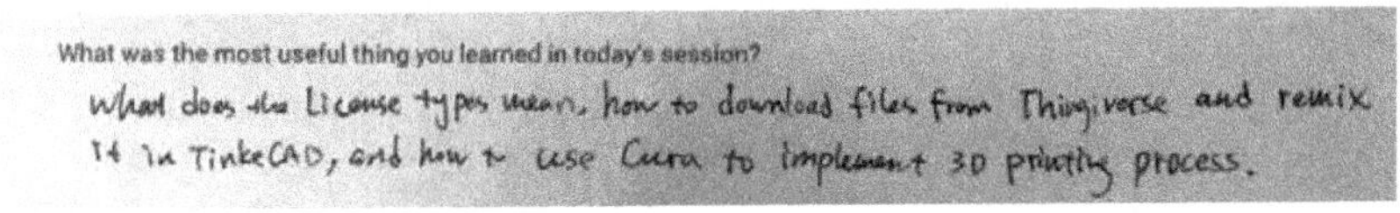
What was the most useful thing you learned in today's session?

What does the License types mean, how to download files from Thingiverse and remix it in TinkerCAD, and how to use Cura to implement 3D printing process.

Conclusion

We have adopted this approach to integrating information about sharing and ownership into all aspects of the NCSU Libraries instruction and outreach work. For example, we address these concepts in high-traffic workshops such as our music-making workshops. We have also incorporated them into the programmatic instruction provided for undergraduate science communication courses. This approach aligns with the findings of the ACRL white paper *Intersections of Scholarly Communication and Information Literacy*, which acknowledges the needs for students at all levels to understand the social life of information along with the rights and responsibilities they enjoy as creators of information resources.[3] By teaching students that sharing and promoting their work are core to engaging with their communities from the beginning of their research or making process, we are able to encourage students to take an active role in preserving and promoting their work.

Notes

1. David Wiley, "Defining the 'Open' in Open Content and Open Educational Resources," Opencontent.org, accessed March 15, 2018, http://opencontent.org/definition/. This material is based on original writing by David Wiley, which was published freely under a Creative Commons Attribution 4.0 license at http://opencontent.org/definition/.
2. Scholarly Publishing and Academic Resource Coalition (SPARC) and the Right to Research Coalition, *OpenCon2016: Empowering the Next Generation to Advance Open Access, Open Education and Open Data: Community Report* (SPARC and Right to Research Coalition, 2016), http://www.opencon2017.org/community_report.
3. Association of College and Research Libraries Working Group on Intersections of Scholarly Communication and Information Literacy, *Intersections of Scholarly Communication and Information Literacy* (Chicago: Association of College and Research Libraries, 2013), http://www.ala.org/acrl/sites/ala.org.acrl/files/content/publications/whitepapers/Intersections.pdf.

Bibliography

Association of College and Research Libraries Working Group on Intersections of Scholarly Communication and Information Literacy. *Intersections of Scholarly Communication and Information Literacy: Creating Strategic Collaborations for a Changing Academic Environment.* Chicago: Association of College and Research Libraries, 2013. http://www.ala.org/acrl/sites/ala.org.acrl/files/content/publications/whitepapers/Intersections.pdf.

Scholarly Publishing and Academic Resources Coalition (SPARC) and the Right to Research Coalition. *OpenCon2016: Empowering the Next Generation to Advance Open Access, Open Education, and Open Data: Community Report.* SPARC and Right to Research Coalition, 2016. http://www.opencon2017.org/community_report.

Wiley, David. "Defining the 'Open' in Open Content and Open Educational Resources." Opencontent.org. Accessed March 15, 2018. http://opencontent.org/definition/.

Section IV

Articulating the Value of Student Work

CHAPTER 19

Valuing Student Work

Amy S. Jackson, Cindy Pierard, and Suzanne M. Schadl

Contributors to this book share a commitment to promoting, sharing, and preserving student work. This section seeks to articulate why such commitments are valuable for learning and why libraries are well positioned to play leading roles in such efforts. Contemporary attentiveness to emerging scholarship and increased transparency makes this articulation of value timely. Diversity studies have also opened doors for critically evaluating how instructors validate and share knowledge, particularly in the classroom. As we all become more aware of what and whom we do not know, we find ourselves relying more readily on others' experiences—including those of students and community members—and valuing their contributions as essential for seeing errors in our traditional ways and opportunities for transformation.[1]

Innovation and change drive the Students as Producers movement. Mike Neary, who led the University of Lincoln's initiative, suggests that re-engineering the relationship between teaching and research can revitalize the purpose of higher education by establishing connections that "enable students to learn through active engagement in research processes and outcomes."[2] This argument underscores the now twenty-year-old Boyer Commission report, *Reinventing Undergraduate Education*, which champions the idea that "everyone at a university should be a discoverer, a learner."[3] Evidence supports this approach, showing that students who participate in inquiry-based learning are more likely to persist, to experience intellectual gains, and to feel satisfied with their education.[4]

The chapters in this section offer examples of libraries that put student works front and center in teaching and learning environments. Discussions include the social and educational value of making undergraduate research publicly available and the ethics of open access, especially for student producers. One question that emerges is this: How can libraries disseminate gray literature and culturally or personally sensitive information without misrepresenting people or disrupting their privacy? This issue is illustrated in chapters addressing a faculty-reviewed undergraduate writing journal, library engagement with student coursework, and an undergraduate research project made available in an institutional repository. Voices emanate from librarians (Swift, Dawson, Waller, Cross), undergraduate students (Hackenberger, Kramer), disciplinary faculty (Miller), and writing center administration (Marken).

If the library is an inspirational force, as Derek Bruff suggests, how might its physical spaces, public audiences, and tools for disseminating academic production increase creativity and learning? Several chapters suggest that high-quality research products emerge when students occupy the same spaces as other established scholars engaged in the complementary processes of teaching and learning. Experiences presented throughout this book offer evidence of success as well as ideas for improvement. Several themes or patterns emerge from these case studies to map the roles libraries are uniquely positioned to play in supporting student work, and by extension effective learning. As one professor in Miller and colleagues (chapter 21) notes, in reference to student theses in Claremont's digital repository: "I just want to emphasize that this is a stupendous teaching tool—not only because it is a repository of knowledge and an illustration for students of the vast diversity of topics that they might pursue. But it also 'raises the ante' for them really taking their thesis very seriously in the knowledge that it will be memorialized as well as scrutinized by future students." Claremont students Hackenberger and Kramer also express variations on this theme. Additionally, faculty and students at NCSU recognize the efficacy of teaching and learning simultaneously, with one student noting that the creativity the Viz Studio facilitates "greatly improves the quality of the presentations and the interest level of those watching." This same student recommends the space for others, stating, "The Viz Studio made me more comfortable in presenting to my peers since they weren't focused on me but on the walls surrounding them. More classes should get to use this room for presentations." (Dakota Frisby, quoted in Waller and Cross [chapter 22]).

Chapters in this section also share the value students place on opportunities to produce as well as consume knowledge with their professors and librarians. Miller and colleagues (chapter 21) argue that publicly disseminating undergraduate research produces an "enduring record of academic achievement" even as it presents an "empowering pedagogical tool" for developing transferable skills for the "next generation of leaders, scholars, artists and citizens." They present this development of "intellectual agency, cultural literacy, and digital citizenship" as "the academic trifecta." Engaging with students in their work enables educators, including librarians, to serve as partners connecting learning experiences with professional development. As NCSU states, we can strive to "be a leader in connecting theory to practice, coursework to careers, and personal passions to global engagement." Their visualization studio offers an example of how library spaces can inspire exploration in creative presentation styles. Libraries can also facilitate learning and creativity by making previous student work available as examples for current students.

In this respect and others, libraries can play unique roles in supporting student engagement. Chapters within this section, and others throughout this book, highlight excellent opportunities. NCSU contributors, for example, illustrate how their central physical spaces and their infrastructure enable students to share their work with campus and community audiences that surpass the reach of most academic departments. Together, with contributors from Duke, they also address the value of cultivating resources that are not commonly available on campus, like an expert programming team. Additionally, authors from Duke note the importance of project management skills and illustrate their methods for engaging this skill set in support of individual and team research. Authors in other sections of this book articulate the value of libraries as a central campus resource supporting all departments and units. Academic libraries can leverage their publishing roles to scholars in order to facilitate traditional and nontraditional modes of sharing information, research, and learning.

In all of these roles, libraries (and their partners) strive to perfect high-impact practices explored within learning communities and capstone courses. Indeed, this book offers several examples of these practices at work in libraries. Miller and colleagues (chapter 21), for example, note the impact of setting high expectations and requiring accountability, while Morse, Temnyalova, and Gordon (chapter 4) highlight the importance of offering timely and constructive feedback and interaction. Wong-Welch and colleagues (chapter 5) illustrate the effectiveness of connecting student work with real problems and audiences, while Apata (chapter 11) and Cruces (chapter 12) demonstrate the opportunities for learning through diversity. Most chapters articulate the value of reflection and integrative learning as well as public displays of competence.

Finally, although the ACRL *Framework for Information Literacy* focuses on information literacy in the classroom, several frames, including "Scholarship as Conversation," "Information Creation as a Process," "Authority Is Constructed and Contextual," and "Information Has Value," can be successfully pursued in library spaces.[5] "Scholarship as Conversation" is supported by using institutional repositories to archive student journals and research and capstone projects. Students who archive their work reflect an awareness of their responsibilities to other scholars as well as to their subjects, acknowledging their prospective reach in larger academic and popular conversations, and they begin to "contribute to scholarly conversation at an appropriate level."[6] "Information Creation as a Process" is demonstrated through student participation with both author and editor roles in student journals. As Dawson and Marken (chapter 20) argue, "They have an insider understanding of how scholarly publishing works. This means that when they submit future research to professional journals they are better prepared for potentially harsh reviews of their work, several rounds of revisions and editing, and long wait times until publication." "Authority Is Constructed and Contextual" becomes clear to students as their work is downloaded, cited, and used as a foundation for future scholars. Miller and colleagues (chapter 21) comment on "Information Has Value" while referencing the "disruptive act" of making student scholarship openly available and note the power dynamics in play when bringing scholarship to those who previously did not have access. Also in chapter 21, Kramer notes the power of giving final research back to those who helped her gather information.

An interesting dichotomy emerges in these chapters through differing approaches to scholarship and the context of information. Dawson and Marken (chapter 20) describe an open-access undergraduate research journal on their campus: "Many students lack the confidence to submit their work to a full-fledged professional journal at this point in their career, and so having a locally produced journal for undergraduate research provides a venue to bridge this gap." Miller and colleagues (chapter 21) also describe open-access undergraduate research made available through the institutional repository. However, in their case, students feel that writing for the general public is more demanding than writing for an academic journal: "The requirement to make our theses available to the general public set the academic and intellectual bar quite high" due to wide reach and public availability, measured through download reports and anecdotal conversations. This dichotomy may be related to the context of the research: the undergraduate research journal groups together several articles, while undergraduate research projects exist independently in the repository. In the academy, the impact of scholarly publications has traditionally been calculated through citation counts. However, emerging scholars are less entrenched in scholarly traditions and are more likely to measure their successes through other means, including download reports and other alt-metrics. Their research is clearly being used for projects in the local community or in their respective communities of practice. Download reports are becoming more sophisticated, and some repository software can track downloads by country, institution, or government agency, enabling immediate citation metrics, personal connections, and feedback. While established scholars take pride in these download reports, emerging scholars appear more humbled by the reach of their scholarship.

These chapters also explore complex ethical considerations, including the importance of trust in relationship building and information sharing. Because we have the technical ability to reach anyone with Internet access, it is important to ask what is appropriate to share? Students in Miller and colleagues (chapter 21) grapple with the complexities involved in making others' opinions publicly available. Are they representing the opinions correctly? Are the opinions intended to be shared with a wider audience? NCSU questions the ethics of sharing content that may be found inappropriate by others, from female genital mutilation to nationalism and Islamophobia in France. From librarians' points of view, how can they facilitate institutional review board applications for limited-time undergraduate research? Do libraries have the responsibility to monitor IRB clearance for all work published through their platforms? How can libraries respect the students' future rights to their work, when they are established and may not want their early works publically available? How can experiences in our own libraries help others work through policies and best practices? NCSU contributors (chapter 22) note that "Faculty and students may also need guidance in considering future consequences of having created, shared, and saved these works so that they reach audiences beyond others who are in the immediate classroom." In their visualization lab case study, they mention an inability to find "models to guide us, as a library, in thinking through how to disseminate and save sensitive material tied to student content creators and producers." This area seems ripe for further exploration.

How do we understand when we are providing high-impact educational experiences by engaging in and supporting student scholarship? One student from Dawson and Marken (chapter 20) comments that "the knowledge from publication [of an undergraduate research journal] was more concrete than what I learned in class," while another notes that "identifying the strengths and weaknesses in other undergraduate work has greatly improved my own writing." Dawson and Marken also found encouraging feedback in a survey sent to authors and editors, which included stronger positive feelings than initially expected of the experience: "Working on a team toward a goal was not a huge motivator (24 percent), but 76 percent felt that they did so. In the same vein, 43 percent wanted a connection with other students interested in research or publishing, and by the end of the year, 52 percent felt that they made that connection." Authors in this study report "the strongest learning happening around scholarly publishing and writing in general." Similarly, NCSU students (chapter 22) report that the libraries "are the only place on campus where they are able to show their work to others outside of their classrooms." Miller and colleagues (chapter 21) demonstrate that student agency in research and methodological development blended with requirements for posting scholarship online "inculcates an individual sense of responsibility and accountability for one's ideas that, when taken together, adds up to a collective transformation." These comments illustrate our values as educators and librarians and demonstrate the value that we provide to emerging scholars.

At a campus level, libraries are contributing to student engagement and retention by engaging in high-impact practices and collaborating with other campus units, illustrating that the library is relevant, engaged, and active in the campus community. By working with other departments and units across campus, libraries can also learn from their strengths and fill gaps in their knowledge bases. Dawson and Marken (chapter 20) state that "collaboration …helps the broader campus community understand the contributions of the library and writing center to the research mission of the institution." They also reflect on librarians as faculty and researchers who "conduct research and disseminate the results, but have substantially less time allocated for these activities compared to teaching faculty…. Therefore, the other ways that the library supports research output on campus increase in significance." Separately, NCSU Library collaboration with classroom instructors (chapter 22) "has increased student engagement, enhanced student presentation skills, and enabled students to learn new presentation tools." Waller and Cross state "at the NCSU Libraries we are working collaboratively with faculty to develop assignments and curricula that support nontraditional methods of information sharing. This also informs the way that we design and use library spaces and services." Hackenberger (chapter 21) offers a student assessment on bridging gaps between academic theory and the built environment through interdisciplinary thesis research, writing and publication: "Open-access research can not only expand access to the academy, but can actually put the power of academia to work for the community." Campus collaboration provides value to the students, the library, and other campus as well as community stakeholders.

There are many added benefits to promoting student work within and beyond the library. Through its unique roles, the library demonstrates its value to the campus and becomes an active participant in engaged learning by sharing knowledge through laboratory, forum, and archival experiences. Libraries demonstrate the values of the ACRL *Framework for Information Literacy* within the cocurriculum by offering students hands-on experiences with scholarship. They earn their place as the cultural center of the university by engaging in and sharing university ideas and projects. In turn, students acquire experience with authentic assignments that can be shared broadly, lending to recognizable impact. Society gains access to works written by emerging professionals, previously obscured in library stacks or professors' filing cabinets. Overall, the value of sharing the work of emerging scholars is substantial to everyone involved, and libraries are well positioned to become leaders in this activity.

Notes

1. Gary R. Howard, *We Can't Teach What We Don't Know* (New York: Teachers College Press, 2016).
2. Mike Neary, "Project Proposal," Student as Producer, University of Lincoln, accessed March 28, 2018, http://studentasproducer.lincoln.ac.uk/project-proposal.
3. Boyer Commission on Educating Undergraduates in the Research University, *Reinventing Undergraduate Education* (Stony Brook: State University of New York at Stony Brook, 1998), 9, https://dspace.sunyconnect.suny.edu/handle/1951/26012.
4. Christopher Justice et al., "Inquiry in Higher Education: Reflections and Directions on Course Design and Teaching Methods," *Innovative Higher Education* 31, no. 4 (2007): 201–14.
5. Association of College and Research Libraries, *Framework for Information Literacy for Higher Education* (Chicago: Association of College and Research Libraries , 2016), http://www.ala.org/acrl/standards/ilframework.
6. Association of College and Research Libraries, *Framework*, 8.

Bibliography

Association of College and Research Libraries. *Framework for Information Literacy for Higher Education*. Chicago: Association of College and Research Libraries, 2016. http://www.ala.org/acrl/standards/ilframework.

Boyer Commission on Educating Undergraduates in the Research University. *Reinventing Undergraduate Education: A Blueprint for America's Research Universities*. Stony Brook: State University of New York at Stony Brook, 1998. https://dspace.sunyconnect.suny.edu/handle/1951/26012.

Howard, Gary R. *We Can't Teach What We Don't Know: White Teachers, Multiracial Schools*. New York: Teachers College Press, 2016.

Justice, Christopher, James Rice, Wayne Warry, Sue Inglis, Stefania Miller, and Sheila Sammon. "Inquiry in Higher Education: Reflections and Directions on Course Design and Teaching Methods." *Innovative Higher Education* 31, no. 4 (2007): 201–14.

Neary, Mike. "Project Proposal." Student as Producer, University of Lincoln. Accessed March 28, 2018. http://studentasproducer.lincoln.ac.uk/project-proposal.

CHAPTER 20

Beyond Consumers
The Value of Engaging Undergraduate Students in Journal Management and Authorship

Diane (DeDe) Dawson and Liv Marken

Introduction

In 2011, a group of University of Saskatchewan (U of S) students proposed the establishment of a multidisciplinary undergraduate research journal. The Office of the Vice President of Research (OVPR) saw alignment with its Undergraduate Research Initiative (URI) and agreed to fund the journal. The *University of Saskatchewan Undergraduate Research Journal (USURJ)* is a double-blind faculty-reviewed, open-access journal.[1] It is based in the Writing Center, which is part of the University Library at the U of S. Each year, an average of twenty student editors gain experience in academic publishing processes. Dozens more students submit papers and experience the rigors of undergoing faculty review and editing a manuscript to publishable quality. This library-based partnership ensures a rich, immersive experience from which student editors and authors gain valuable skills transferrable to life after graduation.

There are few opportunities for undergraduates to participate meaningfully in the dissemination of scholarship. Typically, they are limited to the role of consumers of literature and are authors of papers that only their professors will read. *USURJ* provides an opportunity for undergraduates to begin to see themselves as content creators and contributors to professional scholarship—whether by critically evaluating the contributions of their peers or by submitting a paper themselves.

A successful, sustainable undergraduate journal requires a home on campus and stable funding for continuity.[2] *USURJ* benefits from staff oversight and mentorship from a writing center coordinator, a librarian, and a science faculty member, as well as financial support from the University Library, the OVPR, and the College of Graduate and Postdoctoral Studies. These partnerships and contributions ensure that students receive mentorship, expertise, and guidance in a range of writing, editing, and scholarly communication topics, an experience of value not only to them but also to libraries, institutions, the academy, and society.

This chapter articulates this teaching and learning value, relates the experience of the journal's first years and lessons learned and offers practical advice should other libraries want to establish similar partnerships to support undergraduate research journals.

Background

The University of Saskatchewan is the largest postsecondary institution in the province of Saskatchewan, Canada, with over 21,000 students. It is a public medical-doctoral institution, and a member of the U15 group of research-intensive universities in Canada, which advocates for the advancement of Canadian research and innovation.[3] Undergraduate research has become a key initiative at the U of S, leading to the institutional support for *USURJ*.

Since 2014, *USURJ* editorial boards of approximately twenty undergraduate students are mentored and engaged in the process of producing a scholarly publication each year. By the spring of 2017, eighty-six students (unique), including seven graduate student mentors and three graduate student editors-in-chief, have worked for the journal at a commitment of five to twelve hours per week over eight months. In that time, the journal has published six issues and fifty-nine articles, with additional artwork from six undergraduate students featured. *USURJ* publishes continuously, but articles are collected into two issues per year, allowing for student editors, authors, and the campus community to profile and celebrate student work at winter and spring receptions.

All but three positions on the journal's editorial board are reserved for undergraduate students. The editorial board includes a librarian faculty advisor, a writing center staff advisor, a graduate and an undergraduate student editor-in-chief, six undergraduate senior editors (according to disciplinary category or task), several undergraduate student associate editors, a web ed-

itor, layout editors, and communications editors. *USURJ* editors also gain
as-needed advice from former *USURJ* editors, now in graduate studies. As the
journal's editors-in-chief and staff advisor tend to be from writing-intensive
humanities disciplines, a science professor acts as an intermittent advisor.

Student editors receive training from the faculty advisor, staff advisor,
and editors-in-chief throughout the year. An intensive training session in
the fall, followed by weekly team meetings, occasional workshops, and social
events, prepare students to work as journal editors and to function well as a
team. Some teams will request training topics that are suited to their specific
concerns. A comprehensive training manual is required reading and a useful resource for editors; it covers such topics as delivering negative messages,
anonymizing manuscripts, and using the Open Journal Systems (OJS) platform. Finally, *USURJ* editors complete parts of PKP School, which is a suite
of online, self-paced courses on publication for journal editor and journal
managers using the OJS platform.[4] The editors-in-chief, senior editors, and
faculty and staff advisors meet each week to share updates, concerns, ideas,
and plans, and the senior editors meet each week with their associate editors
to work on paper edits, find reviewers and brainstorm ways to garner submissions for their section. Graduate student mentors sometimes help at these
section meetings, as do the faculty and staff advisors and the editors-in-chief.

During the spring and summer, a new graduate editor-in-chief and the
faculty and staff advisor maintain communication with authors and reviewers, engage in assessment and planning activities, and refine training. This
spring and summer activity allows the journal to keep its publication cycle
from stalling and to improve its operations each year, making it a more ful-
filling and productive experience for authors and editors alike. Additional
past projects for the graduate editor-in-chief have included completing PKP
School courses, interviewing deans and department heads to determine how
best to promote the journal, and revising the *USURJ* training manual.

The Student Voice

Each year, we assess the journal's impact in terms of its teaching and learning
value via anonymous editor and author surveys. The findings from these assessments help us to articulate our value to funders and plan improvements
from year to year. The feedback and ratings from students have been crucial
to improving the educational value, training, and operations. Student feedback has led to minor and significant changes to journal operations, and it
has helped us to see the larger value, and potential, of the journal's activities.

A survey request to all *USURJ* authors and editors from the past two years
(2015–2017) garnered forty-seven author and twenty-one editor responses on

topics related to specific learnings around publication processes; how the role of scholarly publication contributes to the research community; and writing, including the writing process, revision, citation, and organization.[5] We concentrated on these topics not only to measure the value of having writing center and library involvement but also to report to the journal's funders on the depth of learning that was occurring. More broadly, we wanted to know the teaching and learning impact of the journal: what authors and editors learned and experienced, and whether they were satisfied with the experience when comparing their intentions (for submitting or getting involved) to the actual outcomes. We will incorporate some of the results of the 2015–2017 assessments in the following sections.

Scholarship as Conversation

Our experiences with *USURJ*, and what we gleaned from the survey responses, indicate that undergraduates can benefit considerably from being included in content creation. Nevertheless, undergraduate students are typically limited to being passive consumers of scholarly information. Traditional information literacy instruction is often skills-based and practical: introducing students to the concept of primary sources, such as journal articles, and how to locate, assess, and access such sources for use in assignments. But the processes underlying the production of journal articles remains abstract and mysterious to most students. Library outreach on scholarly communication topics related to the dissemination of research results is more frequently directed at faculty and graduate students. Undergraduates have been largely excluded from these conversations.[6] However, undergraduates benefit when they are included in both the dissemination of their scholarly work and in outreach on issues related to the scholarly publishing ecosystem. The ACRL *Framework for Information Literacy in Higher Education* encourages engaging undergraduate students in this way.[7]

The *Framework* was developed by an ACRL task force in response to the rapidly changing higher education environment. One of the elements that is changing is the extent to which undergraduate students are participating in research and knowledge creation on campus: "Students have a greater role and responsibility in creating new knowledge, in understanding the contours and the changing dynamics of the world of information, and in using information, data, and scholarship ethically."[8] Student participation as authors and editors in an undergraduate research journal such as *USURJ* has the potential to fulfill objectives in several of the six frames of the ACRL *Framework,* but perhaps most meaningfully in "Information Has Value" and "Scholarship as Conversation." Both concepts express the importance of students seeing themselves as contributors to scholarship.

Students as Authors

Involving students in dissemination activities completes the cycle of undergraduate knowledge creation on campus, and "with the production of original scholarly or creative work comes the expectation to disseminate and share the new knowledge or creation with the scholarly community."[9] Many students lack the confidence to submit their work to a full-fledged professional journal at this point in their career, and so having a locally produced journal for undergraduate research provides a venue to bridge this gap. *USURJ* enables undergraduates to "contribute to scholarly conversation at an appropriate level" and "see themselves as contributors to the information marketplace rather than only consumers of it."[10] These are key dispositions of the "Scholarship as Conversation" and "Information Has Value" frames (respectively).

For most authors, contributing to *USURJ* is their first experience submitting a work to a scholarly journal. It is an eye-opening and memorable experience. Some are surprised that the paper that got them a great grade in class may be highly criticized by reviewers or that the publication process can be so long and grueling. One *USURJ* student author commented, "I thought my paper and research was rock solid when I handed it in and was at first a little disheartened to see so many comments, but the comments made me dig deeper into my research, think more broadly about my topic, and even change some of my arguments." Another remarked on the authenticity of the experience: "I learned a lot more about the process of research and writing research articles. The knowledge from publication was more concrete than what I learned in class."

The most obvious benefit to student authors is the intensive writing and editing experience they receive in preparing their papers for a broader audience, outside the walls of the classroom: "I was able to look at my own work in a more detached manner, which helped me learn a little more about how to evaluate my own work objectively." Apart from the writing skills improved through working on their papers, improvements to authors' professional communication were a secondary outcome; one student noted that she "learned about how to communicate professionally with editors, staff, etc."

In our annual surveys, student authors (47) reported a range of general and specific learnings,[11] with the strongest learning happening around scholarly publishing and writing in general, such as writing for professional publication and writing for an informed public audience, and the process for publishing in a scholarly journal (see table 20.1). More specific learnings around writing, including revision, citation, formatting, and organization, were less significant, possibly because some of the respondents did not make it to review, or through review to publication.

TABLE 20.1
USURJ Author Learnings

"I LEARNED ABOUT"	Positive Response (%)
How to write for professional publication	72
How to write for an informed public audience	79
The process for publishing in a scholarly journal	83
How scholarly publication contributes to the research community	68
How to support points with evidence	64
How to revise intensively, following reviewer feedback	70
How to cite and document a paper properly	57
How to improve the organization of a paper	60
How to write a better abstract	64
How to manage the writing process in general (from research question to final proofread)	70

Students as Editors

Frequently, the discussion surrounding undergraduate research journals focuses on the benefits to students as authors, but we believe that the more intensive learning comes from involving students as editors on their own journal. It is a unique and rich experience, giving students exposure to the behind-the-scenes operations of a real scholarly journal. And there is evidence that students value "learning about scholarly communication in the context of 'real-life' research experiences."[12]

Editors also witness the rigors of the peer review process—but from a different angle. Over the course of an academic year working on the journal, student editors will manage several papers through the publishing process, from submission to publication. They will see a range of reviewer behaviors, from careful and constructive to harsh and overly critical. It is an entirely realistic introduction to peer review. Editors need to develop skills of diplomacy and discretion in interacting with these reviewers, as well as in selectively communicating their comments to the authors. Delivering negative news, including rejection, is an especially delicate skill that students have an opportunity to develop and practice.

An accepted paper will usually undergo significant revisions. The editors work with the authors to ensure that the revisions are made and other copyediting is done. Evaluating academic writing and providing constructive feedback are not skills commonly addressed in classrooms.[13] Throughout the revision process, editors are developing their abilities to "critically evaluate contributions made by others in participatory information environments," a knowledge practice in the "Scholarship as Conversation" frame.[14] Students are learning highly transferable communication, writing, editing, and critical-thinking skills in an immersive environment. One editor remarked, "In three years of school I have had almost zero experience reading other students' work. Identifying the strengths and weaknesses in other undergraduate work has greatly improved my own writing."

Running a journal is a team effort, and team members need to be in continual communication to facilitate the collaboration.[15] *USURJ* student editors work in disciplinary teams led by another undergraduate student who acts as the senior editor for their section. The sections meet weekly to discuss the papers under their purview. It is a considerable time commitment for busy undergraduates, and they need to adhere to strict and sometimes tight timelines to meet publication schedules. This involves the collaboration of team members and the leadership of the senior editor to ensure all members of the section are engaged and on track, which can be challenging during lull times when waiting for reviews or revisions. One student editor noted, "[Teamwork] wasn't my motivation at the beginning, but I really grew to appreciate the team dynamic." Student editors also receive mentorship in their activities from the editors-in-chief, graduate student advisors, and staff and faculty advisors. *USURJ* is a student-run journal, but the advisors invest considerable time in guiding and facilitating the students' work.

From our annual survey results, approximately half (21) of all editors from 2015 to 2017 reported on learning similar writing skills to authors, in addition to topics specifically related to editorial work. One editor commented, "Working together with others definitely helped me improve my writing." Possibly due to the regularity, depth, diversity, and range of work they did throughout an eight-month period, editors had more positive responses, showing richer and deeper learning compared to authors (see table 20.2). As noted, most research around student learning outcomes for undergraduate research journals has focused on authors' experiences. If our surveys are any indication, editors have a richer learning experience compared to authors, further enhancing their self-identification with scholarly producers.

TABLE 20.2
USURJ Editor Learnings

"I LEARNED"	Positive Response (%)
About the process for publishing an article	100
How to evaluate the credibility of authors of articles	92
When to cite other authors in a paper	79
How to use at least one formatting and citation style	75
How to work collaboratively	100
How to write constructive feedback	96
How to use Open Journal Systems	96
How to edit in groups	100
How to prepare my own work for publication	100
How to communicate with professors	96
How to write about research for an informed public audience	92
The process for publishing an article in a scholarly journal	96
How scholarly publication contributes to the research community	75
How to support points with evidence	92
How to revise intensively, following reviewer feedback	100
How to cite and document a paper properly	79
How to improve the organization of a paper	100
How to write a better abstract	71

Student Intentions versus Outcomes

Student editors have many motivations and expectations when applying to work on the journal, as do student authors. We were curious to know whether the authors' reasons for submitting work to the journal—and the editors' reasons for getting involved with the journal—were satisfied and whether there were unintended outcomes for them. This is what we learned from the annual surveys.

Authors

Of the options given, the strongest reason for authors (47) submitting their work was around developing their skills to an end: CV-building or applying for graduate studies. Of authors, 66 percent wanted to "gain skills for graduate studies," with 43 percent reporting that they did. In submitting their work, most wanted to "build a stronger CV or resume" (89 percent) and 70 percent felt that they did.

Other highlights included the following:

- 36 percent wanted a challenging learning experience, and 38 percent felt that they did get one.
- 47 percent wanted to be competitive as a graduate school applicant and 1 percent (4 out of 47) used the process of review or publication to get into graduate school.[16]
- 34 percent wanted more intensive feedback on their work, with 36 percent feeling that they got that feedback.
- 81 percent wanted to learn more about academic publishing or publication processes, with 77 percent feeling that they did.

Editors

Particularly relevant to this chapter, of the editors (21) surveyed, the strongest reasons for applying to work with the journal were wanting to "contribute to a culture of undergraduate research on campus" (95 percent) and holding an "interest in publishing and publishing processes" (90 percent). By the end of the year, all respondents felt that they did contribute to the culture of undergraduate research and had satisfied their interest in publishing. Of the editors, 91 percent wanted to improve their editing and proofreading skills, and 86 percent felt that they did.

Interestingly, working on a team toward a goal was not a huge motivator (24 percent), but 76 percent felt that they did so. In the same vein, 43 percent wanted a connection with other students interested in research or publishing, and by the end of the year, 52 percent felt that they made that connection. Only 29 percent were motivated by wanting to connect with faculty, but 43 percent felt that they gained that connection. One student editor commented, "I really enjoyed working as an editor with USURJ. It was a great experience and I was able to develop a network of research-oriented people."

Other highlights included the following:

- 48 percent wanted to help other students, and 76 percent felt that they did.
- 48 percent wanted to get student work out there, and 81 percent felt that they did.

- 66 percent wanted to be competitive as graduate school applicants; 14 percent successfully used the experience to get into graduate school.[17]
- 52 percent wanted a challenging learning experience; 66 percent felt that they gained a challenging learning experience.

In sum, author and editor feedback contributes to our understanding of the depth of learning experienced for each, which helps us to understand how to increase student involvement with the journal, realize learning outcomes, and assist returning editors and editors-in-chief in creating a more meaningful experience. Furthermore, it helps us to articulate the value of *USURJ* to our funders.

Transferable Skills

Whether as an author or an editor, students develop numerous transferable skills by being involved in the production of an undergraduate journal. These transferable skills are often called "graduate attributes" in the higher education sector. Hill and Walkington define graduate attributes as "a framework of skills, attitudes, values and knowledge that graduates should develop by the end of their degree programmes."[18] Such competencies are intended to help students succeed after graduation—whether academically in graduate school or in their careers outside academia—and, of course, as informed and productive citizens. At the U of S, graduate attributes clearly map to what we call "Core Learning Goals" in the Learning Charter.[19] This document provides a framework to optimize student learning on campus and is intended to guide the development of further policies for teaching and learning.

Several of the Core Learning Goals in the U of S Learning Charter can be met by student involvement in *USURJ*, including the following:

- Apply critical and creative thinking to problems, including analysis, synthesis, and evaluation.
- Utilize and apply their knowledge with judgement and prudence.
- Exercise intellectual integrity and ethical behaviour.
- Recognize and think through moral and ethical issues in a variety of contexts.
- Communicate clearly, substantively, and persuasively.
- Share their knowledge and exercise leadership.[20]

The students that seek out publishing or editorial opportunities with *USURJ* tend to be high achievers with plans to continue to graduate school. A published article or editorial experience is an impressive inclusion on a CV or graduate school application, but the students are also simply better prepared for a research career. They have an insider understanding of how scholarly publishing works. This means that when they submit future research to professional journals, they are better prepared for potentially harsh reviews of their work, several rounds of revisions and editing, and long wait times until publication. In our surveys, one *USURJ* editor remarked, "I learned so much about the process of creating an academic journal. I had no idea what to expect going in and was very pleased."

Some of our students will not go on to become researchers, but teaching them about scholarly communication issues through participation in an undergraduate research journal will ensure that they "become better information consumers. Their ability to critically evaluate what they read is instantly valuable in all aspects of life, regardless of their profession."[21]

Articulating Value

In these times of budget reductions and increased emphasis on outcomes, it is becoming vitally important for academic libraries to demonstrate their value to their institutions and other stakeholders.[22]

Benefits to Library and Writing Center

Producing an undergraduate research journal is an opportunity for libraries and writing centers to articulate their value through concrete support of the research mission and specific strategic initiatives of the institution.

The 2013 ACRL white paper *Intersections of Scholarly Communication and Information Literacy: Creating Strategic Collaborations for a Changing Academic Environment* emphasizes the need for academic libraries to develop new collaborations on campus to lead our constituents in responding effectively to the rapidly changing digital information environment.[23] The white paper argues that this is a role that is uniquely situated to libraries and where we can demonstrate leadership and articulate our value to the university and academia—especially at a time when many question the purpose and continued existence of a library.

> In order for academic libraries to demonstrate alignment with and impact on institutional outcomes, librarians must accelerate the transition to a more open system of schol-

arship and transform student learning, pedagogy, and instructional practices through creative and innovative collaborations.[24]

As noted above, *USURJ* is based in the writing center, part of the University Library, but is also supported by the OVPR and Graduate Studies, a
partnership that evolved over time, due in no small part to the efforts and
advocacy of staff and student champions within Student Learning Services
and the OVPR. This collaborative partnership among several units is vital
to the sustainability of the journal, both financially and through the yearly
turnover of undergraduate student editors. But the collaboration also helps
the broader campus community understand the contributions of the library
and writing center to the research mission of the institution. As Hensley,
Shreeves, and Davis-Kahl report from their survey of campus coordinators of
Undergraduate Research Programs, libraries are "well positioned to provide
the intellectual and technical infrastructure support for the dissemination
of undergraduate research; and, where these services are offered, they were
of high value to the respondents."[25] The authors also predict the demand for
libraries to offer these services will continue to increase.[26]

Research output is another strategic consideration of most higher education institutions. The U of S is a member of the U15 group of research-intensive universities in Canada. As such, it experiences considerable pressure on
each college of the institution to contribute to the production and dissemination of original research to maintain this status. The University Library at
the U of S is a college and faces the same pressure. Our librarians are faculty
and researchers. They conduct research and disseminate the results, but have
substantially less time allocated for these activities compared to teaching faculty, so output is lower. Therefore, the other ways that the library supports research output on campus increase in significance. Contributing to the success
of researchers, scholars, and practitioners is a Core Strategy of the University
Library's Strategic Plan.[27]

Benefits to Institution

Undergraduate research activities are good examples of high-impact educational practices. These are teaching and learning practices that have been
shown to be beneficial to university students from a wide range of backgrounds.[28] High-impact practices (HIPs) are effective because they typically
involve experiential or active learning situations that provide opportunities
to integrate, synthesize, and apply knowledge, thus engaging students in
deep, meaningful learning. These activities often culminate in some kind of
performance or other output.[29] It can easily be seen how undergraduate jour-

nals fulfill this last criterion. HIPs also create circumstances where students interact with faculty and other students on a substantive task over an extended amount of time—often requiring them to devote considerable time and effort to the task. This deepens the student's investment in the task and its outcome and understandably increases his or her engagement.[30] The editorial teams working on *USURJ* would appear to fit this description as well.

HIPs have been shown to increase rates of student retention and engagement, so they are of great interest to university administrators.[31] One assessment even established a connection between student success and participation in an undergraduate research journal.[32] And Hensley, Shreeves, and Davis-Kahl assert that "there is a growing body of evidence indicating that scholarly disengagement can be reversed when students participate in high-quality, discipline-oriented undergraduate research programs."[33] Furthermore, undergraduate research initiatives and journals have the potential to be used as recruitment tools to attract bright prospective students or in fundraising campaigns as a good news story about innovative research.[34] The U of S has promoted its Undergraduate Research Initiative (URI) in recruitment activities, and it has proved to be a popular topic among potential students.

The URI, a collaboration between the OVPR and the Office of Vice-Provost Teaching and Learning (OVPTL) at the U of S, promotes undergraduate involvement in original research on campus and provides some funding each year to *USURJ*. The journal clearly supports the mission of the URI in providing students with a local outlet to which to submit the results of their research. *USURJ* is not alone; many universities now support undergraduate research journals. The Council on Undergraduate Research (CUR) maintains a lengthy list of such journals.[35] There are numerous benefits to institutions in establishing and supporting undergraduate research journals.

Benefits to the Academy

Perhaps the most obvious benefit to academia in general is the preparation of students for graduate school, then as early career researchers. The Boyer Commission recommended that "as undergraduates advance through a program, their learning experiences should become closer and closer to the activity of the graduate student."[36] Ideally, these experiences would enable the smooth transition from senior to graduate. Indeed, the College of Graduate and Postdoctoral Studies at the U of S is particularly excited about the role that *USURJ* plays in nurturing future graduate students. Graduate students who have some prior experience in the research and publication process are likely to be more successful. There are major changes developing in the scholarly communication system though, and students need to be prepared for these, too.

The current journal publishing system is inequitable and financially unsustainable.[37] Librarians have been advocating for change to this system for more than a decade now, but our primary audience for this kind of advocacy has been those who are most active in disseminating research: graduate students and faculty. We need researchers as allies since they are major stakeholders in the system and have more real power to bring about fundamental change. However, culture in academia is entrenched in tradition and slow to change. But "libraries have an opportunity to engage and influence future scholars during the formative undergraduate research process."[38] It is our hope that engaging undergraduates in these issues during their work on *USURJ* will create future champions for positive changes in journal publishing.[39]

> Undergraduate students are a prime audience for outreach and education efforts around scholarly communication issues. They are highly aware of the cost of their education and resources that support and enrich it, especially when it comes to the cost of textbooks and student loans. College students are also highly attuned to issues of social justice and are more likely to be involved in civic engagement initiatives.[40]

An overhaul of the scholarly publishing system is a long-term benefit to the academy as a whole—in efficiency, equity, and cost-effectiveness.

Benefits to Society

Graduates with attributes outlined above have the potential to be better citizens overall, benefiting society. Universities are under pressure to show stakeholders how they produce graduates with qualities that are useful to society and that prepare them for life after graduation, whether that be in the workforce or in graduate school.[41] Information literacy skills that students learn while working on *USURJ*, such as critically reading and evaluating information, will enable them to be better information consumers. This is especially important today as disreputable publishers and fake news outlets proliferate online.

Good Practices

Advice for journal editors is abundant online but typically directed at those involved with traditional scholarly publishing outlets. These best or good practices include guidance for editors on dealings with authors, reviewers, and the journal's publishers or owners and advice on various ethical and policy considerations (for example see COPE's *Code of Conduct and Best Practice*

Guidelines).[42] While many of these topics can inform library staff who are supporting undergraduate research journals, there are also unique concerns that such advice does not address. The first three years of *USURJ* were not without bumps in the road, but staff involvement and a stable home for the journal has made that road smoother with each passing term. In the setup of a student journal, there is an array of one-time tasks—some challenging and some simple—that we assisted student editors with in the early days. These tasks include setting up hosting; registering in the Directory of Open Access Journals; completing Open Journal Systems site setup; beginning the construction of a reviewer database; creating peer review, copyright, privacy, and security policies; crafting author guidelines; obtaining an ISSN; creating layout templates and publication agreements; designing a workflow; and assigning DOIs. After these one-time tasks, the ongoing help of staff has been invaluable in meeting the shared challenges of journal sustainability and quality.

Maintaining Journal Quality

Staff involvement, whether it is from writing centers, libraries, or faculty, can translate to improved undergraduate research journal quality. It is important, though, that staff and faculty do not sweep in to "fix" problems, but rather they should teach and mentor students to be independent as time goes by. For the maximum educational benefit to editors, undergraduate journals should be student-run. Library, faculty, and writing center professionals, often published authors themselves, can mentor student editors in

- editing and proofreading processes and group editing strategies and logistics
- vetting papers
- imparting knowledge about information literacy, researcher profiles, new media, and research skills
- educating around academic integrity and citation practices
- understanding copyright and open access
- demystifying the world of scholarly publishing, making it less intimidating
- interpreting reviews
- assisting with technical infrastructure
- assisting with crafting constructive feedback and delivering negative news
- finding reviewers (Staff and faculty are more likely to have established networks and can encourage student editors not to be intimidated.)
- articulating transferable skills in CVs and learning portfolios

This mentoring makes for a richer educational experience for student editors and reduces the chance that they will lose interest in the endeavor as they wait long days for a reviewer or author response or struggle with unexpected communication and editing demands.

Ensuring Journal Sustainability

Writing center and library support for undergraduate research journals is not unprecedented. According to an environmental scan currently being conducted, 13 percent of the fifty-one North American undergraduate research journals surveyed work with a writing center or a writing program, and 41 percent work with libraries or librarians.[43] The involvement of staff and faculty effects better continuity for undergraduate journals, which tend to have spotty publication records and cohorts of students with different levels of enthusiasm, morale, and commitment from year to year. Weiner and Watkinson, writing about the *Journal of Purdue Undergraduate Research* (JPUR),[44] emphasize concerns about sustainability in the formation of their journal (emphasis ours):

> How to sustain a new publication was one of the central topics of discussion of the faculty group. An analysis of the list of undergraduate research journals on the Council for Undergraduate Research (CUR) website revealed that almost half of the 65 publications listed in 2009 either had broken links or displayed "current issues" over two years old. A consistent feature of the journals that were struggling was that they appeared to be entirely student-run, with the inevitable problems of staff turnover, *while successful and sustainable publications always had a permanent home within the institution,* usually within a dedicated office of undergraduate research.[45]

JPUR is student-produced but works through a partnership between the university's press and libraries, the Purdue Writing Lab (Department of English), and the marketing and media office. Also noting the risk of discontinuity for undergraduate journals, Buckland advocates "partnerships with faculties or departments [to] help prevent the fly-by-night publication of journals" and emphasizes the "importance [of] someone in the faculty who will ensure that when the current editors of the journals graduate, there is someone to step into their place."[46]

Of course, though Buckland emphasizes faculty involvement, staff involvement can effect the same continuity, as we have seen in the context of

USURJ. Our involvement in *USURJ* has affected sustainability and continuity, as we possess skills and abilities in

- managing the turnover of undergraduate editors via record keeping and established hiring practices
- helping student editors to navigate the practicalities of physical space: booking rooms for editing, events, information sessions, meetings, and training
- assisting with the maintenance of morale (Staff involved can take the long view as they have seen the kinds of twists and turns that are a normal part of journal management, including waiting for faculty reviewers and dealing with disgruntled authors.)
- helping to troubleshoot Open Journal Systems, or other journal management systems, as these platforms tend to be unintuitive and challenging to the occasional user
- remembering and keeping records of traditions and celebrations held from year to year (For example, *USURJ* has two student-run receptions annually, and without the help from staff, some of the logistics and challenges might be a deterrent to editors who are already busy with journal management.)
- advocating for the journal in terms of funding, for example, in helping to prepare reports and structure assessment in a consistent way from year to year (Staff could advocate for increased Undergraduate Research Initiative funding for *USURJ* in its third year and for multiyear funding from the College of Graduate and Postdoctoral Studies.)

Conclusion

Library, faculty, and staff involvement can contribute to the sustainability of a student journal, provide a richer learning experience for authors and editors, and improve its quality. In turn, a strong undergraduate journal helps to fulfill common institutional priorities, around such areas as research intensiveness, student retention and engagement, and learning outcomes. As student authors and editors can begin to see themselves as content creators, not just consumers, their involvement in scholarly dissemination activities fulfills many objectives in the ACRL *Framework for Information Literacy*, particularly in the frames "Information Has Value" and "Scholarship as Conversation." Stephanie Davis-Kahl writes, "Though student journal publishing requires a high degree of faculty-librarian-student dedication, time commitment, and investment of financial and human resources, it can be a valuable and exciting experience for all involved."[47] In articulating their value to others, librarians, faculty, and writing center coordinators might also realize the value to themselves. Helping student scholars is energizing in that it reminds us of why we do the work we do, and the endeavor can bring richness and learning to us as professionals and scholars. We have been fortunate to see journal development through the eyes of developing scholars and have grown professionally and have gained deeper insights into the assumptions, practices, and traditions of the scholarly marketplace.

Notes

1. *University of Saskatchewan Undergraduate Research Journal* homepage, accessed June 4, 2018, http://www.usask.ca/urj/.
2. Sharon Weiner and Charles Watkinson, "What Do Students Learn from Participation in an Undergraduate Research Journal? Results of an Assessment," *Journal of Librarianship and Scholarly Communication* 2, no. 2 (2014): eP1125, https://doi.org/10.7710/2162-3309.1125.
3. U15 Group of Canadian Research Universities, "About Us," accessed June 4, 2018, http://u15.ca/about-us.
4. PKP School homepage, accessed June 4, 2018, http://pkpschool.sfu.ca/.
5. Many survey questions referred to in this paper were the same as those shared by Weiner and Watkinson, "What Do Students Learn," 17–31.
6. Amy Buckland, "More Than Consumers: Students as Content Creators," in *Getting the Word Out: Academic Libraries as Scholarly Publishers*, ed. Maria Bonn and Mike Furlough (Chicago: Association of College and Research Libraries, 2015), 193–202; Merinda Kaye Hensley, Sarah L. Shreeves, and Stephanie Davis-Kahl, "A Survey of Library Support for Formal Undergraduate Research Programs," *College and Research Libraries* 75, no. 4 (2014): 422–41, https://doi.org/10.5860/crl.75.4.422; Scott Warren and Kim Duckett, "'Why Does Google Scholar Sometimes Ask for Money?' Engaging Science Students in Scholarly Communication and the Economics of Information," *Journal of Library Administration* 50, no. 4 (2010): 349–72, https://doi.org/10.1080/01930821003667021.
7. Association of College and Research Libraries, *Framework for Information Literacy for Higher Education* (Chicago: Association of College and Research Libraries, 2016), http://www.ala.org/acrl/standards/ilframework.
8. Association of College and Research Libraries, *Framework*, 2.
9. Hensley, Shreeves, and Davis-Kahl, "Survey of Library Support," 423.
10. Association of College and Research Libraries, *Framework*, 6, 8.
11. We surveyed authors regardless of whether they had only submitted and then were rejected outright; had gone through the review process but had not been published; or had been published. Future surveys will compare the responses to these categories.
12. Catherine Fraser Riehle and Merinda Kaye Hensley, "What Do Undergraduate Students Know about Scholarly Communication? A Mixed Methods Study," *portal: Libraries and the Academy* 17, no. 1 (2017): 170, https://doi.org/10.1353/pla.2017.0009.

13. Adrian K. Ho, "Creating and Hosting Student-Run Research Journals: A Case Study," *Partnership: The Canadian Journal of Library and Information Practice and Research* 6, no. 2 (2011): 1–17, https://doi.org/10.21083/partnership.v6i2.1516.

14. Association of College and Research Libraries, *Framework*, 8.

15. Ho, "Creating and Hosting Student-Run Research Journals."

16. We administered the survey in the spring, before final exams, and not all authors were graduating, applying to graduate school, or already receiving replies to graduate school applications.

17. The survey was given in spring, before final exams, and not all editors were graduating, applying to graduate school, or already receiving replies to graduate school applications.

18. Jennifer Hill and Helen Walkington, "Developing Graduate Attributes through Participation in Undergraduate Research Conferences," *Journal of Geography in Higher Education* 40, no. 2 (2016): 222, https://doi.org/10.1080/03098265.2016.11401 28.

19. University of Saskatchewan, "Core Learning Goals," University of Saskatchewan Learning Charter, June 17, 2010, http://teaching.usask.ca/about/policies/learning-charter.php#CoreLearningGoals.

20. University of Saskatchewan, "Core Learning Goals."

21. Buckland, "More Than Consumers," 201–2.

22. Association of College and Research Libraries, *Value of Academic Libraries: A Comprehensive Research Review and Report*, researched by Megan Oakleaf (Chicago: Association of College and Research Libraries, 2010).

23. Association of College and Research Libraries Working Group on Intersections of Scholarly Communication and Information Literacy, *Intersections of Scholarly Communication and Information Literacy* (Chicago: Association of College and Research Libraries, 2013), http://www.ala.org/acrl/sites/ala.org.acrl/files/content/publications/whitepapers/Intersections.pdf.

24. Association of College and Research Libraries Working Group, *Intersections*, 3.

25. Merinda Kaye Hensley, Sarah L. Shreeves, and Stephanie Davis-Kahl, "A Survey of Campus Coordinators of Undergraduate Research Programs," College and Research Libraries 76, no. 7 (2015): 988, https://doi.org/10.5860/crl.76.7.975.

26. Hensley, Shreeves, and Davis-Kahl, "Survey of Campus Coordinators."

27. University Library, University of Saskatchewan, "Our Organization," University Library Strategic Plan, http://library.usask.ca/info/strategicplan.pdf (page discontinued).

28. George Kuh, *High-Impact Educational Practices* (Washington, DC: Association of American Colleges and Universities, 2008).

29. Kuh, *High-Impact Educational Practices*.

30. Kuh, *High-Impact Educational Practices*.

31. Kuh, *High-Impact Educational Practices*.

32. Weiner and Watkinson, "What Do Students Learn."

33. Hensley, Shreeves, and Davis-Kahl, "Survey of Library Support," 422.

34. Weiner and Watkinson, "What Do Students Learn."

35. Council on Undergraduate Research, "Undergraduate Journals," accessed June 4, 2018, http://www.cur.org/resources/students/undergraduate_journals/.

36. Boyer Commission on Educating Undergraduates in the Research University, *Reinventing Undergraduate Education* (Stony Brook: State University of New York at Stony Brook, 1998), 17, http://reinventioncollaborative.colostate.edu/the-boyer-report/.

37. For example: David W. Lewis, "The Inevitability of Open Access," College and Research Libraries 73, no. 5 (2012): 493–506, https://doi.org/10.5860/crl-299; Peter Suber, *Open Access* (Cambridge, MA: MIT Press, 2012); Jonathan P. Tennant et al., "The Academic, Economic and Societal Impacts of Open Access: An Evidence-Based Review," *F1000Research* 5 (2016): 632, https://doi.org/10.12688/f1000research.8460.3.

38. Hensley, Shreeves, and Davis-Kahl, "Survey of Library Support," 423.

39. Ho, "Creating and Hosting Student-Run Research Journals."

40. Stephanie Davis-Kahl, "Engaging Undergraduates in Scholarly Communication: Outreach, Education, and Advocacy," *College and Research Libraries News* 73, no. 4 (2012): 212, https://doi.org/10.5860/crln.73.4.8744.

41. Hill and Walkington, "Developing Graduate Attributes through Participation."

42. COPE: Committee on Publishing Ethics, *Code of Conduct and Best Practice Guidelines for Journal Editorship* (COPE: Committee on Publishing Ethics, 2011), http://publicationethics.org/files/Code%20of%20Conduct_2.pdf.

43. Courtney Ballantyne, Linda Huard, and Liv Marken, "Environmental Scan of North American Undergraduate Research Journals" (working paper, University of Saskatchewan, Saskatoon, 2017).

44. *JPUR: Journal of Purdue Undergraduate Research* homepage, accessed June 4, 2018, http://docs.lib.purdue.edu/jpur/.

45. Weiner and Watkinson, "What Do Students Learn," 3.

46. Buckland, "More Than Consumers," 198.

47. Davis-Kahl, "Engaging Undergraduates," 213.

Bibliography

Association of College and Research Libraries. *Framework for Information Literacy for Higher Education*. Chicago: Association of College and Research Libraries, 2016. http://www.ala.org/acrl/standards/ilframework.

———. *Value of Academic Libraries: A Comprehensive Research Review and Report*. Researched by Megan Oakleaf. Chicago: Association of College and Research Libraries, 2010.

Association of College and Research Libraries Working Group on Intersections of Scholarly Communication and Information Literacy. *Intersections of Scholarly Communication and Information Literacy: Creating Strategic Collaborations for a Changing Academic Environment*. Chicago: Association of College and Research Libraries, 2013. http://www.ala.org/acrl/sites/ala.org.acrl/files/content/publications/whitepapers/Intersections.pdf.

Ballantyne, Courtney, Linda Huard, and Liv Marken, "Environmental Scan of North

American Undergraduate Research Journals." Working paper, University of Saskatchewan, Saskatoon, 2017.

Boyer Commission on Educating Undergraduates in the Research University. *Reinventing Undergraduate Education: A Blueprint for America's Research Universities.* Stony Brook: State University of New York at Stony Brook, 1998. http://reinventioncollaborative.colostate.edu/the-boyer-report/.

Buckland, Amy. "More Than Consumers: Students as Content Creators." In *Getting the Word Out: Academic Libraries as Scholarly Publishers.* Edited by Maria Bonn and Mike Furlough, 193–202. Chicago: Association of College and Research Libraries, 2015.

COPE: Committee on Publishing Ethics. *Code of Conduct and Best Practice Guidelines for Journal Editors.* COPE: Committee on Publishing Ethics, 2011. http://publicationethics.org/files/Code%20of%20Conduct_2.pdf.

Council on Undergraduate Research. "Undergraduate Journals." Accessed June 4, 2018. http://www.cur.org/resources/students/undergraduate_journals/.

Davis-Kahl, Stephanie. "Engaging Undergraduates in Scholarly Communication: Outreach, Education, and Advocacy." *College and Research Libraries News* 73, no. 4 (2012): 212–22. https://doi.org/10.5860/crln.73.4.8744.

Hensley, Merinda Kaye, Sarah L. Shreeves, and Stephanie Davis-Kahl. "A Survey of Campus Coordinators of Undergraduate Research Programs." *College and Research Libraries* 76, no. 7 (2015): 975–95. https://doi.org/10.5860/crl.76.7.975.

———. "A Survey of Library Support for Formal Undergraduate Research Programs." *College and Research Libraries* 75, no. 4 (2014): 422–41. https://doi.org/10.5860/crl.75.4.422.

Hill, Jennifer, and Helen Walkington. "Developing Graduate Attributes through Participation in Undergraduate Research Conferences." *Journal of Geography in Higher Education* 40, no. 2 (2016): 222–37. https://doi.org/10.1080/03098265.2016.1140128.

Ho, Adrian K. "Creating and Hosting Student-Run Research Journals: A Case Study." *Partnership: The Canadian Journal of Library and Information Practice and Research* 6, no. 2 (2011): 1–17. https://doi.org/10.21083/partnership.v6i2.1516.

JPUR: *Journal of Purdue Undergraduate Research* homepage. Accessed June 4, 2018. http://docs.lib.purdue.edu/jpur/.

Kuh, George. *High-Impact Educational Practices: What They Are, Who Has Access to Them, and Why They Matter.* Washington, DC: Association of American Colleges and Universities, 2008.

Lewis, David W. "The Inevitability of Open Access." *College and Research Libraries* 73, no. 5 (2012): 493–506. https://doi.org/10.5860/crl-299.

PKP School homepage. Accessed June 4, 2018. http://pkpschool.sfu.ca/.

Riehle, Catherine Fraser, and Merinda Kaye Hensley. "What Do Undergraduate Students Know about Scholarly Communication? A Mixed Methods Study." *portal: Libraries and the Academy* 17, no. 1 (2017): 145–78. https://doi.org/10.1353/pla.2017.0009.

Suber, Peter. *Open Access.* Cambridge, MA: MIT Press, 2012.

Tennant, Jonathan P., François Waldner, Damien C. Jacques, Paola Masuzzo, Lauren B

Collister, and Chris H J Hartgerink. "The Academic, Economic and Societal Impacts of Open Access: An Evidence-Based Review." *F1000Research* 5 (2016): 632. https://doi.org/10.12688/f1000research.8460.3.

U15 Group of Canadian Research Universities. "About Us." Accessed June 4, 2018. http://u15.ca/about-us.

University of Saskatchewan. "Core Learning Goals." University of Saskatchewan Learning Charter. June 17, 2010. http://teaching.usask.ca/about/policies/learning-charter.php#CoreLearningGoals.

University of Saskatchewan Undergraduate Research Journal homepage. Accessed June 4, 2018. http://www.usask.ca/urj/.

University Library, University of Saskatchewan. "Our Organization." University Library Strategic Plan. Accessed November 8, 2017. http://library.usask.ca/info/strategicplan.pdf (page discontinued).

Warren, Scott, and Kim Duckett. "'Why Does Google Scholar Sometimes Ask for Money?' Engaging Science Students in Scholarly Communication and the Economics of Information." *Journal of Library Administration* 50, no. 4 (2010): 349–72. https://doi.org/10.1080/01930821003667021.

Weiner, Sharon, and Charles Watkinson. "What Do Students Learn from Participation in an Undergraduate Research Journal? Results of an Assessment." *Journal of Librarianship and Scholarly Communication* 2, no. 2 (2014): eP1125. https://doi.org/10.7710/2162-3309.1125.

CHAPTER 21

Beyond the Sandbox

Student Scholarship, Digital Citizenship, and the Production of Knowledge

Char Miller, Allegra Swift, Benjamin Hackenberger, and Anna Kramer

Introduction

When academics engage and value students as scholars, those students prove better equipped to assimilate the practices of information-literate citizens. Catherine Fraser Riehle and Merinda Kaye Hensley find that "active, experiential learning, including high-impact educational practices such as undergraduate research experiences, often requires students to interact with information in complex, authentic ways."[1] This complexity can fundamentally alter the dynamics of teaching and learning as they occur in classrooms and libraries. Part of that alteration, as Mark Caprio asserts, is to deconstruct the privilege of knowledge production that scholars often claim is their sole purview. The very attributes that undergraduate institutions hope to instill and cultivate in their students, he argues, such as "critical thinking, complex problem-solving and written and oral communication skills, parallel those developed through engagement with the scholarly research process….They are, in fact, attributes of the scholar."[2] That being so, part of our collective

291

challenge is to develop pedagogical strategies that bring together students, faculty, and librarians in a fluid curricular enterprise that advances student scholarship and promotes its public presentation and digital preservation. Acting on the opportunities created by these strategies will benefit undergraduates long after their graduation, inspiring them to remain strong advocates for higher education, intellectual engagement, and conscientious scientific analysis. These outcomes are crucial in an era of rising acrimony toward science, increasing anti-intellectualism, and the troubling concept of "alternative facts." Undergraduates who feel trusted and supported as public scholars, can become more empathetic humans and productive digital citizens. That charge is as robust as it is expansive: Mike S. Ribble, Gerald D. Bailey, and Tweed D. Ross, for example, exhort educators to "prepare students to be members of a digital society or digital citizens" by providing strategies that build on the International Society for Technology in Education's National Educational Technology Standards (NETS). These standards are designed to help students understand "the ethical, cultural, and societal issues related to technology," and "practice responsible use of technology systems, information, and software."[3]

Librarians in scholarly communication and instruction recognize this evolution in the academic agenda. As a result, they work with faculty and students to build a more robust understanding of digital citizenship and the learning and life outcomes that can flow from it.[4] The Association of Colleges and Research Libraries *Framework for Information Literacy for Higher Education*, for example, explicitly links the roles and responsibilities of librarians with those of students and faculty to address questions of information privilege, knowledge creation and access, as well as information ethics and essential attribution.[5] The *Framework*, as it has been devised, "draws significantly upon the concept of metaliteracy, which offers a renewed vision of information literacy as an overarching set of abilities in which students are consumers and creators of information who can participate successfully in collaborative spaces."[6] This metaliteracy "demands behavioral, affective, cognitive, and metacognitive engagement with the information ecosystem" and sets the stage for the practice of "critical self-reflection" that can lead students to become "more self-directed in that rapidly changing ecosystem."[7] Or, as Stephanie Davis-Kahl observes: "Developing a holistic approach to educating and developing awareness around scholarly communication issues in the curriculum, in the library, and on campus can help to create a culture of sharing that will impact the scholarly landscape of the future."[8]

The authors of this chapter—a scholarly communications librarian, a liberal arts professor, and two recent alumni of the environmental analysis program at Pomona College—take this broad framework, and its implicit pedagogical charge, seriously. In what follows, we relate our integrated experiences with this complex educational mission through the collaborative development of classroom assignments framed around information literacy and privilege, critical thinking, and analytical rigor set within the instruction of the senior-thesis capstone course in the college's environmental analysis major. The chapter then describes the advancement of digital citizenship and the responsibilities that such a concept embodies through the subsequent publishing of the award-winning scholarship of two alumni on the Claremont Colleges' digital platform, Scholarship @ Claremont.[9] By its authorship and argument, then, this essay reveals its commitment to the very subject it explores.

Preparing the Next Generation of Digital Citizens: A Librarian's Point of View

The benefits of undergraduates' active participation in research have been valued for several decades.[10] Such participation is an "effective educational strategy" that benefits these emerging scholars, the faculty, institutions, and the larger society.[11] Yet communicating and disseminating students' research results has not been a priority, this despite the 1998 Boyer Report recommendations that "dissemination of results is an essential and integral part of the research process" and that communication should be integrated throughout a student's academic career.[12] By taking advantage of the internet's reach, for instance, it is possible to communicate undergraduate research and scholarship on a global scale. Yet educators often perceive the range of access to be much more constrained, limited to interactions between the educator and the student, in and out of class. This constraint runs counter to what one's alma mater hopes—that its graduates are equipped to engage productively and positively with society. That optimism weaves its way through the words of James A. Blaisdell, the fourth president of Pomona College, chiseled into the college's front gates: "They only are loyal to this college who, departing, bear their added riches in trust for mankind."[13] The other colleges in the Claremont Consortium make similar claims about the social purposes of their academic mission (see figure 21.1), nurturing "responsible citizens of the world" who have a "clear understanding of the impact of their work on society."[14]

To respond to the accelerated need for an educated citizenry living in a globalized world, librarians and faculty are beginning to collaborate in new ways. This is particularly true of their shared interest in critical information literacy pedagogy.[15] As part of that aspiration, libraries, which traditionally have supported and disseminated faculty research, are recognizing the value in doing the same for undergraduate researchers and scholars. Among these initiatives are the construction of collaborative physical spaces with an ar-

FIGURE 21.1
The five undergraduate Claremont Colleges mission statements in a word cloud.

ray of technology and experts to provide the tools for conducting high-end research and the creation of digital systems to collect, preserve, and disseminate all scholarship an academic community generates. This commitment has forced a shift in orientation: until recently, most librarians and faculty thought of undergraduates as consumers or users of information and not as creators who have a voice, agency, and place in the scholarly conversation. No more: Julia Bauder and Catherine Rod are among those urging librarians to facilitate undergraduates entering scholarly conversations and understanding the value of scholarly communication. Even so, their particular assertion limits this engagement to classroom assignments.[16] A number of institutions are going a step farther by collecting and broadly disseminating the products of student research and scholarship, projecting this important work to a worldwide audience.[17]

An example of this dramatic alteration in educational enterprise and the emerging desire—even demand—to facilitate undergraduate scholarship occurred at the Claremont Colleges during the first decade of the twenty-first century, when some faculty and allied departments, along with two of the five undergraduate colleges, decided that it was essential to disseminate and archive undergraduate research. Publicly disseminating undergraduate research not only ensures an enduring record of academic achievement. It also provides an empowering pedagogical tool for the development of transferable skills for a more publicly engaged next generation of leaders, scholars, artists and citizens.[18]

The Claremont Colleges are a consortium of seven institutions—five undergraduate liberal arts colleges and two graduate institutions. The Claremont Colleges Library collectively serves each by aligning strategic initiatives with the educational and research missions of these colleges.[19] Since the creation of the Claremont Colleges Digital Library in 2006 and participation in the first international Open Access Week in 2008, the Claremont Colleges Library has been a champion for the democratization of information and the support of faculty and student scholarship and publication. In 2012, the library embarked on the initial stages of a Mellon Digital Humanities grant that signaled the beginning of several collaborative initiatives that contribute to faculty and student success and the distinction of the colleges. The first principal investigator (PI) for the ultimately successful grant, Jacqueline Wernimont (formerly of Scripps College), practiced the democratization of information by exploring new methods of publication and credit. Through her class, students explored archival material, experimented with digital platforms such as Scalar and Omeka, and engaged with the material in ways that transformed their undergraduate research experience. Wernimont collaborated with librarians whose expertise in digital platforms, digital literacy, and scholarly communications could help support and empower her students as nascent digital citizens. Beatriz Maldonado, Scripps College '15, wrote how she initially felt that she could not contribute to the production of academic scholarship and that people would criticize her if she shared her work publicly. Maldonado overcame her fear and found agency because of her strong desire to share what she had learned about the student protests in Claremont in the Scripps College Denison Library's Student Unrest Archives. "Not only did I learn new information, but I was also able to present it in such a way that it became accessible to the rest of the world.... I too had to become part of the cycle of opening the gateways to knowledge and make a place for myself.... Now I know that I hold the power, I hold the agency, I hold the voice."[20]

In 2010, the Claremont Colleges Library built a digital platform with the capabilities for indexing through Google Scholar, establishing an important starting point for faculty and student research. While academic libraries have been collecting their faculty publications since they established libraries within colleges and universities, this digital initiative collects scholarship regardless of format and shares it beyond the library's brick-and-mortar walls so that others can benefit from this work. The impetus for this project came after a prominent Claremont McKenna College (CMC) alumnus was unable to locate a hard-copy version of his senior thesis, leading the college's president to direct the registrar to make all future senior theses available online. Claremont College Library staff collaborated with the relevant deans at CMC to create a policy whereby the academic record of the college was preserved and accessible. Scripps College and a sampling of departments and intercollegiate programs soon followed suit. The impact has been profound (see figure 21.2).

FIGURE 21.2
Screenshot of the map of CMC senior theses downloaded around the world from Scholarship @ Claremont (http://scholarship.claremont.edu/), taken May 2017.

Frequent access of this scholarship provides evidence of the startlingly widespread impact of the decision to digitize and post senior theses. Over the past seven years, institutions from around the world—68 percent from the education sector—have viewed or downloaded the published work of CMC students 310,005 times.[21] This data does not tell the whole story, either, because student authors have the option to provide open access or keep their scholarship restricted to the Claremont Colleges. Traditionally, academics measure impact by citation counts, but data drawn from requests for access to restricted theses shows that a wider readership is interested in these restricted works, too.[22] The library receives a constant stream of emails from educators, students, and researchers who believe the restricted thesis they have discovered through a simple Google search is important enough to make a request for access or to contact the author. The following are quotes from emails sent to the manager of Scholarship @ Claremont:

- From a Midlands State University student in Zimbabwe: "I am writing a dissertation on the feasibility of using bitcoin as an alternative parallel form of currency to try to combat the cash crisis that Zimbabwe is facing."
- From a Claremont Colleges professor: "I just took a look at the repository of past student theses…. I just want to emphasize that this is a stupendous teaching tool—not only because it is a repository of knowledge and an illustration for students of the vast diversity of topics that they might pursue. But it also 'raises the ante' for them really taking their thesis very seriously in the knowledge that it will be memorialized as well as scrutinized by future students. This is bound to 'up' the competitive juices of most students."
- From a university professor in Florida: "My team has been spending some time thinking about the future of autonomous vehicles. This piece of research "Who Will Be the First to Buy Autonomous Vehicles? An Application of Everett Rogers Diffusion of Innovations Theory" is one of the better-reasoned pieces of publicly available literature available on this topic, and I am hoping to connect with the author. I think a conversation with the author of this paper would be interesting and potentially mutually beneficial."
- A Claremont McKenna College professor emailed that an analyst for the Library of Congress Congressional Research Service responsible for providing reports to Congress on Mexico and Latin America discovered a senior thesis and remarked, "This thesis is amazing." The thesis was also cited by a commander at the US Naval War College: "Her work, and that of other outstanding CMC students, can make an important contribution to scholarly research and discussion, which has reached relevant audiences only through digital, online access."

These requests reveal the global reach of and need for accessible research that Scholarship @ Claremont is meeting, and the site's readership data and activity maps illuminate the geospatial nature of that demand (see figures 21.3 and 21.4).

Unless another author's work is accessed over 165,000 times, Kendyl Klein's CMC senior thesis on Scholarship @ Claremont will remain as one of the top five downloaded Claremont Colleges works of all time, easily surpassing statistics for faculty and student work. As a result of the visibility online, Klein's thesis has been quoted in *Elle* magazine and by her alma mater's media

FIGURE 21.3
Screenshot of a senior thesis about an environmental issue in Vietnam that was accessed and downloaded in Vietnam from Scholarship @ Claremont (http://scholarship.claremont.edu/), taken May 2017.

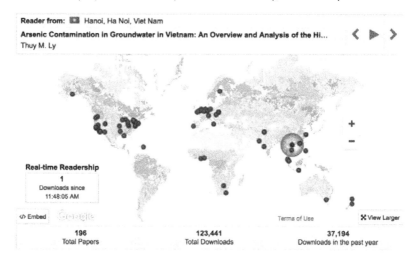

FIGURE 21.4
Screenshot of a senior thesis about an environmental issue in Ghana that was accessed and downloaded in Ghana from Scholarship @ Claremont (http://scholarship.claremont.edu/), taken May 2017.

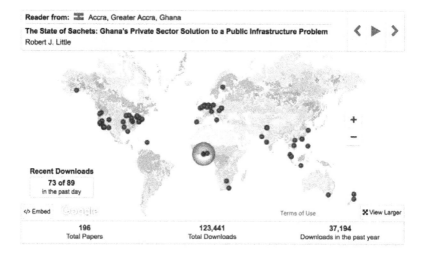

relations, and she has been interviewed by bepress, the software company that supplies the backend to Scholarship @ Claremont. In the interview with bepress, Klein remarks on how this experience has inspired her to continue this line of study. She notes that her "research could be useful in schools: clearly this could turn into some kind of program aimed at parents, teachers, and preteens." Her work and its impact are sources of pride for Klein, "it reminds me of who I am and what I care about."[23] Her insights, like those of others, underscore that undergraduates, by participating in a community of practice and publishing their scholarship online, are adding their voices to "the conversation as researchers and scholars."[24] Also, they are, not incidentally, embodying the Claremont Colleges' academic missions.

Pursuing a Passion: A Teacher's Perspective

Students can engage in this critical conversation only if their work is publicly accessible, which is why it has been so important to establish a digital space in which to publish their scholarship. Otherwise, their work is invisible, much like that of two undergraduate senior theses completed at the Claremont Colleges twenty-eight years apart. When I completed mine at Pitzer College in the spring of 1975, my three faculty readers assessed and graded the final draft and then placed the official version either in a file cabinet or on a bookshelf, somewhere. At least my son's senior thesis, completed in 2003 at Pomona College, can be located on the shelf with others in his major, where it is currently gathering dust in the history department's library. Although my son and I wrote our respective theses in response to primary sources and other archival records, and in dialogue with contemporary academic debates, no one outside of faculty or family ever interacted with these texts' arguments, findings, and insights. Since their production, neither has seen the light of day.

That has not been true for the scholarship that my students produce in partial fulfillment of their major in the environmental analysis program at the Claremont Colleges—they are required to post their work on Scholarship @ Claremont. I instituted this requirement in 2011 when I began teaching the senior thesis class, in part because I did not want my students' ideas languishing in a file cabinet or on a shelf, as mine had. Yet my reasoning actually was more pedagogical than personal, dovetailing with the academic goals of the environmental analysis program, in which I taught. EA, as it is known, is a five-college major and offers a highly interdisciplinary curriculum; I routinely mentor and advise thesis students each fall from three of the undergraduate institutions (Pomona, Scripps College, and Claremont McKenna Colleges).

The first thing I tell them on the very first day of the senior-thesis class is that writing a thesis is their chance to establish their intellectual legacy. I note that this semester-long project provides an unparalleled opportunity for them to demonstrate to themselves and the larger world how they (1) integrate the skills necessary to devise and develop an important intellectual initiative of their own making, (2) conduct the relevant research, and then (3) craft a set of arguments that are as powerful as they are persuasive. To reinforce their theses' significance, the second thing I tell them is that because their scholarship will be posted on Scholarship @ Claremont, their arguments will not disappear into the void.

The fact that their final drafts will be public—and will remain so—comes with a series of obligations and responsibilities (and not a little anxiety) as pressing and pertinent as those that their faculty must take on every time they put their fingers to a keyboard. Open access, for example, raises the stakes by reinforcing the meaning of information literacy and research accountability; scholars at whatever age and level of education must own and defend their arguments in the civic arena.[25] Publishing student scholarship also demands a transparency from these writers about what constitutes excellent work: however innovative their claims, accessibility enables others to see if they supported their perspectives in relation to the relevant primary and secondary literature. It also enables others to answer the following questions: Have they done their due diligence in citing the textual and illustrative resources they have employed? Have they scrupulously edited their final manuscript? Digitizing student scholarship, in short, inculcates these and other critical academic values. At the same time, this process can also help subvert traditional hierarchies of knowledge production that privilege faculty-created scholarship over all others.

Achieving these ambitious ends requires intense collaboration, and the EA program in Claremont has been lucky in the extraordinary level of support its students annually receive from colleagues in the Claremont Colleges Library. Beginning in 2012, librarians and EA faculty developed an information literacy skill set (and later a critical-thinking score sheet) that lays out the rubrics by which faculty thesis readers assess the senior theses (metrics that are shared with the students from the get-go so that they understand the standards by which their work will be evaluated).[26] Each fall, librarians come to the first weeks of the thesis class to identify and highlight library resources—human and reference-based—that will aid students in their research and writing. They also construct a program-specific webpage targeting the varied subjects that a particular year's seniors are exploring, including a robust set of links that stimulate and facilitate the students' initial explorations. Periodically, the librarians and faculty reevaluate the rubrics and other support systems to insure that they continue to meet the needs of student researchers and the program's pedagogical goals. In the past, this self-analysis has also entailed a group of librarians and faculty reading a series of theses to help evaluate and normalize the grading process. This latter initiative has had an unexpected consequence of reducing grade inflation due to heightened expectations on the part of faculty who serve as readers of senior theses.

Whatever students may feel about the possibility of more stringent grading, they have reported that the experience of writing a senior thesis was one of, if not the, most important in their undergraduate careers. In the fall of 2016, in advance of the EA program's ten-year self-study, the program sent out a survey to 270 alumni who had graduated in the past decade. One of the questions probed their memories of the process of writing a thesis and the postgraduation value of their scholarship. Nearly 80 percent of respondents indicated that the required class, and the writing process itself, contributed "quite a bit" or "very much" to their understanding of the academic field. More compelling data, embedded in their written comments, demonstrate that their intellectual engagement has paid dividends that are both personal and professional:

- "My thesis was the most valuable part of my education in terms of preparing me for work. It gave me real experience and showed that I could accomplish something."
- "The thesis was a very important step in my academic career, giving me an undergraduate research experience that I have found many others did not have available."
- "My focused research for my thesis, which included some fieldwork, some lab work, and some policy research, is the main thing I have been able to cite as skills on a resume or in cover letters or interviews. That research allowed me to focus on one topic …which I could claim more expertise in when applying to jobs."
- "The senior thesis was another pivotal class for me because of the independence …to create my question and develop a methodology to address it. I learned so much from that experience and it has been a well-received story in interviews for jobs in the environmental field."

Not all alumni agreed with these positive assessments—one even urged the EA program to "take out the senior thesis requirement or make it substitutable with an internship or summer job. There was slightly too much focus on research skills which have limited use outside of academics." Yet, in the main, the alumni's strongly supportive comments affirm the program's pedagogical commitment to the process of thesis writing and to its dynamic implications for these young scholars.[27] Digital publication of their theses, moreover, amplifies and globalizes that dynamism. By going public with their ideas, students can and do recognize their potential impact on a community of practice. They learn firsthand what it means to participate in, contribute to, and perhaps disrupt academic paradigms. By writing for a wider audience and gaining confidence in their voice and expertise, these emerging scholars assert their intellectual agency, cultural literacy, and digital citizenship—the academic trifecta.

Theory, Practice, and Engagement: An Emerging Scholar's Perspective

I began my thesis research, as many do, with ambition and confusion. As Professor Miller mentioned on the first day of our senior thesis seminar, the thesis was our first opportunity to write a work that could contribute to an intellectual legacy. At the beginning of senior year, I had a strong sense of what I had learned thus far as an undergrad, but very little idea of where I wanted to take this knowledge after graduation. I knew that I wanted to go into a design profession, but like most liberal arts students, I was keenly aware that my knowledge was more theoretical than practical. I had trouble envisioning how I could turn my interests in things like urban history and theory, environmental studies, and performance art into a coherent paper. After four years of studying sustainability at a liberal arts college, I wanted to find a way to synthesize some of the environmental frameworks and urban theories I learned into a nuanced argument about the "real" development of Claremont.

Although my instinct was to try to narrow my ideas from the beginning, my thesis readers, whose interest in sustainability represented three distinct personal and disciplinary perspectives, pushed me to begin my investigation broadly. Ultimately, I—like many other EA majors—settled on a defined geographical place situated at the intersection of multiple environmental and social systems. I chose to write about a large, conspicuously empty gravel pit immediately east of the Claremont Colleges. I wondered why, given the extensive urban sprawl of the Inland Empire, this cavernous open ground—a gap—had remained undeveloped. How had it resisted the pressure of the real estate market? How had this obviously underused patch of land escaped development? The short answer was that backfill and development had been cost-prohibitive, up until this point. My training in environmental analysis pushed me to develop iterative ways of thinking about this piece of land to expose the nuance in the longer answer. This land was all of the following:

1. Acreage surveyed through some means and brought into an American system of property rights;
2. A design problem with sociopolitical and technical narratives attached;

3.   Terrain that, by virtue of its "otherness," served as a site for various unrealized and illicit uses that could potentially say something about a narrative struggle between dominant and oppressed/out groups.[28]

I knew I wanted to draw on the various disciplines of my advisers—history, landscape architecture, and architecture, and I knew that I wanted to enter a design discipline. Thus, I began my literature review by trying to understand how design and planning disciplines account for leftover spaces like the large quarry I was assessing. As any student who has conducted research will know, the "literature review" phase of research can be intimidating. I spent my first month imagining myself writing to an academic audience of historians, architectural theorists, and planners. I thought that the goal, as it was in my other academic papers, was to present a concise and accurate analysis and evaluation of relevant arguments. As this work progressed, however, I began to feel stuck between the banality of my place (it was a hole in the ground) and the seemingly groundbreaking scholarship I was reading. I thought; "How could I write something original about this hole in the ground that anyone would want to read?" As I struggled to understand how I would enter this conversation, my anxiety over writing a thesis with an original academic argument grew. I felt like I was spinning my wheels, and further, I felt like I was neglecting my original research topic: the gravel pit next to the Claremont Colleges.

On the advice of my advisors, I turned to the Claremont Colleges Library Special Collections. Although diving into the archive could not relieve my anxiety about creating an original argument about urban design and planning, it replaced this worry with a straightforward research task: find information about the gravel pit. I thought, "This, I can do." Of course, I quickly realized that what appeared straightforward actually was a collection of hundreds of moments in which I could draw connections to the scholarship I had experienced in my coursework. Ultimately, this trust in my advisors and my ability to bridge their diverse academic interests was the key element in helping me access the breadth of knowledge and research skills I had gained over my undergraduate education.[29]

Working in the archives was an open-ended method of research. My interests followed what I found: I was able to develop a close investigation of local mutual water companies at the turn of the twentieth century at some points, and, at another, a survey of the Claremont Colleges' planning history. As more documents piled onto my cart, I experimented with different ways of taking notes and documenting information. Most documents contained first- or second-person accounts of events and expansion plans, and I followed these narrative threads through my unruly pile, piecing together an historical narrative around key landowners and hydrogeological engineers.

My developing understanding of Claremont and improving skill in locating historical documents allowed me to identify the formative impact that late-nineteenth-century Claremont still has on the contemporary built landscape.

Viewing myself as an archival scholar also led to patterns of thinking that helped me follow multiple strains of scholarship. As I probed the specifics of water-rights litigation, the parameters of my arguments became more obscure, but their relevance to modern issues grew, compelling me to double down on the work of contextualizing my analyses and arguments. My archival research revealed that the story of urban development in the Inland Empire is not a straightforward narrative of land speculation, industry, and conservation, but rather a contested territory of overlapping and conflicting claims of access and ownership. Because my task was, in some senses, to mine these archival collections and scholarly analyses for any relevant information from these multiple strains of inquiry, I was able to develop a more theoretically complex understanding of the cultural dimensions of land use and development.

As any student or educator with exposure to college and college-prep curricula will recognize, learning to write to an academic audience is a goal that has long been central to undergraduate education.[30] Even though I had the support of my advisers, who provided both traditional feedback and collaborative brainstorming, the basic challenge of producing an academically relevant argument stood between a successful thesis and me. Knowing that my scholarship would be publicly available allowed my advisers and me to consider a broader audience for this history of Claremont. Instead of pursuing a traditionally narrow research topic, I was allowed to "play" in the archives and follow multiple strains of research. Paradoxically, writing to a general-knowledge audience about the history of Claremont allowed me to cover more academic ground. In the archives, I was investigating histories of hydrogeology and flood management, the underpinnings of property rights and development in colonial and imperial systems of thought, the significance of art movements in the 1960s, and several other threads that formed the basis of my account of Claremont's development. Ultimately, the primary-source-to-digital-publishing framework of the senior thesis provided an intellectual framework and long-term motivation for what would become my first piece of published scholarship, a coauthored article entitled "Watershed Politics: Groundwater Management and Resource Conservation in Southern California's Pomona Valley."[31] The EA program's outward focus, paired with its environmental and historical underpinnings, allowed me to dig deep enough into the archives to draw connections between my subject—a gravel quarry with seemingly limited relevance—and the political and socioeconomic systems that guide Claremont's development.

The most valuable thing I took away from my thesis research was this aptitude for bridging academic theory and the actual condition of the built environment. My thesis showed me that careful historical analysis—a skill typically sequestered within the ivory tower—can in fact lead to larger, normative claims about how communities can shape their built environment. This realization has also helped me understand that open-access research not only can expand access to the academy, but also can actually put the power of academia to work for the community. Analyzing my archival findings for a contemporary general audience was a process of unraveling and publicizing an often-ignored history of water and property rights in order to reframe the problem of development for an audience within and beyond the academy.

Since graduating and moving into the design field, I have continued to use these expanded academic skills on a daily basis to understand interactions between design, construction, and regulation. As a novice designer working in the same community I researched, I have watched homeowners, designers, planners, and community leaders think and act in ways that have direct connections to the one-hundred-year-old history I examined in my senior thesis. My undergraduate research nuanced my understanding of contemporary forces shaping the local built landscape. This experience is by no means unique in the EA program. Over half of my peers in the class of 2015, many of whom are close friends whose companionship in writing and thinking remains crucial to my work, wrote similarly nuanced and geographically based analyses. Further, this revelation is not limited to the class of 2015. Rather, it drew inspiration from reading the class of 2014's theses, and it contributed to other works through a number of downloads globally. My research into water rights helped launch another senior's scholarship two years later.[32] Observing these varied connections within my own scholarship and the EA program more generally has expanded my sense of agency as a writer, planner, and designer in a time of seemingly endless political instability.

Picking Up the Paper Trail: A Student Scholar's View

Jan Conn knows a thing or two about agency. She lives alone, in the wooden home, tucked into the hillside amid aspen, that she and her late husband Herb built in 1949. At the bend in her driveway, off a dirt road in the Black Hills of South Dakota, a hand-painted sign nailed to a tree says, "Please honk." The sign is to let her know that someone is coming: at ninety years old, her hearing is slightly less than perfect, which is still above average for that age. Conn is petite, barely five feet tall, and still sprightly: the result of her many decades of rock climbing, caving, and hiking. She wears a navy and green patterned sweater, blue jeans, red socks, and gray sneakers; Conn still walks several miles to her mailbox every day. She sits with her knees tucked up to her chest with an ease and flexibility many sixty-year-olds can no longer attain. Sixty-seven years ago, Conn was the first woman to climb and summit Bear Lodge, also known as Devils Tower National Monument; four years after that, she and Jane Showacre made the first "manless" ascent there. Conn and her husband were the forerunners of a growing "dirtbag" movement among climbers and other outdoor recreationists, living out of their truck for years in the 1940s and 1950s while climbing in Wyoming and South Dakota and exploring the Wind and Jewel Caves of South Dakota. However, Conn says that if she were young nowadays, she does not think she would climb. "It's just too mainstream."[33]

Given her nearly off-the-grid status, Conn was the most difficult to find out of all of those that I conducted oral history interviews with during the summer of 2015, between my third and fourth years as an environmental analysis major at Pomona College. Reaching out to Conn, and to the other rock climbers, National Park Service employees, Northern Plains tribal members, and historians was part of a year-long research process that involved innumerable hours spent in the Claremont Colleges Library, the University of Wyoming Library, and the Wyoming State Archives. This work also entailed plenty of sunny afternoons on the back porches of my interview participants, listening to their stories of Bear Lodge. I had come across the complicated history of this tremendous rock formation, located in northeastern Wyoming, by chance: I overheard a climbing partner discussing the Northern Plains tribal opposition to climbing at the site and began cursory research that led to a formative academic and intellectual experience.[34]

This was, in many ways, a personal project: as a rock climber and devotee of our national parks and other public lands, I was deeply troubled to learn about the problematic history of our public lands during a class with Professor Char Miller my third year of college. The history of our national forests, grasslands, parks, and refuges intertwines deeply with the violent removal of Native Americans from their lands and waters, and while awareness of this dark side of our "national treasures" is growing, it largely remains limited to academia. This realization required a personal reexamination of the history of the national parks. It also forced me to think about how I play in these spaces and how I have understood these landscapes for the majority of my life. The controversy over rock climbing at Bear Lodge revealed, in a more recent context, the ongoing silence—intentional or not—surrounding the contentious history of our public lands, recreation, and Native Americans.

Bear Lodge has been, for time immemorial, a sacred site for the multitude of Northern Plains tribes and remains so today. It is also our first national monument, and one of this country's iconic rock-climbing sites. Controversy over the appropriateness and legality of rock climbing on this sacred site exploded in the 1990s, leading to extensive negotiations and lawsuits that nearly reached the Supreme Court. My research and thesis historicized the arguments made by rock climbers, local white residents, and the National Park Service to understand how arguments about spirituality, tradition, and history itself legitimized claims to this space in the present.[35]

Due to changes in the directions of my thesis over the course of research and writing, the final argument rested less on the oral history interviews I conducted than on archival materials from the National Park Service and other sources. Nevertheless, these interviews were foundational to the research process, and many informed further research and questions pursued over the course of my writing. They continue to inform me as I rewrite and transform my thesis into a journal article. Conducting oral history research on such a topic confronted me with the ethical issues of the researcher's positionality versus that of the participants, as well as the responsibility of the researcher to the participants. As my focus was on a moment in history that nonetheless happened within my lifetime, I had to grapple with the fact that people involved in the controversy were, for the most part, still alive, well, and more than willing to give me their opinion about whatever I wrote in my thesis.

Into this fray enters the requirement of the environmental analysis program to make our completed senior theses publicly available online at Scholarship @ Claremont. Unlike student scholars during Professor Miller's undergraduate days, I did not have the opportunity to make claims about a particular community or group of people without them noticing. Part of this was my commitment in my agreement with my interview participants that I would send copies of the thesis upon completion; the other was the fact that my thesis would become available to anyone who chose to look for it with a quick Google search.

If my fellow EA students and I were merely asked to submit our theses to an academic journal, there would certainly be an amount of pressure to produce exemplary scholarship. Yet, hidden behind paywalls and in library corridors, these journals are still mostly read only within academia. The requirement to make our theses available to the general public set the academic and intellectual bar quite high: perhaps the greatest challenge I faced was that I would be making my arguments about the statements and opinions of my subjects public, potentially causing unforeseen impacts on the people who had very generously agreed to let me interview them. In a number of ways, this exacerbated the already-extensive ethical quandaries of oral history and made an already self-critical and exacting undergraduate even more so. Publishing my completed thesis on Scholarship @ Claremont would not be the end of my journey with the topic; I was accountable for what happened next, and I am still learning, not whether or not, but how much my work has impacted those people and institutions about which I wrote.

My thesis historicized and critiqued the arguments and statements of rock climbers and the National Park Service. I argued that rock climbers and local white residents appropriated the Northern Plains tribes' language of spirituality and tradition. In so doing, these climbers and residents sought to delegitimize tribal claims to this public space and simultaneously legitimize their own use and meanings of Bear Lodge. Despite the obvious efforts on the part of the National Park Service to accommodate tribal beliefs and wishes, and to strike a balance in a highly contentious situation, the Park Service was nevertheless complicit in controlling the discourse of Bear Lodge and in erasing the complex history of the Northern Plains tribal ties to this sacred place.

Two of the people I interviewed are rock climbers and climbing guides with vested economic interests in the continuation of climbing at Bear Lodge. One of these climbers was a litigant involved in the group suing the National Park Service to halt the agency's accommodation of tribal beliefs and practices regarding Bear Lodge. I also interviewed numerous current and former National Park Service employees. As promised, I sent copies of my thesis to all those whom I interviewed, regardless of whether or not information or quotes obtained during a particular participants' interview ultimately appeared in the thesis. I have not heard from either of the two climbing guides, despite several efforts to reach out, while several of the Park Service participants sent feedback. Several were positive, commending my research and arguments. One was concerned about my depiction of the Park Service as complicit—I said as much in the abstract of the thesis—but admitted that once he had read the entire thesis, he understood some of my criticisms of the agency, even though he did not agree with my conclusion.

Those limited comments, and in certain cases silences, were the extent of direct reactions from my participants. Yet the readership reports made available by Scholarship @ Claremont reveal interesting data that has sparked many unanswered—and perhaps unanswerable—questions about downloads, reads, understandings, and utilization of my thesis. According to the report, people in thirty-five countries have downloaded my thesis. This includes people in the United States, Japan, India, Brazil, India, and the Seychelles. The software tracks the institutional association of individuals downloading my thesis, and while individuals at the Claremont Colleges are understandably responsible for the greatest number of downloads, the National Park Service is third on the list of institutions with the most downloads of my thesis. According to the report, the Bureau of Land Management, the US Forest Service, and the Department of Homeland Security have downloaded my thesis, along with individuals at numerous colleges and universities, and even, curiously, Disney. Perhaps a remake of "Close Encounters with the Third Kind" is in the near future?[36]

I certainly could not have, and did not, anticipate such reach because my thesis is publicly available online. Yet the pressure to produce research and writing to the highest academic and intellectual standards that I could achieve, and to be accountable to and respectful of those whom I interviewed and discussed, was eternally present from the moment I learned of this requirement. That my thesis would become public was at once an honor and a challenge. It was my professors and librarians saying that my thoughts and words matter, that despite not yet holding even a bachelor's degree in my hands, I had value as an intellectual, a historian, and a scholar. The public nature of the thesis also meant that my thoughts and words were before the world, and that I had to create an exemplary thesis in which I made convincing arguments backed by sound evidence and theory, and throughout which I was accountable to those whom I discussed in my thesis as well to historical fact.

Such layers of accountability are challenges that shaped my development as a citizen and a scholar throughout my last year of college, and I am continuing to refine my arguments for an article-length publication and for applications to graduate programs in environmental history. While I am currently outside of academia, navigating the working world and personal adventures, the ability, formulated by oral history research and the requirement to make my thesis publicly available, while working across the boundaries of the academic and nonacademic worlds, has proved invaluable. The challenges will continue: while I intend to pursue a PhD in environmental history, I am firmly committed to bridging those boundaries, through exceptional scholarship, intellectual integrity, compassionate and conscientious research, and a dedication to public history and education. These aims were merely distant ideas at the beginning of my research, but they developed over the course of my research, writing, and publication of my senior thesis. When I drove up Jan Conn's driveway in the Black Hills, I was simply a student in search of the past.

Conclusion

No such search is a solo excursion. Whenever librarians, professors, and students launch their research projects, they do so in collaboration with one another. Making that collaborative process more intentional has been one of the goals of the environmental analysis program's senior-thesis project. Another has been to increase student-scholars' awareness of the public nature of their research and the larger audiences to and for whom they are writing. Conscientious citizenship demands no less. It also requires that students be self-aware of the systemic implications of their work and that they understand why making their scholarship fully accessible online can be a disruptive act. "It is crucial to expose students to the structural considerations and power dynamics that underlie contemporary academia and the associated industries that aid its massive production and consumption of information," Scott Warren and Kim Duckett assert.[37] "Doing so gives these future citizens and scholars the ability to evaluate such systems from moral and ethical stances of their own choosing."[38] The pedagogical impact of giving students agency over their research and the methodological frameworks that structure it, paired with a requirement to post their scholarship online, inculcates an individual sense of responsibility and accountability for one's ideas that, when taken together, adds up to a collective transformation. Put differently, student scholarship is not child's play.

Appendix 21A.
Claremont Colleges Mission Statements

The undergraduate Claremont Colleges mission statements used in the figure 21.1 word cloud:

- Claremont McKenna College, "CMC's Mission and Motto," accessed June 20, 2018, https://www.cmc.edu/about/mission-and-motto.
- Harvey Mudd College, "Mission and Strategic Vision," accessed June 20, 2018, https://www.hmc.edu/about-hmc/mission-vision/.
- Pitzer College, "Mission and Values," accessed June 20, 2018, https://www.pitzer.edu/about/mission-and-values/.
- Pomona College, "Pomona College Mission Statement," accessed June 20, 2018, https://www.pomona.edu/about/pomona-college-mission-statement.
- Scripps College, "About Scripps College," accessed June 20, 2018, http://www.scrippscollege.edu/about/.

Appendix 21B.
Information Literacy in Student Work Rubric—Claremont Colleges Library

Learning Outcome	Level of Achievement			
	Highly Developed 4	**Developed 3**	**Emerging 2**	**Initial 1**
Attribution	*Shows a sophisticated level of understanding for when and how to give attribution.* • Documents sources consistently and completely • Uses in-text citation and notes correctly and consistently • Cites non-textual sources consistently • Names and labels figures and/or graphs clearly and completely.	*Attribution indicates understanding of the rationale for and various mechanisms of citation.* • Documents sources throughout with occasional errors or inconsistencies. • Uses in-text citation and notes with occasional errors or inconsistencies • Cites non-textual sources with relative consistency • Usually names and labels figures and/or graphs clearly and completely.	*Missteps in attribution interfere with the argument or point to fundamental misunderstandings.* • Frequently documents sources incorrectly or leaves out some citations. • Frequent errors and inconsistencies with in-text citation and notes • Does not consistently cite non-textual sources • Names and labels figures and/or graphs inconsistently.	*Use of evidence and citation is poor, making it difficult to evaluate the argument or sources.* • Displays fundamental and consistent errors in source documentation • Does not include or contains significant inconsistencies with in-text citation and notes • Does not name, title, or cite non-textual sources • Does not name or label figures and/or graphs.

Learning Outcome	Level of Achievement			
	Highly Developed 4	Developed 3	Emerging 2	Initial 1
Evaluation of Sources	*Source materials employed demonstrate expertise and sophisticated independent thought.* • Demonstrates sophisticated awareness of universe of literature and community of scholarship • Uses a variety of appropriate and authoritative sources • Always distinguishes between types of sources (e.g., scholarly v. popular, fact v. opinion) • Does not over- or under-rely on the ideas of others or the work of a single author • Demonstrates a thorough critical exploration and knowledge of theories and sources selected	*Source materials are adequate and appropriate but lack variety or depth.* • Explores supporting sources and community of scholarship but might overlook important avenues • Sources are used support claim(s) but may not be the most authoritative source to make claim • Usually distinguishes between types of sources (e.g., scholarly v. popular, fact v. opinion) • May over- or under-rely on the ideas of others or the work of a single author • Demonstrates a preliminary critical exploration and knowledge of theories and sources selected	*Source materials used are inadequate.* • Exhibits weak awareness of universe of literature or other sources that could strengthen claim(s) or argument(s) • Relies on too few or largely inappropriate sources • Does not consistently distinguish between types of sources (e.g., primary v. secondary, scholarly v. popular, fact v. opinion) • Clearly selected sources out of convenience • Demonstrates little critical exploration and knowledge of theories and sources selected	*Source materials are absent or do not contribute to claim(s) or argument(s).* • No evidence of awareness of universe of literature or other sources that could strengthen claim(s) or argument(s) • When included, sources are too few or badly inappropriate • No distinction between types of sources (e.g., scholarly v. popular, fact v. opinion) • Does not explore outside sources or present evidence when called for • No evidence of critical exploration and knowledge of theories and sources selected

Learning Outcome	Level of Achievement			
	Highly Developed 4	Developed 3	Emerging 2	Initial 1
Communication of Evidence	*Evidence is integrated and synthesized expertly to support claims.* • Consistently presents evidence to support claim(s) and argument(s) • Synthesizes and contextualizes evidence appropriately for audience • Uses evidence instrumentally towards rhetorical goals • Distinction between own ideas and ideas of others is consistently clear	*Proficient synthesis and integration of evidence.* • Generally employs evidence to support claim(s) and argument(s) • May present some evidence without context • Frequently demonstrates using evidence instrumentally toward rhetorical goals • Distinction between own ideas and ideas of others is usually clear	*Weak attempts at synthesis or integration.* • Sporadically uses evidence to support claim(s) or argument(s) • Frequently fails to put sources into context (e.g. "The World Bank says...") • Usually does not demonstrate using evidence instrumentally toward rhetorical goals • Consistently blurs distinction between own ideas and ideas of others	*No evidence of attempt at synthesis or integration.* • Claim(s) or argument(s) lack necessary evidence • Fails to contextualize quotes and evidence • No demonstration of using evidence instrumentally toward rhetorical goals • No distinction between own ideas and ideas of others

Information Literacy in Student Work Rubric Scoring Sheet—Claremont Colleges Library

Identification

ID Code _____   Reader Name _____

Term/Year _____   Faculty _____

Could not evaluate information literacy (IL) in this work? Check the box and you're done. ☐

Assignment

A. Does the assignment ask students to use evidence outside of assigned course content? *(check one)*
   ☐ Required   ☐ Allowed   ☐ Discouraged
   ☐ No explicit mention   ☐ Assignment not available   ☐ N/A

B. This work is a (e.g., research paper, thesis, report, summary, argument, analysis, reflection, media project, other)

Quality of attribution, evaluation, and communication of IL (see rubric for details):

	Highly Developed (4)	Developed (3)	Emerging (2)	Initial (1)	Comments	Totals
·tribution						
·aluation of ·urces						
·mmunication Evidence						
					Sum:	

OPTIONAL

This work is a particularly representative example of the following (check any that apply):
   ☐ Very robust bibliography
   ☐ Egregious errors in bibliography, in-text citations, notes
   ☐ Clear and consistent citations
   ☐ Little or no attribution of non-textual elements
   ☐ Chose appropriate sources to support claims
   ☐ Inappropriate source(s) used to support claim

☐ Sources are well-integrated and synthesized
☐ Sources not integrated or synthesized (e.g., "patch writing" or excessive block quoting)
☐ Shows awareness of depth of scholarship in area
☐ Sources lack breadth or depth
☐ Over/Undercited claims
☐ Other _____

Elaboration (optional):

Information Literacy in Student Work Rubric/Scoring Sheet Codebook – Claremont Colleges Library
Identification
Fill out any available details regarding student work.

Can we evaluate information literacy in this work?
Even if no sources are cited or the assignment does not call for outside sources, student work may exhibit information literacy if the student is placing their ideas in a broader context using ideas or information from other sources.

Assignment
A. Expectations about use of evidence outside of assigned course reading or other materials provided by professor (use N/A in the case of thesis or other work without defined assignment parameters).
B. Assignment type allows us to determine how to evaluate works that fall outside the "standard" research paper (e.g. a report, thesis, summary, argument, analysis, reflection, media project, or other type of work)

Quality of attribution, evaluation, and communication of Information Literacy
For each category, check the appropriate box. (Highly Developed, Developed, Emerging, Initial)

- **Attribution** refers to how well and consistently the student cites the ideas of others, including non-traditional sources (like lectures, emails, DVD commentaries) and images/figures.
- **Evaluation** refers to the appropriateness or quality of source materials the student chooses to use to support their rhetorical goals (claims or arguments). This includes materials and sources in their bibliography (if available) as well as those used throughout the work. Do the sources, examples, and evidence selected match the purpose of the type of work and argument the student is creating? Is the student aware of the differences between primary and secondary sources, popular and scholarly sources, or fact and opinion? Have they selected the variety and quality of sources appropriate for their argument and work type?
- **Communication** refers to the use and integration of sources as well as the quality of composition, e.g., whether the student has integrated the evidence they're using and has done so in a way instrumental to their claim(s) and argument(s). Does the student paraphrase, summarize, synthesize, use quotes appropriately? Does the student frame quotations using authoritative sources? How are they using sources to ground their claims? This category also addresses how a student integrates their own ideas with those of others.

OPTIONAL—This work is a particularly rich example of the following (check any that apply):

Check an item when the noted characteristics are present and should be flagged as interesting or rich examples for future analysis or conversation. If you see other rich examples, note them as "Other."

Rubric content adapted for the Claremont Colleges by Char Booth (char_booth@ cuc.claremont.edu), Sara Lowe (sara_lowe@cuc.claremont.edu), Natalie Tagge (natalie_tagge@cuc.claremont.edu), and Sean Stone (sean_stone@uc.claremont. edu) from an instrument originally developed at Carleton College. See http:// www.inthelibrarywiththeleadpipe.org/2011/csil-carleton-forensic-librarians-and-reflective-practices/. This rubric version (2012/13) was revised Summer-Fall of 2012 and finalized 8 November 2012.

Appendix 21C.
Critical Thinking Rubric

Critical Thinking Draft 10_11_2016

Critical thinking is just one of many valuable skills faculty at Pomona College teach their students. We care not only about teaching this to our students but also determining the degree of progress they are making in learning it, and so whether some pedagogical interventions might be called for.

It turns out that WASC too requires Pomona College assess critical thinking as part of Pomona's accreditation. WASC's interest is not in how many of our seniors are measuring up to our expectations, but rather in whether Pomona College is engaged in the process of assessing and reflecting on how well our students are doing and whether any pedagogical changes are called for.

On p. 2 is a draft of an assessment sheet for evaluating the critical thinking skills of Pomona College's seniors.

Pomona College needs one common rubric for all departments since WASC asks for a college-wide assessment. But we want the assessment to be useful at the departmental level and thus flexible enough to capture the individual aims of each discipline.

The rubric that the TLC has come up with, with input from many departments and more than one committee, can be used by whoever the department decides is the best person assess the work of the Pomona seniors in its majors (e.g., the primary thesis advisor). The senior work might be a thesis, a paper from a senior seminar, or perhaps even an exam – whatever senior work the department determines is amenable to assessment for critical thinking and that occurs during the Fall 2016 - Spring 2017 academic year.

Here is our working definition of critical thinking:

> Critical thinking is the ability to explore issues, ideas, artifacts, and events skillfully and insightfully and on that basis formulate a well-supported opinion or conclusion.

There are different points in the process of intellectual inquiry, as exhibited in a piece of written work, where critical thinking skills are employed:[1]

- Selection or Formulation of a question
- Design or selection of a method(s) for addressing the question
- Interpretation
- Evaluation

And throughout the process of inquiry the following is key to critical thinking:

- Connection of thoughts in a rational manner

---

[1] Not every sort of intellectual inquiry i) has all of these points or ii) proceeds in this order or iii) exhibits critical thinking skills at that point. Instead, critical thinking *can* be exhibited at each of these points. Also, (iv) the same critical thinking skill can be used at more than one point and (v) some of these points overlap (e.g., evaluation occurs at various stages of inquiry).

Critical Thinking Score Sheet for
Senior Student Work

Pomona Student's Name	Reader	Type of Work (e.g., thesis, lit review, seminar paper, etc.)	Term/Year
_____	_____	_____	_____

See pages 3-4 and 8 for a detailed explanation of how one might understand I-V categories as well as the 1-4 scale.

If one or more of these points of inquiry is not relevant to how you assesses critical thinking in written work, please put N/A in that row on the score sheet below.

	Highly Developed 4	Developed 3	Emerging 2	Novice 1
(I) Selection or Formulation of a question				
(II) Design/Selection of Method(s)				
(III) Interpretation				
(IV) Evaluation				
(V) Connection of Thoughts				

Within each department (not across departments) the scorers will need to discuss and determine:

a) What counts as "highly developed" as opposed to "developed," and so on? See p. 8 for some initial suggestions for how one might articulate this. It would help the TLC to receive a short description of what you decided this 1-4 scale meant.

b) What number is the cut off for satisfactory achievement, i.e., below what number would be cause for concern? Please write that number here: _____. It would help the TLC to know why your department picked this number.

Interpretation of I-V
(2 pages)

The bullets points under each category are examples of how one can interpret each category. We do not imagine every category or bullet point applies in every instance. For each category, you will need to **omit** the bullet points *that are not relevant,* **add** *bullet points that are missing, or* **revise** *bullet points that are below.*

(I) Selection or Formulation of a question
- Guides, shapes, and narrows the research/analysis
- Suggests a complex, unobvious answer
- Uses precise, unambiguous language that is neither leading nor biased
- Can be supported by research/analysis
- Focuses on a dilemma or problem that is motivated and significant

(II) Design or selection of a method(s) for addressing the question
- Formulates a hypothesis or answer to the question
- Breaks a problem into sub-problems
- Selects *or* creates the method, language, bodily movement, theory
    E.g. designs an experiment, selects a movement language or choreography, picks an approach to translation
- Approaches the problem using more than one method or theory
- Derives the importable, testable implications of the theory

(III) Interpretation
- Applies the appropriate method, language, or theory
- Demonstrates an awareness of how (not merely that) information (e.g. data, results, musical or written passages, etc.) can be interpreted in more than one way
- Demonstrates an awareness of how (not merely that) historical, ethical, political, cultural, social, and environmental conditions influence ideas, events, and artifacts
    For example, how venue, gender, race, class, religion and a variety of other factors affect how one reads a work of art and thus that how the meaning of a single work can change.
- Demonstrates comprehension of the meaning or significance of experiences, sounds, colors, textures, situations, data, events, etc.
- Identifies the *intended* relationships among statements

(IV) Evaluation
- Demonstrates an awareness of the *assumptions* of a given model, theory, technique, language, etc.
    o Demonstrate an understanding of how changing the parameters or assumptions (e.g. of a model) will influence the results
- Demonstrates an awareness of the *limitations* of a given model, theory, technique, language, etc.
- Identifies ways in which an estimation, theory, etc. may be biased or unreliable
- Assesses the credibility and strength of an account, belief, opinion, experience, description of a perception, etc.
- Recognizes missing elements of the evidence or that certain important factors were ignored
- Questions key assumptions (e.g. for plausibility, etc.)
- Identifies bugs in a program
- Distinguishes the intended and actual relationships among statements

- Assesses how useful or appropriate the data are to the research question
- Assesses which technique(s) is most appropriate for establishing causality
- Performs robustness checks of results

(V) Connection of thoughts in a rational manner
  - Makes inferences or establishes what the actual relationships are among statements, factors, or variables
  - Presents ideas in well-ordered fashion
  - Demonstrates an understanding of how an abstract idea, a principle, generalization or model *applies to* a particular or concrete case
  - Demonstrates an ability to abstract, generalize, or develop a model *from* concrete or particular cases
  - Appropriately compares and contrasts different theoretical perspectives, movement patterns, styles, languages, theories, particular cases, etc.
  - Demonstrates an understanding of the relation of the parts to the whole
  - Distinguishes cause and effect from correlation
  - Demonstrates an understanding of the implications of theory, method, etc.
  - Demonstrates how to correctly adapt a theory, method, etc. to *new* situations and information (including grammatical patterns and rules)
  - Identifies useful future research that builds on one's results

The following is CHEMISTRY'S current interpretation of I-V, which might be revised in the coming months.

(I) Selection or Formulation of a question [relevant to the literature thesis but not to the experimental thesis]
  - Uses extensive analysis of the literature of identify a gap in knowledge
  - Guides, shapes, and narrows the research/analysis to develop a question, hypothesis and/or specific aim
  - Suggests experimental observations / results that will support a hypothesis or answer a question

(II) Design or selection of a method(s) for addressing the question [relevant to the literature thesis but not to the experimental thesis]
  - Selects the appropriate experimental method(s) that will unambiguously address the question, hypothesis and/or specific aim
  - Includes the appropriate controls, when necessary
  - Provides expected results and interprets what they would mean
  - Provides potential problems that may arise and alternative approaches that can be used to address those problems

(III) Interpretation [relevant to experimental thesis but not the literature thesis]
  - Demonstrates comprehension of the meaning or significance of the data and observations collected
  - Is able to draw appropriate conclusions from the data

(IV) Evaluation [relevant to both the literature thesis and the experimental thesis]
  - Demonstrates an awareness of the *assumptions* of a given model, theory, technique, etc.
    - Demonstrate an understanding of how changing the parameters or assumptions (e.g. of a model) will influence the results
  - Demonstrates an awareness of the *limitations* of a given model, theory, technique, language, etc.
  - Identifies ways in which an estimation, theory, etc. may be biased or unreliable
  - Assesses the credibility and strength of experimental results
  - Recognizes missing elements of the evidence or that certain important factors were ignored

(V) Connection of thoughts in a rational manner [relevant to both the literature thesis and the experimental thesis]
  - Appropriately integrates prior work with proposed or experimentally obtained results
  - Presents ideas in well-ordered fashion
  - Demonstrates an understanding of why this research is relevant to science and society

The following is ENGLISH'S current interpretation of I-V, which might be revised in the coming months.

(I) Selection or Formulation of a question
- Guides, shapes, and narrows the research/analysis
- Suggests a complex, unobvious answer
- Can be supported by research/analysis
- Focuses on a dilemma or problem that is motivated and significant

(II) Design or selection of a method(s) for addressing the question
- Formulates a hypothesis or answer to the question
- Breaks a problem into sub-problems
- Selects *or* creates the method or theory

(III) Interpretation
- Applies the appropriate method, language, theory
- Identifies the intended relationships among statements

(IV) Evaluation
- Demonstrates an awareness of the *assumptions* of a given model, theory, technique, language, etc.
    - Demonstrate an understanding of how changing the parameters or assumptions (e.g. of a model) will influence the results
- Demonstrates an awareness of the *limitations* of a given model, theory, technique, language, etc.
- Identifies ways in which an estimation, theory, etc. may be biased or unreliable
- Assesses the credibility and strength of an account, belief, opinion, experience, description of a perception, etc.
- Recognizes missing elements of the evidence or that certain important factors were ignored
- Questions key assumptions
- Distinguishes the intended and actual relationships among statements

(V) Connection of thoughts in a rational manner
- Makes inferences or establishes what the actual relationships are among statements
- Presents ideas in well-ordered fashion
- Demonstrates an understanding of how an abstract idea, a principle, generalization or model *applies to* a particular or concrete case
- Demonstrates an ability to abstract, generalize, or develop a model *from* concrete or particular cases
- Demonstrates an understanding of the relation of the parts to the whole
- Demonstrates an understanding of the implications of theory, method, etc.
- Demonstrates how to correctly adapt a theory, method, etc. to *new* situations and information (including grammatical patterns and rules)

The following is ECONOMIC'S current interpretation of I-V, which might be revised in the coming months.

(I) Selection or Formulation of a question
- Guides, shapes, and narrows the research/analysis
- Suggests an unobvious answer
- Uses precise unambiguous language that is neither leading nor biased
- Can be supported by research/analysis
- Focuses on a dilemma or problem that is motivated and significant
- Displays a thorough knowledge of previous research on the question

(II) Design or selection of a method(s) for addressing the question
- Formulates a clear hypothesis or answer to the question
- Selects *or* creates the method or theory that can answer the question
    E.g. designs an experiment
- Derives the importable testable implications of the theory

(III) Interpretation
- Applies the appropriate method or theory
- Demonstrates an awareness of how (not merely that) data and results can be interpreted in more than one way
- Demonstrates comprehension of the meaning or significance of experiences, situations, data, events, etc.
Assesses how useful or appropriate the data are to the research question
(IV) Evaluation
- Demonstrates an awareness of the *assumptions* of a given model, theory, technique, etc.
    o Demonstrate an understanding of how changing the parameters or assumptions (e.g. of a model) will influence the results
- Demonstrates an awareness of the *limitations* of a given model, theory, technique, etc.
- Identifies ways in which the estimation, theory, etc. may be biased or unreliable
- Recognizes missing elements of the evidence or that certain important factors were ignored
- Assesses the plausibility of key assumptions
- Identifies the most appropriate technique for establishing causality
- Performs robustness checks of your results
(V) Connection of thoughts in a rational manner
- Makes inferences or establishes what the actual relationships are among factors and variables
- Presents ideas in well-ordered fashion
- Demonstrates an understanding of how an abstract idea, a principle, generalization or model *applies to* a particular or concrete case
- Demonstrates an ability to abstract, generalize, or develop a model *from* concrete or particular cases
- Appropriately compares and contrasts different theoretical perspectives, theories, particular cases, etc.
- Demonstrates an understanding of the relation of the parts to the whole
- Distinguishes cause and effect from correlation
- Demonstrates an understanding of the implications of theory, method, etc.
- Demonstrates how to correctly adapt a theory, method, etc. to *new* situations and information (including grammatical patterns and rules)
- Identifies useful future research that builds on one's results

Different Ways of Interpreting the 1-4 Scale
(not a comprehensive list: these are just suggestions)

Highly Developed	Developed	Emerging	Novice
4	3	2	1

4 = a contender for a departmental prize
3 = not prize worthy, but very good or perhaps ok.
2 = problematic
1 = not acceptable

4 = **very successful** in demonstrating **all** the bullets points in this category
3 = **very successful** in demonstrating **many** of the bullets points in this category **OR somewhat successful** in demonstrating **all** of the bullets points in this category
2 = **very successful** in demonstrating **only one or two** of the bullets points (or the most important bullet points) in this category **OR somewhat successful** in demonstrating **many** of the bullets points in this category
1 = **somewhat successful** in demonstrating **only one or two** the bullets points in this category

4 = shows **exceptional** achievement in all areas of this category (bullet points); document is mature, sophisticated, insightful, and confident
3 = shows **acceptable** achievement in all areas of this category but perhaps only exceptional achievement in one; document is interesting but perhaps ordinary or lacks confidence/sophistication
2 = **underachieved or clumsy** in some of the areas of this category, or acceptable in some areas and completely lacking in others; document shows evidence of underdeveloped thinking, disorganization
1 = **crude and undeveloped** in all/some/many areas in this category; difficult to identify insights, methods, and/or interpretation and analysis

4 = very consistently meets all expectations in this category and does so effectively (for example: ideas are consistently well-ordered; method is applied consistently and at same high level of effectiveness through entire document)
3 = somewhat consistently meets all expectations in this category; is effective when present (i.e. identifies bias in most areas but misses a few; well-ordered ideas except for one or two sections that wander a bit)
2 = inconsistently meets the expectations in this category; may meet all expectations but there are inconsistencies in every area, or may be consistent in one or two areas but scattershot in the rest
1 = only occasionally meets the expectations that belong to the category

4 = extremely effective in this category
3 = moderately effective in this category
2 = occasionally effective in this category
1 = ineffective in this category

Notes

1. Catherine Fraser Riehle and Merinda Kaye Hensley, "What Do Undergraduate Students Know about Scholarly Communication? A Mixed Methods Research Study," *portal: Libraries and the Academy* 17, no. 1 (2017): 3. https://www.ideals.illinois.edu/handle/2142/95723.

2. Mark J. Caprio, "Student Publishing: Future Scholars as Change Agents," *OCLC Systems and Services: International Digital Library Perspectives* 30, no. 3 (2014): 147. doi.org/10.1108/OCLC-01-2014-0003.

3. Mike S. Ribble, Gerald D. Bailey, and Tweed W. Ross, "Digital Citizenship: Addressing Appropriate Technology Behavior," *Learning and Leading with Technology* 32, no. 1 (September 2004): 7, http://files.eric.ed.gov/fulltext/EJ695788.pdf.

4. Riehle and Hensley, "What Do Undergraduate Students Know?"

5. Association of College and Research Libraries, *Framework for Information Literacy for Higher Education* (Chicago: Association of College and Research Libraries, 2016), http://www.ala.org/acrl/standards/ilframework.

6. Thomas P. Mackey and Trudi E. Jacobson, "Reframing Information Literacy as a Metaliteracy," *College and Research Libraries* 72, no. 1 (2011): 70, https://doi.org/10.5860/crl-76r1.

7. Association of College and Research Libraries, *Framework*, 2–3.

8. Stephanie Davis-Kahl, "Engaging Undergraduates in Scholarly Communication: Outreach, Education, and Advocacy," *College and Research Libraries News* 73, no. 4 (2012): 212, https://doi.org/10.5860/crln.73.4.8744.

9. Scholarship @ Claremont website, accessed June 6, 2018, http://scholarship.claremont.edu/.

10. Jeffrey M. Osborn and Kerry K. Karukstis, "The Benefits of Undergraduate Research, Scholarship, and Creative Activity," in *Broadening Participation in Undergraduate Research: Fostering Excellence and Enhancing the Impact*, ed. Mary K. Boyd and Jodi L. Wesemann (Washington, DC: Council on Undergraduate Research, 2009): 41–53; Kerry K. Karukstis, "Pivotal Junctures in the Undergraduate Research Enterprise: CUR Fellow's Address at CUR's 2012 National Conference at the College of New Jersey," *Council for Undergraduate Research Quarterly* 33, no. 1 (2012): 14–19, https://www.cur.org/assets/1/7/331Fall12KarukstisWeb.pdf; John K. Petrella and Alan Jung, "Undergraduate Research: Importance, Benefits, and Challenges," *International Journal of Exercise Science* 1, no. 3 (2008): 91–95, http://digitalcommons.wku.edu/ijes/vol1/iss3/1/.

11. Osborn and Karukstis, "The Benefits of Undergraduate Research," 41.

12. Boyer Commission on Educating Undergraduates in the Research University, *Reinventing Undergraduate Education* (Stony Brook: State University of New York at Stony Brook, 1998): 24, https://dspace.sunyconnect.suny.edu/handle/1951/26012.

13. Pomona College, "Timeline: 1914," accessed September 1, 2017, https://www.pomona.edu/timeline/1910s/1914.

14. Pitzer College, "Mission and Values," accessed June 20, 2018, https://www.pitzer.edu/about/mission-and-values/; Harvey Mudd College, "Mission and Strategic Vision," accessed June 20, 2018, https://www.hmc.edu/about-hmc/mission-vision/; see appendix 21A, "Claremont Colleges Mission Statements."

15. Julia Bauder and Catherine Rod, "Crossing Thresholds: Critical Information Literacy Pedagogy and the ACRL Framework," *College and Undergraduate Libraries* 23, no. 3 (2016): 252–64, https://doi.org/10.1080/10691316.2015.1025323.

16. Bauder and Rod, "Crossing Thresholds."

17. The Undergraduate Research Commons (URC; http://undergraduatecommons.com/) is a portal showcasing outstanding published works authored by thousands of undergraduate students from a variety of academic institutions.

18. Caprio, "Student Publishing"; Amy Buckland, "More Than Consumers: Students as Content Creators," in *Getting the Word Out: Academic Libraries as Scholarly Publishers*, ed. Maria Bonn and Mike Furlough (Chicago: American Library Association, 2015): 193–202.

19. Claremont Colleges Library, "Strategic Initiatives of the Claremont Colleges Library, 2016–2020," accessed September 1, 2017, http://libraries.claremont.edu/site/downloads/_strategic-plan/StrategicInitiatives2016-2020.pdf.

20. Beatriz Maldonado, "Creating a Voice and a Place with Digital Tools," guest post on *Jacqueline Wernimont: Network Weaver, Scholar, Digitrix* (blog), March 8, 2013, https://jwernimont.com/creating/.

21. Data obtained from the manager of Scholarship @ Claremont.

22. Linda Bennett and Dimity Flanagan, "Measuring the Impact of Digitized Theses: A Case Study from the London School of Economics," *Insights* 29, no. 2 (2016): 111–19, https://doi.org/10.1629/uksg.300.

23. Kendyl M. Klein, "Why Don't I Look Like Her? The Impact of Social Media on Female Body Image" (Claremont McKenna College senior thesis 720, 2013), http://scholarship.claremont.edu/cmc_theses/720; Olivia Fleming, "'Why Don't I Look Like Her?' How Instagram Is Ruining Our Self Esteem," *Elle*, November 18, 2014, http://www.elle.com/beauty/tips/a2531/how-instagram-is-ruining-our-self-esteem/; "Kendyl Klein's '14 Senior Thesis Quoted in Elle Magazine on the Impact of Social Media on Female Body Image," Claremont McKenna College Newsroom, January 14, 2015, https://www.cmc.edu/news/kendyl-kleins-13-senior-thesis-quoted-in-elle-magazine-on-the-impact-of-social-media-on-female-body-image; Casey Busher, "Claremont McKenna Alum Uses Dashboard to See Online Citations and Explore Career Options," bepress.com, May 11, 2017, https://www.bepress.com/claremont-mckenna-alum-uses-dashboard-see-online-citations-explore-career-options/.

24. Buckland, "More than Consumers," 197.

25. Char Miller and Char Booth, "Open Access as Undergraduate Pedagogy," *Library Journal*, March 26, 2014, http://lj.libraryjournal.com/2014/03/opinion/backtalk/open-access-as-undergraduate-pedagogy-backtalk/#_.

26. See appendix 21B, "Information Literacy in Student Work Rubric—Claremont Colleges Library," and appendix 21C: "Critical Thinking Rubric."

27. Survey conducted by the Environmental Analysis Department of Pomona College in 2016, available upon request.

28. Benjamin C. Hackenberger, "The San Antonio Wash: Addressing the Gap between Claremont and Upland" (Pomona senior thesis 136, 2015), http://scholarship.claremont.edu/pomona_theses/136/.

29. Hackenberger, "The San Antonio Wash."

30. David Bartholomae, "Inventing the University," *Journal of Basic Writing* 5, no. 1 (1986): 4–23, http://www.jstor.org/stable/43443456; Christopher L. Schroeder, *Reinventing the University* (Logan: Utah State University Press, 2001).

31. Benjamin C. Hackenberger and Char Miller, "Watershed Politics: Groundwater Management and Resource Conservation in Southern California's Pomona Valley," *Journal of Urban History,* OnlineFirst, March 8, 2017, https://doi.org/10.1177/0096144217692986.

32. Frank Lyles, "Climate Change Adaptation for Southern California Groundwater Managers: A Case Study of the Six Basins Aquifer" (Pomona senior thesis 172, 2016), http://scholarship.claremont.edu/pomona_theses/172.

33. Anna Marie Kramer, "The Power of the Tower: Contesting History at Bear Lodge/Devils Tower National Monument," 2016 Claremont Colleges Library Undergraduate Research Award, April 28, 2016, http://scholarship.claremont.edu/cclura_2016/4.

34. Anne Marie Kramer, "The Power of the Tower: Contesting History at Bear Lodge/Devils Tower National Monument" (Pomona senior thesis 151, 2016), http://scholarship.claremont.edu/pomona_theses/151.

35. Kramer, "The Power of the Tower," http://scholarship.claremont.edu/pomona_theses/151.

36. Char Miller, "Landmark Decision: The Antiquities Act, Big-Stick Conservation, and the Modern State," in *The Antiquities Act: A Century of American Archaeology, Historic Preservation, and Nature Conservation*, ed. David Harmon, Francis P. McManamon, and Dwight T. Picaithley (Tucson: University of Arizona Press, 2006), 64–78.

37. Scott Warren and Kim Duckett, "'Why Does Google Scholar Sometimes Ask for Money?' Engaging Science Students in Scholarly Communication and the Economics of Information," *Journal of Library Administration* 50, no. 4 (2010): 369. https://doi.org/10.1080/01930821003667021.

38. Warren and Duckett, "'Why Does Google Scholar?'" 369.

Bibliography

Association of College and Research Libraries. *Framework for Information Literacy for Higher Education*. Chicago: Association of College and Research Libraries, 2016. http://www.ala.org/acrl/standards/ilframework.

Bartholomae, David. "Inventing the University." *Journal of Basic Writing* 5, no. 1 (1986): 4–23. http://www.jstor.org/stable/43443456.

Bauder, Julia, and Catherine Rod. "Crossing Thresholds: Critical Information Literacy Pedagogy and the ACRL Framework." *College and Undergraduate Libraries* 23, no. 3 (2016): 252–64. https://doi.org/10.1080/10691316.2015.1025323.

Bennett, Linda, and Dimity Flanagan. "Measuring the Impact of Digitized Theses: A Case Study from the London School of Economics." *Insights* 29, no. 2 (2016): 111–19. https://doi.org/10.1629/uksg.300.

Boyer Commission on Educating Undergraduates in the Research University. *Reinventing Undergraduate Education: A Blueprint for America's Research Universi-*

ties. Stony Brook: State University of New York at Stony Brook, 1998. https://dspace.sunyconnect.suny.edu/handle/1951/26012.

Buckland, Amy. "More Than Consumers: Students as Content Creators." In *Getting the Word Out: Academic Libraries as Scholarly Publishers*. Edited by Maria Bonn and Mike Furlough, 193–202. Chicago: American Library Association, 2015.

Busher, Casey. "Claremont McKenna Alum Uses Dashboard to See Online Citations and Explore Career Options." bepress.com, May 11, 2017. https://www.bepress.com/claremont-mckenna-alum-uses-dashboard-see-online-citations-explore-career-options/.

Caprio, Mark J. "Student Publishing: Future Scholars as Change Agents." *OCLC Systems and Services: International Digital Library Perspectives* 30, no. 3 (2014): 144–57. https://doi.org/10.1108/OCLC-01-2014-0003.

Claremont Colleges Library. "Strategic Initiatives of the Claremont Colleges Library, 2016–2020." Accessed September 1, 2017. http://libraries.claremont.edu/site/downloads/_strategic-plan/StrategicInitiatives2016-2020.pdf.

Claremont McKenna College Newsroom. "Kendyl Klein's '14 Senior Thesis Quoted in Elle Magazine on the Impact of Social Media on Female Body Image." January 14, 2015. https://www.cmc.edu/news/kendyl-kleins-13-senior-thesis-quoted-in-elle-magazine-on-the-impact-of-social-media-on-female-body-image.

Davis-Kahl, Stephanie. "Engaging Undergraduates in Scholarly Communication: Outreach, Education, and Advocacy." *College and Research Libraries News* 73, no. 4 (2012): 212–22. https://doi.org/10.5860/crln.73.4.8744.

Fleming, Olivia. "'Why Don't I Look Like Her?' How Instagram Is Ruining Our Self Esteem." *Elle*, November 18, 2014. http://www.elle.com/beauty/tips/a2531/how-instagram-is-ruining-our-self-esteem/.

Hackenberger, Benjamin C. "The San Antonio Wash: Addressing the Gap between Claremont and Upland." Pomona Senior Theses 136 (2015). http://scholarship.claremont.edu/pomona_theses/136/.

Hackenberger, Benjamin C., and Char Miller. "Watershed Politics: Groundwater Management and Resource Conservation in Southern California's Pomona Valley." *Journal of Urban History*, OnlineFirst, March 8, 2017. https://doi.org/10.1177/0096144217692986.

Karukstis, Kerry K. "Pivotal Junctures in the Undergraduate Research Enterprise: CUR Fellow's Address at CUR's 2012 National Conference at the College of New Jersey." *Council for Undergraduate Research Quarterly* 33, no. 1 (2012): 14–19. https://www.cur.org/assets/1/7/331Fall12KarukstisWeb.pdf.

Klein, Kendyl M. "Why Don't I Look Like Her? The Impact of Social Media on Female Body Image." Claremont McKenna College senior thesis 720, 2013. http://scholarship.claremont.edu/cmc_theses/720.

Kramer, Anna Marie. "The Power of the Tower: Contesting History at Bear Lodge/Devils Tower National Monument." 2016 Claremont Colleges Library Undergraduate Research Award, April 28, 2016. http://scholarship.claremont.edu/cclura_2016/4.

———. "The Power of the Tower: Contesting History at Bear Lodge/Devils Tower National Monument." Pomona senior thesis 151, 2016. http://scholarship.claremont.edu/pomona_theses/151.

Lyles, Frank. "Climate Change Adaptation for Southern California Groundwater Managers: A Case Study of the Six Basins Aquifer." Pomona senior thesis 172, 2016. http://scholarship.claremont.edu/pomona_theses/172.

Mackey, Thomas P., and Trudi E. Jacobson. "Reframing Information Literacy as a Metaliteracy." *College and Research Libraries* 72, no. 1 (2011): 62–78. https://doi.org/10.5860/crl-76r1.

Maldonado, Beatriz. "Creating a Voice and a Place with Digital Tools." Guest post on *Jacqueline Wernimont: Network Weaver, Scholar, Digitrix* (blog), March 8, 2013. https://jwernimont.com/creating/.

Miller, Char. "Landmark Decision: The Antiquities Act, Big-Stick Conservation, and the Modern State." In *The Antiquities Act: A Century of American Archaeology, Historic Preservation, and Nature Conservation*. Edited by David Harmon, Francis P. McManamon, and Dwight T. Picaithley, 64–78. Tucson: University of Arizona Press, 2006.

Miller, Char, and Char Booth. "Open Access as Undergraduate Pedagogy." *Library Journal*, March 26, 2014. http://lj.libraryjournal.com/2014/03/opinion/backtalk/open-access-as-undergraduate-pedagogy-backtalk/#_.

Osborn, Jeffrey M., and Kerry K. Karukstis. "The Benefits of Undergraduate Research, Scholarship, and Creative Activity." In *Broadening Participation in Undergraduate Research: Fostering Excellence and Enhancing the Impact*. Edited by Mary K. Boyd and Jodi L. Wesemann, 41–53. Washington, DC: Council on Undergraduate Research, 2009.

Petrella, John K., and Alan Jung. "Undergraduate Research: Importance, Benefits, and Challenges." *International Journal of Exercise Science* 1, no. 3 (2008): 91–95. http://digitalcommons.wku.edu/ijes/vol1/iss3/1/.

Pomona College. "Timeline: 1914." Accessed September 1, 2017. https://www.pomona.edu/timeline/1910s/1914.

Ribble, Mike S., Gerald D. Bailey, and Tweed W. Ross. "Digital Citizenship: Addressing Appropriate Technology Behavior." *Learning and Leading with Technology* 32, no. 1 (September 2004): 6–9. http://files.eric.ed.gov/fulltext/EJ695788.pdf.

Riehle, Catherine Fraser, and Merinda Kaye Hensley. "What Do Undergraduate Students Know about Scholarly Communication? A Mixed Methods Research Study." *portal: Libraries and the Academy* 17, no.1 (2017): 145–78. https://www.ideals.illinois.edu/handle/2142/95723.

Schroeder, Christopher L. *Reinventing the University: Literacies and Legitimacy in the Postmodern Academy*. Logan: Utah State University Press, 2001.

Scholarship @ Claremont website. Accessed June 6, 2018. http://scholarship.claremont.edu/.

Warren, Scott, and Kim Duckett. "'Why Does Google Scholar Sometimes Ask for Money?' Engaging Science Students in Scholarly Communication and the Economics of Information." *Journal of Library Administration* 50, no. 4 (2010): 349–72. https://doi.org/10.1080/01930821003667021.

CHAPTER 22

North Carolina State University Spotlight

Part 4, Preparing Students to "Think and Do": Promoting the Value of Student Work at NCSU

Mira Waller and William Cross

North Carolina State University's (NCSU) mission to "Think and Do" has empowered the NCSU Libraries to be a leader in connecting theory to practice, coursework to careers, and personal passions to global engagement.[1] For students, this engagement has taken many forms. Like many libraries, the NCSU Libraries license materials, teach workshops, and provide resources for every stage of student life, and experimental efforts like our Alt-Textbook Project and makerspace program meet students where they are and connect them to communities beyond the walls of our campus.[2] Our emphasis on "Thinking and Doing" is woven into all of these activities, not just supporting traditional student success in the classroom, but as part of holistic engagement with student life. Charged to work on student time, the Libraries have found opportunities to connect with students and empower them to develop projects and tell their stories.

Students value the NCSU Libraries as a place to create and display scholarly and creative works. In fact, some students have reported that the Libraries are the only place on campus where they are able to show their work to others outside of their classrooms. Students use library spaces and services to support traditional research products such as papers or posters. They also use them to create digital media works, experiment in the makerspace, and explore new types of scholarship. Currently, we are working with students to expand the role of the library so it acts as both a hub for the creation of student works and a center for displaying and preserving student works. We see this as an opportunity for students to showcase their work for a larger audience and for the Libraries to provide added value by supplying a trustworthy space and a forum for students to engage, interact, share, and learn from each other as well as from those outside their immediate university community.

This chapter highlights some of the inspiring and empowering ways the Libraries engage with student coursework. Beginning with the case study of the D. H. Hill Library Visualization Studio, we will show how we have intentionally used this space to transform the campus view of student scholarship and creative work. This particular case is but one component of a broader series of programming designed to demonstrate the commitment the NCSU Libraries bring to supporting students as producers, the challenges inherent to this work, and the ways in which the Libraries can support and articulate the value of student creations. While actively exploring and engaging in this space, we do not purport to have the answers and are still investigating how best to provide emerging scholars and creative students with the tools, spaces, and resources to share, save, and disseminate their work.

D. H. Hill Library Visualization Studio

Faculty have taken note of evidence that integration of technology into curricula leads to student engagement. This has increased their interest in developing assignments that require student use of different media technologies.[3]

These assignments offer new ways for students to express their research and present it to an audience that can be much larger than just their instructor, class, or even institution. These types of assignments may also have added benefits such as encouraging collaborative work, increasing student engagement, facilitating student learning, and exposing students to new media technologies. By incorporating technology into classroom teaching and learning, instructors are providing students with another way to actively participate in the learning process. Student learning and engagement are most effective when students are participating with learning activities in a meaningful way.[4] In response to these new initiatives in academia, the role of the subject specialist librarian is evolving to include expertise in emerging technologies and scholarly communication skills. By focusing more on liaison activities, emphasizing active learning during instruction, and collaborating with faculty and students around creating content, subject librarians are able to position themselves as valuable partners for new programs and services.[5]

The knowledge gained from researching and creating works that incorporate emerging technologies can help students set themselves apart in an increasingly competitive and technology-oriented job market. Though clearly beneficial, it can also be challenging for faculty to provide the infrastructure needed to support these types of assignments. At the NCSU Libraries, we are working collaboratively with faculty to develop assignments and curricula that support nontraditional methods of information sharing. This also informs the way that we design and use library spaces and services. The case study that follows describes our collaboration with Dr. Shea McManus, a professor in the department of sociology and anthropology, and the immersive, multimedia-rich research projects being created and presented by her students in the Visualization Studio at D. H. Hill Library, located on NCSU's main campus.

The Visualization Studio is an integral part of the NCSU Libraries' portfolio of high-tech spaces. Created as an immersive and collaborative environment, the studio provides an ideal physical space for arranging, presenting, and studying information visually. The room contains twelve projectors (three evenly spaced per wall) that can be used to display the contents of a single Windows computer screen 360 degrees across the four walls (see figure 22.1). It also has the infrastructure to tie in personal laptops, allowing up to four different users to project on the walls simultaneously. Because the Visualization Studio runs on a standard desktop, it can support a wide range of applications and users from a variety of disciplines with varying levels of computer skills.

FIGURE 22.1
Maeshowe Tomb

In fall 2015, Dr. McManus's "Research Methods in Cultural Anthropology" and "Qualitative Research Methods" students were tasked with a research project that included the following components: choosing a community in North Carolina's Research Triangle area; conducting interviews and engaging in participant observation; and taking photographs, videos, and sound re-

cordings to document and analyze the community. When it came to presenting their projects, McManus wanted students to feel immersed in the topic, the
same way they did when researching their communities. Josephine McRobbie,
then an NCSU Libraries fellow, introduced McManus to the D. H. Hill Library
Visualization Studio as a way to create more immersive and participatory research presentations. McManus quickly realized that the space would be ideal.
"The Visualization Studio makes possible a rich presentation of knowledge
and a more interactive environment for its communication," McManus says.
"I was immediately struck by the creative potential it offered students in my
ethnographic research methods course."[6] McRobbie and Markus Wust, the Libraries Digital Scholarship and Research Librarian, worked with McManus
to introduce her students to the studio and to tools, including Sway, HTML,
Tiky-Toky, Google Slides, and panoramic field images, which would help them
take advantage of the immersive nature of the Visualization Studio.

In 2016, the Libraries' Associate Head of Collections and Research Strategy, Mira Waller, became the subject liaison to the department of sociology and
anthropology and began working with McManus. Since then, McManus has
been working with Waller, Wust, and Shaun Bennett, a library technician, to
integrate the space and its services into assignments developed for several of
her classes, including "Research Methods," the "Intermediate Seminar in International Studies," and "Anthropology of the Middle East"(see figure 22.2) Over
time we have been able to refine our work and create templates and guides, with
help from McManus, that can also be used to assist other faculty and students
who want to use the Visualization Studio to support course assignments.

FIGURE 22.2
McManus's spring 2017 "Anthropology of the Middle East" class in
Visualization Studio.

Direct student feedback, provided throughout the courses, as well as extended conversations with Dr. McManus, has led us to conclude that this collaboration has increased student engagement, enhanced student presentation skills, and enabled students to learn new presentation tools. The partnership has also come with its share of challenges. As with any successful and growing initiative, managing staff time can be tricky. For this particular program, we found the investment in staff time with McManus was significant at first, but decreased as she became comfortable with the space and the tools. On the other hand, new students are constantly cycling through her classes, and each student has a different level of knowledge and comfort with using this space and learning new presentation software. Although we encounter students who have previously used the Visualization Studio or the associated presentation software, every new class has the potential to present to a room full of students who are unfamiliar with the experience and tools. And, while the learning curve for using the Visualization Studio and learning the tools is not high, it does require time and effort on the part of students. Since students can be pushed for time themselves—with other classes, work, and school-related social obligations—it can be challenging to coordinate consultation times, outside the set classroom instruction hours, especially when students seek assistance at the last minute and at times when the space may be less available due to other scheduled engagements or classes.

In addition to operational and procedural challenges, we have had to develop strategies for creating an environment for exploring and addressing the culturally and personally sensitive materials that often are encountered in the classes McManus teaches. For example, students have researched and presented on topics such as female genital mutilation, the Fukushima nuclear power plant meltdown, nationalism and Islamophobia in French culture, and sex and domestic work in the United Arab Emirates. We did not find models to guide us, as a library, in thinking through how to disseminate and save sensitive material tied to student content creators and producers. Faculty and students may also need guidance in considering future consequences of having created, shared, and saved these works so that they reach audiences beyond those who are in the immediate classroom.

This type of collaboration provides the Libraries with a perfect opportunity to build and strengthen relationships with faculty, and provides both McManus and the NCSU Libraries with a way to increase student engagement and to help students learn new skills and tools. The libraries are also well positioned to support faculty in the use of emerging technologies since we understand the types of work that emerging researchers are doing.

"While I wasn't the most interested in wanting to try this," says Dakota Frisby, a student in McManus's seminar class, "[but] getting to learn how to present on four different walls for a presentation without PowerPoint was a

fun learning process. The Viz Studio made me more comfortable in presenting to my peers since they weren't focused on me but on the walls surrounding
them. More classes should get to use this room for presentations, because the
creativity that it allows the students to have greatly improves the quality of
the presentations and the interest level of those watching the presentation."[7]

Furthermore, these types of multimedia research presentations give students an opportunity to build unique works for their portfolio and résumé.
And we see this as a key way for the Libraries to add value to the student
experience, student works, and faculty curricula. However, while this case
study illustrates how we have been successful in facilitating the creation and
dissemination of student works, we have more to do when it comes to saving
student works.

Much of this work is likely to be considered gray literature. As defined
at the Grey Literature Conference, Luxembourg, 1997, and expanded in New
York, 2004, gray literature is "information produced on all levels of government, academia, business and industry in electronic and print formats not
controlled by commercial publishing i.e. where publishing is not the primary
activity of the producing body."[8] Based on this definition, works produced by
students that have not been "published," such as the immersive presentations
being created for McManus's classes, would qualify as gray literature. Because
we do not have an established practice for linking to them, citing them, and
even sharing them on a continuous basis, this work is often ephemeral. Currently, these student works are being saved in Moodle, which is the primary
learning management system (LMS) used at North Carolina State University. The works are being saved by Dr. McManus with the knowledge of the
students. Both Dr. McManus and the students understand that the NC State
University cannot guarantee archival access beyond the semester. Since these
presentations are created often using commercial or proprietary tools, such as
Microsoft Sway, Wix, and Weebly, there may also be access issues if the tools
are no longer available. These challenges remind us that there is much work
still to be done as we move forward in our efforts to support students in the
creation, promotion, presentation, dissemination, and preservation of their
works. At this time, preservation and archiving of student works are beyond
the scope of our Libraries' current strategic focus.

Overarching Themes

The case study of the Visualization Studio, much like the projects and cases
shared by our NCSU Libraries colleagues throughout this book (see Spotlight
chapters across sections), provide but one example of the innovative, collaborative, and creative work done in the Libraries every day. Although these

projects engage different students and for distinct purposes, they are united by several themes, all inspired by NCSU's "Think and Do" mission.

The first theme involves taking a proactive approach. Rather than waiting for students to come to us, we have met students where they are and where their interests lie, whether in their classes or in connection with their student organizations. We have learned what students are passionate about and have worked to help them find ways to share that passion with a broader community.

A second theme is the collaborative nature of the projects. Putting together a presentation for the NCSU Libraries Presents series, sharing ideas at a Music Meet-Up, and developing a new project in the makerspace all leverage communities that support individual students and that are themselves sustained by student engagement. The Libraries' emphasis on open culture makes this theme explicit, as exemplified by the OpenCon event, which framed student work in the context of a community of practice that can help individual students improve a project, connect with collaborators, or even find a job.

The third theme is the importance of new tools and technologies. The Libraries have invested heavily in the technologies and expertise students need, but also in the resources that get students excited. Open licensing, digital sampling, and data visualization are competencies many students need, many more want, and that the Libraries are actively supporting. The Hunt Library provides a unique opportunity to engage with these issues, but any librarian can develop facility with these issues to help engage students with the tools and technologies in their own community.

Each of these themes brings a related set of challenges. Challenges related to resources are evergreen, with staff time, expertise, and funds always at a premium. Another constant challenge is the rapid turnover of students. Every semester some of the most dedicated and engaged students graduate, replaced by a fresh set of students who lack the expertise—and often the awareness—required to engage with these projects. In one sense this is a feature, rather than a bug. After all, the purpose of these projects is to train students and prepare them to try new things. Nevertheless, the programs require a core of expertise as well as a sustained culture of collaboration. Individual librarians obviously have a role in this culture, but we have also developed training materials and resources to sustain institutional memory. We also rely on student workers and other students to refresh our understanding and translate the value of these programs to each new generation of students.

In the end, these programs have been successful because they unite so many stakeholders in exciting shared work. Students connect to a vibrant community and learn skills that advance their passion projects and prepare them for success in their careers. Faculty find a refreshed approach to teaching and a set of projects that students enjoy, rather than simply complete. The

Libraries gain recognition as the hub that makes all of these things possible. Our campus benefits from an environment of innovation and creativity and appreciates the well-told stories that highlight our exceptional students and faculty.

Notes

1. "About Think and Do," North Carolina State University, accessed June 4, 2018, https://www.ncsu.edu/think-and-do/about/.
2. Kristine Alpi et al., "The North Carolina State University Libraries' Alt-Textbook Project: Open Education That Opens a Door to the Library," in *Textbooks in Academic Libraries: Selection, Circulation, and Assessment*, ed. Chris Diaz (Chicago: American Library Association, 2017), 69–89; "Makerspace Press and Publications." NCSU Libraries, North Carolina State University, 2017, https://www.lib.ncsu.edu/makerspace/press.
3. Selim Gunuc and Abdullah Kuzu, "Confirmation of Campus-Class-Technology Model in Student Engagement: A Path Analysis," *Computers in Human Behavior* 48 (July 2015): 114–25, https://doi.org/10.1016/j.chb.2015.01.041.
4. Catherine Fraser Riehle and Sharon A. Weiner, "High-Impact Educational Practices: An Exploration of the Role of Information Literacy," *College and Undergraduate Libraries* 20, no. 2 (2013): 127–143.
5. Association of College and Research Libraries Working Group on Intersections of Scholarly Communication and Information Literacy, *Intersections of Scholarly Communication and Information Literacy* (Chicago: Association of College and Research Libraries, 2013), http://www.ala.org/acrl/sites/ala.org.acrl/files/content/publications/whitepapers/Intersections.pdf.
6. Shea McManus, quoted in Josephine McRobbie and Mira P. Waller, "Anthropology in 360°: Cultural Immersion in the Visualization Studio," NCSU Libraries, April 6, 2017, https://www.lib.ncsu.edu/stories/anthropology-in-360%C2%B0-cultural-immersion-in-the-visualization-studio.
7. Dakota Frisby, quoted in McRobbie and Waller, "Anthropology in 360°."
8. Dominic John Farace and Jerry Frantzen, eds., *Sixth International Conference on Grey Literature: Work on Grey in Progress, GL 2004 Conference Proceedings, New York, 6–7 December 2004* (Amsterdam, Netherlands: TextRelease, 2005): 9-16.

Bibliography

Association of College and Research Libraries Working Group on Intersections of Scholarly Communication and Information Literacy. *Intersections of Scholarly Communication and Information Literacy: Creating Strategic Collaborations for a Changing Academic Environment*. Chicago: Association of College and Research Libraries, 2013. http://www.ala.org/acrl/sites/ala.org.acrl/files/content/publications/whitepapers/Intersections.pdf.

Alpi, Kristine, William Cross, Greg Raschke, and Madison Sullivan. "The North Carolina State University Libraries' Alt-Textbook Project: Open Education That Opens a Door to the Library." In *Textbooks in Academic Libraries: Selection, Circulation, and Assessment*. Edited by Chris Diaz, 69–89. Chicago: American Library Association, 2017.

Farace, Dominic John, and Jerry Frantzen, eds. *Sixth International Conference on Grey Literature: Work on Grey in Progress, GL 2004 Conference Proceedings, New York, 6–7 December 2004*. Amsterdam, Netherlands: TextRelease, 2005.

Gunuc, Selim, and Abdullah Kuzu. "Confirmation of Campus-Class-Technology Model in Student Engagement: A Path Analysis." *Computers in Human Behavior* 48 (July 2015): 114–25. https://doi.org/10.1016/j.chb.2015.01.041.

McRobbie, Josephine, and Mira P. Waller. "Anthropology in 360°: Cultural Immersion in the Visualization Studio." NCSU Libraries, April 6, 2017. https://www.lib.ncsu.edu/stories/anthropology-in-360%C2%B0-cultural-immersion-in-the-visualization-studio.

NCSU Libraries. "Makerspace Press and Publications." North Carolina State University, 2017. https://www.lib.ncsu.edu/makerspace/press.

North Carolina State University. "About Think and Do." Accessed June 4, 2018. https://www.ncsu.edu/think-and-do/about/.

Riehle, Catherine Fraser, and Sharon A. Weiner. "High-Impact Educational Practices: An Exploration of the Role of Information Literacy." *College and Undergraduate Libraries* 20, no. 2 (2013): 127–43.

Conclusion

CHAPTER 23

Conclusion

*Amy S. Jackson, Cindy Pierard, and
Suzanne M. Schadl*

This book shows how libraries across North America actively engage with student-created content while encouraging students to see themselves as producers of information in addition to consumers of the same. The idea of students as producers and creators resonates across higher education institutions, from the University of Lincoln, Vanderbilt University, and the New Media Consortium and Educause's *Horizon Report*.[1] As identified in the *Horizon Report*, acknowledging students as producers provides a path to authentic learning assignments. Nonetheless, "institutions continue to be challenged to generate these opportunities in spaces and with paradigms that still lean on traditional practices."[2] Libraries are in an ideal position to offer new spaces and opportunities outside of traditional practices and fill this gap. They can build upon established resources to develop and create new opportunities and resources for emerging scholars at our institutions. Supporting students enables librarians to engage with student work and create robust environments in which everyone can practice being scholars. By collaborating with others on campus, we can also build campus networks, situating libraries as central spaces for students to create cultures of sharing.

As Bruff notes in the introduction of this book, the opportunity to recognize students as creators involves collaboration across different entities on campus and includes knowledge contributed by many individuals. As a neutral learning environment and trusted partner on the campus, the library is an ideal location to co-locate these diverse sets of expertise, tools, and knowledge domains. Additionally, libraries are already well versed in copyright issues and respect for individuals' intellectual property, no matter the creator's credentials or backgrounds. With these tools, libraries can act as centers for sharing student production, encouraging and inspiring students through library laboratories, forums, and archives, while teaching them about rights to their intellectual property and respecting these rights when presenting their materials. Libraries can become a part of students' learning experiences by providing an environment supportive of their best work, instead of repositories of knowledge created by others with the assumption that students do not meet these standards. Additionally, the trust between established scholars and the library should demonstrate to emerging scholars that the library values their work and will treat it with respect. Opening library doors to resources created by emerging scholars enriches campus environments and invites in the next generation.

Bruff also highlights several elements that are necessary to promote students as producers, including a safe environment for failure, troubleshooting, and trying again. This idea resonates with several student voices in this book, which acknowledge learning from the process rather than from the product. Emerging scholars also benefit from the built-in audience present in library spaces, both online and physical. By providing a broad audience, libraries help make assignments more impactful, and students are more likely to produce high-quality work. Finally, students must be able to direct their own learning processes in order to feel deeply engaged in their work. By offering experiences outside of a classroom setting, libraries are able to let students make autonomous choices, which lead to learning and work that is meaningful to the student.

Students are not the only ones to benefit when their work is included in the library. Libraries also benefit from this new arrangement as they forge connections, gain new expertise, and become part of student and campus culture. By considering students as producers of information, we shift the role of the library from a disseminator of knowledge to an active participant in creating and sharing new knowledge within communities. Instead of gatekeepers of knowledge, in this model, libraries are participants in knowledge production and dissemination. Additionally, the library gains a space in the center of student work and achievement, becoming a trusted partner to students and academic units, as well as a collaborator with others on campus. As this cycle continues to grow, the library emerges as a major center uniting scholarship and creative activities across the campus.

The chapters in this book present some common approaches and best practices to help libraries engage in the student-as-producer culture. Most significantly, nearly every chapter presents some type of cooperative effort. This collaboration may be with course instructors, writing centers, or other units across campus, and it connects undergraduates, graduates, faculty, and staff. Libraries work directly with students producing the work, turn to student employees for expertise and assistance, and connect with undergraduate and graduate students to strengthen networks and campus cultures. Collaborating across campus ensures that we build upon each other's strengths.

Moreover, we can share and acknowledge common goals. By collaborating directly with students, we learn from their knowledge, and in turn share our experiences in scholarly work with them.

Another commonality woven through these chapters is the library's role in supporting high-impact educational practices and student engagement. High-impact practices include writing-intensive courses, undergraduate research, capstone courses or projects, first-year seminars and experiences, common intellectual experiences (core courses), learning communities, collaborative assignments and projects, diversity/global learning, service learning/community-based learning, and internships.[3] These practices support student engagement, resulting in higher retention levels at the university. The library is well positioned to provide resources for almost all of these activities, including support of high-impact practices outside of the classroom curriculum. This book explores activities that allow students to practice becoming scholars in a supportive sandbox environment, developing their careers before graduation—a lofty goal that is realistic when experiencing high-impact practices. By collaborating with others on campus, libraries can also participate in a campus-wide culture that will truly benefit students. Students engaged at the institutional level tend to experience a higher level of learning. They are likely as a result to return for similar experiences.

Frames from the ACRL *Framework for Information Literacy* appear throughout this book despite a focus on examples from outside of the library classroom.[4] Librarians developed the *Framework* to inform classroom teaching of information literacy, but the library also demonstrates these concepts in other settings, thus promoting active learning experiences that occur in both curricular and cocurricular settings. Students can practice and experience "Authority Is Constructed and Contextual" when their work is read and cited as an authority on a subject. They experience "Information Creation as a Process" through involvement in publishing projects such as student writing journals. They can understand "Information Has Value" after experiencing the research process and valuing the time involved, and the legitimacy assigned to others' work. Authentic assignments requiring in-depth research demonstrate "Research as Inquiry." When future students and other scholars build upon student work, it is easy to reflect on "Scholarship as Conversation." Library laboratories, forums, and archives support experiential learning, and information literacy as theory becomes practice in library spaces. By tying these experiences into collaborative high-impact activities, the library becomes a sandbox for emerging scholars, and—ultimately—a significant part of student engagement and retention.

Another common theme across sections of this book is the concept of intellectual property, rights to information, and information ethics. These issues are examined through many lenses, including the ethics of sharing information collected from others, appropriate levels of sharing controversial information without endorsing specific viewpoints, how to make work available for reuse through an open license, and basic rights to intellectual property offered through copyright protections. As the line between information presented in an educational context and in a public context blurs, we must take the opportunity to consider how students, faculty, and librarians are presenting information and who has access to it. The library must examine these questions directly so that we can respect the ethics of information and the intellectual property of everyone represented in the library, including those new to the world of scholarship. We also need to share knowledge about these concepts with emerging scholars to help them understand their rights, management of these rights and the ethics involved with sharing information.

In the introduction to this book, we discussed gaps in library practices where we felt that the library environment did not adequately support emerging scholars. Chapters in this book have shown that this is not unique to our experiences, or to other librarians, classroom instructors, campus collaborators, and even students. They seek means for acknowledging students as producers, with the library acting a natural space for this support. We believe that these case studies help libraries articulate their voices in the students-as-producers movement, leveraging campus connections, library resources and spaces, and established scholarship to inspire authentic experiences to emerging scholars. By acting as a sandbox in which emerging scholars can practice their crafts, we become an invaluable resource throughout a scholar's entire career.

Gaps and Next Steps

Although librarians focus on information and digital literacy as our primary contribution to learning, we can also fill many other gaps on campus, including programs and projects supporting authentic learning assignments and other types of high-impact educational practices. For example, the 2017 *NMC Horizon Report* identifies "Fostering Authentic Learning" as a movement in higher education, but also identifies the challenges of creating these experiences using traditional spaces and paradigms.[5] By making our libraries known as a space on campus where authentic learning happens, librarians can start conversations with others looking for practicum space, eventually filling this identified gap. We can also offer expertise and tools to help students explore new knowledge and experiences, positing our spaces as sites of collaboration, and ourselves as collaborators in assignments. Librarians have invested resources in processes that support established scholars and their work upon graduation, but we must also leverage these resources to help emerging scholars as they participate in these processes before graduation. By publishing in our repositories, presenting in our forums, and practicing in our labs, students engage in the full range of scholarly discourse during their time in our sandbox. Upon graduation, they are thus better equipped to take on the challenges of pursuing a scholarly research agenda, having experienced both successes and failures within the supportive environment of the institution.

Another challenge faced by librarians supporting student work is ensuring that opportunities are available to all types of students and all types of scholarly products. The library has traditionally privileged text-based resources and learners, but how can we change to ensure that all students find representation in our spaces? Beyond text-based documents, we can support images, sounds, artifacts, and other experiential learning, but this will require redesigning learning and other traditional spaces, as well as providing flexible tools for online dissemination and collaboration. Librarians should be aware of all types of learning, from visual and aural to verbal and kinesthetic, in order to provide appropriate supports for all emerging scholars. We can document student work created across a broad spectrum and elevate the importance of new types of work to the same level as traditional, text-based work. As online platforms and infrastructure evolve, we can embrace preservation and dissemination of more types of materials than the traditional, text-based materials that are common in our environment. Additionally, we can break down barriers of degrees and credentials and level the platform to include everyone in the process of disseminating and creating knowledge, including our emerging scholars. As this book demonstrates, myriad works created by students and presented in public spaces can help shape future scholarly and critical discourse.

Derek Bruff refers to the "library as inspiration" in his introductory chapter. This book has identified ways in which libraries can rise to this calling and inspire our emerging scholars to produce impactful work and make a difference in the world while they are students. The library provides spaces for our students in the form of forums, laboratories, and archives, and it is up to us to take full advantage of these opportunities to provide experiences for and inspire our emerging scholars. We are also collaborators and a site of collaboration, offering a space for networking among those on campus, both for students and for those supporting student scholarship. New scholars should be able to look back on the place of the library in their education as a foundation to their careers, a place where they experienced inspiration, authentic learning, and supportive collaboration.

As a sandbox in which students can engage with new ideas and experiences, the library has an opportunity to provide spaces for students to take the stages with a broad community of scholars and advocate for learning.

Libraries can support experimentation, productive failure, and amazing successes. Looking outside of our traditional roles of teaching in the classroom and supporting primarily text-based resources, the possibilities to inspire students as producers in the library are limitless.

Notes

1. S. Adams Becker et al., *NMC Horizon Report: 2017 Higher Education Edition* (Austin, TX: New Media Consortium, 2017).
2. Adams Becker et al., *NMC Horizon Report*, 6.
3. George D. Kuh, *High-Impact Educational Practices* (Washington, DC: Association of American Colleges and Universities, 2008).
4. Association of College and Research Libraries, *Framework for Information Literacy for Higher Education* (Chicago: Association of College and Research Libraries, 2016), http://www.ala.org/acrl/standards/ilframework.
5. Adams Becker et al., *NMC Horizon Report*.

Bibliography

Association of College and Research Libraries. *Framework for Information Literacy for Higher Education*. Chicago: Association of College and Research Libraries, 2016. http://www.ala.org/acrl/standards/ilframework.

Adams Becker, S., M. Cummins, A. Davis, A. Freeman, C. Glesinger Hall, and V. Ananthanarayanan. *NMC Horizon Report: 2017 Higher Education Edition*. Austin, TX: New Media Consortium, 2017.

Kuh, George D. *High-Impact Educational Practices: What They Are, Who Has Access to Them, and Why They Matter*. Washington, DC: Association of American Colleges and Universities, 2008.

Author and Editor Biographies

Amy S. Jackson is Director of Instruction & Outreach at the University of New Mexico, and has previously held positions of Performing Arts & Digital Arts Librarian, Digital Initiatives Librarian, and Metadata Technician. She earned a MLIS from Simmons College in Boston, MA, and a Master of Music from the Peabody Institute of the Johns Hopkins University. She has worked with students in the library and through the institutional repository, and enjoys making connections through the work students are passionate about. She advocates for non-traditional library users, including performing artists, by engaging in their process and offering library resources and spaces. Amy is also writing a book on music research data management, and has published books and articles on music data curation, music history, and metadata.

Cindy Pierard is Director of Access Services & Undergraduate Engagement at the University of New Mexico, where she leads and supports a team that provides public services and collections support across UNM's four main campus libraries. This team also works with other library and campus partners to develop and strengthen services for undergraduates. Cindy previously served as Head of Reference & Research Services at New Mexico State University and in a variety of public services positions at the University of Kansas. She holds an MLIS from Indiana University where she did additional graduate work at the IU School of Journalism. Cindy is energized by the opportunity to share student work within library spaces and has been active in developing and coordinating programs with this focus. Other current projects involve space planning and assessment, and intersections between student employment and student learning.

Suzanne M. Schadl is Chief of the Hispanic Division at the Library of Congress, transitioning from a position at the University of New Mexico as Curator of Latin American collections. Working with specialized materials across disciplines, languages, and communities enables her access to intermediary spaces between differing perspectives and formats. Her work aims to bridge these differences as well as inequities in the information landscape. Suzanne earned her PhD in Latin American studies from the University of New Mexico in 2002. She has also worked as assistant professor of Latin American History at Roanoke College; visiting instructor of Latin American history at the University of Texas in Austin; Director of the Gerald and Betty Ford Library at the Bosque School and teacher of high school Literature, History, and Portuguese. Suzanne is fortunate to have co-authored works with students, while also implementing grants, internships, and exhibitions with other emerging scholars.

Derek Bruff is director of the Vanderbilt University Center for Teaching and a senior lecturer in the Vanderbilt Department of Mathematics. As director, he oversees the Center's programming and offerings for faculty and graduate students, helping them develop foundational teaching skills and explore new ideas in teaching and learning. He also consults regularly with campus leaders about pedagogical issues, seeking to foster a university culture that supports effective teaching. Bruff's research interests include educational technology, visual thinking, and social pedagogies. He blogs on these topics at derekbruff.org, and his book, Teaching with Classroom Response Systems: Creating Active Learning Environments, was published by Jossey-Bass in 2009. Bruff has taught at Harvard University and has a PhD in mathematics from Vanderbilt University.

Memory Apata is the Music and Performing Arts Librarian at Dartmouth College. While pursuing masters degrees in liberal studies and librarianship from Dartmouth and Simmons College, her research focuses on the intersections of librarianship, music, and social change. She is interested in the ways in which silences in library collections, spaces, and outreach affect the demographics and experiences of patrons and library staff. In her scholarly and artistic work, Memory experiments with audible disruptions to the library soundscape which showcase lacunae in collections and university music curricula. At Dartmouth, she has worked on the development and teaching teams of four massive open online courses (MOOCs) on opera and literature. Her experience with MOOCs has made her an advocate for high quality distance learning which creates opportunities for underprivileged students. Outside academia, Memory maintains an active career as a professional actor and musician.

Ann E. Biswas, PhD, teaches courses in medical and professional writing at the University of Dayton as well as courses in the first- and second-year writing program. There, she also served as the English department's Director of Writing Programs from 2013-2017. Her scholarship centers on plagiarism and academic integrity, experiential learning, and faculty development. Ann earned a BA in Communication from Wright State University and an MA in English and PhD in Educational Leadership, Higher Education, from the University of Dayton. Prior to her academic career, Ann worked as a corporate and healthcare communications manager and has extensive experience as a scriptwriter, technical editor, and business communications consultant. In addition to her academic scholarship, she has authored numerous articles, media programs, advertisements, and educational materials for corporate and non-profit organizations.

Talia Cain is an undergraduate at Chapman University majoring in Integrated Educational Studies and English Literature. She is passionate about issues relating to educational equity and social justice and while at Chapman she created the organization Student Alliance for Prison Reform. She has presented research at the National and Western Regional Honors Conference and is currently exploring how school disciplinary procedures impact students differently by race, class, and gender. After Chapman, she plans to attend graduate school and continue researching ways classrooms can disrupt the school-to-prison pipeline. Ultimately, she would like to pursue a career in teaching high school English.

Charles Joseph Casabar is an undergraduate student at San Diego State University pursuing a Bachelor's degree in Electrical Engineering. At SDSU, he works at the library's makerspace, build IT @ SDSU Library. Outside of school, he volunteers with a local high school robotics club, mentoring students and teaching about engineering design and STEM-related topics.

Jessica Clemons began her career as a science librarian at a private liberal arts school where she was deeply engaged with the sciences and supporting digital collections throughout the curriculum. Moving to SUNY College of Environmental Science and Forestry, she planned, implemented, and managed the institution's institutional repository and was a proponent for open scholarship. Currently Jessica serves as the Association University Librarian for Research, Education, and Outreach for the University at Buffalo. She demonstrates leadership and provides strategic direction for arts, humanities, social sciences, science and engineering, and health sciences librarians and library services, special collections, archives, government documents, and scholarly communications. She has published book chapters and articles in academic journals on leadership, digital collections, and scholarly communication, and presented nationally and internationally. She has a Master's degree in library science from Clarion University and a second Master's degree in geographic information systems from Pennsylvania State University.

William Cross is the Director of the Copyright & Digital Scholarship Center in the NCSU Libraries where he guides legal policy and practice and leads digital scholarship and publishing initiatives. Trained as a lawyer and librarian, Will speaks and writes on the intersection of legal issues, innovative library practice, and open culture. He teaches with the ACRL Scholarly Communication Roadshow and in the UNC SILS and has led workshops for international audiences from Ontario to Abu Dhabi. Will serves as co-PI on two IMLS grants focused on developing open educational resources (OER) for teaching scholarly communication and on the development of an "Open Textbook Toolkit" that leverages library publishing services to support open pedagogy.

Lisa Cruces has served as the Hispanic Collections Archivist at the University of Houston since 2014. Prior to joining the University of Houston, Cruces was the Librarian-in-Residence at the University of Notre Dame's Hesburgh Libraries. A first generation Mexican American, Lisa earned dual B.A. degrees from Texas State University-San Marcos in 2009 and her Master of Science in Information Studies, specializing in archives and academic libraries, from The University of Texas at Austin in 2012. Cruces is committed to building an inclusive cultural record and empowering individuals to preserve their experiences through traditional and non-traditional archival practices. Also important to Cruces is preserving and creating access to Spanish-language material. Her service and scholarship focus on diversity and inclusion in special collections and archives, Latinx digital humanities, and outreach and instruction.

Diane (DeDe) Dawson is Science and Scholarly Communication Librarian at the University Library, University of Saskatchewan in Canada. In addition to her MLIS degree, she holds a BSc in Biology and an MSc in Earth Sciences. Driven by her education and research background in the sciences, she has a strong interest in the ways scientists communicate the results of their research and how libraries can support this. DeDe's research program focuses on scholarly communication and open access issues, and her professional practice includes information literacy instruction to undergraduate and graduate students. She also serves as the Faculty Advisor for the University of Saskatchewan Undergraduate Research Journal (USURJ).

Melissa Fierke. I am originally from Northwest Arkansas and have a BS in Environmental Chemistry and a BS in Environmental Biology as well as a MS in Fisheries & Wildlife and a MS in Environmental Science/Water Resources and a PhD in Entomology. I am a forest entomologist at SUNY College of Environmental Science and Forestry (ESF), Department of Environmental and

Forest Biology. Research in my lab has largely focused on introduced forest insects, e.g., emerald ash borer and its parasitoids, while other recently funded work includes landscape variables associated with black legged ticks (BLT) & prevalence of human diseases in BLTs, as well as pollinators associated with powerline rights of ways. I teach Ecology & Organismal Biology and Systematic Entomology as well as co-facilitate two graduate level seminars (fall and spring). I am serving as Director and Academic Program Coordinator of Cranberry Lake Biological Station and am Associate Chair of my Department. I have served on many committees (including founding and chairing ESF's Bike Safety Committee) and I recently termed out after serving four years as Secretary of ESF's Academic Governance. I currently serve on the President's Leadership Council and continue to serve on our departmental Graduate Program Advisory Council.

Marian Fragola. As the Director of Program Planning and Outreach for the NCSU Libraries, Marian Fragola fosters community engagement through a suite of public programs that showcase the creativity, interdisciplinarity, diversity, and value of student and faculty work to the campus community and beyond. These programs build upon communities of practice on campus and strengthen connections between the university and the region. She received her MLS at the University of North Carolina at Chapel Hill and is currently the board chair for the North Carolina Humanities Council.

Heidi Gauder is professor and coordinator of research and instruction at University of Dayton. She chairs the Instruction and Research Teams of Roesch Library, coordinating and scheduling the work of the team members, as well as conducting program assessment for both instruction and research. She is the subject liaison to the History and Political Science Departments, in addition to the Honors Program.

Rita Ghazala is an undergraduate student at San Diego State University. She is studying Art with an emphasis in Multimedia. She works at build IT @SDSU Library, where she enjoys being able to her creativity for multiple work-related purposes and connecting with other students outside her major at San Diego State University. She also works at El Cajon County Library, where she enjoys interacting with a diversity population of patrons. In the future, she wants to become an animator where she designs characters and make animation movies. In her free time, she likes to draw and paint.

Jason Evans Groth is Digital Media Librarian at NCSU Libraries. As part of the Learning Spaces and Services department he helps to support the eleven audio and video production suites and several other high-tech creative multimedia spaces. He earned his MIS/MLS from the School of Library and Information Science at Indiana University in May of 2013. At IU he was the graduate assistant for the Media Preservation Initiative from 2012- 2013, an Assistant Archivist at the Indiana University Libraries Film Archive from 2010-2013, the graduate assistant for the Digital Library Program at IU from 2011-2012, and a teaching assistant for the classes "The History of Rock and Roll: 70s and 80s," "History of the Beach Boys," "History of Frank Zappa," "History of the Blues," and "History of Jimi Hendrix." From 2001-2010 he toured the world as a guitar player and with many bands and artists, including Magnolia Electric Co, Jens Lekman, and The Impossible Shapes.

William Gordon is a New Englander living in Santa Fe. He's an assistant editor at *Outside*. His work has been seen on Esquire.com, MensJournal.com and in *The Morning Call*, a newspaper based in Allentown, Pa. In 2017, he graduated from Lafayette College. As a student, he edited *The Lafayette*, the campus newspaper, and broke a national news story with Ian Morse. Will spent the summer of 2016 studying digital humanities as part of a program through Lafayette College's Skillman Library.

Benjamin Hackenberger is a Master of Landscape Architect Candidate at the Harvard Graduate School of Design. He co-authored a paper with Char Miller published in 2017 in the Journal of Urban History https://doi.org/10.1177/0096144217692986. His research interests focus on the formal expression of ecological and topographical systems in landscapes of leisure. Before moving into Landscape, he was a Global Academic Fellow at New York University, where he worked with student writers in art, geography, and engineering courses. At Pomona College, Hackenberger studied Environmental Analysis with a focus on the built environment http://scholarship.claremont.edu/pomona_theses/136/.

Anna Kramer serves as the Policy Coordinator and Grants Manager for the American Alpine Club. Her undergraduate thesis, "The Power of the Tower: Contesting History at Bear Lodge/Devils Tower National Monument," received a Claremont Colleges Library Undergraduate Research Award in 2016. After graduating with a degree in Environmental Analysis and a concentration in U.S. environmental history from Pomona College, she also worked for the National Wildlife Federation and the Colorado Outward Bound School. She will be pursuing her PhD in U.S. and environmental history at the University of Colorado, Boulder, starting in the fall of 2018. Her research interests include the histories of public lands, indigenous America, outdoor recreation, and rural communities. Links to Kramer's senior thesis, her award winning research, and an interview on the impact of undergraduate research can be found at http://scholarship.claremont.edu/open_access_week/2016/outreach-videos/3/

Liv Marken. As coordinator of writing help programs and services at Student Learning Services at the University of Saskatchewan, Liv Marken manages a team of graduate students. In addition, she teaches the Arts and Science transition course Strategies for Academic Success, and has been a lecturer in the U of S Department of English for several years. Liv is staff advisor for the *University of Saskatchewan Undergraduate Research Journal* (USURJ).

Liz Milewicz heads the Digital Scholarship Services department in Duke University Libraries. Her team partners with researchers and students on digital research, teaching, and publishing projects (http://sites.duke.edu/digital) and provides training and consulting in digital approaches to scholarship. She helped to plan and launch a new space for research, called The Edge: The Ruppert Commons for Research, Technology, and Collaboration (http://library.duke.edu/edge), where project teams pursue interdisciplinary, data-driven, and digitally reliant research.

Char Miller is the W.M. Keck Professor of Environmental Analysis at Pomona College, Claremont, California. She is author and editor most recently of Where There's Smoke: The Environmental Science, Public Policy, and Politics of Marijuana, Not So Golden State: Sustainability vs. the California Dream, America's Great National Forests, Wildernesses, and Grasslands, and On the Edge: Water, Immigration, and Politics in the Southwest. Forthcoming works include San Antonio: A Tricentennial History and the co-authored Ogallala: Water for a Dry Land. Miller established the Environmental Analysis Program's Senior Thesis class in 2011, and developed it in close collaboration with colleagues at the Claremont Colleges Library. Librarians serve as subject-area guides for the student researchers and with program faculty refine an evolving series of rubrics by which to aid these young scholars' work and evaluate the resulting theses, all of which are posted online http://scholarship.claremont.edu/eap_ea_theses/.

Ian Morse graduated from Lafayette College in 2017 with a double major in History and Mathematics-Economics after completing the Digital Humanities Summer Scholar program in 2015. During college he studied in Turkey, which inspired his DH project, and at Cambridge University, which inspired his honors thesis on post-colonial press freedom in Tanzania. During college, he helped drive the college paper's award-winning renovation and broke national stories. He is currently a freelance journalist in eastern Indonesia after completing a yearlong Fulbright English Teaching grant there. He speaks

German and Indonesian, and he continues to bring DH and statistics into his reporting, having given reporting seminars with Indonesian journalists. He tweets @ianjmorse.

Carla S. Myers serves as Assistant Professor and Coordinator of Scholarly Communications for the Miami University Libraries. Her professional presentations and publications focus on fair use, copyright in the classroom, and library copyright issues.

Carolyn Radcliff is the co-founder of Carrick Enterprises, a company that works with colleges and universities to assess student achievement in the area information literacy. Her current work builds on 25 years of experience as an academic librarian at universities in the U.S. Throughout her library career she focused on four areas of academic library work: information literacy, library assessment, reference services, and management. Carolyn has an M.L.S and an M.A. from Kent State University. carolyn.radcliff@gmail.com

Lillian Rigling is the Program Coordinator at eCampus Ontario, a not-for-profit organization supporting equitable access to technology-enabled learning at 45 colleges and universities in Ontario. Lillian has a background in Scholarly Communications librarianship and holds a Master of Information from the University of Toronto. She writes and teaches about developing and sustaining open education work within unique organizational contexts.

Kevin M. Ross, Associate Dean of the Leatherby Libraries at Chapman University, has worked in higher education for over 20 years as a teacher, librarian, and administrator. Kevin's educational background includes a B.A. from St. Ambrose University, an M.L.S. from the University of Iowa, an M.A. from Chapman University, and he is currently completing a Ph.D. at Chapman University. Kevin has worked at the Leatherby Libraries since 2000, holding a variety of positions in the library including Distance Education librarian, Coordinator of Bibliographic Instruction, Web Manager, Head of Reference, Chair of Public Services, and Associate Dean. In his current role, Kevin provides leadership and support for library administrative services; serves as human resources' liaison in collaboration with the campus HR Department; supervises, mentors, and evaluates the library's three chairs and administrative assistant; participates in library advancement activities; and oversees assessment planning, strategic planning, goal setting, and the library's operations budget.

Maureen Schlangen is an institutional repository manager in the University of Dayton Libraries in Dayton, Ohio. A former newspaper reporter and editor, she has worked in higher education communications, advancement, and libraries since 1997. In her scholarly communications work, she educates the university community about open-access scholarship and works with faculty to make their research and data more discoverable and accessible.

Allegra Swift is the Scholarly Communications Librarian at the University of California San Diego Library. In this position and in her previous position as the Scholarly Communications Coordinator at the Claremont Colleges Library, Swift advocates for researchers and scholars from all backgrounds, disciplines, and at all career stages to use, create, and publish scholarship and research in ways that contribute to the transformation of scholarly communication. Swift explores the topics of digital identity and reputation management, publishing undergraduate research, the intersections of information literacy and scholarly communications, open access, and new modes of publishing. She has recently presented and instructed on these topics at national conferences that include ACRL, Digital Initiatives Symposium, Library Publishing Forum, and the FORCE11 Scholarly Communications Institute.Swift holds a MLIS from SJSU and a BA in Comparative Literature with Interdisciplinary option from University of Southern California.

Mila Temnyalova is a Bulgarian national working towards her undergraduate degree in the U.S. She studies Economics and International Affairs with a regional focus on Europe and a thematic focus on global conflict and co-operation and U.S. foreign policy. Apart from academia, she is interested in photography, foreign languages and poetry.

Brittney Thomas is the Manager of the NNLM *All of Us* Community Engagement Center for the NNLM All of Us National Program. Before that she managed the Main Library Learning Commons at the University of Iowa where she coordinated the development and implementation of new services, programs, resources and technologies into the Learning Commons. She received her BA in Art History & Theory from Iowa State University in 2008 and her MLIS from the University of Iowa in 2011. Her background and research interests are in community engagement, student success, learning spaces and digital and media literacy.

Mira Waller is the Interim Department Head of Research Engagement in the North Carolina State University Libraries. She leads an engagement centered team that supports research productivity and flexible modes of learning through access to expert assistance, curriculum integrated instruction, research-enhancing technologies and spaces, and innovative services across the lifecycle of research, scholarship, and pedagogy. Waller was previously

Associate Head of Collections & Research Strategy at NCSU Libraries and Director of Publishing Services for Project Euclid.

Lindsay White is an undergraduate student at San Diego State University, studying Electrical Engineering and Computer Science. She is a student employee at build IT @ SDSU Library, a makerspace that works to teach and assist university students via hands-on activities. Lindsay mentors the Mt. Carmel High School Robotics Club in their efforts to compete in the FIRST Tech Challenge, working with the high school students to develop their skills in robotic design, build, and programming. [use KI6LZN@gmail.com for email]

Brittany Wofford is the Coordinator for The Edge and Librarian for the Nicholas School of the Environment. She connects users of the library's research commons to library staff and resources and provides research support to the Nicholas School of the Environment. She graduated with a bachelor's degree in English from the University of North Carolina at Chapel Hill and a Master of Library Science from North Carolina Central University.

Jenny Wong-Welch is the STEM Librarian at San Diego State University. In addition to her responsibilities of providing research assistance and library instruction for the College of Engineering and the departments of Astronomy, Physics, and Mathematics/Statistics, she is the Director of build IT @ SDSU Library, a student-run makerspace designed to foster creativity and innovation by providing an infrastructure for DIY learning of technology. She has presented and published on the role of libraries as makerspaces on the academic campus and the library's ability to use the process of creating to make information literacy more tangible.